Christopher Gadsden
and Henry Laurens

Christopher Gadsden and Henry Laurens

The Parallel Lives of Two American Patriots

Daniel J. McDonough

SUP

Sellinsgrove: Susquehanna University Press
London: Associated University Presses

Associated University Presses
440 Forsgate Drive
Cranbury, NJ 08512

Associated University Presses
16 Barter Street
London WC1A 2AH, England

Associated University Presses
P.O. Box 338, Port Credit
Mississauga, Ontario
Canada L5G 4L8

The paper used in this publication meets the requirements of the American National Standard for Permanence of Paper for Printed Library Materials Z39.48-1984.

Library of Congress Cataloging-in-Publication Data

McDonough, Daniel J., 1961–
    Christopher Gadsden and Henry Laurens : the parallel lives of two American patriots /
    Daniel J. McDonough.
        p. cm.
    Includes bibliographical references and index.
    ISBN 1-57591-039-X (alk. paper)
    1. Statesmen—United States—Biography. 2. Gadsden, Christopher, 1724–1805.
3. Laurens, Henry, 1724–1792. 4. United States—Politics and government—
1775–1783. 5. South Carolina—Politics and government—1775–1783. 6. United
States. Continental Congress—Biography. I. Title.

E302.5 .M33 2000
973.3′092′2—dc21
[B]

                                                                                    00-025820

Contents

Preface

LITTLE DID I KNOW WHEN I FIRST ENCOUNTERED CHRISTOPHER GADSDEN AND Henry Laurens that these two lives would occupy such an important place in my own life. The present study originated as a doctoral dissertation at the University of Illinois in which I set out to compile a group study of the revolutionary elite of Charleston, South Carolina. The more I read, however, the more intrigued I became with the lives of Gadsden and Laurens. Born days apart and close friends for decades, Gadsden and Laurens shared similar socioeconomic backgrounds. I found myself growing increasingly interested in how, contrary to all of the historical models proposed to explain loyalties during the revolutionary era, Gadsden emerged as the leader of the radical resistance to British policy in South Carolina while Laurens remained staunchly moderate. At the same time, I found that neither of these important figures had received the attention merited by their accomplishments: though Gadsden was the subject of a fairly recent biography, Laurens's story had not been told since the outdated work of David Duncan Wallace in 1915. What follows is a dual biography which chronicles not only the rise and fall of a friendship, but one which emphasizes the political development of two complex revolutionary leaders.

This study could not have been completed without the assistance of many people. Special thanks go to John Pruett, who not only sparked my interest in the topic, but also served as advisor, mentor and friend at the University of Illinois. The same can be said of Robert Johannsen who took time out of his own busy schedule to read parts of this manuscript. More important, however, Professor Johannsen set examples of scholarly and teaching effectiveness, as well as gentlemanly conduct, which I have attempted to follow in my own career. Robert McColley, Walter Arnstein, Vernon Burton, Daniel Littlefield, William Sutton, and Steve White also provided thoughtful and insightful commentary during the revision process. C. James Taylor and David Chesnutt of *The Papers of Henry Laurens* project at the University of South Carolina contributed important suggestions as well as assistance in locating sources. I also appreciate the advice and support of my friends and colleagues at Middle Tennessee State University and the University of Tennessee at Martin. Nor could the work have been completed without the assistance of the staffs of the South Caroli-

7

niana Library, Columbia; the South Carolina Department of Archives and History, Columbia; the South Carolina Historical Society, Charleston; the Library of Congress; and the libraries of the University of Illinois, Middle Tennessee State University, and the University of Tennessee at Martin.

Finally, my most profound thanks go to my family, each of whom became much more familiar with Christopher Gadsden and Henry Laurens than they had ever thought possible. Most particularly, my parents, Lou and Gerry McDonough, who provided consistent encouragement and a quiet hideaway for reflection; my sister, Sharon McGrath, whose fingers probably still hurt from all of the typing she did; most of all, however, my thanks go to Alesia and little Dan for all of their love, support, and patient understanding through all of the long nights and lost weekends that went into this project.

Christopher Gadsden
and Henry Laurens

Introduction

THE AMERICAN REVOLUTION HAS ALWAYS HELD A CERTAIN FASCINATION FOR students of American history. For over two centuries, historians have maintained a lively debate over the varied causes of the Revolution and the importance that should be attached to these causes. Efforts have been made to attribute the Revolution to economic, social, religious, intellectual, and other factors. As quickly as one interpretation gains acceptance, it is challenged by new studies that point out its problems and limitations. Thus, the causes of the Revolution have remained controversial among historians. In any study of the Revolution, one must take into account the general nature of British colonial policy during the 1760s and 1770s: the influence of the Stamp Act and other parliamentary tax measures, the role of the peacetime standing army, as well as other policy developments. These factors played an important and sometimes crucial role in the coming of the Revolution. Yet they do not tell the entire story. John Adams made an insightful observation when he remarked that the cause of the Revolution could not be attributed to a single event, or even to a series of events, but that it lies in the transformation that took place in the hearts and minds of the American people. This development varied from colony to colony and from person to person. While there were important grievances that were common to all of the colonies, there were also important issues that were peculiar to the individual colonies. These local factors are too often overlooked. This is unfortunate, for the local issues were often precisely the ones that provided the revolutionary movement with its greatest impetus.

Local issues were crucial to the development of a revolutionary movement in South Carolina. A formidable protest movement had already appeared in South Carolina before the introduction of the Stamp Act. Smoldering resentment over appointments to local positions had developed into a serious dispute over the relative merits of British regulars and local militia during the Cherokee War of 1759 to 1761. The protest movement solidified in 1762, when Governor Thomas Boone refused to allow the duly elected Christopher Gadsden to take his seat in the South Carolina assembly. Later, during the early 1770s, when the protest movement was stagnant in other colonies, local issues served to maintain the momentum of the movement in South Carolina. Most prominent among these issues was the attempt by the British government to force the assembly to rescind a grant it had made to the defense fund of the notorious English radical, John Wilkes. As a result of the ensuing deadlock, South Carolina was, for all practical purposes, left without an assembly for the remainder of the colonial era.

Just as historians have tended to generalize on the causes of the Revolution, they have also proposed general models to explain individual loyalties during the conflict with Britain. These models often take the form of efforts to distinguish between radical patriots, moderate patriots, and Tories by means of their social, economic, or religious backgrounds. While such models are not without merit, they must be used with care. Just as the thirteen colonies had varying reasons for overthrowing British rule, so, too, did the individuals involved in the conflict base their positions upon various factors. Illustrative of this fact are the lives and careers of Henry Laurens and Christopher Gadsden, two of the most prominent figures in revolutionary South Carolina. Born only days apart in 1724, these two South Carolinians shared similar social, economic, and religious backgrounds. Close friends from their youth until the issues of the early 1760s led them in different directions, both men grew wealthy as leading members of the Charles Town mercantile community and both emerged as open-minded and tolerant leaders in the Charles Town social and intellectual scene. In light of these strikingly similar backgrounds, it is interesting that Gadsden emerged as one of the most radical of patriots while Laurens was among the most firmly moderate.

These two lives clearly demonstrate the limitations of the economic, social, and religious models in the classification of American leaders of the revolutionary era. Neither Gadsden nor Laurens stood to realize any immediate economic gains from the patriot cause. Indeed, both declared themselves prepared to make serious financial sacrifices and, in fact, both eventually did so. Both also held sincere republican principles and, though Gadsden was the more liberal of the two, neither would support social revolution. Under these circumstances, it would seem a difficult task to explain the wide divergences in the positions of the two men during the conflict with Britain. A close study reveals that the behavior of neither man was dictated by economic, social, or religious factors. Rather, the role of personality and differing ideas concerning the role and nature of the British Empire emerges as the crucial element in the developing political rivalry between Laurens and Gadsden and in explaining their divergent responses to the Revolution itself. A study of these factors does much to illuminate and clarify the positions assumed by Gadsden and Laurens, as well as other prominent Americans of the revolutionary era.

Christopher Gadsden developed an extremely independent personality during his formative years. Sent to England as a small boy to be educated, Gadsden was forced to develop a self-reliance that proved unnecessary to Laurens. Hot-tempered, fiery, and self-righteous, Gadsden would tolerate no interference with what he considered to be the rights and liberties of either himself or his country. Though Gadsden took pride in the British Empire, his residence in England inspired no deep love for the mother country and he never demonstrated any desire to reside there permanently. Gadsden would rather see the empire split than allow the impairment of the rights and privileges of America.

Such was not the case with Henry Laurens. Raised in a caring and supportive family environment, Laurens always placed a strong emphasis on family loyalty, parental respect, and subordination to authority. At the same time, he became almost a symbol of the moderate lifestyle, developing an impressive work ethic, as well as conservative business and personal habits. Laurens, too, had spent several years in England, but he had lived there as a young man and, in seeming contrast to Gadsden, had enjoyed the experience. Indeed, his life in England was so agreeable that he hoped to establish himself in business in London. Though these plans collapsed and Laurens returned to South Carolina, he retained a love for England and a devotion to the empire. Thus, Laurens entered into the dispute with Britain with a far greater attachment to the imperial connection than did Gadsden. With a far deeper devotion to republican principle than to the concept of the British Empire, Gadsden was prepared to offer strong opposition to any policy he considered oppressive. Laurens, on the other hand, with his strong feelings toward the empire, was unwilling to endorse the radical measures championed by Gadsden and the Sons of Liberty. Indeed, Laurens diligently sought a peaceful imperial settlement during the early 1770s. Only when this proved impossible did Laurens become a revolutionary. Thus, personality and feelings toward the empire played the crucial roles in leading Gadsden to become a radical and Laurens to become a moderate patriot.

While the major focus of this study is to explain the motivation of these two patriot leaders, another focus is to illuminate the lives and careers of two important, yet relatively neglected, figures. As the "Sam Adams of the South," Gadsden did much to bring about the Revolution in South Carolina, while Laurens's moderate leadership was essential to the success of that revolution. Both men assumed important roles in the Continental Congress, with Laurens serving as president during the bleak period of the Congressional retreat to York, Valley Forge, and the Conway Cabal. Both, too, served as important symbols of British vengeance after capture: Laurens spent over a year in the Tower of London and Gadsden spent almost a year in the dungeon at St. Augustine. It is hoped that this study will provide greater insight into these American heroes.

1

Early Lives and Business Interests, 1724–1758

T<small>HE LIVES OF</small> C<small>HRISTOPHER</small> G<small>ADSDEN AND</small> H<small>ENRY</small> L<small>AURENS SEEMED DESTINED</small> to be intertwined even before their births less than three weeks apart in 1724.[1] Both patriots were the sons of men who migrated to Charles Town during the 1710s, a time when South Carolina was a young colony and Charles Town little more than a frontier settlement. To the ambitious and enterprising, Charles Town was a place of great excitement during the eighteenth century. With an abundance of inexpensive land, continued improvements in indigo and rice planting, and the excellent harbor at Charles Town, South Carolina was rapidly growing into one of the most important British possessions in America. The colony experienced such rapid economic growth that by 1750, it was arguably the wealthiest colony in North America.[2] Thomas Gadsden and John Laurens were among the ambitious individuals who recognized the opportunities offered by Charles Town and set out to take advantage of them.

Very little is known concerning the backgrounds of either the Gadsden or the Laurens families. Almost nothing is known of the Gadsden family before the arrival of Thomas Gadsden, father of Christopher, in Charles Town sometime before 1718. The family originated in Hertfordshire, England, where none rose to prominence despite the fact that several owned land. It is unclear as to where Thomas Gadsden fit into this clan for there is no remaining record of his education, his life in England, or even the names of his parents or the date of his birth. It is known that he was a sailor in the British merchant fleet and had settled in Charles Town by 1718. He must have had some influential friends in England, for he received an appointment as collector of customs at Charles Town in 1722 and held this post until his death in 1741.[3] Even less is known of his first wife, Elizabeth. The only reference to be found of her in the remaining writings of Christopher Gadsden is in a 1797 pamphlet in which he recalled that he was of Irish descent "by the mother's side, whose father was a native of Ireland whom I am named after."[4]

Little more is known of the ancestry of Henry Laurens. Descended from a French Huguenot family from La Rochelle, Laurens could trace his ancestry only to his grandfather, Andrew (Andre) Laurens, who fled to England in 1682 to escape religious persecution. From there Andrew Laurens moved to Ireland and later to New York City before finally settling in Charles Town in 1715. His son John (Jean) Laurens was born in New York in 1697 and married Esther Grasset (also descended from French Huguenots) shortly before migrating to Charles Town with his family in 1715. John Laurens must have achieved some success in New York, for the Grasset family had achieved some prominence. Augustus Grasset, father of Esther, was "a noted merchant and government official," before he was killed during a slave revolt in New York.[5] Henry Laurens remembered his father as an extremely hardworking and ambitious man who was devoted to his family and determined to establish the family both economically and socially. Laurens took great pride in his father and used John Laurens as a model in the development of his own impressive work ethic.[6] This hard work paid off as John Laurens became the largest saddler in the colony. He also became a respected citizen of Charles Town, as reflected in his election as a church warden of St. Philip's in 1733 and as a town firemaster in 1742. The prosperity achieved by John Laurens can also be seen in the fact that he was comfortable enough to retire in his midforties, turning his saddlery business over to his brother Peter Laurens and Benjamin Addison in 1742. John Laurens's will, filed after his death in May 1747, showed the results of a life of diligence. He was able to leave one thousand pounds currency (one-seventh the value of sterling) to his second wife Elizabeth, as well as two thousand pounds to his younger son James, and fifty pounds to each of his three daughters. He had also acquired several valuable tracts of land, which he bequeathed to Henry and James.[7]

Thomas Gadsden also attained a sizable estate before his death in 1741. He took his duties as customs collector seriously and performed them well, with no hint of the customs racketeering that did so much to alienate colonial merchants during the 1760s. He invested much of his money in land and left large tracts, including a valuable town lot, three hundred acres near Dorchester, and another one thousand acres on the Waccamaw River, near Georgetown, to his son Christopher. He might have owned even more property had he not spent much of his free time drinking and gambling. One of the most popular Charles Town traditions concerns Gadsden's loss of the sixty-three-acre tract of land later known as Ansonboro, just north of Charles Town on the Cooper River, to Lord Anson in a card game. Still, despite his vices, Thomas Gadsden died a successful man, leaving an estate valued at nearly five thousand pounds sterling, with much of this going to his eldest son Christopher.[8]

Thus, John Laurens and Thomas Gadsden were both examples of the upward mobility present in South Carolina during the first half of the eighteenth century. Neither came to Charles Town with a fortune, but both managed to become successful through ambition, integrity, and diligence. Though neither man rose into the South Carolina elite, their efforts established the foundations for their sons to do so. But even more important than the financial legacy were the examples these men provided for their sons. Both were ambitious, honest, hardworking, and (despite Thomas Gadsden's fondness for drinking and gambling) deeply religious men, models that their sons followed in the continuing rise of the two families.

Christopher Gadsden was born on February 16, 1724, in Charles Town, the third child of Thomas and Elizabeth Gadsden, but the only one to survive infancy. Elizabeth Gadsden died in 1727 and Thomas married two more times. By his third wife, Alice Mighells, he had two more sons, Thomas and James, who lived to adulthood. Henry Laurens was born on March 6, 1724, in Charles Town, the third child and first son of John and Esther Laurens. He would have one brother and four sisters, all but one of whom lived to adulthood.[9]

Very little information remains about the childhoods of Christopher Gadsden and Henry Laurens. It is clear that the two youths were playmates and that they developed a strong friendship. Years later Laurens's son-in-law, the doctor, historian, and political leader David Ramsay, wrote that the two were

> attached in their early youth to each other by the strongest ties of ardent friendship. They made a common cause to support and encourage each other in every virtuous pursuit, to shun every path of vice and folly, to leave company whenever it tended to licentiousness, and by acting in concert to parry the charge of singularity so grating to young persons. By an honorable observance of a few concerted rules, they mutually strengthened virtuous habits, broke the force of many temptations, and acquired an energy of character which fitted them for acting a distinguished part in the trying scenes of a revolution through which it was the destiny of both to pass under similar circumstances.[10]

Yet, too much emphasis should not be placed upon this early relationship, for they saw little of each other between 1732 and 1748. Gadsden was sent to England to study in 1732 and did not return to Charles Town until 1740. Even then his stay was brief as he was soon apprenticed to Thomas Lawrence, a prominent Philadelphia merchant. Thus, from 1740 until he terminated his training upon his twenty-first birthday in 1745, Gadsden spent most of his time in Philadelphia. After completion of his training he planned to return to Charles Town and enter into business for himself. First, however, he decided to visit relatives in Britain. Since King George's War was raging, Gadsden sailed on the man-of-war *Aldborough* and was appointed purser after this officer died during the passage. Service upon the *Aldborough*, which lasted until the spring of 1748, allowed Gadsden great excitement along the North Atlantic coast: he took part in the capture of Louisbourg and visited Boston and New York, as well as Barbados and Jamaica in the West Indies. These experiences left Gadsden with a broad perspective and could, in part, explain his early nationalism, particularly when compared to his more parochial Charles Town contemporaries. His long absences notwithstanding, Gadsden must have found time for several visits to Charles Town, for he managed to court and, on July 28, 1746, finally marry Jenny Godfrey. His friendship with Henry Laurens also continued to grow during this period, and it was Laurens who watched over Jenny Gadsden, forwarded her letters to her husband, and even informed Gadsden of the birth of the latter's first child in September 1747.[11] While Gadsden was being educated in England, Laurens remained in Charles Town, where he received "the best Education which that Country afforded."[12] In 1744 Laurens was sent to London to receive his mercantile training in the house of James Crokatt, who had been a prominent Charles Town merchant before his relocation to England. Except for a brief trip home during late 1747 and early 1748, Laurens spent the next five years in England. Despite long absences from one another, Laurens and Gadsden clearly developed a sincere attachment based upon mutual confidence, respect, and affection that would make them warm friends throughout the 1750s.

By 1750 Laurens and Gadsden were both launched upon business careers that would propel them into the South Carolina elite. The transition from apprentice to merchant proved to be much easier for Gadsden than it was for Laurens. Gadsden was a shrewd businessman who was already established in trade when he finally settled down in Charles Town in 1748. As early as 1742, while he was still serving his apprenticeship in Philadelphia, advertisements appeared in the *South Carolina Gazette* for a store that Gadsden had apparently opened on Shute's Wharf. This business expanded while he served on the *Aldborough*, where he quickly realized that service in the Royal Navy could be profitable as well as patriotic. His letters to Henry Laurens demonstrate clearly that he saw his service as an opportunity to make money through the seizure of French prizes. Within a year of his return to Charles Town, Gadsden was importing a wide variety of European goods to a store he opened on Broad Street, a prime Charles Town location. His growing prosperity was demonstrated by his taking a house on Elliott Street near the Cooper River, one of the wealthiest areas in the town.[13]

For Henry Laurens the transition was much more difficult and uncertain. He had been happy living with James Crokatt in Cloak Lane, and planned to remain in London as a partner in Crokatt's business. This partnership fell through, however, for reasons still unexplained, and Laurens was left with no alternative but to return to South Carolina. His return only added to his sorrow, for he found that his father had died four days before his arrival at Charles Town. His father's death was a great blow to Laurens for, in addition to losing a "tender and affectionate Parent," he now had to settle the affairs of John Laurens. This left him little time to consider his own business situation.[14] Yet he managed to maintain his composure and was philosophical about his troubles. To a London friend, he wrote that his motto, "*Optimum quod evenit*" (whatever happens, happens for the best), had again proven true: the loss of the partnership was a disappointment, but a fortunate one, for the death of his father would have necessitated his return to America and the probable loss of the partnership anyway. However, he did not consider his return to America to be a permanent move. He realized that he would be detained in Charles Town for some time, perhaps years, but hoped that he would someday return to London to live out his days.[15]

As he prepared to settle in for a long stay, Laurens received an offer that he assumed would change his life forever. In July 1747, little more than a month after his return home, he received a renewed offer of partnership from Crokatt. Laurens jumped at this offer and assured Crokatt that he would make every effort to be in London before the offer expired in April.[16] He spent the next several months in a frustrating effort to settle his affairs and the estate of his father. His confidence in meeting Crokatt's deadline declined as he was repeatedly forced to delay his departure. He finally sailed for London in September 1748, months after the time limit had expired. Not knowing what to expect, Laurens took the precaution of arranging a Charles Town partnership with the rising merchant George Austin, to take effect if the position with Crokatt was no longer available.[17]

Arriving in London in November 1748, Laurens found that his fears had been realized and that Crokatt had taken another man as his partner. Worse still was the discovery that the partnership offer was withdrawn not on account of tardiness, but because Crokatt had received some charges of "cruelty and ingratitude" on the part of Laurens.[18] Though the younger man quickly explained his behavior to Crokatt's satisfaction, the damage had been done: Crokatt now had a partner and no need of Laurens. Crokatt, again solicitous of Lauren's interests, advised him not to make public his recent agreement with Austin in Charles Town, for he would surely receive other offers in London. Laurens certainly thought London preferable to Carolina, but now his honor was involved. In an early demonstration of character, Laurens replied that

> such Conduct would be confirming the Character he gave me of Cruel & ungratefull, for I had promis'd Mr. Austin to be his Partner in case I did not agree with him & therefore thought it out of my Power to accept new proposals from any Person whatsoever Let the Prospect of advantage be ever so great.[19]

And so, after a few months of purchasing goods and establishing business contacts, he sailed home in 1749.

This entire episode was a bitter experience, one that Laurens would remember for the rest of his life. Once again, though, Laurens's belief in serendipity appeared to be justified, for the incident was not without benefit. Though he considered himself a loyal Englishman, he finally concluded that his fortune lay in South Carolina. From this point Henry Laurens was first and foremost a South Carolinian. Never again would he express the desire to live out his days in England. Even a quarter of a century later he could vividly recall this incident when consoling a friend who had lost a partnership.[20]

Laurens returned to a Charles Town that was in the midst of an economic boom that allowed South Carolina to achieve one of the highest rates of economic growth in the world.[21] As business boomed, the Charles Town merchant reached the height of his prestige during the quarter century preceding Lexington. It was the decision of Parliament in 1731 to allow planters to ship their rice directly to European ports south of Cape Finisterre that was primarily responsible for the great increase in trade. With the opening of new ports, rice exports doubled within a decade and continued to rise until reaching a record of 137,400 barrels in 1770. Indigo was another South Carolina export that increased dramatically in value and, by 1770, five hundred thousand pounds of indigo were being exported annually. These two products represented approximately 15 percent of American exports during the 1760s, with rice the third most valuable colonial export and indigo the fifth.[22] Such traffic made Charles Town the busiest port in America, surpassing, by 1770, all of the northern ports in ships cleared and in annual tonnage handled. Bostonian Josiah Quincy was suitably impressed with Charles Town harbor during his visit in 1773. Quincy marveled that, though it was only February, there were some three hundred fifty ships in the harbor, a number that "far surpassed all I had ever seen at Boston."[23]

Laurens understood the potential enjoyed by a shrewd businessman in Charles Town and he quickly embarked upon a career that would establish him among the wealthiest men in America. The foundations for this success had been laid even before he left London. His association with George Austin was an excellent move, as Austin was an industrious, well-connected merchant with an already established business. Laurens also recognized the importance of British contacts and worked hard while in England to establish ties with the leading houses. As a result, the firm of Austin and Laurens began with important contacts with leading British companies, ties that would be crucial to its spectacular success. Without such contacts, a merchant would have to content himself with retailing, as Gadsden was doing. Such a business could be profitable, as it was for Gadsden, but the big money came from serving as a factor for the large British firms. A factor generally had little contact with the consumer; instead, for a commission (usually 5 percent) he received and sold British merchandise to the retailers. He then bought colonial products, such as rice, indigo, and deerskins, for shipment to England. These functions provided the factor with the connections and extensive capital necessary for participation in the lucrative slave trade, a business which would be the cornerstone of the Laurens fortune.

As a partner in the firms of Austin and Laurens (1749–1759), Austin, Laurens, and Appleby (George Appleby, nephew of George Austin, was brought in as a partner, 1759–1762), and later by himself, Laurens became one of the great Charles Town factors. With correspondents throughout the empire and at several European ports, his trade centered around the main Carolina staples of indigo and rice, with significant dealings in deerskins and naval stores. Stuart Stumpf has used the records of the public treasurer to rank 337 Charles Town firms based on the amount of duties paid on imports between 1735 and 1765. Austin and Laurens ranked third on this list, with 121 entries paying £13,834.6 currency in duties. Austin, Laurens, and Appleby, despite the brevity of its existence, was ranked thirty-third with forty-six entries at £3,362.1. Acting alone, Laurens was thirty-ninth on the scale, with payments of £3,123.5 on thirty-two entries. Thus, Laurens was involved in 199 entries on the ledgers of the public treasurer, accounting for £20,320.2 in duties. This would place him as the third most active Charles Town merchant during this thirty-year period, close behind John Savage, but far behind Gabriel Manigault, the undisputed prince of Charles Town trade, who registered 534 entries paying £30,338.7 in duties.[24] It should be remembered, however, that Manigault and Savage were active during this entire thirty-year period, while Laurens did very little business before 1750. Thus, it is quite likely that Laurens was the most active Charles Town merchant between 1750 and the early 1760s, when he began to reduce his business activities.

Perhaps the most interesting aspect of Laurens's mercantile career is his activity in the slave trade. His prominence in this business may come as a surprise to those who read his later statements condemning slavery and the slave trade, but despite the harshness of some of this later commentary, Laurens was an eager participant in the slave trade until the mid-1760s. His letters from England in 1748 and 1749 demonstrate the importance of the slave trade to Austin and Laurens, as Laurens gave special attention to arranging connections with the leading British slave merchants. These efforts produced enormous dividends and contributed much to the success of Austin and Laurens.[25]

That Henry Laurens was far more than a dabbler in the slave trade is clearly proven by W. Robert Higgins in his study of the duties paid upon the slave trade into South Carolina between 1735 and 1775. Despite the relatively short life of the firm (1749–1759), Austin and Laurens ranked first on the list of over four hundred firms and individuals studied by Higgins, paying £45,120 currency[26] in duties on forty-five cargoes of slaves. Austin, Laurens, and Appleby ranked seventh on this list, with sixteen cargoes and £22,890 in duties. Finally, acting alone between 1762 and 1769, Laurens paid £1050 in duties on another seven cargoes. Thus, according to these figures, Laurens was involved in the sale of sixty-eight cargoes of slaves, yielding £69,060 in duties. Accepting Higgins's estimate that the average duty per slave was ten pounds, Laurens was directly involved in the importation of over sixty-nine hundred slaves into South Carolina.[27]

Though he would later downplay his involvement in the slave trade, Laurens was highly regarded as a slave factor and advisor to those interested in the business. His correspondence provides a most insightful view of the late colonial slave trade into South Carolina and demonstrates that the trade could be quite profitable if managed well, though it required extensive capital. The base commission for the slave trade was normally 10 percent, twice that of other products. Yet, there was an element of risk to the enterprise, as the slave trade included several important expenses that were subtracted from the commission of the factor. Most important among these expenses were the responsibility for provision for the slaves between landing and sale[28] and accountability for all bad debts. This latter responsibility was particularly important since few planters could pay cash for their slaves and, thus, the slave trade was essentially a credit business. This fact demanded that slave factors have access to sizable resources, as evidenced by Laurens's claim that he was often in advance for more than ten thousand pounds sterling.[29]

The collection of debts was a critical problem for the slave factor, as he was generally required to transmit his accounts to England at the time they fell due, whether they had been collected or not. Poor harvests or a host of other problems caused delays that had to be borne by the factor. Laurens's innate caution served him well here and his correspondence does not indicate any serious trouble with bad debts. His lending policies were conservative and he insisted that the interest rates be held in strict proportion to the length of credit. He looked upon three or four months as an ideal term of credit and advised that anything longer than six months should be avoided.[30] While these terms served Laurens well, other firms with more liberal lending policies could easily find themselves faced with bankruptcy, as was the fate of the influential house of Middleton, Liston, and Hope during the late 1760s.[31] Thus, expenses could cut into the commission of the factor and even Laurens, as perceptive a judge of men and affairs as there was in Charles Town, reported that he never netted more than a 9 percent commission and that he usually cleared between 8 and 9 percent from the slave trade.[32]

Laurens was often solicited for advice on the slave trade and, in 1755, he summarized what he desired in a slave cargo:

very likely healthy People, Two thirds at least Men from 18 to 25 Years old, the other young Women from 14 to 18 the cost not to exceed Twenty five Pounds Sterling per head. . . . There must not be a Callabar [*sic*] amongst them. Gold Coast or Gambias are best, next to them the Winward Coast are prefer'd to Angolas. We would not choose them sent in the Hurricane Season but rather to come in the month of October or November. Pray observe that our People like tall Slaves best for our business & strong withall. Such as are small, meagre, or other ways ordinary wont sell better here than with you. The difference in price between Men & Women here is never less than £3 Sterling per head, sometimes £6. For your government, young Lads from 13 to 15 Years of age wont bring so much as Men by £5 or 6 Sterling.[33]

In addition to being a good judge of planter desires, the factor had to accurately forecast political and economic trends. Timing was essential to maximizing profits and the factor had to make early assessments of the effects of good or bad harvests, the prospects of war and peace, or other events that could affect the local slave market. The fact that the leading British firms repeatedly turned to Laurens for advice is testimony to the high regard placed on his judgment of the South Carolina scene.

As an adjunct to the slave trade, Laurens also engaged in the importation of indentured servants, though never with the same enthusiasm. This business was not nearly as profitable as the slave trade and could be much more troublesome. His aversion to the servant trade can be easily understood by a look at the experience he had with a shipment of fifty servants from Glasgow during 1767. This voyage was particularly brutal, as the crew nearly mutinied against the officers and, upon arrival, the servants filed complaints concerning their treatment with the governor, council, and the assembly, as well as several prominent local attorneys. Some of the servants openly insulted Laurens on the street and demanded either their freedom or that the bounty collected by Laurens be given to them instead. Laurens was so embarrassed by the episode that he agreed to release forty-eight of the servants.[34] Clearly, he found the sufferings of white laborers more disturbing to his equanimity than the sufferings of slaves. Moreover, there was little profit to be gained from the sale of indentured servants. He could collect a four-pound provincial bounty and a 5 percent commission on sales, but this revenue was largely offset by the expense of maintaining the servants until they could be sold. Laurens looked upon the servant business as more trouble than it was worth and was not disappointed when the trade virtually dried up in South Carolina after the bounty was discontinued in 1768.[35]

In contrast to the collapse of the servant market, the slave trade continued to flourish in South Carolina. The extensive profits produced by the trade inspired a lively competition and few condemned the slave trade as dirty or reprehensible during the mid-eighteenth century. Rather, the opposite is true. That the slave trade was seen as an entirely legitimate, even respectable, business is demonstrated by the participation of so many of the Charles Town elite: Lieutenant Governor William Bull, Jr.; speaker of the Commons House, Peter Manigault; his father, Gabriel Manigault, the most prominent among the pre-revolutionary Charles Town merchants; Christopher Gadsden, who paid the duties upon one cargo of slaves in 1755 and upon another in 1762; and even the Reverend William Tennent can be found among the many prominent names that appear on the list of those who paid the duties on slave cargoes.[36]

The subject of Laurens's retirement from the slave trade is an interesting, if somewhat misunderstood, story. David Duncan Wallace, the prominent historian of South Carolina and biographer of Laurens, accepted the later claims of his subject and argued that Laurens withdrew from the slave trade because of a growing moral repugnance to the business.[37] But, in fact, Laurens's motives in this regard were complex and included a combination of moral, economic, and personal considerations. Admittedly, Laurens had always been aware of the unsavory realities of the slave trade. The business was cruel at its best and could be, at times, brutally savage. Laurens understood these realities and was concerned with them, but it was not until 1763 that he mentioned any intention of retiring from the slave trade. Even then, he found that dissociating himself from the business would be no simple task. His advice and assistance were still valued and eagerly sought by his English friends and, though he did sharply reduce his participation in the trade, Laurens continued to collect commissions for his efforts.[38]

In reducing his participation in the slave trade after 1763, Laurens provided little evidence that he had done so for moral reasons. Not until 1768 did Laurens cite morality as the main reason for his refusal to accept slave cargoes. Until then, Laurens had excused himself on the grounds that he no longer had partners and the business was too difficult for a single man acting alone. This letter of 1764 was typical of those he wrote at this time:

> You must know Gentlemen, that I have in general declined the Affrican [sic] business, altho I have had the most kind and friendly offers from my friends in London, Liverpool, & Bristol & do believe that I might have sold 1,000 or 1,500 last Year & more the Year we are now in if I wou'd ask for them but having no partner I do not chuse to embarrass & perhaps involve myself in concerns too unweildy [sic] for a single Man both on his own & his friends Account. However, a few now & then of a good sort I can Manage well enough for you while the prices keep up of which I shall keep you advised.[39]

The fact that Laurens, quite willingly, continued to handle slave cargoes is further evidence that morality was not yet the crucial element in his decision to withdraw from the slave trade. While Laurens did cut his participation in the slave trade to a minimum during the 1760s, he did pay the duties on seven cargoes of slaves between 1762 and 1769, and it is likely that he assisted in the sale of others.[40]

Nor was his severe castigation of the act passed by the assembly in 1764 to temporarily raise the duty on slaves by one hundred pounds currency the action of a man who opposed the slave trade on moral grounds. This act was essentially a prohibition and it presented a perfect opportunity for a moral opponent of the slave trade to strike a blow against this business. Instead of seizing the opportunity, Laurens opposed passage of the act, condemned it in public and private, and responded to it by arranging the sale of cargoes in Georgia, collecting handsome commissions in the process.[41]

The most important element in Laurens's gradual dissociation from the slave trade was the general contraction of his business interests after 1762. The decisions of George Austin and George Appleby to retire from business and relocate to England caused the dissolution of Austin, Laurens, and Appleby in 1762. Laurens felt that this would be a good opportunity to shift his focus from his mercantile interests to his growing family and his mounting interests in land and planting. The slave trade was a good place to begin this cutback because, despite its profitability, it demanded a much greater investment of time and capital than Laurens felt he could afford. He was forced to further reduce his business interests in 1764 when the death of his brother-in-law John Coming Ball, a close friend and partner in several planting ventures, forced Laurens to take a more active role in the management of his plantations. Not only was Laurens devoting more of his time to his planting interests but, by the early 1760s, he was directing much of his disposable income to the purchase and development of new lands, thereby decreasing the amount of money available to the capital-intensive slave trade.[42]

As Laurens's active participation in the slave trade waned during the 1760s, moral reservations took a more prominent place in his correspondences. By November 1768, his emphasis had clearly shifted:

> I have been largely concerned in the African Trade; I quitted the Profits arising from that gainful branch principally because of many acts, from the masters & others concerned, toward the wretched Negroes from the time of purchasing to that of selling them again, some of which, altho within my knowledge were uncontroulable.[43]

Still, Laurens wavered over his relationship to the slave trade. Despite repeated statements such as the one quoted above, Laurens could be found, as late as September 1770, offering to assist in the sale of slave cargoes.[44] While it would be easy to conclude from such conduct that Laurens was simply a hypocrite, the truth is somewhat more ambivalent. His correspondence between 1768 and 1770 clearly documents a growing dislike of the slave trade. Yet, Laurens valued his contacts among the British firms engaged in the American trade and the high reputation he had achieved among them. He was caught between his growing moral doubts concerning the slave trade and his desire to retain his reputation and serve his British friends. By 1771, these inner conflicts had been resolved and Laurens began to refuse all slave cargoes on moral grounds. Still, these moral reservations only went so far, as he continued to own slaves and never publicly denounced the slave trade. Indeed, he even encouraged the participation of younger friends such as John Lewis Gervais and Felix Warley. In defense of such a glaring inconsistency, Laurens weakly explained that, though he personally disapproved of the lucrative business, it was accepted by the public and, thus, no opprobrium would fall upon those engaged in it.[45]

As Laurens privately denounced the slave trade, he was careful not to offend public opinion with a public attack upon the trade. In 1769, during his bitter pamphlet war with Egerton Leigh, the latter attacked Laurens as an opponent of the slavery system who had withdrawn from the slave trade for moral reasons. Laurens recognized the danger of such an accusation, since such a stance was widely held to be subversive in South Carolina and could result in social and political ostracism. Thus, Laurens vehemently denied Leigh's charges and declared himself a staunch supporter of the South Carolina plantation economy who had removed himself from the slave trade because he was contracting his business interests and because he had no partner and was not inclined to get one.[46] This was an accurate reflection of the reasons he had given for disengagement before 1768, but it was a less than candid reflection of the current situation. Laurens was clearly unwilling to challenge popular opinion by admitting that he was indeed declining the business, as Leigh well knew, on moral grounds. Thus, Laurens's stance upon the slave trade was often ambivalent and sometimes hypocritical. Though he insisted that he had always held moral reservations concerning the slave trade, he did not finally end his own participation until 1770, long after he had grown wealthy from the business. Even then, his decision owed as much to business and personal considerations as it did to matters of conscience.

When Laurens sailed to England in 1771 to oversee the education of his sons, he essentially closed one of the most successful mercantile careers in colonial America. This success had not been achieved by accident. Like Benjamin Franklin, Laurens wasted none of his time and had little patience with those who did. He rarely slept more than four hours a night and carefully avoided balls, horse races, idle conversation, and other social activities that took up so much of the time of many of his contemporaries. A very thorough man, Laurens later told Lafayette that he always sent several copies of his letters, and at least six copies of important communications during wartime.[47] This allowed his business to continue almost uninterrupted while his less-cautious friends suffered losses. Perhaps the best assessment of Laurens the merchant came from David Ramsay, who wrote that his father-in-law

> engaged in trade with spirit, but at the same time with caution and judgment. His scrupulous attention to punctuality not only in the discharge of pecuniary engagements, but in being where and in doing what he had promised was almost romantic. He suffered nothing to interfere with his own engagements, and highly disrelished all breeches of punctuality on the part of others. He was an excellent model for a young man to form himself upon, and was largely trusted in that way by parents who wished their sons to be brought up strictly and in habits of doing business with accuracy. To have served in his counting-house was no small recommendation. He worked hard himself and made all around him do the same. He required less sleep than most men, and devoted a great part of the night to the mercantile pursuits of the day. For the dispatch of business he was never exceeded, perhaps never equalled, in Charlestown.[48]

Laurens took great pride in his work ethic and the example he set for others. He was understandably proud of his reputation for training clerks, and those who did well under him could count upon the assistance of his great influence when striking out on their own.[49]

Laurens's family grew with his increasing prosperity, and he settled into a comfortable and happy family life. On June 25, 1750, he married Eleanor Ball with whom, according to tradition, he had immediately fallen in love when he met her at the wedding of her brother, John Coming Ball.[50] In courting Eleanor, Laurens was careful to conform to the standards of the day. He later recalled that he did not initiate the courtship until he had obtained the consent of the Ball family, for "I should have deemed a contrary conduct a species of dishonorable fraud." The Laurenses experienced all of the joys and sorrows of parenthood in colonial Charles Town during their twenty years of marriage. Before her death in 1770, Eleanor Laurens bore thirteen children, though only four of these survived to adulthood. With a growing family and increasing prominence, Laurens decided to leave his residence in St. Michael's parish for the more fashionable area of town. In 1762 he began to purchase and develop lands near Ansonboro, developing an area called Laurens Square, on the northern edge of the town. He kept a parcel on East Bay Street to himself, and it was there that he built the town house that he would occupy from 1764 until his death.[51] Ironically, the house was located just across the street from that of his old friend Christopher Gadsden.

Though fortunes could be made in business, one was not truly a member of the South Carolina elite until he branched into planting. Laurens took this step in May 1756 when he purchased a half interest in the Wambaw plantation from John Coming Ball.[52] During the next several years the pair combined to purchase several other plantations, which Ball managed. Laurens struck out on his own in 1762 when he purchased the Mepkin plantation for eight thousand pounds currency. Covering three thousand acres on the Cooper River thirty miles from Charles Town, Mepkin would become Laurens's pride and family seat, and it was here that he retired after the Revolution. By 1768 Laurens had developed Mepkin into an efficient and profitable plantation, employing over fifty slaves in the cultivation of indigo, corn, and wheat, yielding about six hundred pounds sterling a year.[53] But this was in 1768. Mepkin was Laurens's first try at plantation management and his inexperience was quickly demonstrated when he sent twenty-five slaves there but neglected to supply them with tools. He wrote to Ball that "I have a poor Notion of Plantation business which I proved pretty fully by sending up those late Negroes without a Tool in their hands, but I may improve my knowledge by study & application."[54] This is precisely what Laurens did, combining his legendary work ethic with advice from his brother-in-law to become a highly competent planter. This experience proved fortunate, for death took John Coming Ball in October 1764, forcing Laurens to take a more active hand in the management of all of his lands. He soon determined that he could have no partner as agreeable as his close friend Ball and decided to plant independently, selling the lands he held with others. By 1770 the only lands he held in partnership were a vast tract of thirteen thousand acres near Ninety Six that he held with his trusted friend, the Hanoverian immigrant John Lewis Gervais.[55] Laurens's appetite for land proved to be almost insatiable and he finally amassed over twenty-four thousand acres in South Carolina and Georgia.[56]

This success in business and planting made Henry Laurens one of the wealthiest Americans of his day. In 1766 he summarized his holdings, coming up with assets of £147,900 currency (or £21,128 sterling), including eighty-eight hundred acres of land, 227 slaves, and varying degrees of ownership in six ships. It has been estimated, however, that these figures represent only about 80 to 90 percent of his total assets, for he had not included his accounts receivable and money lent at interest. He was even wealthier by the time of the Revolution, as he added vast tracts of land that, he estimated, produced an annual income of twenty-five hundred pounds. To put this figure into perspective, it should be noted that the leading doctors and lawyers in Charles Town were making approximately two hundred fifty to five hundred pounds per year, while the leading artisans were fortunate to earn one hundred to one hundred fifty pounds. Thus, Laurens had become one of the wealthiest men in South Carolina and, indeed, in all of North America.[57]

Though Christopher Gadsden shared Laurens's work ethic, he never achieved the brilliant success of his neighbor. This is not to say, however, that Gadsden was a failure. Rather, his success came on a smaller scale, as a prosperous wholesaler and retailer. He owned several stores during the 1750s, including at least two in Charles Town, and one each in Ashley Ferry, Cheraw, and Georgetown. Here he sold a variety of goods imported from the West Indies, Europe, and the northern colonies. His connection with Georgetown was particularly long and important, and during the 1750s, it seemed that he was redirecting his focus to that area. In 1755 he married his second wife, Mary Hassell, a sister of the comptroller of the customs at Georgetown, and the next year he bought a town lot there. In 1757 he purchased thirteen hundred acres on the nearby Pee Dee River that, combined with the land his father had left him in this area, gave him an important stake in Georgetown. Those who saw a move toward Georgetown in all this were soon disabused of the notion when Gadsden, during the early 1760s, announced that he was contracting his interests to Charles Town and closed most of his operations in Georgetown. By the time of the Revolution, Gadsden had sold all of his Georgetown holdings except the one thousand acres left to him by his father. This tract he continued to operate as a thriving plantation for the rest of his life.[58] Gadsden's success as a merchant can also be seen in Stuart Stumph's study of the duties paid to the public treasurers. Gadsden ranked seventy-fourth out of the 337 firms studied, paying £1,431.8 currency on thirty-one entries between 1750 and 1761. This would place Gadsden in the top 20 percent of the importers, indicative of prosperity, but nowhere near the level achieved by great factors like Henry Laurens. In fact, Gadsden paid less than half as much in duties as Laurens did while acting alone after the dissolution of his partnership.[59]

How did Gadsden feel about his neighbor's great success? Did envy play any role in the break between Gadsden and Laurens? These questions are impossible to answer in the light of the destruction of almost the entire correspondence between the two men, and the general scarcity of Gadsden materials from this period. Clearly, Gadsden was an ambitious man who dreamed of entering the world of the great factor and the Charles Town mercantile elite. As he began to contract his business interests during the 1750s, he began planning a bold enterprise that could help him achieve this goal. In April 1758 he paid six thousand pounds currency for fifteen acres of high land and twenty-nine acres of marshy land in northeastern Charles Town. Located directly to the north of Laurens Square, Gadsden proceeded to develop this property as a subdivision that he named Gadsdenboro. As the crisis with Britain deepened during the early 1770s, Gadsden used his subdivision to honor several of his favorite champions of liberty. Thus, he renamed the area Middlesex, in honor of the English county that defied king and ministry by repeatedly electing the royal nemesis John Wilkes to

Parliament. He also saluted other heroes by renaming some of the streets for Wilkes, William Pitt, and Pasquale Paoli.[60]

Gadsden retained two parcels of this land for his own use. On the first he constructed his home, just across the street from that of his old friend Henry Laurens. On a larger parcel along the Cooper River he constructed a wharf that was later described by the *South Carolina Gazette* as a "stupendous work . . . which is reckoned the most extensive of the kind, ever undertaken by one man in America."[61] This wharf was an extensive project in terms of both time and money, and the fact that he financed it independently is solid evidence that he had a considerable fortune at his command.[62] Though Gadsden would later write that the wharf was begun "to relieve my Mind for the almost insupportable Loss of my eldest Son,"[63] there were other reasons as well. He hoped to use this wharf to become a factor and, in 1773, advertised this desire in the Gazette.[64] The wharf was ready for business in 1767 but work continued for years afterwards. In March 1773 he announced that the entire 840-foot front had been completed and that it contained stores that could hold nearly ten thousand barrels of rice. He proudly proclaimed his wharf, even in its incomplete state, to be surpassed by none in North America.[65] Gadsden closely supervised the work and took care that the structure could withstand all of the extremities of the South Carolina climate. The wharf proved so sturdy that the *Gazette* reported that, despite a particularly violent storm, the wharf received no damage at all, "A Proof of its Firmness and good Construction."[66] This wharf brought significant profits to Gadsden in later years and might have established him as a factor had the intensification of the conflict with Britain not intervened.

As Laurens and Gadsden grew in prominence, it was natural that they would gravitate toward the highest social and political circles. Though both men were jealous of their standing within the local social hierarchy, neither interested himself in the more frivolous activities for which Charles Town was gaining a reputation. The Boston patriot, Josiah Quincy, during his 1773 visit, expressed amazement at the intensity of the Charles Town social scene. While impressed by the quality of the balls, concerts, and dinners he attended, Quincy felt that the entire community wasted far too much of its time on leisurely pursuits. He remarked disapprovingly that "cards, dice, the bottle and horses engross prodigious portions of time and attention, the gentlemen (planters and merchants) are mostly men of the turf and gamesters." Such "luxury, dissipation, life, sentiments and manners," Quincy concluded, "naturally tend to make them neglect, despise, and be careless of the true interests of mankind in general." Even more discouraging than the rampant pursuit of pleasure, thought Quincy, was the lax religious principles he observed in the South Carolina capital. After attendance at a brief, sparsely attended, lighthearted Sunday service at St. Philip's, Quincy wrote that

> the state of religion here is repugnant not only to the ordinances and institutions of Jesus Christ, but to every law of sound policy. The Sabbath is a day of visiting and mirth with the rich, and of license, pastime and frolic for the Negroes.[67]

While this assessment has some validity for Charles Town as a whole, the attitudes and practices of Gadsden and Laurens must be excepted. Both regularly attended services of the Church of England and were serious students of the Bible, regularly reading and quoting from the Scriptures. Though dedicated Anglicans, each approached his faith from a moderately Puritan perspective. They shared a belief in a just and omnipotent God whose hand could be seen in all events, both great and small. They also agreed that there would be a future state of rewards and punishments, and each was certain that heaven was to be his final destination. Of the two, Gadsden was the more optimistic, believing that man might escape the awful justice of God, while Laurens was more resigned to divine will. Despite the intensity of their faith, both shared a tolerance for dissenting views that was quite advanced for the time, particularly among those who held strict Christian views. A strong devotion to the free expression of ideas combined with an innate curiosity on religious matters led both men to join the interdenominational religious and literary society that was founded during the 1750s by the Reverend Richard Clarke, the rector of St. Philip's.[68]

As sober, religious men, Laurens and Gadsden were drawn to the more serious, public-oriented societies and each participated in the intellectual life of the community. Both men were active in the Charles Town Library Society, the center of local intellectual life, which loaned books and sponsored scientific experiments. The society possessed a library of between six thousand and seven thousand books and a look at its holdings is instructive in explaining the development of republican tendencies among the local elite, including Laurens and Gadsden. In addition to all of the leading British periodicals of the day, members had the opportunity to consult a wide variety of English political thought. The seventeenth-century classical theorists were well represented and the works of James Harrington, John Locke, and Algernon Sidney were popular among the members. The society also owned a full collection of writings by eighteenth-century radical dissenters, including Trenchard and Gordon's *Independent Whig* and *Cato's Letters*, and the writings of Bolingbroke, Robert Molesworth, and Philip Doddridge, among others. Finally, contemporary French political thought was well represented through the works of Rousseau, Voltaire, and Montesquieu. Laurens and Gadsden also belonged to the South Carolina Society, a prestigious organization among the local elite. The South Carolina Society engaged in numerous philanthropic activities and had originated as a French Huguenot club before opening its doors to the elite as a whole.[69]

Both men also served in positions that combined the religious or social element with the political. Laurens was elected a vestryman of St. Philip's, serving from 1751 to 1753, and both men were elected to this position from 1755 to 1758. Laurens had also served the parish as a churchwarden between 1753 and 1755. Each man also devoted time to the military. Laurens was appointed a lieutenant in the militia in 1757 and was promoted to lieutenant colonel of the provincial regiment in 1760.[70] Gadsden was one of the founders of the colorful and controversial Charles Town artillery company and commanded this body as captain from its origin in 1756 until he went to the Continental Congress in 1774. He took this position seriously and the company won widespread praise, including praise from the Commons House and Lieutenant Governor William Bull, Jr. Unfortunately, the company was unable to participate in the Cherokee War, due to the inability of the Commons House and Governor William Henry Lyttelton to agree over whose responsibility it was to charter the company.[71]

In September 1757, Gadsden and Laurens both achieved the top honor that could be bestowed by their fellow citizens—election to the Commons House of Assembly. They were elected from St. Philip's parish and took their seats on October 6, 1757. Both appear to have been held in high regard, for both (particularly Laurens) were trusted with important duties almost from the time they entered the House. The esteem in which Laurens was held by his colleagues was immediately recognized when he, along with his friend Gabriel Manigault, was given the honor of informing the governor that the House was in session. He was then chosen to the committee that drew up the reply to the governor's opening message.[72] Governor Lyttelton paid his compliments to both Laurens and Gadsden by appointing them, along with Benjamin Smith (the Speaker of the Commons) as commissioners of fortifications. This was a committee of importance, for the colony was at war and the commissioners would see to the defense of Charles Town and the province.[73] Quite clearly both men were recognized to be men of influence who could get things done. The financial abilities of Henry Laurens were particularly recognized by the Commons and he was regularly appointed to the most important financial committees, particularly those selected to audit the public accounts.

By 1760, Henry Laurens and Christopher Gadsden had brought their friendship into politics and each had become a prominent member of the Commons House. But 1760 was an important year in South Carolina politics, as new issues were beginning to emerge that would destroy the relative harmony of the local political scene and shake the very foundations of the British Empire. These issues would have important ramifications for rising individuals such as Laurens and Gadsden, placing pressure on old friendships such as the one enjoyed by these two men. As a young man in 1747 Henry Laurens had casually observed that "the people in this Province are generally very fickle, especially in respect to Governours Spiritual or Temporal, soon pleas'd & soon disgusted."[74] Little did Laurens realize in 1747 that he would get a firsthand taste of just how accurate this observation could be. He would spend the early 1760s locked in a bitter political controversy with a fiery old friend who had emerged as the tribune of the people. This friend turned out to be Christopher Gadsden, and the friendship between these two men would be one of the first to be tested by the issues of the 1760s.

2

The End of a Friendship:
The Cherokee Conflict, 1759–1762

THE FRENCH AND INDIAN WAR BROUGHT GREAT VICTORIES AND VAST NEW territories to the British Empire, leaving Great Britain the most powerful nation in the world. Within twenty years of this tremendous victory, however, the empire would be humbled and dismembered by revolution. Though the American colonies happily joined the patriotic celebration of 1763, seeds of revolution had already been sown. Indeed, some colonies, including South Carolina, had already been the site of serious attacks upon British authorities. The major threat to South Carolina during the war came not from the French, but from the Cherokee Indians who threatened the frontier between 1759 and 1761. The resulting Cherokee War proved costly in both lives and money, and it became a serious issue in provincial politics, one that pitted local pride against imperial authority. By the time the war ended, Christopher Gadsden had emerged as the leading critic of British Cherokee policy, particularly the performance of Lieutenant Colonel James Grant during the campaigns of 1760 and 1761, while Henry Laurens found himself in the forefront of the defenders of Grant and the Indian policy. The resulting conflict would ultimately destroy their long-standing friendship.

As the conflict with France opened in 1755, Laurens identified three major projects that, he felt, would exhaust the human and financial resources of the colony. First, a recent hurricane had virtually annihilated the Charles Town defenses, which now had to be rebuilt at an estimated cost of forty to fifty thousand pounds sterling. Second, the French had been active in stirring up the Creek Indians on the frontier, and this combination was threatening the destruction of the Chickasaw tribe. Such aggression could lead to frontier chaos, necessitating a provision of men and money to counter the threat. Finally, the Crown had earlier agreed, in exchange for the surrender of some Cherokee territory, to build a considerable fort on the Tennessee River to protect the Cherokee from the French. This promise was to be carried out through the construction of Fort Loudoun, which would cost another six to seven thousand pounds sterling. Thus, Laurens believed, South Carolina was in no position to assist the general cause and might even need help if threatened with attack.[1]

Laurens and Gadsden both hurried to the defense of their colony and were tireless in their efforts to ensure its safety. Both entered the Commons House of Assembly in 1757 and both were appointed, in 1758, to oversee the Charles Town defenses as commissioners of fortifications by Governor William Henry Lyttelton. Both also assumed roles in the military establishment: Gadsden as a founder and captain of the artillery company and Laurens as an officer in the militia. Both would also participate in the Cherokee War, though Gadsden did so as a volunteer, since the charter of his artillery company was delayed while Governor Lyttelton and the assembly argued over who had the power to grant the charter.

The entire Cherokee War might have been avoided had South Carolina been governed by a less rash and more skillful man than William Henry Lyttelton. The trouble began as a dispute between the Cherokees and the Virginians when the Indians, returning from the 1758 expedition against Fort Duquense (from which they had deserted two days before reaching the fort), lost some of their horses and appropriated some of the Virginians' horses for their use. After the Virginians responded by killing a dozen of the warriors, the outraged Cherokees, encouraged by the French, retaliated by falling upon the Carolina frontier. Yet many of the Cherokees desired peace and, after Lyttelton called out the militia, sent a delegation to Charles Town for negotiations. Unfortunately, Lyttelton was in a belligerent mood and, against the advice of Lieutenant Governor William Bull and many other provincial leaders, insisted that the Indians be taught a lesson.[2]

It would have been difficult for Lyttelton to make peace at this point, for the recent news of Wolfe's capture of Quebec and the fact that South Carolinians had as yet made few personal sacrifices in the war combined to create a martial atmosphere among the people. Add to this the governor's desire for military glory and his contempt for the Indians and his course of action was predictable. Yet Lyttelton would have been wise to listen to the advice of Bull and the Carolinian leaders. Though there was some sentiment in favor of war among the Cherokee, the sending of the chiefs to the capital was a clear sign that the majority favored peace. But Lyttelton wanted his military expedition and, rather than negotiate, he humiliated the chiefs by insisting that they return to the frontier under his "protection." The Indians were then forced to march as virtual prisoners until the small army reached Fort Prince George, at which time they were confined as actual prisoners.[3]

Neither Lieutenant Governor Bull nor the Commons House was pleased with the militant stand of the Governor. Bull, a capable observer of the Carolina scene, understood that serious grievances existed among both the Cherokee and the white frontiersmen. He felt that a policy of intimidation should be avoided, as it might produce a treaty, but one that the Cherokee would feel free to renounce at the first opportunity. Instead, advised Bull,

Lyttelton might acknowledge the legitimate grievances of the Indians and negotiate an agreement that would result in a lasting peace. The Commons House, while not as generous to the Indian position as the lieutenant governor, were also opposed to a belligerent stance. Indeed, the Commons had been engaged in a continuing battle with the governor over control of Indian policy. Thus, it consistently slashed his requests for men and money.[4] Even after rumors of Cherokee outrages began drifting in during July 1759, the assembly insisted upon cutting defense spending. Lyttelton asked the Commons to continue the current establishment, a regiment of seven hundred men, in service until January 1. Realizing that this suggestion would meet with opposition, the governor added that he, as well as Prime Minister William Pitt, considered the provincial regiment necessary to the security of the colony. As an added inducement Lyttelton offered to waive the salary of thirty-five thousand pounds currency paid him by the assembly in order to help defray the cost. The Commons refused this offer and consented to the continuance of only three companies of the regiment (about three hundred men) and approximately fifty rangers to patrol the frontier. Lyttelton was extremely disappointed with such a provision and predicted that the assembly could expect to be called into special session if a more substantial assistance was not offered.[5]

This prediction proved accurate when the Cherokees erupted on the frontier and the assembly was called into special session in October 1759. The Commons House remained unhappy with the warlike demeanor of the governor and, though it reluctantly agreed to raise fifteen hundred men for a military expedition, asked him not to go to war until all hope of peace was exhausted. To demonstrate its seriousness, the Commons once again severely slashed Lyttelton's requests for funds. Though the governor estimated the cost of the expedition to be twenty thousand pounds sterling, the Commons provided only twelve thousand pounds currency. Lyttelton exploded in rage when he heard of this and sent the assembly a stinging note challenging its patriotism. This had little effect other than to anger the legislators and stiffen their desire to avoid increased expenditures. Such a stance necessitated the raising of a public subscription, which brought in forty-five thousand pounds currency during November 1759. Even this was not nearly enough to cover the actual cost of Lyttelton's expedition, which has been estimated at twenty-five thousand pounds sterling, the equivalent of £175,000 currency.[6]

Two men whose patriotism could not be questioned at this time were Henry Laurens and Christopher Gadsden. Though Laurens was probably among those counseling caution, he was also among the most generous contributors to the subscription when it became clear that Lyttelton was bent upon a military campaign. The firm of Austin, Laurens, and Appleby contributed seven thousand pounds, which tied them with Gabriel Manigault and the company of Middleton and Brailsford as the leading subscribers. Gadsden, too, was a likely supporter of the governor's measures against the Indians, as indicated by his later writings and by the fact that he quickly volunteered to serve during the campaign.[7]

The Lyttelton expedition was a disaster for the colony. The Governor left Charles Town on October 26, 1759 with fifteen hundred troops, twenty-six Indian chiefs, and Christopher Gadsden. The march to Fort Prince George was a difficult one of forty-five days, during which over two hundred men either deserted or became too ill to continue. By the time he arrived at the fort, Lyttelton was in command of a demoralized, mutinous army in the midst of serious measles and smallpox epidemics. Realizing that this force was in no condition to fight, he had the chiefs incarcerated and summoned Attakullakulla (known as Little Carpenter) for negotiations. Lyttelton gained nothing in the resulting treaty that could not have been achieved months earlier in Charles Town. It was agreed that the twenty-six chiefs would be held as hostages to be released when the Cherokee surrendered those responsible for the frontier murders. With this treaty in hand Lyttelton proclaimed himself the victor and quickly returned to a hero's welcome at Charles Town.[8] Despite the lack of concrete gains, the people of the capital seemed genuinely satisfied with the military results of the Lyttelton expedition. Soon afterward many of the leading citizens, Gadsden and Laurens included, signed a complimentary farewell address as the governor prepared to vacate his position in order to assume the post of governor of Jamaica in April 1760.[9] Yet, there remained one aspect of the Lyttelton expedition that terrified the residents of Charles Town: the small army brought the smallpox with them, creating the most serious epidemic in the history of the town. Since the last serious epidemic had come in 1738, relatively few of the residents had built any immunities to smallpox. Thus, despite a desperate inoculation campaign, smallpox ravaged the capital during the winter and spring of 1760. By the time that the epidemic had run its course in June 1760, three-fourths of the population was taken ill and over seven hundred (approximately 9 percent of the population of the town) were dead.[10]

Lyttelton's diplomacy was in little better condition, as his shaky peace collapsed even before he left the province. In February 1760, after the Cherokee threatened Fort Prince George and ambushed and killed its commander, the garrison panicked and massacred the chiefs. As a result, a unified Cherokee nation exploded in rage and rushed upon the frontier. Realizing that the colony was too weak to handle the Indians alone, a shaken Lyttelton called for assistance from General Jeffrey Amherst, the British commander-in-chief in America. Though Amherst was busy planning his own campaign in Canada, he did send a force of twelve hundred men under Colonel Archibald Montgomery. Still, he was impatient for the return of Montgomery's force and he ordered the colonel to defeat the Cherokee quickly and return to New York as soon as possible. Under no circumstances was Montgomery to engage in defensive operations. Montgomery was dismayed by the inadequate state of preparation when he arrived at Charles Town. The colony was supposed to have supplied a regiment of soldiers, but had raised only 335 rangers. Nor had the province made much of a provision for supplies or transportation. The infuriated Montgomery threatened to return immediately to New York if the colony did not properly provide for his campaign. The assembly finally agreed to raise the necessary supplies and transportation, but the smallpox epidemic made it impossible to raise more troops.[11]

Setting out in April 1760, the Montgomery expedition achieved little more than Lyttelton had and left the colony in even more trouble. The army destroyed several of the lower settlements of the Indians, and finally relieved Fort Prince George. Finding the Cherokee unwilling to negotiate, Montgomery set out to relieve Fort Loudoun (in present-day Tennessee), burning several of the middle settlements along the way. Finally, in late June, the small army was ambushed near the town of Etchoe. Montgomery held the field and burned the town, but suffered almost one hundred casualties in the process. After considering the mountainous terrain that would have to be traversed to reach Fort Loudoun, he decided that the Indians had been defeated and returned to Charles Town. In so doing he "Stole a March upon them [the Indians] in the Night" in order to be through the mountain passes, which he recognized as good places for ambush, before the Indians knew what was happening. This night retreat served only to increase the confidence of the Indians, making them even more dangerous and difficult to deal with. Colonial leaders begged Montgomery to remain in the province, but the colonel, citing his orders, was determined to return to New York. Though Montgomery was finally prevailed upon to leave four companies of soldiers on the frontier, this force was clearly not sufficient to protect the colony from the confident Cherokee.[12]

Fearing that Montgomery's expedition had only added fuel to the Indian fire, Lieutenant Governor Bull, who had assumed governance of the colony upon Lyttelton's departure, thought it best to go over to the defensive while making another effort at negotiation. With Montgomery gone, the colony was left almost defenseless, and the war had already cost the province almost £317,000 currency with little to show for such great expense.[13] The Commons, however, had changed their position and now saw that the honor of the colony was at stake. They bitterly denounced Bull's suggestion of negotiations and insisted upon a vigorous prosecution of the war. Many of the assemblymen, including Gadsden, were still smarting under the charges that the colony had done little to help defend itself. Nor were matters improved by the criticisms passed by British officers upon the

provincial troops. Particularly harsh commentary was offered by Lieutenant Colonel James Grant, the second-in-command, who informed Bull that
almost fifty of the rangers deserted before the army even marched and the
rest, to a man, ran off once the fighting began.[14]

Such commentary made Grant a very unpopular figure with men such as
Gadsden, who now increased their determination to prove the courage and
patriotism of South Carolinians. The Commons quickly raised the bounty
on Cherokee scalps to one hundred pounds currency, voted to raise a force
of one thousand men, and even gave serious consideration to a plan to arm
five hundred black men to help fight the Indians, the latter resolution failing
only by the vote of the speaker.[15]

Despite the unmistakable mood of the Commons, Bull continued to press
for negotiations. This policy was undermined by the surrender of Fort
Loudoun to the Cherokee and the resulting massacre of many of the prisoners. After this, even Bull agreed that another expedition was necessary
and appealed to Amherst for aid. The British commander again responded
with a regiment, this time to be led by Lieutenant Colonel James Grant.
Though Grant was a competent soldier, the seeds of trouble were present in
his appointment. Some Carolinians were still resentful of the remarks
Grant had made about the South Carolina rangers during the previous
campaign, while others were upset that Grant had been given command of
the campaign in spite of the fact that he was outranked by the commander
of the South Carolina regiment, Colonel Thomas Middleton. Such examples
of British haughtiness were particularly rankling to men such as Christopher Gadsden and would figure prominently in Gadsden's newspaper assault upon Grant.

The colony was much more serious about preparing for this offensive
than it had been for the previous one. Henry Laurens received his commission as lieutenant colonel of the South Carolina regiment in September
1760 and immediately set out on a recruiting mission that included much of
both Carolinas. This trip lasted several months and was fairly successful, as
the South Carolina regiment soon contained twelve hundred men.[16] In June
1761, Grant led over twenty-eight hundred men along the same route used
by Montgomery. He was attacked in almost the same spot as Montgomery
had been and, like his predecessor, fought the Cherokees off with substantial casualties. But, unlike Montgomery, Grant determined to forge ahead
and, rather than simply destroying the lower and middle settlements, he
destroyed the Indians' corn fields. Though Grant killed few Indians, he
considered his campaign a success:

> Fifteen towns and all the plantations in the country have been burnt—above
> 1,400 acres of corn, beans, pease, etc., destroyed; about 5,000 people including
> men, women, and children drove into the mountains to starve. They have

nothing left to subsist upon but a few horses which they contrived to keep out of our way; but we found the remains of numbers of them, which had been killed by themselves almost in every place we went to. Luckily nothing was left to be done on this side. It would have been impossible for us to proceed further. Our provisions were almost expended and our men were wore out and unable to act.[17]

Grant was pleased with the performance of the South Carolina troops and, while not retracting his earlier comments, praised them in his report to Amherst:

The Provincials have behaved well, as I always expected they would do and the Rangers, who I had not so favourable an opinion of, have been very usefull and alert, they never made a difficulty and they seem now to despise the Indians as much as they were suspected to fear them before.[18]

Grant's assessment of his campaign was proven correct when the Cherokees sent a delegation to him to discuss peace terms. As Amherst had specifically ordered him to leave the negotiation of peace to the provincial leaders, Grant directed the Indians to Lieutenant Governor Bull at Charles Town. Henry Laurens was designated to accompany the Cherokees to the capital and, since Charles Town was in the midst of another bout with smallpox, he led them to Ashley Ferry, two miles from the city. Here, on September 15, 1761, Bull and the council met the chiefs to discuss the terms of peace. Also present at this meeting was Henry Laurens, who was there to present Grant's advice, and an extremely dissatisfied Christopher Gadsden, whose appearance was apparently uninvited and unwelcome. Gadsden was unhappy for two reasons. First, he was angry that Grant had been content with the destruction of the Indian towns and fields, rather than the physical annihilation of the Cherokee. Second, he was upset that the council had rejected a bill that would continue the South Carolina regiment so that another, more effectual, campaign could be launched. The resulting peace treaty only infuriated Gadsden further and a serious argument broke out between him and Laurens at Ashley Ferry that marked the end of their friendship and almost ended in a duel.[19]

While there is little direct evidence, it is likely that the break came over the treatment of the Indians. The Cherokee were willing to admit defeat, and Laurens was in full agreement with Grant's advice that moderation was the best way to maintain peace in the future. Thus, Grant and Laurens suggested that since the Indians had already been severely punished through the destruction of their fields and homes, the demand that warriors be executed in retaliation for the frontier murders could be dispensed with. Gadsden represented the opinion of the Commons House when he insisted that this demand, insisted upon from the start of the war, be included in the treaty. He was adamant in his belief that the war could not be considered a victory without the executions and without severe restrictions placed upon the Cherokee. Bull agreed with his military advisors that insistence upon executions had already prolonged the war and that further inflexibility on this point would only sow the seeds of future trouble. Thus, the demand for executions was removed from the treaty.[20] It is not difficult to imagine the blunt and hot-tempered Gadsden launching a vicious harangue at his old friend Laurens, not only for the advice offered to the lieutenant governor, but also for supporting the hated Grant. Laurens, while not as excitable as Gadsden, could be every bit as biting, and he apparently confronted Gadsden with an unspecified previous incident in which the conduct of the latter was cast in a very poor light. Though the intervention of friends later brought an apology from Laurens, the two men left Ashley Ferry with their long and close friendship in ruins.[21]

Gadsden quickly reported the proceedings at Ashley Ferry to the members of the Commons House, many of whom agreed with his views on the treaty. He was appointed to a committee of the House that declared a treaty without executions to be "useless and dishonorable" and announced that "no Peace ought to be made with the Cherokees upon any other Terms." The House as a whole agreed in principle with this report but, after considering that the terms had already been offered to the Cherokees and that the military establishment had been virtually dissolved, reluctantly agreed to the treaty as it stood.[22] Yet, the assembly felt cheated of victory and for this the blame was placed squarely upon Grant. The Commons criticized his strategy and also denounced him for ignoring the advice of Colonel Middleton, commander of the South Carolina regiment and currently a member of the assembly.[23] While the official protests against Grant quickly died down, the public dispute was only beginning. Tempers were so high, Grant wrote, that while waiting to embark for New York he was insulted every time he appeared on the streets of Charles Town. Grant soon lost patience with the attacks on his character being launched by Gadsden, Middleton, and others, and ended up fighting a duel with Middleton. Here, Grant reported, "tho he had used me worse than any Man ever did Another, I gave him his Life, when it was Absolutely in my Power."[24] Grant departed the province shortly afterward, but the dispute only intensified as Gadsden continued his attacks upon the British officer, while Henry Laurens stepped forward in defense of the colonel.

Gadsden's contributions to this conflict took the form of two long essays signed Philopatrios ("lover of homeland"), which appeared in December 1761 and May 1762. In these essays he set out to prove several important points. First, he charged that Grant was an incompetent officer who had implemented a defective strategy that cheated the colony of certain victory. Second, he argued that Grant had not only botched his own campaign, but had assumed primary direction of the Montgomery expedition and ruined that as well. Third, Grant had repeatedly ignored and insulted Colonel Middleton and the South Carolina regiment, virtually forcing Middleton to leave the army. Finally, despite large expenditures that now must be provided for, Grant had left the colony in worse condition than when he had first arrived.[25] Henry Laurens vigorously denounced these charges as a collection of half-truths, misrepresentations, and outright lies in a long unpublished manuscript signed "Philolethes" ("one who loves obscurity"), which he circulated privately in Charles Town.

In summarizing Grant's services, Gadsden concluded that he

> was sent to us the first time, and did worse than nothing: He was sent to us again, a second time, and did twice as much: And 'tis probable, he has not yet shewn us half he can do in the same way; another expedition may be still necessary; . . . and does the province want any thing more, than his presence a third time, as a commander in chief, to make all our estates as purely negative.

Gadsden insisted that Grant feared the Indians and had no intention of bringing them to battle. Instead, "the colonel's chief dependance, *from the very beginning*, was, on the *known* cowardice of the Indians." Grant's entire attitude and his strategy of burning towns and fields, Gadsden argued, served only to enrage the Indians and make them more confident in their roles as "conquerors."[26]

Laurens was shocked at such commentary and wondered if he and Gadsden were discussing the same campaign. In his view, the Grant expedition had been an extremely successful venture. He scoffed at the idea that Grant had pursued a defensive strategy, pointing out that the army moved ahead even after the ambush. Nor was Grant afraid of the Indians. To Gadsden's criticism that Grant had not killed enough Indians, Laurens replied:

> they kept aloof, & saved their Scalps by flight to such places as insur'd their safety. But yet I would not exchange the Towns & Fields that were destroy'd for five times the number of Heads that he wishes for, over & above what were really taken; because I am certain that the Loss as it now stands is greater & the Chastisement will be much longer.[27]

By burning the fields Grant did great damage to the Cherokee, forcing them to flee into the mountains faced with the choice of surrender or starvation. True, he admitted, these tactics probably enraged the Indians, but this hardly made them more formidable. Indeed, the Cherokees had been reduced to the necessity of eating their horses. Was this the way of "conquerors"? Laurens thought not, and he assured his readers that the Indian will had been broken and that all the Cherokees wanted now was peace.[28]

Laurens did not attempt to dispute the charge that Grant exercised ineffective command of the Montgomery campaign, for he had not accompanied this force and did not consider himself an authority on the subject. He did, however, think it quite odd that Gadsden, who was not a firsthand observer of either the Grant or Montgomery expeditions, could now be such an expert on both. Though it was impossible for Gadsden to prove that Grant had the command of Montgomery's march, he did effectively portray Grant as a self-seeking opportunist who took credit for successes while passing the blame for failures. In attempting to demonstrate "that none and the same great negotiating genius . . . presided throughout," Gadsden merely turned to the reports Grant made to Lieutenant Governor Bull during the Montgomery campaign. He demonstrated Grant's tendency toward self-promotion in the following devastating passage:

> The only one in either letter where col. M———y is even permitted to appear to have the sole direction, which he is honoured with just before *"we stole a march upon them in the night"* to get *safe* back to Kechowee: a most auspicious illfavoured junction indeed: "in this situation: (we are told) *"col. M———y thought it adviseable to return to Fort Prince George"* &c No I, no We here! what modesty! what self-denial! When the action was a little more conspicuous, as in a pretty little affair at the close of this letter, who but *"I was obliged to march a company of light infantry into the fort to bring them to reason."*[29]

Thus, Gadsden was able to use Grant's own letters to show that the British colonel was a self-seeker who would bend the truth, if necessary, to promote himself.

Gadsden shared with many of his fellow Carolinians a belief that Americans were unappreciated by the British and could always expect to be blamed for failures, regardless of the truth. He viewed Grant's criticism of the provincials during the Montgomery campaign as yet another example of this and set out to set the record straight. He admitted that some of the provincials had deserted in the early stages of the campaign but pointed out, correctly, that most remained with the army throughout and performed well under attack. The fact that Grant ignored the latter fact while emphasizing the former was, to Gadsden, further evidence that the colonel wished to blame the provincials for the failures of himself and his men.[30]

Gadsden went on to bitterly criticize Grant for what he saw as poor treatment of Colonel Middleton, considering this case a confirmation that no American, no matter how deserving, could ever expect to achieve a position of real importance. He thought it ridiculous that Grant, an outsider with little knowledge of the colony or the Cherokee, could be placed above a prominent provincial officer who outranked him. Gadsden praised Middleton for submitting to this arrangement, particularly after Grant refused to consult with him and rejected his objections out-of-hand. Considering that Lieutenant Governor Bull had given Middleton permission to leave the regiment if he found it necessary, Gadsden marveled at the restraint of the provincial colonel under repeated insults. Still, Gadsden denied any implication that the provincial soldier was better than the British regular. He did feel, however, that Americans might possess some insights on warfare, especially Indian warfare, which merited at least some consideration.[31]

While Laurens agreed that British officers could be arrogant, he was certain that British arrogance had not been the problem in this case. He disagreed wholeheartedly with Gadsden's praise of Middleton, complaining that he had seen little from this officer during the campaign that merited compliment. Indeed, if the conduct of any officer warranted investigation, wrote Laurens, if was that of Middleton. Nor was the provincial colonel entitled to any special praise for submitting to Grant's command for "he had no alternative, but that one, of staying at home, because Genl Amherst did not rate his Value so high as to make it a matter of any consequence whether he went with the troops or not." Laurens displayed a clear bias in favor of the regulars when he added that Amherst had not sent a commanding officer and a considerable body of troops to take lessons from a provincial colonel who, for all he knew, may have been a shopkeeper the day before.[32]

Laurens admitted that Middleton had not been consulted on basic strategy but explained, weakly, that it was Grant's custom to keep his own counsel and, therefore, he did not ask any of his officers for advice on strategy. Still, Laurens insisted that Grant has always treated Middleton with respect, keeping him well informed of plans and welcoming objections or suggestions from any of the officers. Laurens expressed surprise at Gadsden's claim that Grant had rejected all of Middleton's objections, for he could not remember the provincial colonel making any suggestions or demonstrating any ability at all. His strongest criticism of Middleton's conduct, however, was reserved for the colonel's leaving the army before the end of the campaign, an act that Laurens considered indefensible. Though Gadsden and Middleton both claimed that the latter had left the army because of Grant's continued insults, Laurens could recall no such insults. As Middleton's second-in-command, Laurens assumed that he would surely have known of any serious difficulty between the two officers. He felt that Grant had consistently treated Middleton with respect and had definitely not forced the colonel to leave his regiment. Nor did Middleton's letter to Grant informing the latter of his decision to leave the army support his later story. Here, the emphasis was placed upon pressing family and business concerns, an excuse that Laurens found to be completely unacceptable.[33] But even if one accepted the colonel's story that he left because of the incompetence and tyranny of the commander, his actions were still incomprehensible. If Middleton really believed this of Grant, asked Laurens, was it not his duty to remain with the army to try to check any bad moves made by the commander, or at least to look out for the safety of his men? Any way that one viewed this episode, Middleton was guilty of a gross dereliction of duty, and Laurens suggested that the attack upon Grant was only a smoke screen to protect the provincial colonel from a fully warranted investigation of his own conduct.[34]

Nor was Laurens very impressed with the performance of the South Carolina regiment, particularly when compared to that of the British regulars. He scoffed at the idea that the regulars did not know how to fight Indians and needed training for this purpose from the colonials. Rather, the opposite was true. Laurens pointed out that Grant led a force of seasoned professionals who had spent the past few years fighting the Canadian irregulars and northern Indians. It was they who trained the provincials, few of whom had ever seen an Indian, and many of whom had never been outside of Charles Town. Also, Grant had made great efforts to prevent discord between the provincials and the regulars, going so far as to share his supplies after the colonials had run out. Despite this, Gadsden had held Grant responsible for the fact that many of the provincials had to go without blankets, camp kettles, and other items. Laurens admitted that the provincials were forced to live without these items, but insisted that this was hardly the fault of the commander. He explained that each man had started with these supplies but, when the Indians attacked, many of the provincials threw off their backpacks and some even tossed their bayonets away. Such conduct had disgusted Laurens and he "used every means in my power to prevent it, except shooting them which I was once so near doing as to Cock my Fusil for the purpose but all in vain."[34] Finally, Laurens lowered the boom on Gadsden, remarking that the latter must have been a very recent convert to the merits of the provincial soldier. He recalled that Gadsden had once remarked in the assembly that

> I have seen so much of these people (says he) in the expedition with Mr. Lyttelton, that if we had been attacked by the Cherokees, & that I could have had it in my own choice, I would rather take my chance to be on the side of 500 Regular Troops to oppose the Indians, than to be with 1500 of them (the Rangers or Militia).[36]

Laurens was also unhappy with Gadsden's claim that only the executions of Cherokee warriors would ensure that the Indians would remain peaceful. The opposite was true, said Laurens. It would gain the colony nothing and only increase the resentment of the Indians. He assured his readers that the Cherokee had been so thoroughly frightened by Grant that they had no desire to fight again and, if the colony would let well enough alone, its Indian problem was at an end. Of course, only the future could settle this argument and, as Laurens occasionally pointed out with satisfaction, events did prove him correct. By the end of the decade Laurens could report that even Gadsden seemed to be accepting the fact that he had been wrong. As Laurens wrote to Grant in 1768:

> As to the farcical Campaign & Sham Treaty in the Cherokee Country I have some reason to believe that no Man is more convinced of his errors, than Philopatrios himself is, of his mistakes in asserting things of that sort. He has his Passions & Mad fits as well as other People & almost as often, but he has likewise his Lucid intervals & too much candour than to deny the proofs of "Facts & Dates."[37]

This was a good assessment of Gadsden. An honest, well-meaning man, he sometimes allowed his zeal and temper to affect his judgment. Once he assumed a position to be correct, it was nearly impossible to convince him that he had been mistaken. Such was the case with the Cherokee War. His distrust and dislike of Grant blinded him to the very real benefits produced by this campaign. In comparing the Grant campaign to the Montgomery expedition, Gadsden had made the mistake of equating two nonequals. Though there were many similarities between the two offensives, there were also some important differences. Grant destroyed twice as many villages as Montgomery but, more important than that, he had also burned the Indians' fields, leaving them no choice other than surrender or starvation. The cooler and more even-tempered Laurens quickly realized that Grant had achieved the same results, at a far lower cost, than a bloody campaign aimed at the destruction of the Cherokee. Unfortunately, this position became unpopular as Grant's supposed mistreatment of Colonel Middleton brought the subject of British arrogance, a sensitive matter to many Carolinians, into the fray. When Laurens defended the British commander few viewed this, as he did, as an honest attempt to protect the reputation of a man deserving gratitude rather than abuse. Many looked upon Laurens as a traitor who was supporting the pretensions of British placemen over the claims of his own people. The result was a serious loss of popularity for Laurens, evidenced by his failure to win reelection to the Commons House in January 1762.[38]

Things turned out much better for Christopher Gadsden. Though most would agree that he got the worst of this debate, the controversy established him as a leading protector of the rights of his colony. Though there was no direct attack upon the British government, South Carolinians made a clear statement that they were tired of being forced into an inferior role in their own colony. They were growing impatient with arrogant British placemen of questionable competence who monopolized the positions of influence, while the local men of talent could expect to rise no higher than the Commons House. These men had found a spokesman in Christopher

Gadsden and were preparing to resist any further attacks upon their rights by the placemen. They did not have long to wait. Before the furor over the Cherokee War had completely subsided, a new and more threatening crisis arose and, once again, Christopher Gadsden was at the center of the conflict.

3

Christopher Gadsden and the Birth of the Protest Movement, 1762–1764

LONG BEFORE THE LOUD DISPUTE OVER THE CHEROKEE WAR AROSE, AN ALMOST imperceptible, though far more threatening, attack upon the royal prerogative was in progress in South Carolina. The power of the Commons House of Assembly had been increasing steadily in the decades before 1760. This rising influence came at the expense of the governor and, more particularly, the council, a body whose place in the government had never been clear. The relative powers and responsibilities of the assembly and the council had been in dispute before 1760 and would become a major problem in the 1760s and 1770s. The crucial struggles had occurred over finance. As in other colonies, the Commons House had emerged as largely victorious by 1760 and had used the power of the purse string to further enhance its influence. Still, the Commons lacked a key element used by colonial legislatures to achieve dominance: control over the salary of the governor. Of the fifteen-hundred-pound salary of the governor of South Carolina, only one-third was provided by the assembly. While a permanent salary allowed the governor some independence, the assembly possessed other weapons that might be deployed to bring the governor to their point of view. Most important was the tax bill: a recalcitrant governor might be willing to sacrifice a third of his salary to make a point, but a refusal to pass a tax bill, which would leave the government without operating funds, usually brought concessions.[1]

The British government was taking steps to reclaim lost authority even before the French and Indian War. Believing James Glen (1738–1756) too weak to implement the necessary reform, the ministry replaced Glen with William Henry Lyttelton. To insure that there was no confusion over their intentions, the ministry specifically instructed Lyttelton to roll back the gains of the assembly and bring the colony under tighter British control. Upon his arrival in 1756, Lyttelton found the assembly and council locked in a bitter dispute over the selection of the colonial agent in London. Anxious to proceed with the public business and slow to comprehend the important implications of the conflict, Lyttelton intervened upon the side of the assembly. When William Wragg, a blunt and outspoken counselor, ob-

47

jected to the decision, Lyttelton removed Wragg from the council and replaced him with a British placeman. Though the contentious Wragg had
never been popular with his fellow Carolinians, his removal increased the
resentment of the local elite over the growing tendency toward appointment of placemen over qualified local candidates. This seemingly minor
affair had important consequences for Lyttelton and his successors, as it
severely weakened the influence of the council, a body that was usually an
important source of executive support.[2]

The performance of the colony during the French and Indian War did
nothing to alter British perceptions of local conditions. Despite the colony's
tax per adult, highest in the American colonies, British officials complained
that the war would have been shorter and cheaper had local authorities
been more cooperative in furnishing men and supplies. A painful
demonstration of parliamentary dissatisfaction came when Parliament
made financial reimbursements for wartime expenses proportionate to
enlistments, leaving South Carolina little assistance in retiring its debt.[3]

As the French and Indian War concluded in America, the British government decided that the American colonies would have to be brought more
firmly under imperial control. South Carolina was to be a particular target
of this crackdown, and Governor Thomas Boone arrived in Charles Town
in December 1761 determined to implement the new policy. Few anticipated trouble upon the arrival of the new governor, and many viewed his
appointment as ideal for calming tensions after the Cherokee War. Boone
had strong and important local ties and was a descendant of the Colleton
family, one of the oldest and most prominent in the colony. Born and raised
in England, he first came to South Carolina as a young man in 1752 to
oversee estates he and his brother had inherited from his powerful uncle,
Joseph Boone. He remained in the colony for two years before going home
to England. Returning to South Carolina in 1759, he married a local woman
before leaving to become governor of New Jersey later that same year.
After a successful tenure of eighteen months in that position, Boone returned to govern South Carolina.[4] The enthusiasm with which Boone was
greeted is understandable as the colony, fresh from a bitter dispute over the
competence of British placemen, would now be governed by a man with
strong local ties and proven administrative ability. It seemed that harmony
would again reign in South Carolina.

The first six months of Boone's administration went smoothly, as Boone
established strong relationships with both the council and the assembly.
Trouble began, however, when Boone examined the Election Act of 1721
and found it to be "loose and general" and in need of revision. The Election
Act defined the entire electoral process in South Carolina, from the establishment of voting and office-holding qualifications to the designation of
constituencies to the regulation of the electoral process. According to the

act, the parish was the unit of representation and the local church wardens would serve as the election officials. After taking special oaths before justices of the peace, the church wardens would oversee the elections and then execute the writs of election issued by the governor and council to certify the results. When Boone, in March 1762, suggested that the Commons draw up a new election act, the assembly refused to consider such action, insisting that the current act was adequate and unobjectionable.[5] Boone bided his time, awaiting an opportunity to demonstrate the weakness of the Election Act. This came with the election of Christopher Gadsden in a special race to fill a vacated seat for St. Paul's parish in June 1762. Three candidates had stood in this election and Gadsden had won a clear and undisputed victory, capturing seventy-six of the ninety-four votes cast. When the assembly met again after a two-month recess in September, it found the election return from St. Paul's to be blank. The Commons sent for the church wardens, who confirmed that Gadsden had been duly elected by the parish. Further investigation disclosed that the church wardens had not taken the oath required by the Election Act. Technically, this constituted a violation of the Election Act. Yet there had been no hint of irregularity in the election and, thus, the spirit of the law had not been violated. Observing that members had been admitted in the past after elections in which the church wardens had not been sworn, and that there was no complaint of fraud, the Commons approved Gadsden's election.[6]

This was precisely the sort of situation that Boone had been awaiting. It was just such a technical violation that could most effectively prove his point that the Election Act needed to be defined more strictly. That it was the election of Christopher Gadsden, whose recent activities had identified him as a troublemaker to British authorities, which had been called into question further attracted Boone's attention. As required under the law, the Commons administered their oath to Gadsden and sent him to Governor Boone for the state oath. Boone refused to administer the oath to Gadsden, expressing amazement that the House would admit him after the violation of the Election Act. In a message to the assembly, the governor made his position perfectly clear:

> Was I to pass over Gentlemen this violation of a Law, which you seemed before so tender of, I should not discover that regard to Laws in General which it is my duty to encourage in others in order therefore to manifest in as publick a manner as I can, my disavowal of so undeniable an infraction of the Election Act.

Continuing, Boone made an unfortunate observation concerning the Election Act, calling it "an Act of Assembly, to a rigid execution of which your Body owes, or ought to owe, its existence." Then, Boone dissolved the House.[7]

In taking such strong action the governor raised two very important constitutional points. The first concerned the right of the assembly to control its own elections and membership. The English House of Commons had asserted this right as early as 1604, and the colonial assemblies had attempted to do so since birth. The South Carolina Commons House had exerted authority in this area since at least 1692 and by 1711 had set up a standing committee on elections and privileges. Yet the requirement that the governor administer the state oath retained the possibility that he could exert a veto by refusing to give the oath. Still, only once before the Gadsden case did a governor refuse to administer the oath to a man whose election was recognized by the assembly. In this previous case, however, the individual in question was under a bill of indictment, a much different circumstance than that of Gadsden. Also, the governor in the earlier case had relented after the Commons cited an English precedent in which an indicted member was allowed to retain his seat until convicted. Even more ominous was Boone's implication that the representative assembly existed not by the natural rights of the people, but by a law sanctioned by the Crown. Acceptance of such a theory could place the very existence of the Commons House in jeopardy, for rights bestowed by the Crown could be taken away at the pleasure of the monarch.[8]

The election of the new assembly was a clear indication of popular support for the Commons, as thirty-seven of the forty-eight members of the previous House were returned. In St. Paul's parish, Gadsden was returned with an even greater percentage than he received in the earlier election. After being prorogued following a brief meeting in October, the assembly met on November 22. Governor Boone made no reference to the Gadsden case in his opening address, indicating a desire to drop the matter. Instead, he stuck to formalities and recommended business for the consideration of the assembly. The Commons, however, greatly alarmed by the implications of Boone's previous actions, refused to end the controversy without informing the governor of its position. After presenting a mild reply to the governor's speech, the assembly proceeded to appoint a committee on privileges and elections to prepare a report on the Gadsden case and the surrounding issues. The importance of this issue is evident in the composition of the committee, which included chairman John Rutledge, Rawlins Lowndes, Peter Manigault, Charles Pinckney, William Wragg, and, to irritate the governor, Christopher Gadsden. A committee of correspondence, which included both Gadsden and Henry Laurens, was appointed to communicate with Charles Garth, the colony's agent in London, if it became necessary to make an appeal over the head of the governor.[9]

Six days later Rutledge reported from the committee that "it is the undeniable fundamental and inherent right & privilege of the Commons House of Assembly of this Province Solely to examine and finally determine the

Elections of their own Members." The committee declared that there had been no violation of the Election Act in the Gadsden case. Since the church wardens had been sworn to faithfully execute the laws at the time of their election it would be "unnecessary and unreasonable" to require special oaths for every election, the original oath being sufficient for this purpose. But even if the law did require a specific oath of the church wardens, failure to take such an oath was not in itself cause for voiding an election. This would punish an entire parish, as well as the successful candidate, for something over which they had no control. The committee felt that the church warden himself might be punished for such a failure, citing a 1757 example of such action, but it was ridiculous to void an entire election over such a technicality. As Gadsden had won an overwhelming majority of the votes and no complaints of fraud had been received, it was clear that he had been duly elected and should have been qualified to serve. The committee proceeded to denounce Boone's implication that the existence of the assembly rested upon the Election Act, basing their stance upon both the British constitution and the colonial charter.[10]

The committee finally suggested four resolutions that were, after debate, accepted by the Commons. These resolutions included (1) that the right to determine the validity of elections belonged solely to the Commons House, (2) that the governor could only constitutionally take notice of affairs in the House by reports set before him by the assembly, (3) that Boone had breached the privileges of the Commons by refusing to administer the state oath to Gadsden after the House had declared him elected, and finally, (4)

> that the abrupt and sudden Dissolution of the last assembly for matters only Cognizable by the Commons House, was most precipitate, unadvised, unprecedented procedure; of the most Dangerous Consequences being a Great Violation of the Freedom of Elections, and having a manifest Tendency to Subvert and Destroy, the most Essential and most invaluable rights of the people, and reduce the Power and Authority of the House, to an abject dependence on, and Subserviency to the will and opinion of a Governor.

The assembly then expressed its seriousness by waiting upon the governor as a body to present these reports and resolutions.[11]

If Boone had earlier hoped that the entire business would blow over, he now refused to modify his stance in any way. He answered the Commons, stating that it was only with great reluctance that he replied at all, "for I never knew of any good effect from altercations of this sort." He then repeated that Gadsden had not been legally elected due to the failure of the church wardens to be sworn, and pointed to the differences between the two oaths to explain that the initial oath was insufficient to cover the execution of the election writs. He reminded the Commons that he, too, had registered disapproval of the Election Act as it stood, but since it had not been modified or replaced, it stood as law and had to be enforced. Nor would he budge on his statement that the existence of the House was due to the Election Act and added that if the act were disallowed the colony would be left without representation. Boone also denied that the Commons held sole power in the determination of elections, arguing that the governor's commission required him to supervise elections and that, without this check, the assembly might decide an election in opposition to the law. By accepting the election of Gadsden the Commons had done precisely this, assuming a power to which it had no right. It was not his purpose to engage in a debate about the various privileges of the House, Boone wrote, only to explain the law on this one. The governor concluded by congratulating himself on checking this "Dangerous Usurpation" of the Commons and suggested that they refer any further complaints to the king.[12]

Such a message was hardly conciliatory and the assembly ordered the committee on privileges and elections to prepare a reply, suspending all further business. On December 9, Gadsden reported from the committee, commenting that "Our anxiety must necessarily be very great, as we apprehend, Our all is at Stake." They again insisted that Gadsden's election was valid and denied that the Commons House owed its existence to the Election Act. Indeed, if the current Election Act were disallowed the assembly could base its existence upon previous election acts all the way back to the proprietary charter, a document that confirmed the natural right of the people to representation. As for the governor, the committee scolded that "we are far from thinking that Your Excellency has prov'd the last House guilty of any, much less a 'Dangerous Usurpation' which we humbly apprehend ought to have been done before Your Excellency coud [sic] with any Propriety applaud yourself for having Constitutionally check'd it."[13]

By this time Boone had grown weary of the conflict and, unwilling to give in, but with nothing to add to his previous comments, gave a brief, oral reply:

> Gentlemen, I must here refer you to my former answer, if you think that forty such Messages can be of any Service to the Province, I am ready to receive them, but give me leave to rely solely & absolutely on the Inefficacy of any thing you can do or say, to sully my Character or Conduct.[14]

Convinced that they would receive no satisfaction from petitions or appeals to reason, the Commons turned to more drastic measures. On December 16, the assembly, in a thinly attended session, voted twenty-four to six to suspend all further business with the governor until he apologized for violating the rights and privileges of the House. In addition, the committee of correspondence was directed to transmit a full account of the affair to Charles Garth in London, who would circulate it in influential English circles.[15] Nor was Boone inactive at this time. During the early months of 1763, the governor busied himself with making vast land grants along the Altamaha river, a coveted area that was still disputed between South Carolina and Georgia. While it may be that Boone was simply in a generous mood, the large grants to prominent members of the assembly suggests the involvement of political considerations.[16]

With Boone and the assembly stalemated, it was clear that the issue would have to be settled by British officials in London. The Board of Trade was concerned with the early reports of Boone's rash conduct, but deferred judgment until the governor submitted information to justify his behavior.[17] Meanwhile, the suspension of business, though approved by most South Carolinians, was not universally popular. Henry Laurens was one prominent citizen who opposed the measure, and it is likely that he joined William Wragg in the minority voting against it in the assembly. Though Laurens was among the recipients of Boone's landed generosity, receiving a warrant for three thousand acres along the Altamaha, it seems that his stance on the issue was as motivated by principle as was Gadsden's.[18] Laurens supported the assembly on the constitutional question, but felt that a complete disruption of the public business was an overreaction that could result in severe consequences for the colony. Once again Laurens and Gadsden prepared to square off on opposite sides of an important and extended public dispute. And once again it was Laurens who took a moderate line, Gadsden who championed the more combative position. As the committee of correspondence prepared its reports, the controversy moved from the state house and into the press. It was Gadsden who first took to the newspapers when, on December 11, he mischievously published an advertisement under the signature "Auditor Tantum" in the *South Carolina Gazette* in which he satirized Boone's position in highly overstated terms.[19] Such shenanigans aside, the duel in the press did not begin until the new year. The main issue was not Boone's conduct, for few could be found to defend this, but the question of whether such provocations were sufficient cause for a complete cessation of the public business. Laurens, Wragg, and others who felt that the assembly had overreacted published their ideas in Robert Wells's *South Carolina Weekly Gazette*, the main source of conservative thought during the crisis with Britain. Gadsden and his supporters made use of Peter Timothy's *South Carolina Gazette*, a paper that was rapidly becoming the leading organ of the South Carolina protest movement.

William Wragg fired the first shots with a letter to his constituents in the January 5, 1763 issue of the *South Carolina Weekly Gazette* in which he explained and justified his vote against the suspension of business. He felt that suspension was a hasty action that carried far more serious consequences than many of its supporters realized. With business halted the government would have no money and the colony might be reduced to chaos. Under such conditions, the bounties used to encourage immigration would be curtailed and the government would not be able to support the garrison defending the frontier at Fort Prince George. Nor would the government be able to pay its debts or even meet the daily responsibilities of running the colony. Finally, Wragg argued, a suspension would have harmful effects on the current negotiations of the colony's agent in London for South Carolina's share of the parliamentary grant covering expenses incurred in the late war. He concluded that such dislocations were too high a price to pay merely "because we happen to be displeased with his excellency's conduct; which, for ought we know, may in his majesty's judgment merit his highest commendation."[20]

Gadsden stepped forward to answer Wragg in a lengthy letter to his constituents of St. Paul's parish, published on February 5, 1763, in the *South Carolina Gazette*. This letter is important not only as a defense of the assembly's position, but also as an early exposition of the natural rights philosophy, which would shortly be used so effectively by the protest movement against British policy. He assured his readers that the effects of a suspension of business had been exaggerated and that the Commons had taken care to provide sufficient funds to continue the immigration bounties and maintain the garrison at Fort Prince George. Nor was there any more negotiating to be done for the parliamentary grant covering war expenses, as Charles Garth had recently reported from London that the money had already been distributed among the other colonies.[21] Gadsden went on to express complete support for the behavior of the Commons House throughout the dispute with Governor Boone and declared the final step

absolutely necessary, and the only step that a *free* assembly, *freely* representing a *free people*, that have any regard for the preservation of the happy constitution handed down to them by their ancestors, their own most essential welfare, and that of their posterity, could *freely* take.[22]

Gadsden next set out to demonstrate that a free assembly was essential to individual liberty and that no assembly could be free without the power to rule on its membership. This issue was the basis of any free assembly, Gadsden wrote, and any hardship or inconvenience, either individual or collective, would be worthwhile in defense of this point.[23] He also expressed surprise that Wragg could even suggest that the king might support Boone in his unconstitutional actions. Such a suggestion was insulting to the Crown and contrary to his own observations of George III, which, of course, would soon change:

Thank God! we have as good a king upon the throne as ever graced it, who has given the earliest and most endearing signs of the tenderest regard for the liberties and privileges of his subjects, and has thereby manifestly shown, his inclination is, to reign solely *in* the hearts of *free* people, not over a parcel of *slaves, free* men I *say*, who have an *inherent* not *promissive* right to be so.[24]

Gadsden insisted that the Act of Settlement had guaranteed the right of representation in a free parliament to all Englishmen. This was a natural and inherent right, and it was ridiculous to assume that such rights were indisputably held by those living in England, but forfeited forever by the courageous souls who settled the American wilderness. If such an idea had been commonly accepted, "the sons of Britain would have been thinly, very thinly, scattered on this side of the Atlantic ocean." No, he wrote, the natural rights of Englishmen were the birthright of all British subjects, regardless of where they lived. This included the right of free representation, and since Americans were not represented, and could not with practicality be represented in Parliament, the colonial assemblies were the only logical alternative. Indirectly denouncing the theory of virtual representation, Gadsden argued that the colonial assemblies were miniature parliaments entitled to the same rights and privileges as the English House of Commons. He found it distressing that anyone could object to this idea, exclaiming "What? A son not have a right to imitate his good parent, when nature tells him it ought to be his chief pride, as it most certainly is his chief duty!"[25]

Gadsden then proceeded to a lengthy recapitulation of the election dispute behind the crisis, placing particular emphasis upon how silly it was to void an entire election for no other reason than that the church wardens had not been sworn. Though Governor Boone was attempting to pose as a crusader against corruption, Gadsden was not so sure. He felt that Boone's interpretation of the law opened the electoral process to a new and dangerous threat of corruption. It would be far easier to corrupt a church warden or two than an entire parish, and "when the election is over, if the church-warden likes it, all is right, if not, then he has only to confess he was not sworn, and of course 'tis set aside."[26] Nor could Gadsden resist the temptation to take a final shot at Boone, attributing this crisis, and similar problems in other colonies, to inexperienced governors who lacked understanding of their local constitutions and arrogantly rejected any counsel that contradicted their narrow views. As a possible remedy, Gadsden advocated the appointment of one general American agent in London. Already anxious to achieve a unified American opposition to violations of their natural rights, Gadsden felt that a general agent would give the colonies more influence by placing the combined weight of America behind their complaints. Were this to be done, "we might hear, *now and then*, of an instance of [a] governor being severely and publickly censured, for *too bare-faced* stretch even of the prerogative."[27]

Gadsden's letter was answered by anonymous letters from Henry Laurens and former Chief Justice William Simpson in the February 28, 1763 issue of the *South Carolina Weekly Gazette*. While there are no known extant copies of this issue, the contents of the letters may be surmised through Gadsden's reply in the *South Carolina Gazette* of March 12, 1763. Each of these letters appears to have been primarily a personal attack, with little attention to the public issues. In his letter, Gadsden identified Laurens as the author of an eighteen-paragraph attack upon him and proceeded to dispute it paragraph by paragraph. The main issue seems to have been whether or not Laurens had allowed his unpublished writings on the Cherokee War to be used against Gadsden in a political campaign. Gadsden wrote that after the argument at Ashley Ferry, mutual friends had arranged a truce between the former friends, insisting that "if we could not be again at an amicable footing, we should at least, for the sake of our common friends, let all matters subside." Both men agreed to this, but Laurens had apparently considered something in Gadsden's recent letter of February 5 as aimed at himself. Thinking that Gadsden had broken the engagement, Laurens published his letter of February 28 attacking Gadsden's conduct during the Cherokee War controversy and threatening to publish his writings on the subject. Gadsden responded that even if he had made negative inferences to Laurens in his letter, it was the latter who had broken the agreement by privately circulating his criticisms of Gadsden. He then challenged Laurens to publish his charges so that he could respond publicly to them. Additionally, it appears that Laurens also accused Gadsden of being a leader in mob activity, even at this early date, a charge that Gadsden vehemently denied.[28]

Finally, Gadsden briefly summarized his past and present relationship with Laurens:

> I was for many years a warm, sincere, and disinterested friend to Mr. *Laurens*, and defy him to produce one instance wherein my actions, in all that time, failed of my professions; or what friend or friends of his Iago-like, I ever exerted any artifice or stratagem to separate from him. Mr. *Laurens* was I acknowledge, reciprocally my friend too. I thought him, I found him so, upon several occasions. His gross and public affronts, several years since, without making any concessions, convinced me he wanted candour at least; these occasioned the first breach between us. I am very sorry his behavior since, has not appeared to me in such a light, as to regain my good opinion, of no importance to him I dare say, and therefore beg to drop the subject, first desiring him to burn all my old papers, for fear of *more* mistakes. I assure him I have not one letter of his by me, that I know of, of an older date than June 1760.[29]

With this exchange the relationship between Christopher Gadsden and Henry Laurens, at best tenuous since the dispute at Ashley Ferry, collapsed entirely, never to be resurrected. Though the two would remain civil toward one another, the relationship would henceforth be one of mutual misunderstanding and recrimination.

As the controversy raged in the newspapers, both sides presented their cases to officials in England. The Board of Trade, already doubtful of the wisdom of Boone's conduct, received his defense in March 1763. While not yet ready to censure either side, the board did inform the governor that it still did not see sufficient cause for the original dissolution of the assembly. In the meantime, the House's committee of correspondence finally completed its report on February 14 and, without the signatures of Laurens and Wragg, sent it to Charles Garth in London. Garth published the report in a pamphlet entitled "A Full State of the Dispute Betwixt the Governor and the House of Assembly," which he circulated privately before submitting it to the Board to Trade in July 1764.[30] Meanwhile, serious difficulties were beginning to emerge in South Carolina as a result of the halt to public business. Henry Laurens complained in June 1763 that the closure of the public treasury was causing financial problems for him and others who were having trouble collecting money from men who used the situation as an excuse to avoid paying their debts. He reported that, though nine thousand pounds sterling fell due to him at this time, he could collect barely enough to keep himself out of debt. Indeed, he had recently been forced to draw bills for seven hundred pounds sterling in London, which he would have avoided if possible.[31]

The Commons House showed no signs of departing from its resolution and did not even muster a quorum between the suspension of business in December 1762 and September 3, 1763, when Boone urgently called it into session to look into outrages committed by the Creek Indians on the frontier. Though the Commons refused to consider the Indian problem, it did take advantage of the situation by insulting the governor. Observing the custom of sending two previously qualified members to witness the taking of the state oath by a new member, the assembly sent Gadsden and William Moultrie to watch Sir John Colleton take the oath. The appearance of Gadsden upset the governor, who angrily stated that the Commons had no right to order anyone into his home. Inviting Colleton to remain and transact his business, Boone insisted that the other two gentlemen leave and personally showed them to the door. Besides this deliberate insult to the governor, the only other business of note conducted by the assembly was the preparation of an address to the king, denouncing Governor Boone and holding his refusal to apologize for trampling on the rights of the House responsible for the suspension of business, now in its eighth month. After asking the king to redress their grievances, the members of the Commons accepted the address on September 13. This accomplished, many of the members returned home, once again leaving the assembly without a quorum.[32]

Boone made another effort to restore relations with the Commons after a

Christmas Eve raid by the Creeks resulted in the death of fourteen people at the frontier settlement at Long Canes. Addressing the Commons on January 4, 1764, Boone was careful to say nothing to upset the House. Instead, he outlined the Indian outrages and the chaotic state of the frontier, begging the assembly to support its countrymen. Once again, however, the Commons refused after defeating a motion to repeal the resolution suspending business.[33] Henry Laurens was among those who were shocked and dismayed by such a disgraceful dereliction of duty. Placing the blame largely upon Gadsden, Laurens denounced his neighbor in a bitter letter to a friend:

> Our public disputes are still maintained & God only knows when there will be an end to them. One poor rash headlong Gentleman who has been too long a ringleader of people engaged in popular quarrels lately declared in full Assembly that he would rather submit to the distruction of one half of the Country than to give up the point in dispute with the Governor. His judgement must be very nice & much refined to discover that just one half of our Lives would be a sufficient compensation for the loss of that point which he has in view, which perhaps may prove to be no more than the miscarriage of his own vain opinion, but it happens that he lives within the walls of Charles Town. If he was a settler at long Canes or even had one Thousand pounds at stake then he would sing a different note. Our Frontier inhabitants are not very much obliged to him for his tenderness altho the Indians may be. This Gentleman could not have produced a stronger argument to convince me that he is not a fit person to judge of public affairs, but this being the unhappy situation or present circumstance of our Province we must all submit with patience until it pleases God to deliver us from the calamity of domestic broils, which we have long suffered under & which in my sentiments are more awful than Fire, Pestilence, or Foreign Wars.[34]

This was perhaps the harshest commentary that Laurens would ever pass on Gadsden. Yet it was understandable under the circumstances, as Laurens felt strongly that the assembly, dominated by Gadsden, had violated the public trust in failing to protect the frontier from the Indian menace.

It was now painfully obvious that no public business would be transacted while the governor remained in the province. Faced with this fact and desirous of an explicit decision by the Board of Trade, Boone left for London on May 11. As Lieutenant Governor William Bull again took charge of the government, the Commons decided to resume business.[35] Finally, on July 16, 1764, the Board of Trade reached its decision in which it quite properly criticized the conduct of both sides. The board had no sympathy for the position of Governor Boone, declaring that he had "taken up the matter in dispute with more zeal than prudence and in the process of it to have been actuated by a degree of Passion and Resentment inconsistent with good Policy, and unsuitable to the dignity of his situation." As for the members of the Commons House, they had "allowed themselves to be so far provoked as to forget their Duty to His Majesty & to their Constituents." The board, as expected, refused to support the Commons in its suspension of the public business, declaring the measure "equally unjustifiable in itself and disrespectful to His Majesty."[36] Still, the board was clearly more sympathetic to the position of the Commons than to that of the governor, and this represented a victory for the assembly. Though the board did not explicitly guarantee the sole right of determining the validity of elections to the Commons, this decision and the subsequent removal of Governor Boone effectively confirmed this right to the House.

The controversy was not yet over, however, for there remained the question of the salary of the governor, who had received no pay at all from the assembly during his tenure in South Carolina. An item had appeared in the tax bill to pay the governor seven thousand pounds currency for two years' salary, but was promptly removed by the assembly. The council refused to pass a tax bill unless some provision was made to pay Boone's salary.[37] Stalemated again, the Commons appointed a committee, headed by Gadsden, to prepare an answer to the council. The furious Gadsden reported from the committee that the traditional payment to the governor was not a salary, but a gratuity from the people, and it would be "stupid" for them to confer it upon a governor who had attempted to deprive them of their dearest rights. He then offered a strong denunciation of the council, questioning its legislative authority and informing it that "we most highly applaud your profound Sagacity in discovering the Great abilities and merit of a Governor who (in our opinion) has not been exceeded by any of his Predecessors in the arts of Haughtiness and Despotism." Gadsden concluded with an angry refusal to restore the allowance for Boone's salary, "NO! not even for your favorite Governor!"[38] Though the House toned down the violence of Gadsden's language, they agreed that the salary should not be paid. Upon hearing of this, Boone petitioned the Board of Trade for two-and-a-half years salary of twelve hundred fifty pounds sterling, suggesting that this be paid from the South Carolina quitrents. After asking the advice of the Privy Council, on February 25, 1766 the Board of Trade issued an additional instruction to the governor of South Carolina, directing him to recommend strongly to the assembly that they pay Boone's salary. Lord Charles Greville Montagu, the newly appointed governor, presented this instruction to the assembly upon his arrival in the colony in June 1766. The Commons, though refusing to admit error in withholding the salary, nevertheless agreed to comply as a demonstration of goodwill and gratitude for the removal of Governor Boone and the repeal of the Stamp Act.[39]

Thus ended the Gadsden election controversy. Though a seemingly ridiculous dispute over a small matter, the importance of this episode to the development of the revolutionary movement should not be underestimated. The crisis provided valuable experience in opposition politics for the members of the South Carolina Commons House, many of whom would assume key roles in the protest movement. The case also served to increase the already surging confidence of the assembly: the condemnation and subsequent removal of Governor Boone proved to the House that it was strong enough to take on any opponent who dared attack its rights. When the British government decided to tax the colonies without their consent, South Carolina was ready to defend itself and had the organization in place to do so effectively. The spirit of opposition that had manifested itself against Governor Boone proved easily transferable to Parliament. So, too, were the strategies and arguments of opposition, which were constructed and refined during the struggle with Boone. Though the Commons had been careful to assure the British government of its loyalty throughout the crisis, it can be truly said that the South Carolina revolutionary movement was born during the Gadsden election controversy.

The issue also served to further define the characters and positions assumed by Christopher Gadsden and Henry Laurens. Gadsden had once again confirmed himself as the leading and most daring defender of the rights and privileges of his province against the pretensions of outsiders. In his typically blunt and fiery manner, Gadsden anticipated many of the arguments that Americans would employ throughout the constitutional dispute with Britain. Most notable among these was his reliance upon natural rights and his rejection of the theory of virtual representation. In his proposal for the appointment of a general agent to represent shared American interests in London, Gadsden also demonstrated a continental vision far in advance of most of his contemporaries. Willing to look beyond local interests, Gadsden understood early that united action was essential if the American colonies were to successfully defend their rights. Finally, Gadsden's refusal to support a resumption in business in the face of Indian outrages on the frontier demonstrated the best and the worst in his character. While demonstrating a single-mindedness of purpose and a willingness to sacrifice (though in this case, the sacrifices were to be borne by others), Gadsden again allowed his zeal to interfere with his judgment.

The controversy also provided further confirmation of the general moderation and levelheadedness of Henry Laurens. Despite his agreement with the assembly on the constitutional question, Laurens felt that the disruption of business was an extreme move that could prove counterproductive. He hoped that other measures might be found that would yield similar results without the dislocations of a complete interruption of the public business. The problems experienced by the colony during the controversy confirmed him in this opinion. He was particularly distressed with the assembly for its refusal to come to the assistance of the frontier, an action that he considered indefensible, regardless of the provocations offered by the governor. As the Cherokee War marked the end to the friendship between Gadsden and Laurens, the Gadsden election controversy inspired the development of a strong political rivalry between the two men. This rivalry intensified as the radical Gadsden and the moderate Laurens turned their attention from the provocations of Governor Boone and toward the innovations of the British Parliament. In their thoughts and actions on the Stamp Act, Gadsden and Laurens would again stand as symbols of the wide divergence between the radical and moderate positions.

4

The Stamp Act Crisis, 1764–1766

THE FRENCH AND INDIAN WAR HAD CREATED LITTLE GOODWILL IN OFFICIAL British circles for the American colonies. Rather, British leaders saw the Americans as selfish and ungrateful, people who had prolonged the war by trading with the enemy and who did little fighting, even in their own defense, until Parliament agreed to underwrite the costs. The war had been as beneficial to the colonies as to the mother country, yet the Americans had not shared the financial sacrifices endured by their fellow citizens in England. To men such as George Grenville, the new first minister and chancellor of the exchequer, the colonies were getting a free ride, growing rich and strong, while Britain was exhausted and burdened by taxes. It seemed only fair that Americans, already demanding the political rights of British citizenship, also assume part of the financial responsibility of that citizenship.[1]

To Grenville and Charles Townshend, president of the Board of Trade, it was not only desirable and just that America contribute more to the costs of imperial government, but absolutely necessary. The British national debt had nearly doubled during the late war and taxes, already high in Britain, would have to be raised just to pay the interest on the debt. Though the American debt was not nearly as oppressive as Britain's, Grenville was not yet prepared to insist upon American support in payment of the national debt.[2] He did feel, however, that Americans should assume more of the costs of imperial government, specifically the ten-thousand-man army stationed in America. The annual cost of the army was estimated at £220,000 and Grenville thought it reasonable that America assume at least part of the expense because, after all, it was for their own defense. The source of this American revenue was a more difficult issue. Grenville rejected any reliance upon the traditional method of requisition, as it had never proven adequate in the past. The customs service provided little better prospect, as it was rife with corruption and was producing, on average, the ridiculously low sum of eighteen hundred pounds per year.[3]

In his search for an American revenue, George Grenville was certainly no innovator. His entire program, from the standing army to the Stamp Act, had been promoted for years by men more familiar with colonial affairs than he. Grenville began with reforming the customs service and insisting

upon strict enforcement of the Navigation Acts. Realizing that these revenues would be insufficient, Grenville searched for new taxes that might be
suitable to the colonies. His attention quickly focused upon extending the
stamp duty to America. Stamp duties had been levied in England since the
reign of Charles II and were currently yielding a revenue of approximately
£260,000 per year. That such a tax was relatively easy and inexpensive to
collect made it even more attractive. In designing the Stamp Act, Grenville
was careful to tailor it to meet the likely American objections. Believing
that it would be difficult for Americans to resist paying a tax paid by
Englishmen for nearly a century, he reduced the rates in America, hoping to
make the tax more palatable. He assured the colonies that all revenue
collected under the act would remain in America and that the act would be
administered by Americans rather than British placemen.[4]

Grenville delayed implementation of the Stamp Act for a year, hoping to
obtain the general consent of the colonies, along with any suggested modi-
fications. Charles Garth, the agent in London, informed the South Carolina
assembly that Parliament was set upon the Stamp Act and would accept no
arguments concerning either an inability to pay or challenging the authority
of Parliament to levy such a tax. Garth added the counsel that, given the
circumstances, the assembly would be wise to assent to the Stamp Act and
hail it as a valuable constitutional precedent that would require consultation with the colonies before passage of any revenue legislation affecting
America.[5]

The assembly was startled at the idea of a stamp duty and immediately
appointed a committee, which included Gadsden, to prepare a reply to the
agent. The committee rejected Garth's advice, denouncing the Stamp Act
on precisely the grounds that Grenville had declared nonnegotiable. The
major argument was constitutional: "The first, and in our opinion, the
principal reason, against such a measure, is its inconsistency with that
inherent right of every British subject, not to be taxed but by his own
consent, or that of his representative." Emphasizing the natural rights of
Englishmen, the committee expressed a desire to submit to all the acts of
Parliament, yet hoped "that when that august body come to consider this
matter they will view it in a more favorable light, and not deprive us of our
birthright, and thereby reduce us to the condition of vassals and
tributaries."[6]

The committee also forwarded the plea that the colony was already
burdened with taxes and was not able to support another tax. They pointed
to the large debt incurred during the Cherokee War, much of which had
been assumed upon the positive promise of parliamentary reimbursement.
That Parliament appeared to be reneging on this promise increased the
economic hardship of the province, as did the restrictions placed upon
them by the Navigation Acts. Though it may be suspected that the commit-

tee exaggerated the economic problems of the colony in an attempt to avoid the Stamp Act, this was not really the case. South Carolina was undergoing some difficult economic times during the 1760s. There was a genuine shortage of money in the colony, and the Currency Act of 1764, which prohibited any emission of legal tender currency without the permission of Parliament, contributed to the problem. In the same letter in which the Commons expressed opposition to the Stamp Act, Garth was directed to obtain approval for the printing of currency equivalent to forty thousand pounds sterling. As expressed by the committee, the colony was faced with a severe shortage of money, with only £106,500 currency, equal to £15,214 sterling, in circulation.[7] In addition to the monetary problem, taxes were being raised precipitously, particularly in Charles Town. The population of the capital nearly doubled between the 1750s and 1770s, and this population increase was accompanied by a great increase in the numbers of the poor. Requests for relief from the church wardens of St. Philip's rose 300 percent while taxes increased almost 700 percent between 1751 and 1773.[8] Under these circumstances the committee had hardly exaggerated the precarious economic condition of the colony. The committee concluded with a sharp denunciation of the Stamp Act, wondering why "a British Parliament, instead of alleviating, parent-like, the many hardships and difficulties peculiar to her sons settled in this hot and unhealthy climate" would increase those hardships through "so baneful an expedient" as an internal tax.[9]

It is doubtful that the Commons expected such arguments to have much effect and, as Grenville had predicted, Parliament refused to hear any petition that questioned its authority to tax the colonies. The Stamp Act became law on March 22, 1765 and was scheduled to go into effect on November 1. Few men in either England or America expected a severe outcry against the act. Most agreed with Benjamin Franklin, who, after fighting the act in London, felt that Americans would complain at first, but finally pay the tax.[10] Franklin notwithstanding, the South Carolina Commons House provided clear signs that its members would not accept the act mildly. The first order of business was the election of a speaker, generally a formality, as it was customary that the previous speaker be returned to the chair if he so desired. In this case, however, the previous speaker, Rawlins Lowndes, was defeated by Peter Manigault. While this contest has sometimes been explained as a personal struggle between the two men, the political implications cannot be ignored. Lowndes agreed that the Stamp Act was unconstitutional, but was unwilling to do more than petition for repeal while counseling compliance. Manigault, on the other hand, was prepared to support more active opposition.[11]

The importance of the assumption of the speaker's chair by Manigault was soon evident. On July 19, 1765, a circular letter was received from the speaker of the Massachusetts assembly in which the colonies were invited to send delegates to a special meeting to be held in New York in early October. The topic would be parliamentary taxation, and the meeting would attempt to unify American objections to the innovations of Parliament. Gadsden was chosen to chair the committee selected to consider the Massachusetts letter. A week later he reported that such a conference was "prudent and necessary" and recommended that the Commons appoint delegates. A dramatic debate followed, finally resulting in the approval of the meeting and the appointment of Gadsden, Thomas Lynch, and John Rutledge to represent the colony in New York. Though the journal of the Commons House did not record the results of the vote, it appears that several members, including Henry Laurens, voted against participation in the Stamp Act Congress.[12] The opponents of the Congress were unable to carry the day, largely because of the efforts of Christopher Gadsden. As David Ramsay wrote, Gadsden's "talents for speaking did not exceed mediocrity, yet there was in him so much honest zeal, ardor, and energy, that he had no small share of the merit of bringing the House into that important measure."[13]

Of all of his services during the revolutionary era, Gadsden was proudest of his role in bringing about the Stamp Act Congress. He viewed the Congress as the critical factor in the birth of the intercolonial protest movement and felt that he and his colony had played crucial roles in making it a reality. In 1778 he reminded William Henry Drayton that "no man in America ever strove more (and more successfully) first to bring about a Congress in 1765 and then to support it ever afterwards than myself."[14] In 1779, he assessed the significance of South Carolina's quick response in the calling of the Congress in a letter to Samuel Adams, writing that "Massachusetts sounded the Trumpet, but to Carolina is it owing that it was attended to; she immediately in 1765 flew to the appointed Rendezvous and had it not been for her I believe you are well convinced no Congress wou'd have then happen'd."[15] Certainly the South Carolina delegation was enthusiastic, for they were the first to arrive in New York, landing on September 15 after a voyage of eleven days. The Congress did not open until October 7, giving Gadsden time to meet and size up the other delegates as they arrived. What he found may have been somewhat discouraging, for South Carolina was the only colony south of Maryland to be represented at the Congress. Even worse, with the exception of James Otis, there was little radical representation at the meeting. Under these circumstances the usually inflexible Gadsden realized that he would have to compromise in order to achieve the unity he knew to be essential to success.[16]

There were two major areas of dispute that divided the Congress. First, there was disagreement over whether the main emphasis in the Declaration of Rights and Grievances should be placed on natural rights or charter rights. Gadsden felt that reliance on charter rights was a dangerous proposition that would likely end in catastrophe. True, the colonies might point to the Maryland charter, which expressly prohibited parliamentary taxation, but the British could counter with the Pennsylvania charter, which specifically allowed this power to Parliament. And where would this leave the colonies whose charters were silent on the issue? Also, were not charters issued by the Crown also subject to revocation by the Crown? Reliance on the charters, argued Gadsden, would destroy American unity and probably condemn the protest movement to failure. The Congress, said Gadsden, should base its opposition on the grounds of the natural and permanent rights of Englishmen. Then, there "would be no New England man, no New Yorker, etc. known on the Continent, but all of us Americans."[17] Such commentary represents a further extension of Gadsden's developing nationalism, a principle that would continue to grow throughout the rest of his life. It was also a sensible and effective position and, realizing this, the Congress decided to emphasize natural rights over the charters.

He was not to be so successful on the second issue, that of whether application should be made to the king alone, or whether Parliament should be included. Gadsden quickly placed himself in a minority by denying the authority of Parliament in any area other than the regulation of trade. Claiming that all British authority in America came from the Crown, Gadsden opposed making any admission that would imply recognition of parliamentary authority. Not that petitioning Parliament would have any effect anyway, insisted Gadsden, reminding the Congress that the House of Commons had refused to even hear colonial objections to the Stamp Act a year earlier. Though successful in defeating the first draft of the Declaration of Rights and Grievances, in which parliamentary legislation was specifically accepted as obligatory, Gadsden was unable to achieve a complete renunciation of parliamentary authority. Rather, the final draft of the declaration was a compromise agreement in which "all due Subordination" was granted to Parliament. Nor was Gadsden able to prevent the Congress from sending petitions to Parliament, as petitions were sent to both Houses as well as to the king.[18]

Still, Gadsden had reason to be content with the final results of the Stamp Act Congress, for the resolutions and petitions largely conformed to his views. Though disliking the implied recognition of parliamentary authority, he could find little else that was unsatisfactory. The arguments were based primarily upon natural rights, and the Congress asserted that no taxes could be placed upon the colonies without their consent. The theory of virtual representation was directly denounced and the idea of colonial representation in Parliament was dismissed as impractical. The Congress declared that the power of taxation belonged solely to the colonial assemblies and ridiculed the notion that the people of Great Britain could grant the property of Americans to the Crown as "unreasonable and inconsistent with the principles and Spirit of the British Constitution." The Congress also insisted upon the right of jury trial and grouped the extension of the courts of admiralty, together with the Stamp Act and other parliamentary taxes, as acts having a "Manifest tendency to Subvert the Rights, and liberties of the Colonists." Finally, it was pointed out that Americans already contributed to the treasury through the Navigation Acts. These cost enough and, combined with the shortage of specie and the strict enforcement of the Currency Act, made payment of further taxes "absolutely impracticable." Were such measures to be enforced, the result could only be the ruin of America, and the Congress reminded the government that such an event would be catastrophic to British merchants and manufacturers as well as the colonies.[19]

The Congress adjourned on October 25 after the adoption of the resolutions and petitions. Having received information that the South Carolina Commons House was to meet on October 28, the delegation decided that Gadsden should sail immediately to Charles Town to report to the House before adjournment. Unfortunately, his journey lasted longer than expected and he did not arrive until November 13, only two days before Lynch and Rutledge and long after the House had completed its session. The assembly met again on November 26 and took the proceedings of the Congress into immediate consideration. The resolutions and petitions were introduced by the delegates and quickly accepted by the assembly, with only one dissenting vote.[20] While the American colonies generally shared the satisfaction of the Commons House with the results of the Congress, the British government had a different view. Considering the Congress to have been an illegal assembly, the administration was not about to hear petitions that again challenged the authority of Parliament to tax the colonies. Using a technicality that required all petitions to be signed in person, the government refused to allow the petitions to be read in Parliament.[21]

While Gadsden was in New York, events moved quickly in Charles Town. As November 1 approached it became increasingly evident that execution of the Stamp Act would be resisted, by force if necessary. The threat of violence came mainly from the mechanics, the local artisans who were forming themselves into a secret organization called the Sons of Liberty. The Charles Town mechanics were the backbone of local society, a sturdy, hardworking, and prosperous middle class who were often the most affected by restrictive British legislation. By the mid-1760s, the mechanics were clearly feeling the pinch of British mercantilism. The Currency Act of 1764 was particularly distressing, for the contraction of the money supply made it difficult for the mechanics to collect or pay debts, purchase tools, and expand their businesses. The Stamp Act and the precedent it set for future parliamentary taxation promised to worsen an already difficult situation. Despite the fact that many of the mechanics owned property, and some had considerable holdings, the group had no representation in the assembly, and thus were blocked from the legitimate means of resistance. Yet the mechanics had never submitted quietly to their fate. Though not as prone to violence as their peers in some of the northern cities, the Charles Town mechanics were not above using riots and disorder to voice their sentiments.[22]

As the Sons of Liberty prepared to forcibly resist the Stamp Act, the question arose as to the relationship between this organization and Christopher Gadsden. Clearly, Gadsden had important contacts with the mechanics long before the introduction of the Stamp Act. He was a member of the Fellowship Society, a benevolent and charitable organization founded in 1762 and consisting largely of mechanics. Also, many of the members of his artillery company were artisans who would also belong to the Sons of Liberty. One member of the Sons of Liberty later recalled that Gadsden had first discussed politics with the group in 1764, a likely date as they were then joined in opposition to the Currency Act.[23] Gadsden certainly appreciated the usefulness of the mechanics, "whose worth no man in the city, perhaps, is better acquainted with than myself." Near the end of his life, he recalled their services, stating that "From the first of, and throughout the revolution, none have shewn themselves more firm and steady in the most dangerous and trying occasions, in short, had it not been for their assistance, we should have made a very poor figure indeed."[24]

Unquestionably, Gadsden and the mechanics were closely allied and mutually supportive. Yet it is a mistake to assume that the Sons of Liberty were mere puppets, dominated by Gadsden and other radical leaders. While supporting Gadsden as a prestigious and influential political leader whose views on British policy coincided with their own, the mechanics maintained their own identity. Gadsden was their spokesman and leading candidate, but only as long as they could agree on policy. When irreconcilable differences arose in 1778, the mechanics broke with Gadsden and aligned themselves with leaders who were more sympathetic to their goals.[25] But this rupture lay in the future. In 1765, Gadsden and the mechanics were joined in opposition to the Stamp Act. While it is probable that Gadsden met with the Sons of Liberty before leaving for New York, it is unlikely that his connection with their subsequent activities went beyond a general approval of the use of violence. The actions of the mob appear to have been largely spontaneous responses to events, which would preclude any further involvement by Gadsden.

News of disorders in Boston and other northern towns increased the determination by the Sons of Liberty that no stamps be landed at Charles Town. As early as September 28, Peter Timothy had predicted in the *South Carolina Gazette* that the stamp officers would resign immediately upon their arrival.[26] The ship carrying these officials, and supposedly the stamps,

arrived late on the night of October 18 and settled under the guns of Fort
Johnson in the harbor. By sunrise a gallows had been erected in front of
Dillon's Tavern at the intersection of Broad and Church streets. Hanging
from the gallows were three effigies—a stamp distributor, hung between
the devil on one side and a boot (symbolic of the hated Lord Bute, A Scot
advisor to the king and the individual whom many Americans held responsible for the Stamp Act) on the other. On the front of the gallows was a sign
that read "LIBERTY and no STAMP ACT," while another sign was placed on
the back of the effigy of the stamp distributor reading, "Whoever shall dare
attempt to pull down these effigies, had better been born with a mill stone
about his neck, and cast into the sea." The figures were displayed in this
manner throughout the day, before being cut down as night fell. The effigies
were then placed in a cart drawn by eight or ten horses and carried, before
a crowd of over two thousand people, in a procession from Broad Street to
the Bay. Moving into Tradd Street, the procession halted in front of the
house of George Saxby, one of the stamp distributors. The crowd demanded to know if there were any stamps in the house. When no answer
was received, some of the windows were broken, and it took some effort to
prevent members of the crowd from burning the house. Finally, the doors
were opened and the house was searched for stamps. Finding none, the
crowd continued to the green, where the effigies were burned. The bells of
St. Michael's were rung throughout the day and, earlier, another crowd
buried a coffin inscribed "American Liberty." Still, Timothy hastened to
add, no damage had been done except for the broken windows at Saxby's
house, and even this would have been avoided if the occupants had answered sooner.[27]

While much of Charles Town rejoiced at these proceedings, there were
some who disapproved of such antics. Prominent among the latter was
Henry Laurens, who, though an opponent of the Stamp Act, urged that it be
obeyed until it could be repealed by lawful means. Upset by the violence in
Boston, Laurens hoped that it would not "be feebly imitated by some tur-
bulent spirits in this Metropolis." A week before the arrival of the stamps,
Laurens summarized his position for a friend:

> Conclude not hence that I am an advocate for the Stamp Tax. No, by no means.
> I would give, I would do, a great deal to procure a repeal of the Law which
> imposes it upon us, but I am sure that nothing but a regular, decent, becoming
> representation of the inexpediency & inutility of that Law will have the desir'd
> effect & that all irregular seditious practices will have an evil tendency, even
> perhaps to perpetuate that & bring upon us other Acts of Parliament big with
> greater mischiefs. Resignations which people here build so much upon can
> answer no good end. The Act must be executed & indeed a suspension of it
> while it is in force would prove our ruin and destruction. . . . In short there
> remains nothing for us at present to do but to shew a graceful obedience to the

Law until we can procure its annihilation in a constitutional way or to beat to Arms & I defy all the grumbletonians from Quebeck to West Florida to point out a medium.[28]

Thus, Laurens saw no other options but compliance or open, even armed, defiance and, under these conditions, urged compliance until the law could be repealed. Believing in the benevolence of the British government, he had no doubt that the act would be repealed once the American objections were offered in a respectful, constitutional manner. Still, Laurens was not surprised at the disorders in Charles Town. Rather, he was disappointed that nothing was done to crush the malcontents. Though he had been out of town and did not witness the events, he was convinced that "Six Men of Spirit could in the beginning have crushed the whole shew. Whereas meeting with no opposition they carried their point with a high hand."[29] He would soon have cause to wish that the government had acted against the mob, for he was about to receive a firsthand taste of just how insolent the Charles Town Sons of Liberty had become.

On October 23 a report circulated in Charles Town that the stamps had been secretly landed and hidden in the home of Henry Laurens. At midnight of that night, Laurens reported, he heard the approach of a crowd, many of whom were shouting "*Liberty, Liberty & Stamp'd Paper, Open your doors & let us Search your House & Cellars.*" He met the crowd and assured them that he possessed no stamps and had no connection with them. When this response failed to appease the mob, he angrily charged them with cruelty to his sick wife, who was in the latter stages of pregnancy.[30] This,too, failed to have any effect, as the mob replied that they

Loved & respected me, would not hurt me nor my property but that they were sent by some of my seemingly best friends to search for Stamp'd Paper which they were certain was in my custody advised me to open the door to prevent worse consequences.

Laurens hesitated to open the door, but the cries of his wife, combined with his belief that they would knock the door down, led him to comply. His reward for this action was "a brace of Cutlasses across my breast." Yet he managed to maintain his composure and turned the tables on the people of the mob by studying their faces and, despite their disguises, called several of them by name. This disconcerted the mob and they proceeded to "a very superficial search or no search at all" of the premises. Finding no stamps, the mob demanded that Laurens swear an oath that he did not know the location of the stamps. Despite repeated curses and threats of physical punishment, he absolutely refused any oath, responding that his sentiments on the Stamp Act were widely known and he "had voluntarily given my word & honour but would not suffer even that to pass my Lips by compulsion." Finally, after an hour and a quarter, the mob departed, but not before praising him highly and raising three cheers. The ordeal over, Laurens was amazed that the mob, which he estimated at between sixty and eighty men, "did not do one penny damage to my Garden not even to walk over a Bed & not 15/ damage to my Fence, Gate, or House."[31] Even while the mob threatened his property, Laurens was certain that he knew who had set them in motion. He discovered this when one of the men grabbed him by the shoulders and

> said they loved me & every Body would Love me if I did not hold way with one Governor Grant. This provoked me not a little as it exhibited to me the Cloven foot of a certain malicious Villain acting behind the Curtain who could be reached only by suspicion.[32]

That this Governor Grant was the same James Grant, now royal governor of East Florida, who had been so prominent in the dispute between Laurens and Gadsden over the Cherokee War, has led to the widespread acceptance of the mistaken idea that Laurens blamed Christopher Gadsden for the invasion of his home.[33] While Laurens certainly was convinced that Gadsden had close ties with the mob, he did not hold his neighbor responsible for this incident. He realized that the visit of the mob had been a reaction to the rumor that the stamps were hidden in his home. As Gadsden had been out of the province for well over a month, it would be difficult to connect him to this event. Rather, in a letter to Grant, Laurens specifically identified Peter Timothy as the man who "put your name into the Mouths of those Anti-Parliamentarians if he was not the sole projector as well as prompter of the Play." He told Grant that he was so upset by this and other injuries received from Timothy that he was strongly considering using his influence to have the radical printer removed from his position as secretary of the Charles Town post office.[34] Though Gadsden did not set the mob upon Laurens, neither did he denounce its actions. Rather, in a letter written shortly after his return to Charles Town, he embraced them:

> Our people have behaved as firmly in the common cause as any upon the Continent, without having done the least mischief, and I make little doubt of their continuing so to do, though we have a number of cunning, Jacobitical, Butean rascals to encounter with, that leave nothing untried to counterwork the firmness and loyalty of the true sons of liberty amongst us.[35]

While it is unlikely that Gadsden numbered Laurens among these "infernal Fiends," Laurens's opposition to the developing protest movement over the past few years likely raised doubts that enabled Gadsden to approve the actions of the Liberty boys.

The attack upon Laurens's home, and a similar assault upon the home of Chief Justice Charles Shinner that same night, convinced Lieutenant Governor Bull that some action was necessary to prevent further disturbances. Thus, on October 24, Bull announced that the stamps had been deposited at Fort Johnson, where soldiers would resist any attempt to destroy them.[36] Even then, however, the situation remained tense as news of the arrival of stamp distributor George Saxby was received. Saxby was aware of the unpopularity of the Stamp Act and offered to suspend execution of his duties until the king and Parliament could respond to the colonial petitions. This offer was accepted and, on October 28, amid great cheering and celebration, Saxby and his fellow distributor Caleb Lloyd publicly promised not to perform their duties.[37] Operation of the Stamp Act was now effectively frustrated in South Carolina. But what was the next step? The law provided strict penalties for anyone, even the governor, who transacted business without stamps. Since there were no stamps, ships could not be cleared and, as of November 1, the port of Charles Town was forced to close. The civil courts also required the use of stamps and were forced to suspend business, though the criminal courts, which did not require stamps, continued in operation. Even an opposition leader such as Peter Timothy was unwilling to risk the penalties of noncompliance, so publication of the *South Carolina Gazette* was also suspended.[38]

Lieutenant Governor Bull, in his report to the Board of Trade, blamed much of the disorder upon the northern colonies. He held Peter Timothy responsible for much of the trouble, identifying the *South Carolina Gazette* as the "conduit pipe" through which "some busy spirits" had poisoned the entire colony with ideas "imbibed & propagated from Boston & Rhode Island." Nor was Gadsden overlooked by the lieutenant governor, and it was likely he to whom Bull alluded when he declared that the mob was "animated by some considerable man who stood behind the curtain." Bull saw little hope of immediate improvement and he informed the Board that Charles Town would persist in its resistance until the fate of New England was known.[39] News of violence and mob disorder was not well received in London. Charles Garth notified the assembly that the violence was adversely effecting the prospects of repeal and advised that the best course was to discontinue mob action and rely upon the petitions circulating among British merchants and manufacturers who were suffering from the loss of trade.[40] The use of violence was further discouraged when Bull sent the assembly a letter from Henry Seymour Conway, one of the secretaries of state. Conway, though himself a leading opponent of the Stamp Act, informed Bull that submission to further violence would not be "suitable either to the safety or Dignity of the British Empire." He instructed Bull to tolerate no further disorder and, if any more violence was perpetrated, to use force to combat it. If he needed more troops, Conway directed him to call upon General Thomas Gage, the commander of the British army in America.[41]

Perhaps most important to the disciplining of the mob was the example that the use of violence set for other dissatisfied groups. Particular concern was focused upon the slaves, a constant source of alarm during troubled times. When rumors flew of a slave insurrection planned for the Christmas holidays of 1765, Lieutenant Governor Bull acted forcefully to prevent any rebellion. Henry Laurens felt the threat exaggerated, the result of an over-reaction to some slaves who "had mimick'd their betters by crying out *Liberty.*" Yet, Laurens saw a positive side to the threat, as he reported that it had exercised a calming influence upon Gadsden, Timothy, and other local hotheads.[42] Laurens was not mistaken on this point, for the fear of slave revolt had indeed given Gadsden pause for thought. Though he had earlier applauded the performance of the Charles Town Sons of Liberty, by April 1766 Gadsden was expressing concern over the weakness of the colony. Much of this weakness he attributed to the presence of such a large body of slaves, and he hoped that, in the case of South Carolina, the enslavement of blacks would not cause the enslavement of whites.[43] In addition to slaves, there was trouble with the approximately fourteen hundred unemployed sailors who had found themselves stranded in Charles Town after the closure of the port. As these men grew increasingly disorderly, it fell to the leaders of the protest movement to keep the seamen in line. This they did efficiently, suppressing the sailors when they became unruly and tossing the ringleaders into jail.[44]

As the new year opened, Gadsden and other protest leaders sought to relieve some of the pressure caused by the Stamp Act. Hoping to convince the lieutenant governor to open the port and the courts, the Commons House seized upon a technicality and, on January 22, 1766, asked Bull if he had received official notification of the Stamp Act. Bull replied that he had received a copy of the act from Egerton Leigh, attorney general of South Carolina, in June and another copy from Governor Boone in August, and he considered these sources sufficient to confirm the authenticity of the act. Unsatisfied, the Commons chose Gadsden to chair a committee to prepare an answer. On January 24, Gadsden reported that copies transmitted by Leigh or Boone could not be considered sufficient to oblige enforcement of the act. Only notification from official channels, specifically the secretaries of state or the Board of Trade, could be accepted as authentic. Gadsden asserted that, since proper official notification had not been received, the lieutenant governor should relieve the "very great hardships" of his people by suspending enforcement of the Stamp Act. After consulting the council, Bull answered that by a vote of five to two it had decided that, since the copies of the act were printed by His Majesty's Printing Office, they could be assumed to be authentic. Thus, the Stamp Act would continue as law.

Shortly afterwards, however, Bull did consent to the issuance of certificates that, after payment of a duty equal to the price of stamps, would allow the clearance of ships. This concession effectively opened the port.[45]

Though the opening of the port was a victory for the protest movement, a new danger arose with the news that the Stamp Act was in operation in Georgia. Gadsden recognized the implicit threat to American unity and again took to the press, publishing an essay over the signature "Homespun Free-Man" in the February 11, 1766, issue of Charles Crouch's *South Carolina Gazette and Country Journal.* He sharply criticized the Georgians, insisting that the placeman-dominated colony had played directly into the hands of a Parliament that was attempting to conquer the colonies by dividing them. Upset at how the Georgians had "out-cunninged themselves" and had been "so easily deluded and bullied" out of their liberties, Gadsden pleaded with South Carolinians to persist in their resistance, if not for their own sake, then for that of their posterity. Concluding, Gadsden urged his countrymen to promote American manufactures and to demonstrate their patriotism by wearing homespun.[46]

Gadsden followed this letter with another three weeks later in which he congratulated a group of local merchants who had refused to sell supplies to Georgia. Looking upon this as a good start, he encouraged the entire colony to follow the example of some of the northern colonies, which had formally boycotted Barbados for accepting the stamps. He then warned his readers against "insidious Opportunity-watching Liberty-Sellers" who, like Henry Laurens, urged peaceful compliance until the law could be repealed:

> I know you are not to be frightened, but beware of being cajoled by pretended Friends, who would seem to be more concerned for you, than you are, or at least ought to be, for yourselves; who modestly expect their Advice to be followed before that of all unstampt America, in order to screen the unnatural and preposterous Opinion and Conduct of some of their Friends here and at G———a.[47]

Such commentary led some to believe that Gadsden had lost his senses. John Moultrie informed James Grant that "Your old friend Philo [patrios] I think is now ten times mader [*sic*] than ever he was. I'm sure he thinks himself nothing less at this time than Brutus & Cassius."[48] If Gadsden's public letters led some to suspect that he had gone insane, a look at his private letters, which contained much harsher language, would have convinced them. In a letter to an English friend, Gadsden launched a bitter attack upon the ministry:

> Your late Ministry the previous Introducers of this pestilential Tax must most certainly have thought us Americans all a parcel of Asses & very tame Asses

too, or they never would have ventured on such a hateful, baneful Expedient. Or did they imagine us like themselves such dastardly self- interested Fools that by laying a Trap to deprive us of our Estates & brand us with hard Rebellious Names we by that hellish ministerial Artifice might be scar'd out of our Senses & intimidated into any Thing. [49]

Gadsden was clearly losing patience with the refusal of Parliament to redress American grievances. If the government was so insensitive to the suffering of the colonies, he wrote, the only recourse would be a complete boycott of trade with Britain. If it came to this, Gadsden felt that the result could be "a free & open Trade with all the powers of Europe," a fate that Britain would richly deserve for "treating us already worse than the Aegyptian Task Masters of old did the Israelites." Unsure whether or not the British would use force to uphold the Stamp Act, Gadsden left no doubt that he would continue in opposition, regardless of the consequences. Viewing this as "a Cause worthy an honest Man to die in," he declared it his "highest Ambition" to die for the cause of liberty, if this became necessary.[50]

Such sacrifices were not yet called for, however, and Gadsden turned his attention to a plan for the reopening of the local courts. The civil courts had been closed since November 1, as Chief Justice Charles Shinner adamantly refused to do business without stamps. The Commons House, led by Gadsden, insisted that the lieutenant governor appoint assistant judges who would sit with Shinner and outvote him, thereby opening the courts. Bull resisted this pressure until late February when he finally relented and appointed Rawlins Lowndes, Benjamin Smith, and Daniel Doyley to act as assistant judges. These men quickly outvoted Shinner and the court resumed hearing cases. Still, the victory was not yet won, as Dougal Campbell, the clerk of the court, surprised everyone by refusing to enter the judgments into the record. Campbell had been a model clerk and had always treated the judges with proper respect. But, as he pointed out, the Stamp Act specifically named his office as one subject to heavy penalties for disobedience. Refusing to accept this explanation, Lowndes fined Campbell one hundred pounds proclamation money, and the assembly demanded that the lieutenant governor remove the clerk. Bull was once again placed in a difficult position: his inclination was to support the authority of the court, but Campbell had only been obeying the law, and his removal could incur royal displeasure. After consulting the council, Bull refused to fire Campbell, explaining that the clerk's refusal to obey orders was due to "the Superior Authority of an Act of Parliament."[51]

Bull's refusal brought the wrath of Christopher Gadsden down upon the head of the Lieutenant Governor. The frustrated Gadsden sized up Bull, writing that "Our Lt. Governor in his private character is a very agreeable polite man and very well beloved, but as a Governor is and always has been the weakest and most unsteady man I ever knew, so very obliging that he never obliged."[52] This characterization was far too harsh and could only have been made by a zealot like Gadsden. Bull was greatly respected in South Carolina, and he was hardly a weak man. Indeed, Bull was the most effective governor that South Carolina had during the two decades before independence. His disinterestedness and concern for the welfare of his colony, of which he was a native, was as unquestioned as his loyalty to the king. What Gadsden saw as weakness was really a flexibility that allowed Bull to relieve the hardships of the people while upholding British authority. Bull's skill as a governor contrasted strongly with the conduct of his predecessor, Thomas Boone, and his successor, Lord Charles Greville Montagu. While these two governors were practically expelled from South Carolina, Bull retained the respect of his people, even after the outbreak of armed conflict. Had William Bull received an appointment as governor of South Carolina, Gadsden and other radical leaders would have found it far more difficult to organize a revolutionary movement in South Carolina.

Tension over the court evaporated quickly, however, with the fortunate arrival of news of the repeal of the Stamp Act in early May. Still, the court remained closed, as Chief Justice Shinner, using a tactic previously employed by the Commons, refused to do business until official news of the repeal was obtained. This proved to be a fatal mistake for Shinner, as it brought the full anger of the Commons House upon him. It was Gadsden who took the lead in the movement to secure the removal of the chief justice. In April 1767, Gadsden presented a report to the assembly that charged Shinner with gross incompetence and poor knowledge of the law. Despite the obvious political motivation, it seems that the charges had some validity, as the report passed the House and received the approval of governor Montagu.[53] News of the repeal was greeted with "universal Joy" in Charles Town. Gadsden was so overcome at the news that he almost fainted upon hearing it.[54] The Commons House celebrated by appropriating funds for portraits of Gadsden, John Rutledge, and Thomas Lynch to be hung in the assembly room in recognition of their service as delegates to the Stamp Act Congress. Money was also voted to commission a statue of William Pitt, to be erected in gratitude for his role in securing the repeal of the act. Laurens reported that a motion to erect a statue of George III was not even seconded and its mover, William Wragg, was "derided for his presumption."[55] As publication of the *South Carolina Gazette* resumed, Peter Timothy provided a full account of the celebration of the repeal. The morning was ushered in by the ringing of bells and the general display of colors. The militia, a company of light infantry, and Gadsden's artillery company were reviewed by the lieutenant governor, the council, assembly, and other public officials. Afterwards, Lieutenant Governor Bull held a "very elegant entertainment" for the above officials at Dillon's Tavern, during which "many loyal and constitutional toasts were drank, amongst which the best friends to Britain and America were not omitted." The evening concluded with a "grand and general" illumination.[56]

Despite the great celebration, the victory had not been complete. Parliament, as was clearly manifested in the accompanying Declaratory Act, had by no means surrendered its claim to legislate for the colonies. Indeed, the repeal of the Stamp Act passed the House of Commons by a vote of 240 to 133, a comfortable, though hardly commanding, majority. Nor was this repeal due to any widespread sympathy for the American cause. Rather, it was achieved largely because of the domestic economic crisis and the realization that the only alternative was force and the possibility of civil war.[57]

The significance of the Declaratory Act was not lost upon either Laurens or Gadsden. Laurens viewed the conduct of Parliament as "irreconcilable" and foresaw future trouble, declaring a few months later that "all America will undergo many pangs yet before there is a hearty reconciliation."[58] Gadsden shared the belief that the Declaratory Act was an ominous sign and, as usual, determined to take action. He met with members of the Sons of Liberty at the Liberty Tree[59] and, as recalled forty years later by one of those present, "harangued them at considerable length, on the folly of relaxing their opposition and vigilance, or of indulging the fallacious hope that Great Britain would relinquish their designs and pretensions." The gathering then joined hands around the Liberty Tree and solemnly swore resistance to future tyranny.[60] Whatever satisfaction Gadsden might have felt at the repeal of the Stamp Act was soon turned to grief by the death of his eldest son, Christopher Gadsden, Jr., in August. Gadsden's great sorrow was shared by his old friend turned foe Henry Laurens, who observed that "my Neighbor Gadsden has met with a very affecting stroke indeed in the death of a fine lad his eldest Son, last night."[61]

The Stamp Act crisis was over and had seemingly ended in victory for the protest movement. Yet the adoption of the Declaratory Act led many, including Christopher Gadsden and Henry Laurens, to doubt the significance of the victory. Their fears were indeed justified, for the British government had by no means given up its struggle to reassert control over America, as its actions in the near future would amply demonstrate. Still, the Stamp Act had been repealed, and this strengthened and increased the prestige of the protest movement. Much of the credit for the firm stance of South Carolina can be assigned to Gadsden, whose fame as a defender of American liberty had spread throughout the colonies. Not only had he dominated the resistance in South Carolina, he also traveled to New York and joined James

Otis in enunciating the radical position in the Stamp Act Congress. In this role Gadsden grew as a political leader, setting aside his typical intransigence and compromising on important issues in order to safeguard American unity.

Some have argued that Gadsden was a proponent of independence, even at this early date. This seems unlikely. Perhaps, in one of his more passionate moments, Gadsden did make a statement indicative of a desire for independence. But it must be remembered that Gadsden was an emotional man who had a tendency, in the heat of the moment, to make comments that exaggerated his true feelings. As biographers E. Stanly Godbold and Robert H. Woody have pointed out, Gadsden prided himself on his honesty and was far too honest to repeatedly, in private as well as in public, declare loyalty to Great Britain and her king, while secretly plotting revolution. What Gadsden was seeking at this time was freedom to enjoy the natural and constitutional rights of British subjects, including that of self-government in internal matters. This was essentially a demand for home rule within the empire, not independence.[62] Still, if Gadsden was faced with a decision between continued loyalty to Great Britain or American liberty, he had made it clear that he would choose the latter. But it had not yet come to this and he hoped that it never would, though he was beginning to doubt that this would always be so. The future would only increase these doubts.

Henry Laurens emerged from the Stamp Act crisis in a far less enviable position than Gadsden. Though repeatedly asserting his opposition to the Stamp Act as an unconstitutional innovation, he could not support the methods of opposition. Particularly appalling was the violence of the Sons of Liberty, which Laurens viewed as illegal and extreme, and likely to bring harsher measures from Parliament. For his efforts, Laurens saw his popularity decline and his devotion to American liberty called into question. No one could question his courage, however, as evidenced by his defiance of the mob that invaded his home in a futile search for the hated stamps. This experience demonstrated that, though he may not have had the devotion of the people, Laurens retained their respect. His conduct was explained well by David Duncan Wallace, who wrote that "he was not a worse patriot than his fellows, he was a better prophet. As a loyal subject of the British Empire he was already grieving lest his children be called by some new name."[63] Laurens was concerned about the questionable wisdom of British policy and could not reconcile the repeal of the Stamp Act with the Declaratory Act. As he considered this situation he, like Gadsden, found little evidence that American rights had been permanently secured. This represented a much greater dilemma for Laurens than it did for Gadsden. The latter's devotion to liberty was so strong as to take precedence over all other considerations, be it loyalty to Great Britain or even life itself. While Laurens was as devoted to American rights as Gadsden, his allegiance to Britain was more intense and much more difficult to cast aside. Henry Laurens would spend the next decade hoping that he would not have to make a choice between liberty and loyalty. Ironically, it would be the conduct of British officials, rather than the urgings of Gadsden and his associates, that would set Henry Laurens on the road to rebellion.

5

The Making of a Rebel: Henry Laurens and the Vice-Admiralty Court, 1767–1770

JUST AS THE STAMP ACT CRISIS LED CHRISTOPHER GADSDEN TO SERIOUSLY question whether the American colonies would long remain a part of the British Empire, the activities of the customs officers and the local vice-admiralty court played the same role for Henry Laurens. Imperial officials had long been aware that the Navigation Acts were widely evaded in America, particularly in the northern colonies. Few registered any serious concern, however, until the French and Indian War, when American merchants were bitterly attacked for trading with the French West Indies and thereby prolonging the war. These attacks were focused mainly upon Rhode Island and, to a lesser degree, several northern towns that appeared to be ignorant of the fact that a war was in progress. As these merchants nonchalantly went on with their business, William Pitt, in 1760, insisted that an end be put to the smuggling trade. As the war drew to a close it became clear that strict enforcement of the Navigation Acts would continue as a peacetime policy. For a government desperately seeking the means to increase revenues and determined to reassert its control over the colonies, such a course was logical and reasonable. Thus, in 1763, the practice of absenteeism in the customs service was ended and all colonial customs officers were ordered to either relinquish their positions or assume their posts in America. Instructions were given to the colonial governors to put an end to smuggling, and an act of Parliament was passed authorizing the use of the navy against colonial smugglers. These reforms created considerable alarm in areas such as Rhode Island, Boston, and New York, as the increasing number of seizures threatened the smuggling business with ruin.[1] Yet there was little that these merchants could do but grumble, for though the Navigation Acts had been evaded, they had been accepted for generations as legitimate and constitutional.

Had the British been satisfied with this, there would have been little justification for widespread opposition. The government, however, went further and introduced innovations that were unacceptable to Americans and opened the door to the abuses that created new and legitimate grievances. The Revenue Act of 1764 and the changes it brought to the Navigation system was primarily responsible for this state of affairs. The Revenue Act extended the authority and jurisdiction of the vice-admiralty courts, allowing customs officials to bring their cases before a single admiralty judge, rather than the notoriously sympathetic local juries that had previously handled the cases. Such provisions created grievances among Americans who argued that they were being treated unfairly, pointing to the retention of the jury trial in the admiralty courts in Great Britain and Ireland. Perhaps more disturbing was the fact that the burden of proof in these cases was shifted to the defense. Even if a judge did not condemn a cargo, he could rule that there had been probable cause for seizure. Under such a ruling the defendant would have to pay the court costs, which could be quite expensive, and was prevented from taking any legal action against the prosecutors. This was an invitation for trouble. Freed from the threat of suit for false arrest or of having to pay the costs of an acquittal or dismissal, a corrupt and enterprising customs officer might succumb to the temptation to supplement his income through customs racketeering.[2]

Though the many rivers and creeks of South Carolina made it difficult for the customs service to effectively patrol the coast, illicit trade does not appear to have been a problem in the colony. There was little temptation for the Charles Town merchants to smuggle, as they generally prospered under the Navigation system. The Acts of Trade were a complicated set of laws, but effective management by upright men such as Thomas Gadsden and Hector Berenger de Beaufin prevented any significant problems. Highly respected among the mercantile community, both men pursued fair and consistent policies that, though not always in conformity to the letter of the law, were always in accord with its spirit. This situation prevailed until March 1767 when Daniel Moore assumed the post of collector.[3] Moore would have preferred to remain on good terms with the local merchants, but was also determined to use his position to increase his personal wealth. When he discovered that it would be impossible to achieve both goals, he teamed up with the customs searcher, George Roupell, to "set a new standard for rapaciousness."[4] Under these conditions, the customs house was set upon a collision course with the Charles Town merchants.

Moore was a personification of another important problem that has earlier been alluded to: the monopolization of important offices by British placemen of questionable competence. This problem had already created considerable frustration among the South Carolina elite during the 1750s and its intensification during the 1760s and 1770s should not be ignored as a contributing factor to the growth of the protest movement. The frustration of the local elite was noticed by Josiah Quincy, who, after a visit to Charles Town during the early 1770s, reported hearing many say that "We none of us, when we grow old, can expect the honors of the State; they are all given away to worthless poor sycophants."[5] Many of these placemen could be found on the Royal Council, seats that, before the Lyttelton-Wragg dispute, were considered a tremendous honor and were actively pursued by many among the Carolina elite. By the time that Henry Laurens received an appointment to the council in 1764, however, these seats had lost most of their former luster. Laurens personified this development when he declined the appointment, due, in large part, to "injudicious appointments" that caused the prestige of the council to sink "almost below contempt."[6] The prestige of the council continued to plunge, deteriorating to such an extent that, in 1770, Lieutenant Governor Bull informed the earl of Hillsborough that it was extremely difficult to fill vacancies on the council, as none of the leading citizens would accept such an appointment.[7]

Among the most prominent of these placemen was Egerton Leigh, a capable official whose main problem was not competence, but multiple office holding, which left him open to charges of conflict of interest. Leigh accompanied his father to Charles Town at the age of twenty in 1753, and even this event created controversy. Upon the death of the chief justice in 1752, Governor James Glen appointed the eminent local attorney Charles Pinckney to the post. This was a popular choice until Pinckney was forced to step aside six months later upon the arrival of Peter Leigh (father of Egerton), who carried a royal commission to assume the position of chief justice. The dissatisfaction created by this unfortunate event was enhanced by information that Leigh had recently been forced to resign his position as high bailiff of Westminster under a cloud of corruption. Though Leigh proved to be a competent chief justice and there was no hint of scandal during his tenure, his replacement of Pinckney was irksome to many in South Carolina and has been called the beginning of the placemen problem in the province.[8]

Despite his father's problems, Egerton Leigh rose rapidly into the South Carolina elite. He practiced law and served briefly as clerk of the court of common pleas, a position in which he made many important contacts. He was elected to the Commons House in 1755 and retained his seat until promoted to the council in 1760. In 1755 he assumed the position of surveyor general and in 1761 became judge of the vice-admiralty court. In 1765 he returned from a visit to England with a commission to serve as attorney general for the province, as well as with the first copy of the Stamp Act to appear in South Carolina. An extremely ambitious man, Leigh took time from his accumulation of offices to arrange an advantageous marriage to Martha Bremar. Though the tie to the Bremar family gained him little, it was important that his wife was the niece of Henry Laurens. This marriage led to a close relationship with Laurens, who brought much of his legal business, and that of many of his friends, to Leigh. Thus, through hard work, ambition, and contacts, Leigh became one of the wealthiest men in the province.[9]

Leigh's problems began during the Stamp Act crisis when he, almost alone among the Charles Town legal community, supported the refusal of Chief Justice Shinner to open the courts without stamps. This was a costly stance, as it led to a serious decline in his legal business. It also provoked the Commons House, which noted his holding of several offices that were supposed to act as checks on each other, to direct Charles Garth in London to secure his removal from some or all of these positions.[10] Among the leaders of the movement against Leigh was Christopher Gadsden, who delivered a stinging attack in the Commons House that, among other things, attacked the memory of Leigh's father. It was Henry Laurens to whom the shaken Leigh turned with complaints about Gadsden's performance. Laurens pitied his weeping friend and, as he later wrote, "I endeavoured to console him by saying that Mr. G——— was a man of warm passions—his Reflexions had met no Marks of Approbation, and I was persuaded that he himself was sorry for what he had said."[11] Gadsden was certainly a passionate man, but he was not sorry for his attack upon Leigh. Nor would it be long before Laurens himself would be offering even harsher commentary, after he had gained firsthand experience of the implications of Leigh's plural office holding.

Laurens's problems with the customs house began with the arrival of Daniel Moore in March 1767. Moore was particularly interested in the coastal trade: traffic along the coast of a single or nearby colonies. Such trade was crucial to the plantation economies of South Carolina and Georgia, as it was the means by which planters supplied their estates and shipped their produce to Charles Town. To insist that vessels engaged in this trade enter and clear the customs house would have been inconvenient and quite expensive. Not until the Revenue Act of 1764 placed the coastal trade upon a footing equal to the ocean trade was such a requirement written into the law. Even then, however, the customs officers, realizing that there was little fraud in the coastal trade and aware of the harmful effects rigid enforcement would have on the economy, did not enforce these provisions.

Moore set out to reverse this policy and quickly seized the schooner *Active* for carrying enumerated goods between the South Carolina ports of Charles Town and Georgetown without bonds or certificates. Uncertain of his legal grounds, Moore had attempted to obtain the advice of the attorney general before making the seizure. Here the plural office holding of Egerton Leigh became a problem, as Leigh refused to advise Moore on a case that he would have to decide as judge of the vice-admiralty court. Thus, the unscrupulous Moore was left to balance his legal uncertainty with his hunger for seizure money. When greed won out, the entire mercantile community joined in support of the *Active*, raising a defense fund and using their influence to prevent the customs officers from gaining adequate legal counsel. When the case went to court, Leigh declared that there was no reason to believe that the *Active* was engaged in illicit trade and released the vessel. Still, he protected Moore from legal action by certifying a probable cause for seizure. This left the unhappy owners of the *Active* to pay the costs of the case, which came to one hundred fifty pounds sterling, in order to regain a vessel worth no more than eighty pounds.[12] Thus, Moore may have lost the battle, but the decision did nothing to deter him from continuing the war.

Laurens had been on friendly terms with Moore until the collector implemented his tight navigation policy. Moore informed Laurens that he had the authority to insist that every vessel engaged in the coastal trade enter and clear the customs house on every trip it made to and from the plantations. Laurens replied that such a course would "create a great deal of Trouble to the People in Carolina" while doing nothing to further the interests of the Crown. Under these circumstances, Laurens told Moore, it would be unwise to risk alienating the people over such a point. Laurens also doubted whether Moore actually possessed the authority he claimed. His suspicions increased when, despite repeated requests, Moore failed to produce his authorization. Laurens soon began to question Moore's honesty after discovering that the collector was inconsistent in his charges for permits to engage in the coasting trade. The final straw came when Moore charged him exorbitant fees to clear ships and then failed to make restitution, even after admitting that the charges had been too high. Thus, when Moore seized the *Active*, Laurens took a leading role in the defense of the vessel and the rights of the Charles Town mercantile community.[13]

The dispute with Moore intensified when the collector seized two ships owned by Laurens, the *Wambaw* and the *Broughton Island Packet*, within a two-week period in July 1767.[14] Both of these ships were engaged in the coastal trade, carrying provisions to Laurens's plantations along the Altamaha River in Georgia. Laurens was careful to comply with the trade regulations and went personally to the customs house to clear both ships. While clearing the *Broughton Island Packet*, Laurens engaged in a heated dispute with the collector, which ended with Moore challenging Laurens to a duel.[15] With his ships cleared, Laurens traveled on the *Broughton Island Packet* to inspect his Georgia estates. Upon arrival in Georgia, he found that the master of the *Wambaw* had loaded the vessel with fifty thousand shingles for the return voyage to Charles Town. Though these shingles were placed aboard largely for ballast, it was agreed that they would be sold upon arrival. Since there was no customs house within forty miles, Laurens posted bond and obtained clearance papers from two local magistrates who, in accordance with custom and local statute, were allowed to perform these duties in remote areas. Despite these precautions, Moore ordered his searcher, George Roupell, to seize the *Wambaw* for not clearing a customs house before leaving Georgia. Moore then sent word to James Laurens (brother of Henry) and Gabriel Manigault, who were acting as Laurens's representatives during his absence, that he would release the ship if they asked him to do so as a "great Favor." Recognizing that Moore was attempting to use Laurens as an example to gain acceptance of his stance on the coastal trade, these friends indignantly refused the offer.[16]

While these events were transpiring, Laurens supervised the loading of the *Broughton Island Packet* for its return from Georgia. This ship was loaded with logs and chunks of wood and, since this was used entirely as ballast, no bonds or clearances were obtained. Moore was determined to seize this ship, too, but was unsure of making another seizure while the fate of the *Wambaw* was undecided. Thus, he again turned to Leigh for advice. After some hesitation, Leigh told Moore that if the circumstances of the two ships were the same, his actions should be consistent in both cases. Moore accepted this as advice to seize the *Broughton Island Packet* and promptly did so.[17]

Both cases were tried in the vice-admiralty court and the decisions were returned on September 1, 1767. Citing the fact that the shingles were to be sold, Leigh condemned the *Wambaw*, ordering the vessel sold and the proceeds to be divided equally between the king, the governor, and George Roupell. This decision upset Laurens who, though he admitted that the shingles were intended for sale, insisted that the customs officers had told him when he cleared the *Wambaw* at Charles Town that he did not have to post bond for nonenumerated goods. Laurens was also ordered to pay the costs of the suit, almost seven hundred pounds currency. Prospects for the *Broughton Island Packet* appeared bleak, for Leigh had earlier declared that the two cases would stand or fall together. It came as a surprise, then, that Leigh acquitted this ship, accepting Laurens's word that the wood was used entirely for ballast. At the same time, however, Leigh ordered Laurens to pay two-thirds of the costs, with Roupell paying the other third. Most important, Leigh neglected to declare a probable cause, leaving Roupell open to a lawsuit for damages.[18] Though Leigh hoped that his decisions would be a compromise acceptable to both sides, they satisfied neither. Indeed, both sides were left with a sense of grievance. Moore and Roupell felt betrayed by a judge who had advised them to seize the *Broughton Island Packet* and then acquitted the vessel in court. Laurens, too, was amazed and angry at the decisions. He was upset that Leigh had condemned the *Wambaw*, especially after the judge admitted that Laurens had done everything possible to comply with the law. He was also baffled by the fact that, though the *Broughton Island Packet* was acquitted, he was ordered to pay two-thirds of the costs.

Though Laurens was disappointed in Leigh, his fury was directed mainly at the customs house and its "good for nothing Collector," Daniel Moore, who "in the space of Six Months has given more plague to the Trading people here than all the Officers of Customs put together since the memory of the oldest Merchant among us—ten to one."[19] In a long letter to his Georgia friend James Habersham, Laurens expressed sorrow that, despite his honest attempts to avoid disagreeable controversies, he was too often drawn into them. He insisted that he bore no malice towards his opponents, but would defend himself against oppression, taking consolation from the fact that "all those folks who through party heat in 1761 & 1765 affected to be very angry are now upon good terms with me & that without any particular seeking or deviation on my part." He recounted the problems with the customs house since the arrival of Moore and insisted that the merchants had made every effort to reach an accommodation with the collector. These were all doomed to failure, however, because "the Collector's pride & obstinacy would allow him to submit to no terms but his own & even these varied as often as the Weather Vane."[20] The clash with the customs house affected Laurens very deeply, and he told Habersham that "such Officers are the most likely instruments to effect a disunion between the Mother Country & her American offspring." After all, he continued, if Americans had been so upset at the Stamp Act, how much angrier would they be with officials who robbed the people and then declared, as Moore had done, "I can sweat them at Law with their own Money?"[21]

Laurens's anger quickly led him into another embarrassing incident with Moore. Shortly after the conclusion of the vice-admiralty court hearings, Laurens confronted Moore and sharply reproved him for his behavior. When Moore responded with insults, Laurens instinctively grabbed the official by his nose and twisted it before a large crowd of people. Though embarrassed by the incident, Laurens justified his conduct to his friend, the Philadelphia merchant William Fisher:

> You will perceive that the Act was not premeditated, that it fell out accidentally, & that I do not glory in having been the Actor, if my friends barely excuse me it is all that I can expect. Those rapacious, haughty, insolent, & overbearing Men, such as our Collector certainly was during his short Six Months residence here, are great troublers of quiet minds, but they sometimes meet with rewards, suitable to their demerit.[22]

In addition to physical punishment, Laurens and the merchants were preparing to prosecute Moore for illegal extortion of fees. Faced with several lawsuits and realizing that the community was against him, Moore sailed for London to lay his case before the imperial authorities. The Charles Town merchants responded with a report entitled *A Representation of Facts*, authored primarily by Laurens, which they circulated among their correspondents on both sides of the ocean. The Commons House sent a copy to Charles Garth with instructions to use it to defend the province against any charges made by Moore.[23]

With Moore gone, Laurens turned his attention to Roupell and sued him for damages arising from the *Broughton Island Packet* case. The suit was heard in May 1768 and, though Roupell was defended by Egerton Leigh, Laurens won a judgment for fourteen hundred pounds currency. Laurens was pleased with the decision and he reported that the award was sufficient to cover his costs in the *Wambaw* case as well as the *Broughton Island Packet*. With Roupell ordered to pay another one hundred twelve pounds in court costs, Laurens hoped that this setback would reform the conduct of the customs officers.[24] Still, his anger at the customs house, and Moore in particular, continued unabated, and he warned Richard Oswald in England that similar appointments should be avoided in the future. He was convinced that

> Such men as that one in Office are the greatest Enemies to Britain of any Man in America & as one Vile Priest does more injury to the cause of Religion than two Rakes, so does one such Officer or Man in power more prejudice to the Interest of Britain in America than twenty Mouthing Liberty Boys.[25]

Unfortunately, the judgment against Roupell had the opposite effect from what Laurens had hoped. Rather than reconsidering his conduct, Roupell was left with a burning desire for revenge. Roupell began biding his time, waiting for an opportunity to strike against his adversary. The chance finally arrived in June 1768. Laurens supervised the loading of the *Ann*, which he owned with several partners, with rice and other enumerated goods. After posting bond for enumerated goods, he received a permit to load and set out for Georgia, leaving the completion of the loading to his young clerk, John Hopton. Afterwards, and without the knowledge of Laurens, several nonenumerated goods—one pipe and one barrel of Madeira wine, one barrel of pink root, one barrel of rum, and a parcel of cattle horns—were placed on board. As the ship prepared to sail, the captain presented the manifest to the deputy collector, Roger Peter Handasyde Hatley, who pointed out that no bond had been given for nonenumerated goods. Hopton offered to sign a bond, but was refused because he was too young, though he was informed that another man who was of age might sign the bond. When Hopton left to find a surety, Hatley quickly sent word to Roupell that the *Ann* had loaded nonenumerated goods without first posting bond. When Hopton shortly reappeared with a local merchant, Edmund Head, Hatley told him that he was too late; the ship had been seized.[26]

Such a seizure was ridiculous, and the motivation behind it was insultingly clear to all but the willfully blind. The best that could be said for the conduct of the customs officers was that it was inconsistent. Laurens pointed out that it was the practice of the customs house to clear ships carrying nonenumerated goods if the bond had been posted for enumerated articles. Hatley himself had signed an agreement with the merchants that expressly sanctioned the continuation of this practice. Thus, when the case came to trial, Hatley shifted his ground and declared that the *Ann* was seized because bond was not posted before the ship was loaded. Once again, however, testimony clearly demonstrated that this technicality had not been enforced and that it was the practice to take the bond when the ship was loaded and ready to sail. Indeed, a ship had been cleared in this manner the day before the *Ann* was seized. Testimony clearly proved that Laurens and Hopton had made every effort to comply with the law as it was applied by the customs house and were only prevented from doing so by the actions of the customs officers.[27] The true reason for the seizure became clear when Gabriel Manigault visited the customs house with the captain of the *Ann* to inquire into the case. In reply to Manigault's questions, Roupell

asked Mr. Manigault if he did not know that Mr. Laurens had obtained a Verdict against him, and held a rod over his Head? —and with an Exalting Bounce— replied to Capt. Forten's Entreaties on Behalf of the innocent Owners of the Ship, "Now Sir! Mr. Laurens may pay himself—he may take £1400 out of one Pocket and put it into the other."

Within days, several friends of the absent Laurens were approached by Hatley with offers that Roupell would agree to release the *Ann* if Laurens would relinquish the judgment he had won against the searcher.[28] When these offers were angrily refused, the case went to trial.

Roupell and Hatley would have been wise to withdraw the case at this time, for the evidence against them was overwhelming. As testimony mounted the issue quickly turned from the fate of the *Ann* to whether or not it would be possible to decree a probable cause and protect Roupell from another expensive damage suit. Leigh finally resorted to the rarely used oath of calumny, in which Roupell was required to swear before the court and before God that he had seized the ship out of a sense of duty, rather than from malice or resentment. After Roupell took the oath, Leigh acquitted the vessel and, in open court, read a severe chastisement to the customs officers. This lecture was so severe that it merits reproduction in some detail here:

That it appears to me, by the proofs and exhibits in this cause, that the practice of the Customs . . . has been various, fluctuating, and uncertain: that the Merchants have been at one time told, by the Custom House Officers, that bond must be given *before* the lading such goods on board, and, at another day, that it might be done *at the time of clearing out*, that such uncertain conduct in the officers may (if allowed and permitted) work the most dangerous effects, as they, by such occasional and partial dispensing with, or relaxions of, the laws, may have it in their power to draw unwary persons into snares, and involve the most innocent in ruin. FORASMUCH ALSO, as the Claimant's manifest contains the very non-enumerated goods informed against, as well as those for which bond had been given, it clearly contradicts every suspicion of fraud or design: That the Claimant, by his conduct, discovered the most ready inclination to comply with the terms required of him by the officers of the Customs; and the evidence affords me some violent presumption, that matters were so artfully conducted, that the Claimant was not able to conform thereto, before an actual seizure was made for a non-compliance with the terms required; which circumstances induces a strong suspicion, that there was more of design and surprize, on the part of some officers, than of any intention to commit a fraud, on the part of the Claimant.

Leigh went on to praise Laurens's character as a merchant free from any suspicion of fraudulent practices and hoped that other innocent men would not be similarly "trepan'd" in the future.[29] Then, in spite of this severe indictment of the customs officers, Leigh declared a probable cause and ordered each side to pay their own costs.

Once again, Leigh hoped that both sides would accept the decision as a compromise and, again, the decision satisfied neither. Roupell, who might have been expected to be happy to get off this lightly, immediately informed the customs commissioners at Boston that effective enforcement of the Navigation Acts was impossible under current conditions at Charles Town. He placed the blame squarely upon Leigh who was, Roupell wrote, more interested in protecting his personal position than in enforcing the law. Thus, the customs service was forced to operate without the advice and support of the attorney general and the judge of the vice-admiralty court.[30] Henry Laurens was even more bitter. He considered it shocking enough that Leigh would offer an oath of calumny to a man whom Leigh had recently labeled a "damn'd perjured Villain" and threatened to prosecute for perjury. Yet he could hardly believe his ears when Leigh, after his scathing denunciation of the customs officers, ordered him to pay half of the costs (his share of which he estimated at sixty pounds sterling) and prevented him from taking any legal action against Roupell.[31] Laurens, too, traced his problems to Leigh's plural office holding and was now convinced that the situation would not improve until these offices were separated and filled with more public-spirited men.[32] He informed Leigh that he planned to circulate the records of the *Ann* case among his friends and correspondents and might even publish them if necessary. Leigh's immediate reaction was to threaten Laurens with criminal prosecution if such a publication was not "properly" handled. Finally, however, after a series of letters passed between the two men, Leigh informed Laurens that he could publish what he pleased.[33]

On August 1, 1768, Laurens sent a lengthy report on the *Ann* case, which would serve as the basis for two separate pamphlets entitled *Extracts from the Proceedings of the Court of Vice-Admiralty in Charles-Town, South Carolina* to his friend, and a co-owner of the *Ann*, William Fisher in Philadelphia. He denied that he was motivated by personal resentment at Leigh's decisions, observing that it was "no agreeable task" to publicize the misconduct of a relative with whom he had long been friendly. Such a publication was necessary, he wrote, to prevent any further damage by the rapacious customs officers at Charles Town and throughout America:

> Every Man in America is more or less concerned at this critical Time in such Events, & the avidity of these Locusts, as you justly term them, should be rectified by some wholesome Medicine. Nothing less than a halter will cure some of them.[34]

Leigh had been in a perfect position to apply some of this "medicine," but he had shirked this duty in order to protect his personal position. Numerous complaints had arisen against Leigh's multiple offices and Laurens wrote that he often warned his friend that he should resign some of these positions to avoid compromising his character. But Leigh was too addicted to the high life to see the wisdom of such advice. Laurens was certain that if Leigh had not been both attorney general and judge of the vice-admiralty court, the *Ann* would not have been seized. Even if it were, he asserted, he would have received justice in the trial. Such a peculiar decision could only have been the result of a desperate effort by the judge to prevent any further complaints about his plural office holding from reaching London.[35]

Laurens was particularly incensed at Leigh for allowing, indeed almost forcing, Roupell to take the oath of calumny. Leigh did not even mention such an oath until the seventh session of the court, after all of the evidence had been taken. If the application of this oath was at all justified, and he refused to believe that it was, Laurens argued that the logical time was at the beginning, rather than the end, of the proceedings. The only possible purpose of such a charade, as Leigh practically admitted from the bench, was a final desperate attempt to set up a probable cause for the seizure. The administration of the oath was, as described by Laurens, equally ridiculous. Leigh explained the oath to Roupell and informed him that if he did not take it the case would be dismissed. When Roupell hesitated and attempted to avoid the oath, Laurens and his attorneys, John Rutledge and James Parsons, heatedly objected. Laurens was particularly opposed to the oath and declared that he "would rather loose the Subject in dispute, than to impose such an oath upon Mr. Roupell." Undeterred, Leigh angrily gave Roupell the choice of taking the oath or stopping the prosecution. Roupell answered that if these were his choices he would take the oath and, to Laurens's dismay, did so. In denouncing the oath, Laurens explained what the consequences of refusal would have been for Roupell: first, this would have been a virtual acknowledgment that he had seized the vessel out of malice, an act that would have been fatal to his public and private character. Second, it would have ended the prosecution, leaving Roupell liable for the entire cost of the case and opening him to another expensive damage suit. Thus, Roupell stood to gain a great deal by taking the oath. Laurens proceeded to quote several prominent scholars, including Francis Bacon and Samuel Pufendorf, to support his contention that such an oath could not be administered under these circumstances.[36]

Laurens then addressed himself to the decree endorsed by Leigh in the decision, finding it impossible to reconcile the final decision with the severe indictment the judge passed upon the customs officers. He attacked Leigh's statement that the customs officers were inconsistent in sometimes demanding that bond be posted before loading and at other times before the ship cleared. Laurens contended that it was far worse than this, as it had been the constant practice to allow bond to be posted when the ship was ready to sail. Laurens pointed to the testimony of several prominent merchants, which indicated that Hatley perjured himself in stating that bond had sometimes been demanded before loading. He felt that an impartial judge might have settled the matter of this conflicting testimony by calling for the books of the customs house, which would have clearly proved that Hatley was lying. Leigh's failure to do this convinced Laurens that the judge was less interested in justice than in shielding Hatley and his fellow rogues from the consequences of their misdeeds.[37]

Laurens then scoffed at Leigh's declaration that the inconsistent conduct of the customs officers set dangerous precedents for the harassment of innocent merchants. He certainly agreed with the statement itself, but felt that Leigh's subsequent actions made such commentary ridiculous. The certification of a probable cause did nothing to deter and much to encourage such practices in the future. Nor could Laurens accept Leigh's remark that he had been "trepan'd" for some "private & inexplicable reason," commenting that

The private reason for trepaning an Innocent Owner in this case was not inexplicable. Every person the least conversant in Affairs knew & assigned the reason aloud. The Court resounded with the reason. Four, Five, nay twenty Witnesses were ready to bear testimony of the true reason. It was impossible for the Judge, nice in perception, quick in discovery, & perfectly acquainted with late transactions between the Prosecutor & Owner, to be unacquainted with the true reason, but his Honour did not wish to have reasons explained, and when he discovered that there was some danger of such an explanation, he effectually preclosed it by the *Oath of Calumny*, unseasonably extorted, unreasonably insisted upon in manner as hath been repeatedly described.[38]

Thus, Laurens insisted, the issuance of a probable cause in the case of the *Ann* was a blatant miscarriage of justice. It was naive to think that Leigh would reform his conduct in the future. Therefore, it was imperative that he be relieved of some of his positions.[39]

Laurens asked Fisher to gain the advice of the Philadelphia legal community on the propriety of publishing the report. Before he could receive an answer, however, he learned that Roupell had sent an account of the story to the customs commissioners in both America and Britain. In response, Laurens directed Fisher to publish his paper and circulate it throughout New England, New York, and Pennsylvania.[40] Fisher decided to publish the extracts of the *Ann* case without much of Laurens's commentary. Instead, he added an introduction and conclusion that contained some harsh criticism of the Navigation system and, in November or December 1768, published the pamphlet entitled *Extracts from the Proceedings of the Court of Vice-Admiralty in Charles-Town, South Carolina*. Though the introduction and conclusion have been attributed to Laurens, it appears that, though Laurens approved them, they were actually written by Benjamin Chew, attorney general and, later, chief justice of Pennsylvania.[41] As Fisher prepared to publish the Extracts, it was learned that the British government had privately ordered Leigh to resign either his judge's commission or his position as attorney general. Leigh chose to resign his seat on the bench because, according to Laurens, it was the less profitable of the two.[42] Emboldened by Leigh's resignation from the bench and disappointed that Fisher had omitted so much of his commentary, Laurens decided to suppress the Philadelphia edition of the *Extracts*. In its place he would publish a second edition that would include the case of the *Ann*, along with several other cases, including the *Wambaw* and *Broughton Island Packet*.

The second edition of the *Extracts* was published in Charles Town in February 1769 and contained more severe criticism of Leigh than had appeared in either the Philadelphia edition of the *Extracts* or in Laurens's August 1 letter to Fisher. Laurens distributed the pamphlet among his friends, correspondents, and officials in Britain and America.[43] Laurens continued his assault on Leigh, stating that honest merchants and corrupt customs officers alike had reason to be unhappy with such a "selfish double dealing" judge. After pages of abuse, Laurens concluded his pamphlet with two lines virtually guaranteed to arouse the wrath of Leigh: "Friendship and Party with a weak and corrupt Judge Is Enmity against God and opposition to the publick Good."[44]

Leigh was infuriated by the *Extracts* and announced that he would shortly publish a response. This he did in May 1769 in a pamphlet entitled

The Man Unmasked, a performance that marked the deterioration of the conflict into a bitter, public battle in which personal attacks were emphasized over the issues.[45] Asserting that to "argue law with Mr. Laurens, would be like a physician disputing with a quack," Leigh refused to discuss the cases, other than answering the remarks that touched upon his character. He expressed dismay that Laurens, whom he had always thought of as a friend, would attempt to rob him of his reputation and ruin a large family to which he was related. Such conduct could only be the product of the "evil workings of a cruel and malignant heart."[46] Leigh insisted that Laurens was pursuing a vendetta against him in a desperate attempt to regain his popularity, lost since the Cherokee War. He characterized Laurens as a "man of plodding parts and tolerable sense" who, through application and hard work, had made himself into a skilled and successful merchant. Yet Laurens yearned for something more and his ambition led him to attempt to become a military man. This was a fatal mistake, Leigh incorrectly asserted, for his performance as a soldier destroyed his reputation among the people.[47]

Leigh attacked Laurens as a cynical hypocrite who went to great pains to hide his malignant heart and present himself to the public as a virtuous, deeply religious man. To this point, he had been remarkably successful in this charade, for his many acts of charity, his generosity in public subscriptions, and his willingness to help aspiring merchants, all gave him the appearance of a good and honorable man. Yet his recent publications served to remove the mask, revealing the heartlessness and sinister brutality of the real Henry Laurens.[48] This character could be seen in Laurens's continued professions of concern for Leigh's welfare. There could be no greater presumption, Leigh felt, than that exhibited by Laurens in asking Leigh to consent to his libelous publications:

> The world, with all its follies, can scarce equal *this;* and it is hardly credible, that a man should, in one view, represent a judge as partial, and in another situation wish to have him for *his counsel; abuse him,* and say he did not *mean it; libel him,* and ask his assent to the publication of it; if we did not call to mind *Solomon's fool,* who, in a frolicsome and *silly* mood, cast *fire-brands* and *arrows* and *death,* and cried *"it is in sport."*[49]

Such behavior might have been expected from Laurens, wrote Leigh, pointing to the dispute with Gadsden over the Cherokee War as another demonstration of why Laurens "has little reason to talk of ingratitude, or the unfaithfulness of any man in the course of private friendships."[50] This was the real Henry Laurens, Leigh insisted, a man who "never wages a dispute but the ruin of his antagonist is the motto of his banner." He warned his readers not to be deceived by the almost universal display of affection for Laurens in Charles Town, for this proceeded not from respect, but from the fear of arousing the displeasure of such a merciless foe.[51]

Nor could Leigh resist the temptation to comment upon his rival's moral qualms about the slave trade:

> The goodness of his heart persuades him one moment that a certain branch of his profession is odious, nay, repugnant to all *sound doctrine*. He reads the Revelations, which speak of divers articles of merchandize, and finding that *slaves* and the souls of men are also in the enumerated list, swears that St. John meant, in his *vision*, the pernicious practice of the *African trade;* he therefore withdrew himself from the horrid and barbarous connection, retaining however, to himself, a few of those *jewels* which he had heretofore amassed, some of the *wages* of this *abominable trade.*[52]

Finally, after passing more commentary on Laurens's character, Leigh took his leave of the "wicked brute" who had made use of "every subtle, vindictive and diabolical art and stratagem which he had been able to devise" to destroy Leigh's good name and ruin his innocent family.[53]

Laurens was incensed by this pamphlet and rejected several offers of accommodation from Leigh that would have included private concessions of error. Only a public apology would be acceptable in light of the scandalous nature of *The Man Unmasked.* If this was not received, Laurens promised that he would publish a reply that would "fix him dumb to his Seat, unless he has more impudence than I even yet think he has."[54] Thus, on August 3, 1769, Laurens published two pamphlets. The first was a second edition of the Charles Town version of the *Extracts*, in which he presented a text similar to the first edition, but with more severe language. The second publication was an answer to the charges of *The Man Unmasked*, entitled *Appendix to the Extracts.*[55] Laurens ridiculed Leigh's work, asserting that his case was so weak that he had not even attempted to defend his own conduct. Instead, Leigh resorted to the use of deceptions, half-truths, and outright lies in a vicious and futile effort at character assassination. As a demonstration of how Leigh had manipulated the evidence in a clumsy attempt to distort the truth, Laurens pointed to the correspondence between the two men over publication of the *Extracts.* Leigh had printed an edited version of this correspondence, which he claimed to be an accurate summation of the letters. Laurens published this correspondence in its entirety. These letters offered devastating proof that Leigh had grossly misrepresented the substance of the correspondence to portray Laurens in a far worse light than the facts warranted. Such shenanigans led Laurens to observe that there was only one thing that Leigh had asserted that he could almost agree with: "that I was an Ass for putting the smallest Confidence in *him.*"[56]

Laurens was deeply hurt by Leigh's reflections on his character and offered a convincing defense of his conduct. He disputed the charge that he never waged a dispute without trying to ruin his foe, insisting that, though he had engaged in as much business as anyone in the province, he rarely sued to collect debts and had never sent a man to jail for debt. Only once, in the case against Roupell, had he brought suit at common law or in chancery. Noting that Leigh was in a position to know all of this, he offered to forfeit one thousand pounds sterling if Leigh could substantiate his charge of cruelty. If he could not, then he was a liar and should acknowledge the fact publicly. As Roupell was the only man against whom Laurens had brought suit, he assumed that this must be the case in question. Laurens denied that he tried to ruin Roupell, though he agreed that he certainly could have done so were he so inclined. He explained that Roupell was unable to pay the fourteen hundred pounds that had been awarded to Laurens. The searcher asked for time to present a request to the customs commissioners at Boston that allowed him to pay the sum out of the American chest. Though Laurens was under no obligation to grant this delay, he did so, despite the urgings of friends who insisted that Roupell's past or subsequent conduct merited no indulgence. Laurens refused this advice because he did not wish to distress Roupell or his family by sending the searcher to prison. Roupell finally settled the debt ten months later and, even then, he included a challenge of a duel. Laurens failed to see how his conduct in this case constituted persecution. If anything, he felt that, given the circumstances, he might be censured for being too indulgent.[57]

Laurens then turned his attention to his withdrawal from the slave trade, asserting that

> If from "the Goodness of my Heart," as he sarcastically affirms, I had persuaded myself that I had been engaged in an unlawful Traffick, and therefore stopped short in the very Prime of my Day, when I might have amassed many Thousands more, surely it would be no Proof of the *Goodness of Mr. Leigh's Heart* to expose me to Redicule for making a Sacrifice of *Gain* to my *Conscience*. Will *Mr. Leigh* ever follow such an Example?

Contending that he could "claim no such particular Merit," Laurens explained that he had left the slave trade because he was contracting his mercantile activities and because he had no partner and was not disposed to get one. Though this was an accurate reflection of the reasons he had given in 1763 and 1764 for his disengagement from the slave trade, he was careful not to mention that he was currently declining this business on moral grounds.[58]

Nor was Laurens happy with Leigh's attacks on his service in the Cherokee War. He pointed out that his troubles at this time were related not to his military conduct, but to his "Abhorence to the groundless Aspersions" cast upon the direction of the campaign. He offered to produce certificates from several officers, including James Grant, who commanded the expedition, and Thomas Middleton, who had commanded the provincial regiment, that proved that his performance was honorable. He took particular care to note that Middleton had sanctioned his conduct while the two men were engaged in the controversy on opposite sides. Such conduct might be expected from Middleton, who, unlike Leigh, "was too generous to impute Faults or Crimes to me which I had not been guilty of merely because he and I did not agree in Sentiments."[59]

Finally, Laurens denied that his attacks on Leigh were motivated by a desire to regain popularity with the people. He admitted that his positions during the conflict over the Cherokee War and the Stamp Act crisis had been sharply criticized by some people. Yet he felt that most of these men still respected him as an honorable man and insisted that he had been reconciled to most of them. If he remained unpopular with some people at this time, he attributed it to his recent defense of Leigh against the attacks of Gadsden and others, rather than to these earlier incidents.[60]

The public battle between Laurens and Leigh was now at an end. Neither man had distinguished himself in this scathing public dispute, but Laurens clearly had the better argument. Though he had also engaged in personal abuse, he had at least assumed and defended a position on the issues. Leigh was a better writer than Laurens, but he realized that his case could not stand serious scrutiny and, thus, refused to engage in a debate centered upon the issues. His effort to cloud the issues was largely unsuccessful as the overwhelming majority of the community supported Laurens in this controversy.

Laurens would angrily remember this disagreeable affair for a long time to come. In late 1769, he was still bitter in his denunciation of the customs service, writing that "the King never had in this Province so vile a set of Servants in the Customs House as there are at present, persons who are bound by no Oaths nor moved by any considerations but Such as tend immediately to their own Interest."[61] He realized that his problems with the customs house were not necessarily over, as Roupell remained in the province and was even promoted to collector after the removal of Daniel Moore. The battle with the customs officers disturbed Laurens to the extent that he determined to avoid future trouble by cutting his trade back as far as possible. When he did engage in commerce, Laurens was careful to specifically warn his ship captains to avoid violation of even the slightest technicality in order to avoid seizure.[62] With these precautions (and a long absence from the colony), Laurens managed to avoid any further difficulties with the customs service.

Unfortunately, he was not destined to have similar luck with Egerton Leigh. In December 1772, while in England to oversee the education of his sons, Laurens received word that his young niece, Molly Bremar, had given birth to an illegitimate child. Even more disturbing was the news that the father had been Leigh, the husband of Molly's elder sister and the man who had recently taken Molly into his home after the death of her mother. Laurens immediately instructed his brother, James Laurens, to confront Leigh with the charges. If Leigh's reply was unsatisfactory, Laurens directed his brother to lodge official complaints with the governor, the council, and the assembly. Meanwhile, he would investigate the matter and prepare to take the case all the way to the king, if necessary.[63] The irate Laurens also wrote to "the Perjured, Adulterous, Incestuous, Murderer— Egerton Leigh" a bitter letter demanding that Leigh assume responsibility for Molly's pregnancy and for the subsequent death of the child shortly after birth.[64]

This unhappy affair dragged on for over a year and a half, as Leigh repeatedly denied all responsibility for Molly's condition. Not wishing to involve Leigh's large family in his ruin, the Laurens brothers were left with few weapons with which to pressure Leigh into an acknowledgement of his actions. Increasingly frustrated, Laurens grew more convinced than ever that his former friend was a "Compound of Knave & Fool in the extreme of each."[65] While Laurens simmered in London, Charles Town became an uncomfortable place for Leigh, as few believed his denials and he was ostracized from society. He was insulted in the streets and William Henry Drayton and Edward Rutledge publicly insulted him in the council and in open court, respectively.[66] Yet, anxious to avoid any possibility of a meeting with Henry Laurens on the streets of London, Leigh stubbornly refused to leave Charles Town. Only when rumors that Laurens had sailed for South Carolina were received did Leigh depart for England.[67] Unfortunately for Leigh, there was no truth to these rumors and, in September 1774, he was faced with a meeting with Laurens. Though Leigh at first professed innocence, Laurens reported to his brother, he soon broke down and tearfully admitted responsibility. When Leigh asked forgiveness and offered six hundred guineas as reparation, Laurens declared himself satisfied, though he refused to accept the money. Then, after a sharp admonition to reform his conduct, Laurens forgave Leigh, putting an end to this long and distasteful scandal.[68]

The conflict with Egerton Leigh and the customs officers was the major catalyst in propelling Henry Laurens toward the revolutionary movement. Before this point, Laurens acknowledged that the British government had made mistakes, but he considered these unintentional errors that would be corrected as soon as the ministry discovered the true facts about America. This belief in the benevolence of British officials was severely shaken by the rapaciousness of the customs officers and his inability to receive justice in the vice-admiralty court. His confidence was further shaken when two of the men whom he considered most culpable, Leigh and Roupell, were rewarded with honors and promotions, rather than punished for their misdeeds. As a merchant who prided himself on honesty and respect for the law, Laurens was shocked when he found himself victimized by officials who acted more like pirates than servants of the king. Certain that he would find justice in court, he instead found a judge who was more concerned with advancing his own selfish interests than in ensuring that an old friend was treated fairly. Though Leigh severely chastised the customs officers for their actions, Laurens was certain that nothing had been done to prevent similar conduct in the future.

Leigh's assertion that Laurens was motivated, in this conflict, by a desire to regain lost popularity has some validity, but is misleading as an explanation for his behavior. It is true that Laurens's ideas on imperial relations had conflicted with those of a large segment of the community during the 1760s. It is also true that Laurens realized that his stance on this issue would do much to restore his reputation with these people. Yet his correspondence during this period provides little evidence that this was the predominant concern. Laurens continued to express his distaste for the radicalism of Gadsden and the Sons of Liberty and had little inclination to join in sentiment with this group. He was convinced, however, that the corrupt and arbitrary placemen represented a far greater threat to the interests of Great Britain than did the the Sons of Liberty. Laurens took no pleasure in exposing the deficiencies of royal officials, but he felt that the very existence of the empire would be endangered if the government continued to employ rogues in responsible American positions. The failure of imperial authorities to respond satisfactorily to his pleas for reform, combined with Leigh's personal attacks, served to further alienate him from the British government. The misconduct of Egerton Leigh, Daniel Moore, and George Roupell produced an effect that the urgings of Gadsden and the Sons of Liberty had always failed in: turning Henry Laurens toward the opposition movement.

6

The Nonimportation Movement, 1769–1770

Even as Laurens battled Egerton Leigh and the customs house, a new issue had arisen that would provide the intercolonial protest movement with fresh momentum. In 1767, Charles Townshend, now chancellor of the exchequer, won parliamentary approval for a new plan of colonial administration. The Townshend program emerged from the continuing search for a colonial revenue, a problem that was becoming increasingly urgent. The issue of imperial finance remained unresolved and, indeed, was intensified as the annual cost of the American army approached four hundred thousand pounds, almost twice the original estimate. Increased costs, along with continuing challenges to British authority, led to a parliamentary consensus that some assertion of British power was necessary. Thus, debate centered upon the nature and extent, rather than the desirability, of a new system. The Townshend plan had several advantages that commended it to Parliament. First, the new taxes could be defended as trade duties, thus circumventing the arguments used in opposition to the Stamp Act. Second, the duties would be relatively inexpensive to collect and could be expected to provide an annual revenue of forty thousand pounds. Thus, despite some opposition and a long debate, Parliament agreed to the Townshend Duties Act (technically the Revenue Act of 1767) in June 1767.[1]

Few Americans were fooled, however, by Townshend's efforts to disguise the taxes as measures to regulate trade. John Dickinson reflected the views of many Americans when, in his *Letters from a Pennsylvania Farmer*, he differentiated between duties designed to regulate trade and taxes to raise a revenue. Dickinson insisted that the former served a useful and valuable function that had always been accepted by Americans. He denounced the latter taxes as unconstitutional innovations, for Americans had never agreed to the raising of a revenue amongst them without their consent.[2] Americans were also quick to recognize that the Townshend Duties Act was far more threatening than the Stamp Act. While the latter was designed to raise revenue for the support of the army in America, the revenue from the Townshend duties was to work a complete reform upon the colonial administrative system. Indeed, the main purpose of the act was to provide for the support of imperial officials in America, hopefully relieving them from dependence upon the colonial assemblies. Such a policy would have serious consequences for the assemblies, as it would deprive them of an important form of leverage in dealing with British officials.[3]

The Townshend duties promised to be detrimental to South Carolina, which continued to suffer under the effects of the Currency Act. Already faced with a severe money shortage during the early 1760s, the repeated refusals of Parliament to sanction an emission of currency intensified the problem. As the Townshend duties threatened to remove more money from the colony, South Carolina was faced with a monetary crisis. The mechanics, the group most dependent upon ready money, were the first to feel the effects of this situation. By 1769, however, the merchants and planters were also experiencing significant difficulties.[4] Under these circumstances, serious opposition to the new program might have been expected from South Carolina. The Commons House immediately ordered Charles Garth to join with the other American agents to obtain the repeal of the act. Yet the Commons, perhaps waiting to learn what measures other colonies might take, adjourned without taking any further action.[5]

It was Boston that once again took the lead in organizing the opposition and the Massachusetts assembly sent a circular letter inviting the other colonies to join in protest. The speaker of the Commons House, Peter Manigault, received this and a similar letter from the Virginia House of Burgesses while the assembly was in recess. As the House was not likely to meet again until the fall elections, there was little that Manigault could do but inform both assemblies that he would place the letters before the Commons at the first opportunity. The general response to the Massachusetts letter was not encouraging and matters might have developed differently were it not for the overreaction of the British ministry. The Massachusetts letter offended and infuriated the earl of Hillsborough, the new secretary of state for the colonies, and he angrily instructed Governor Francis Bernard to demand that the assembly rescind it. Hillsborough then wrote a circular letter of his own in which he directed the other governors to order their assemblies to ignore the Massachusetts letter. Bernard dutifully presented Hillsborough's demand to the Massachusetts assembly, which, by a vote of 92 to 17, refused to obey and was promptly dissolved.[6] Hillsborough's bungling policy played right into the hands of colonial radicals such as Gadsden, who could then point to the proceedings in Massachusetts as exactly the type of situation that the Massachusetts letter had warned against.

The election of a new Commons House was set for October 5, 1768, and Charles Town buzzed with excitement as the day approached. A considerable amount of electioneering was carried on by radicals and moderates alike, as both sides sought to control the seats for the Charles Town parishes of St. Philip's and St. Michael's. The mechanics, particularly determined to elect men who supported vigorous opposition to the Townshend duties, met at Liberty Point on October 1, in what amounted to a nominating convention. The mechanics agreed to a slate of candidates for each parish, with Gadsden, Thomas Smith, Sr., and Hopkin Price chosen for the three St. Philip's seats. Afterwards, the gathering enjoyed a barbecue provided by Gadsden and others. Later, they moved to the Liberty Tree where "many loyal, patriotic, and constitutional toasts were drank, beginning with the *glorious* NINETY-TWO *Anti-Rescinders-of Massachusetts Bay.*" When night fell, the Liberty Tree was decorated with forty-five lights and forty-five rockets were fired in honor of John Wilkes and his *North Briton No. 45.* The company finally proceeded to Dillon's Tavern

> where the 45 lights being placed upon the table, with 45 bowls of punch, 45 bottles of wine, and 92 glasses, they spent a few hours in a new round of toasts, among which, scarce a celebrated Patriot of Britain or America were omitted.[7]

This festival was greeted with distaste by many of the more conservative residents of Charles Town. Among these was Henry Laurens, who took another jab at Gadsden when he informed James Grant that

> We are become very important in this Town in the Electioneering business. To day a Grand Barbecu is given by a very Grand simpleton, at which the members for Charles Town are to be determined upon. Therefore if you hear that I am no longer a Parliament Man, let not Your Excellency wonder, for I walk on the old Road, give no Barbecu nor ask any Man for Votes, and my inmost wish is now to retire from that sort of bustle.[8]

This letter is interesting for two reasons. First, despite his continuing problems with British officials, it is clear that Laurens remained unwilling to align himself with Gadsden and the radicals. There was, however, evidence that his reputation had been at least partially restored among the mechanics, for his name was placed in nomination at the Liberty Tree meeting. The fact that he was defeated by a comfortable margin indicates, however, that he had not yet regained their confidence.[9] The letter also provides a good example of how Laurens could sometimes be hypocritical by assuming a "holier than thou" attitude. His criticism of the electioneering of Gadsden and the radicals appears praiseworthy until it is discovered that Laurens himself paid Robert Dillon £370 for expenses at Dillon's Tavern during the elections of October 1768 and March 1769.[10]

The increased political activity of the mechanics worried the merchants and planters, and these groups launched a campaign for their own slate of candidates, which included Laurens. The result was basically a draw, as the mechanics won two of the three seats for St. Michael's and lost two of the three for St. Philip's. They might have lost all three seats in the latter parish had Christopher Gadsden not been at the head of their ticket. Gadsden, whose social position made him acceptable to the merchants and planters, and whose politics were popular among the mechanics, received the support of both sides to finish far ahead of other candidates in St. Philip's. Yet the strength of the merchants and planters was demonstrated by the fact that Laurens, who finished second, could give twenty of his votes to Charles Pinckney. These votes allowed the eminent attorney to defeat Hopkin Price, a prosperous tanner whom the upper social order, including Laurens, regarded as unqualified for a seat in the assembly.[11]

The mechanics quickly found that their doubts about Laurens's principles were largely unfounded. The refusal of the British ministry to redress American grievances combined with current frustrations to work a transformation upon Laurens's ideas on imperial relations. His writings on the Townshend Acts bore a much different tone than had his thoughts on the Stamp Act. His description of the situation throughout the colonies, in an October 1768 letter to Lachlan McIntosh demonstrates this change:

> The Cloud is gathering thick in the North, & will soon spread over America if not dispel'd by wise Measures in Britain. New England is in Arms. New York slumbers but will not sleep if there shall be a necessity for her Appearance. Pensilvania is divided but the most powerful Part is on the Side of Liberty. Mary-Land, Virginia, & N. Carolina are confirmed in their Principles declared in 1765 & will support them in 1768. South Carolina & Georgia, weakest Sisters will not subscribe to the Right of a British Parliament to lay internal Taxes upon America, & tho' feeble, have gather'd Strength among themselves, will be keen in asserting their Liberty, & sullenly & stubbornly resist against all ministerial Mandates & admonitions tending to enslave them.[12]

Such commentary was much different from that offered by Laurens in 1765 and was a clear signal that he was now prepared to support measures of opposition.

The Commons House demonstrated similar resolution when it met again in November 1768. Governor Montagu, in obedience to Hillsborough's directive, opened the session by warning the Commons to treat with contempt any seditious letters or papers it might receive. After appointing a committee, which included Laurens and Gadsden, to prepare a reply to the governor's speech, the assembly turned to the Massachusetts and Virginia letters. Peter Manigault read the letters to the House, which directed the letters to the same committee chosen to reply to the governor's speech.[13] This committee assured the governor that the Commons would ignore any seditious papers that appeared before it. It did not, however, feel that the Massachusetts and Virginia letters fell within this category, explaining that

> the said Letters are replete with Duty and loyalty for his Majesty, Respect for the Parliament of Great Britain, Sincere affection for our Mother Country,

Tender care for the preservation of the rights of all His Majesty's Subjects, and founded upon undeniable Constitutional Principles.

Finally, the committee suggested that Manigault be directed to inform the Massachusetts and Virginia assemblies that the Commons House approved of their measures, and that the king be petitioned for a redress of grievances. The South Carolina Commons House was notorious for the sparse attendance at its early sessions and this assembly was no exception. Though only twenty-four of the fifty-five members were present to consider this report, the recommendations were unanimously accepted. These proceedings alarmed Governor Montagu, who quickly summoned the assembly and informed it that the king considered the Massachusetts letter

a measure of the most Factious Tendency, calculated to inflame the minds of his good Subjects in America, to promote an unwarrantable Combination, and to encourage an open Opposition to, and denial of the Authority of Parliament.

He again warned the Commons to ignore the letter in order to "avoid any disagreeable Consequences that may attend the Contrary." The assembly responded by ordering the address to be printed and made public, along with the Massachusetts and Virginia letters and the resolutions of the House. Not surprisingly, the furious Montagu dissolved the House.[14]

The popular mood was evidenced by the reelection of Laurens, Gadsden, and the other twenty-two members who had voted for the resolutions. Yet, due to a series of prorogations by the governor, the assembly did not meet again until June 26, 1769. The Commons House protested these repeated prorogations, arguing that the fact that the House had sat for only five days during the previous fourteen months was a dangerous and illegal precedent that threatened the independence of the assembly.[15] Under these circumstances, it is surprising that the Commons House did not pass a nonimportation agreement and, indeed, took little further notice of the Townshend Acts. One exception came in August 1769 when the Commons refused to provide for a group of British soldiers that had spent the winter of 1768 in Charles Town before proceeding to St. Augustine. The assembly pointed out that these soldiers had performed no services within South Carolina and that neither the people nor their representatives had been consulted about their presence. Furthermore, the Commons argued, it was for such purposes that the Townshend Acts had supposedly been passed and, as long as this unconstitutional program remained in effect, the revenue should come from this source.[16] Beyond this, however, the opposition to the Townshend Acts was largely carried on outside of the assembly.

The mechanics took the lead in opposing the Townshend Acts, adamantly demanding that all British manufactures be prohibited. The planters promised their support for nonimportation, but efforts were frustrated by the refusal of the merchants, whose consent was crucial to the success of any nonimportation plan. Boston had adopted a nonimportation agreement as early as October 1767 and most of the northern colonies had soon followed their lead. Yet, not until July 1769 could the Charles Town merchants be prevailed upon to consent to such a plan. In October 1768, Lieutenant Governor Bull informed Lord Hillsborough that the invitation from Boston to join the nonimportation movement was met with "silent Neglect." Yet Bull warned Hillsborough that this spirit was not necessarily lasting, for the principles spread from Boston promoted "a kind of enthusiasm very aft [*sic*] to predominate in popular Assemblies and whose loud cries silence the weaker voices of moderation."[17] Once again Bull had demonstrated his keen insight, for this was precisely what happened in Charles Town during the next several months.

The early months of 1769 were a trying period for Christopher Gadsden. His efforts to bring the merchants into a nonimportation agreement had failed and there appeared little hope of a change of heart in the near future. Realizing this, the mechanics decided, in late January 1769, to enter into a nonconsumption agreement among themselves. They hoped to promote economy and keep money within the province by refusing to buy British goods (including slaves), promoting manufacturers within South Carolina and throughout America, and discontinuing unnecessary and expensive customs such as the wearing of mourning and the providing of entertainments after funerals.[18] Without the merchants, however, this was little more than a gesture, and Gadsden and the mechanics continued to press for a nonimportation agreement that would bind the entire colony. While the mechanics prepared their nonconsumption plan, Gadsden was forced to deal with another personal calamity when his second wife died in late January after a long illness. Gadsden had married Mary Hassell on December 29, 1755, and the couple had four children together. It is impossible to measure how deeply the life and death of Mary Gadsden affected her husband, for his surviving writings contain no information on this subject. Gadsden did use this opportunity, however, to promote the recent resolutions of the mechanics. The funeral of Mary Gadsden was a simple and inexpensive affair, and Gadsden stood at the grave dressed in blue homespun, rather than the traditional black mourning cloth imported from Britain. This gesture was reported as far as Boston as an example of how dedicated Americans in general, and the people of Charles Town in particular, were to the promotion of economy and American manufactures.[19]

Gadsden and the mechanics continued to press for a nonimportation agreement and used the pages of Peter Timothy's *South Carolina Gazette* to bombard the public with their pleas. The movement gathered momentum during the next few months and even Henry Laurens grew convinced that a boycott would be implemented if Britain did not make concessions.

The extent to which Laurens had been alienated by British policy is seen by the fact that, though he did not take a leading role in the nonimportation movement, he did support it at this time.[20] Matters came to a head in June 1769, as the *Gazette* announced that the mechanics and "many other inhabitants of the town" were about to hold a meeting to enter into "patriotic associations" like those of the northern cities. A week later the *Gazette* reported that "several Societies of Gentlemen" in Charles Town had agreed to dress in homespun and boycott all British goods that could be manufactured in America.[21] Still, the merchants remained opposed to a boycott, and any nonimportation agreement would be futile without their participation.

Gadsden responded to this situation with a public letter that appeared in the June 22, 1769 issue of the *Gazette*. Over the signature "Pro Grege et Rege" (for the people and the king), he presented the case for nonimportation. Gadsden informed his readers that the Townshend Acts represented the renewal of the efforts of a wicked ministry to enslave the American colonies. He reminded the people of the distinguished role they had played in the opposition to the Stamp Act. "But," wondered Gadsden, "what is become of this spirit, my friends?" He implored his readers to awaken to these dangers before it was too late. In arousing the people to defend their rights, however, Gadsden specifically denounced the use of violence, as disorders "will do infinetly more mischief than good." Only a nonimportation agreement, supported with unity and spirit, could rescue American liberty from the clutches of the British Parliament.[22]

Gadsden then launched another attack on British tyranny, expressing amazement that the government seemed to be doing everything possible to drive the colonies "to some desperate act." He was offended by reports that the ministry had contemptuously rejected American petitions with the assertion that, if it came to force, one or two regiments would be sufficient to subdue the entire continent. Gadsden warned the British that they had grossly underestimated American strength and resolve and that serious consequences could result from programs such as the Townshend Duties:

Again, She certainly does not consider that, by these oppressive and unconstitutional acts, she imprudently tries to *dissolve* the *principal* the *strongest* tie of our dependence. For in other respects, particularly those of a mercantile nature, are not several powers of Europe better customers to some of the colonies, for their productions than she is? For instance, what an insignificant part of our main staple, Rice, is consumed in Great Britain? Not above five thousand barrels at most. And can she be so blind, or absurd, as to think, that if distress, dispair, and self-interest should co-operate with any fair and safe opportunity, that in the course of some future war, may be given a better customer, who possibly may have *more* than *two* regiments ready to land in America, that such dastardly wretches, as we are insinuated to be, may not only be afraid to refuse, but glad to jump at a change that we are sure, in such circumstances, cannot be for the worse?[23]

Gadsden again attributed much of the responsibility for both British tyranny and the lack of a spirited response to "that detestable *Stuart* race" of Scots, "a race of pedants, pensioners, and tyrants." After a final admonition to defend colonial liberties and avoid being fooled by the tricks of Scottish traitors, Gadsden presented the nonimportation agreement that had been agreed to by the mechanics and planters.[24]

As it became clear that some sort of agreement was to be implemented, both sides set out to prepare their proposals. The mechanics and planters had already agreed to an Association, and the *Gazette* reported that the response was encouraging, as many, including at least twenty-five members of the Commons House, had signed. The same issue of the *Gazette* contained advertisements calling for the merchants to meet at Dillon's Tavern and the mechanics and planters at the Liberty Tree to discuss the situation. The merchants met first and constructed an agreement that was unacceptable to the others, who then decided that anyone who did not sign the earlier Association should be boycotted. This reaction startled and infuriated the merchants. In the July 13 issue of the *Gazette*, the merchants agreed that taxation without representation was a legitimate grievance, but protested that a boycott was

an unjust attempt, of one part of the community, whose wants are already supplied, to throw a burden upon the rest, more grievous than ever was conceived by the most arbitrary minister of the most despotic King.[25]

The merchants continued to believe that they would shoulder the brunt of any boycott, but realized that failure to reach an agreement with the mechanics and planters could result in even worse consequences. With this in mind, the merchants declared themselves ready for compromise.

Gadsden presided over the July 22 Liberty Tree meeting at which the two sides accepted a unified Association. This agreement was among the most comprehensive in America and represented an almost complete surrender by the merchants. The Association encouraged economy and American manufactures, and prohibited importation of any European or East Indian goods, except only a few necessary items that could not be produced in America. All orders to British firms were to be countermanded and signers were pledged not to raise their prices. Slave importations from Africa were banned after January 1, 1770, and from the West Indies and other places after October 1, 1769. Trade with transients was banned after November 1, and all signers pledged to boycott anyone who did not sign within a month. Anyone who broke the agreement was to be treated "with the utmost contempt," and the Association would remain in effect not merely until the

Townshend Acts were repealed, but until all American grievances were redressed. Gadsden read the Association to the gathering twice, once for information and once for a point-by-point discussion. Apparently, there was little debate, for the *Gazette* reported that the crowd quickly approved the Association "with a Unanimity scarce to be parallelled." Then, several copies were produced and signed by everyone present, including every member of the assembly who was currently in Charles Town. Finally, the meeting turned to the question of enforcement. It was agreed that a General Committee composed of thirty-nine men, equally divided between the merchants, planters, and mechanics, would perform this task. Gadsden was nominated to serve as a representative of the planters, but he declined, though he did agree to help circulate the Association.[26]

Henry Laurens was another who signed the Association but did not serve upon the General Committee. Though his economic interests suffered from the boycott, he remained a staunch supporter throughout the life of the Association. In October 1769, Laurens explained that the major question in dispute was

> Whether it be consistent with natural right and Justice or with the constitution of the Realm that one part of the Subjects of that Realm should be Taxed without their own consent by the other part, who are not only to be excepted from any part of the burthen of such Taxation, but are themselves to be benefited thereby.[27]

Such statements did not represent any major transformation for Laurens, as he had expressed similar thoughts during the Stamp Act crisis. What had changed was his relationship with the protest movement. It was a difficult decision for Laurens to participate in the resistance to British policy, and his current troubles with Egerton Leigh and the customs house played a significant role in it. Yet, other important factors must not be ignored. Laurens had opposed the Stamp Act as oppressive, but saved his sharpest condemnation for the tactics employed by Gadsden and the protest movement. He was shocked by the disorderly conduct of the mob, and he was certain that the British government would redress American grievances if opposition was carried on in a proper and respectful manner. His observations since 1765 led him to conclude that he had placed too much confidence in the benevolence of British officials. As protest leaders demonstrated an ability to control the Liberty Boys, Laurens was prepared to support stronger measures that he earlier would have denounced.

The Association was quite successful in South Carolina, so much so that the *Gazette* reported on August 10 that almost the entire population had signed. A month later the *Gazette* announced that, excluding Crown officials, only thirty-one inhabitants of Charles Town had refused to subscribe. As promised, these names were published and the nonsubscribers soon found themselves unable to sell their merchandise.[28] This brought a loud and troublesome, though hardly threatening, attack from the nonsubscribers. Leading this charge was William Henry Drayton, a twenty-seven-year-old planter whose refusal to subscribe to the Association left him without a market for his crops. The son of a member of the council and nephew of Lieutenant Governor William Bull, young Drayton hailed from one of the most prominent families in the province. Educated in England, Drayton had developed expensive tastes and a fondness for gambling that left him deep in debt. Though a member of the Commons House, Drayton was, in the words of Robert M. Weir, "a rather frivolous young lightweight, unable to get his life in order."[29] Upset at his ostracism, Drayton leveled an attack against the Association in a public letter published in the August 3, 1769 issue of the *Gazette*. Drayton assailed the publication of the names of nonsubscribers as an infringement on individual rights, insisting that only the legislature could brand a man an enemy of his country. He singled Gadsden out for special criticism as a local tyrant who hoped to use the issue as a means for personal advancement. Drayton ridiculed "our patriot" as "either a *traitor* or *madman*" who looked upon himself as a monarch, "in his opinion at least, *the ruler of the people*." He concluded with the suggestion that, in the interest of all concerned, Gadsden be locked in an insane asylum at the public expense until the next change of the moon.[30]

This hostile assault marked the beginning of yet another long and disgraceful newspaper battle in which the combatants generally ignored the issues in favor of personal abuse. This war was fought in the pages of the *Gazette* from August through December 1769 and featured Drayton and William Wragg on one side and Gadsden and John Mackenzie[31] on the other. Gadsden responded to Drayton on August 10 and wasted no time defending the Association. He chided "Master Billy" as a dishonest and immature individual who lacked "every trace of public spirit and generosity." He declared that Drayton must have been deceived by "naughty men" who took "advantage of the known 'weakness of poor Billy's head'; a head visibly not calculated to undergo the fatigue of 'thinking and reasoning, and acting in conformity thereto.'"[32]

When the names of the nonsubscribers were finally published in September, both Wragg and Drayton published letters in the *Gazette* of September 21. Of the two, Wragg was by far the calmer and more controlled. He found it difficult to understand the rationale behind the locking up of his property, observing that he had done nothing to threaten the peace of society and had no concern with the Association other than to privately observe that he thought it counterproductive to the desired goal. He asked if he was not within his constitutional rights in "withholding my assent to propositions I disapprove of, and which are in their nature altogether discretionary." If so, he could see no justice in the efforts of the subscribers to ruin him.[33]

Drayton was less restrained and far more belligerent. He refused to be bullied and welcomed the publication of his name as a testimonial of his "resolution and integrity." Finding it arrogant in the extreme for the General Committee to assert that it was defending American liberty, Drayton insisted that this body was doing the opposite, for it "hath violated the first principles of liberty" by acting in a "despotic and unjust manner." He agreed that the subscribers had the right to act according to their consciences. But, by the same token, Drayton argued that he possessed the same right and could not be publicly censured for exercising it. He then turned to the publication of the names of the nonsubscribers, declaring that

> If these proceedings are not arbitrary and unjust, I confess that I am ignorant of the idea which these epithets convey—Is this a land of liberty? Who ought to be called lovers of liberty? Those who violate its first principles? Or those who religiously maintain them?

Wragg and Drayton had both constructed reasonable arguments and might have met with some success if Drayton had been content to stop there. Yet, he demonstrated his lack of judgment when he ridiculed the participation of the "profanum vulgus" in the General Committee. He refused to allow his thoughts to be regulated by men whose talents lay in "how to cut up a beast in the market to the best advantage, to cobble an old shoe in the neatest manner, or to build a necessary house." He concluded that nature had never intended such men to engage in the formulation of public policy and suggested that they stick to the trades for which they had been trained.[34]

The response to this tirade was fast and furious. John Mackenzie was the first to step forward, assuring Drayton that there had been no attempt by the "profanum vulgus" or anyone else to control his opinion. He defended the Association and insisted that the General Committee had every right to warn against individuals who were plotting to betray the liberties of their fellow citizens. Mackenzie also denied that the Association was arbitrary or unjust, pointing out that it violated no laws and that the people had as much right to join the Association as Drayton had to stay away.[35] Far more scathing, however, was the mechanics' reply. This letter upset Drayton to such an extent that when he published the relevant materials in a book entitled *The Letters of Freeman*, it was the only document that was excluded. The mechanics asked Drayton how much merit he claimed from gaining a large estate from marriage and inheritance, rather than from his own efforts or talents. They asserted that Drayton would find himself in a difficult position indeed were he ever faced with the necessity of earning a living. He might, if he applied himself, survive as a manual laborer, but would be utterly helpless if faced with any task that required skill. The mechanics concluded with the same generous offer that Drayton had earlier extended to Gadsden: a rent-free room in the building for the insane.

During his stay, however, "he must be debarred of pen, ink, and paper (dangerous implements in unskillful hands) lest they should aggravate his disorder."[36]

Drayton would have been wise to allow the matter to drop there. Instead, he produced another letter in which his main object seems to have been to correct the grammar and literary style of Gadsden and Mackenzie. As for the mechanics, Drayton ignored them except to state that he considered them to be useful members of society, so long as they remembered their place. He then reasserted his previous statement that the artisans should mind their own business and stop meddling in political matters for which they had no competence.[37] Two weeks later, Drayton was back in an effort to prove that the Association was a violation of the theories of John Locke, one of the favorite political writers of the opposition leaders. Here Drayton raised an important and insightful point: that effective power was being transferred from the legislature to an extralegal organization among the people. This, he felt, was an illegal and treasonous attempt to overthrow the established government and constitution.[38]

This charge brought a long answer from Gadsden, his most important published thoughts during the nonimportation crisis. Here he finally settled down and provided an effective defense of the Association. Gadsden denied that the American colonies desired independence, but he no longer considered such a solution to be out of the question. He suggested that if the British ministry was really interested in retaining the affection of the colonies, this would be difficult to tell from their conduct. He insisted that the British had learned nothing from past mistakes, and their repeated oppressive measures did more to encourage thoughts of independence than discourage them. Still, though Americans did not want independence, he left the door open, stating that this "would be the greatest misfortune which could befall them, excepting that of losing their rights and liberties: that indeed is, and must be, confessedly a greater." He pointed out that Americans had repeatedly petitioned for a redress of grievances, but had met with such scorn that further efforts were discouraged.[39]

Gadsden also looked to Locke, and he reminded his readers that government was established to protect the rights and property of the people. When governors ignored these obligations, they forfeited the allegiance of the governed. He maintained that Americans continued to love and revere the king and were confident that he had no intention of wronging his loyal American subjects. The same could not be said of the ministry, however, as these "selfish, arbitrary, and designing counsellors" were doing everything in their power to alienate the king's faithful subjects throughout the realm. This cunning, diabolical, and wretched ministry had so misrepresented the American situation to the king that Americans had "nothing, absolutely nothing, left to depend upon, but our own union, prudence, and virtue." The

Association was a last, desperate attempt to bring the ministry to its senses through the means of economic pressure. Gadsden denied that there was anything illegal or unconstitutional in such a policy, for every man possessed the right to decide for himself which articles he would purchase. If he decided to patronize American manufactures, this was his privilege. He saw nothing arbitrary about the Association, noting that only those who violated the agreement after subscribing to it were to be treated with contempt. The nonsubscribers were left to their own consciences and the names were published to prevent them from gaining an unfair advantage over those who did sign.[40]

Several more letters, consisting largely of personal attacks, were published before Drayton finally wearied of the struggle and sailed to England in early January 1770. None of the participants had covered themselves in glory in this controversy, and the dispute did little to clarify the important issues in question. Henry Laurens was among those who were dismayed by the spectacle, and his commentary was an excellent summation of the dispute:

> You see in the Newspapers the sparrings between some of our Party Men who like many other Men in such circumstances have each taken aside [sic] and seem to have forgot the subject upon which they began to dispute. Their contest is not now in defence of Liberty and the constitution, but about false concord and ungrammatical blunders. How often have you seen Religion in the same manner made the Stalking Horse to a couple of quarrelsome fellows who were writing volumes unintelligible in every part except there [sic] reciprocal invective.[41]

Such commentary might seem odd coming from a man who was himself engaged in the early stages of a similar contest with Egerton Leigh, but such sentiments were quite suitable to the occasion. Perhaps the most bizarre twist to this tale, however, concerned the future activities of William Henry Drayton. Returning to South Carolina in 1772 as a member of the council, Drayton quickly rejected his previous position and became a close associate of Christopher Gadsden and the radical wing of the protest movement.

More serious trouble arrived with the new year, as accusations were made in early 1770 that the Association was unevenly enforced, to the benefit of several leading members of the general committee. In January the case of Mrs. Ann Mathews brought some severe criticism upon the committee. Mrs. Mathews was a widow who suffered under the boycott and received a shipment of merchandise after the Association had gone into effect. She had ordered her goods before the Association was adopted and, due to circumstances beyond her control, received them at this time. When permission to sell the goods was denied, she sold them anyway, pointing to the fact that several prominent supporters of the Association, including John Edwards and John Rutledge, had received goods after her, yet were not required to store or reship them. She wondered why she was singled out for such treatment and concluded that the reason might have something to do with the fact that she lived near a prominent merchant on the committee with whom she sometimes competed for business.[42] A second problem arose in late January when the Dutch-born Charles Town merchant Alexander Gillon attempted to sell one hundred pipes of wine that he had recently received. At a general meeting chaired by Gadsden at the Liberty Tree, the committee ordered Gillon either to store or reship the wine. This Gillon refused to do, arguing that he had ordered the wine in May and should not be punished for circumstances beyond his control. The question was then put to the people, and Gillon complied with the unanimous demand that the wine be stored. The charge that the Association was selectively enforced appears to have had some validity. Yet, it was politics, rather than economics or favoritism, that largely determined the selection of targets. Gadsden and his enforcement cronies recognized the destructive effects that a failure or two of enforcement might have upon the Association. Thus, targets were selected carefully and individuals such as Gillon and Mrs. Mathews were chosen because they lacked the ability to offer effective resistance.[43]

In March 1770, the *Gazette* reported that "Ministerial writers" were asserting that merchants were withdrawing from the Association in several colonies. The publisher of the *Gazette*, Peter Timothy, denied these rumors and claimed that British merchants were clearly feeling the effects of the boycott, having lost more than two hundred thousand pounds sterling on the refusal to purchase slaves alone.[44] Even Lieutenant Governor Bull could find little evidence of backsliding at this time. He reported to Hillsborough that the association was still rigidly enforced and expressed the weak hope that "distress will awaken the generality of them from their dreams" within a year.[45]

When news was received of the impending repeal of all of the Townshend duties except that on tea, there was some question as to whether the Association should be continued. Consideration of this question was complicated by reports that several colonies and towns, including Boston, planned to end their boycotts. Thus, a meeting was held on May 14 at the Liberty Tree to explore the situation. This was an important event in the life of Henry Laurens, as his acceptance of the chair at this meeting marks his assumption of a leadership position in the protest movement. It was quickly pointed out that, though most of the Townshend duties were being removed, the tax on tea, and thus the principle of parliamentary taxation, remained. It was also noted that nothing had been done to redress other grievances, such as the standing army and the vice-admiralty courts. In light of these circumstances, it was decided that South Carolina would remain steadfast in support of the Association, and the other colonies were to be informed of this resolution. As a demonstration of this firmness, the gathering decided that, since Georgia had withdrawn from the boycott, any slaves purchased there would be seized and forfeited.[46]

There could be no greater demonstration of the conversion of Henry Laurens to the protest movement than his thoughts and actions during May 1770. This was a tragic period for Laurens, as his beloved wife Eleanor suffered from a difficult childbirth and died on May 22. That Laurens would leave the side of his desperately ill wife to chair the May 14 meeting at the Liberty Tree is evidence of his strong feelings on this issue. Shortly afterwards, Laurens informed a friend that the Association was as strong as ever and hoped that the people would have the resolve to continue until Britain redressed all American grievances.[47] There is little record of Laurens's thoughts on the events of the next few months, for his grief over the death of his wife led to an almost complete suspension of his public activities.[48] This is unfortunate, as it would be interesting to read his reaction to a renewal of mob violence in June. The arrival of news that Rhode Island had broken the Association led the Sons of Liberty to fear a similar occurrence in Charles Town. Thus, on June 18, an effigy was hung between Dillon's and Gray's Taverns with an attached note promising similar treatment to anyone who violated the Association. A "venerable old Gentleman, clothed with Authority" had the effigy removed and placed in the guardhouse. It did not remain there for long, however, for in the evening the effigy was rescued and paraded through the streets before being burned upon the green. The *Gazette* reported that many of the moderates were unhappy with this spectacle and would have prevented it if possible. This was not possible, however, as Peter Timothy explained that the majority were determined to make it clear that it would be unsafe to break the boycott.[49]

The summer and fall of 1770 witnessed the crumbling of American unity behind the Association. Georgia and Rhode Island had already broken their agreements, and news soon arrived that Boston, New York, and Philadelphia were about to follow this example. Yet South Carolina stood firm and denounced the deviation of the northern colonies and even threatened to boycott several of them.[50] Laurens was among the most discouraged by these events and he vented his frustration in a letter to William Fisher:

> I am so disappointed in my Expectations of several Colonies North of this relative to their late important Resolutions that I am in a humour to disbelieve the Sincerity of the Majority of all Politicians and to conclude that the few who are really sincere in the Pursuits for Public Good are always intended to be made Tools and Dupes for the Imolument of the designing ones, and thence almost to admit a Possibility that our little Parliament here may relax under some unseen Operations of Ministerial Art before January next, and surrender

those essential Rights of their Constituents which you allude to. God forbid this should happen among us.[51]

Yet happen it did, and even sooner than Laurens had feared.

Lieutenant Governor Bull informed Hillsborough on December 5 that there was considerable division among the people. Many of the merchants had empty shelves and accusations were circulating that some, including James Laurens, were secretly importing goods. Bull felt that most of the merchants and some of the planters were ready to end the boycott. The leaders of the General Committee were becoming apprehensive, Bull also reported, under threats of lawsuits by those suffering under the Association. Bull had little respect for John Neufville, the chairman of the General Committee, whom he described as a "man of straw." The real "tribunes of the people," Bull asserted, were the trio of Thomas Lynch, John Mackenzie, and Christopher Gadsden. Bull was particularly wary of the latter, reporting that Gadsden "is a violent enthusiast in the cause," one who viewed all British policy "with a suspicious and jaundiced eye, and maintains with great vehemence the most extravagant claims of American exemptions."[52] On December 13, Laurens was chosen to preside over a Liberty Tree meeting at which the continuation of the Association was debated. Bull sent a complete account of the meeting to Hillsborough, stating that Thomas Lynch rode fifty miles to Charles Town and "exerted all his eloquence and even the trope of Rhetorical Tears for the expiring liberties of his dear country, which the Merchants would sell like any other merchandize." Despite the support of Gadsden and Mackenzie, who wished to continue the Association and import goods from Holland, the gathering decided to discontinue the boycott on all items except tea. The meeting then agreed to send a bitter letter to the northern colonies complaining of their conduct in breaking the Association. Finally, a committee consisting of Gadsden, Lynch, Mackenzie, Thomas Ferguson, and, as chairman, Laurens, was appointed to establish and promote South Carolina manufactures. Then the meeting adjourned after thanking Laurens for his "impartial and faithful conduct" as chairman.[53]

The nonimportation movement proved successful throughout the continent. Enforcement was effective in all of the major towns, and, except for the duty on tea, the Townshend duties were repealed.[54] There was a price, however, for these tactics cost the colonies many of their friends in England. The colonies had earlier possessed the sympathy of many of the merchants involved in the American trade. Yet these men found it difficult to understand why the Americans insisted upon drawing their English friends into bankruptcy and ruin to make their point. Many of these merchants began to question exactly what it was that the colonies hoped to achieve, fearing that this might be the overthrow of the Navigation system, if not complete independence. In future crises, the colonies could no longer depend upon any significant support in England.[55] Still, despite their inability to force a complete surrender, Gadsden and his associates could add another victory to an increasingly lengthy list of triumphs. The prestige of the movement was further enhanced by the addition of new converts who, like Henry Laurens, brought a touch of moderation and legitimacy to the cause.

The nonimportation movement marked a watershed in the career of Henry Laurens. He had long questioned the wisdom of British policy, but had retained the hope that officials would recognize the futility of oppressive policies and rectify the errors. The Townshend Acts, together with his experiences with the customs house and the vice-admiralty court, had served to crush his hopes. By 1770 it was no longer possible to attribute British mistakes to a lack of information or understanding of the colonies. Imperial officials had sufficient time and opportunity to familiarize themselves with American objections, yet they continued to repeat the same mistakes. This convinced Laurens that only a thorough reformation of the British government could restore the affection between the mother country and her colonies. Laurens seriously doubted if such a change would soon be effected and thus, he was prepared to support, and even take a leading role in, programs he would have denounced a few years earlier. His conversion to the protest movement was warmly welcomed by Gadsden and the resistance, and Laurens assumed a place of honor at several Liberty Tree meetings. While he was happy to again enjoy the confidence of the people, Laurens remained unwilling to make common cause with the Sons of Liberty. He continued to express his dislike of the blustering and enthusiasm of this bunch, and certainly shared Drayton's view that politics were beyond their competence.

Despite Laurens's progress, he was still left far behind by Christopher Gadsden, who continued to evolve as a revolutionary leader. Gadsden's performance during this period was yet another demonstration of the essential features of his character. His disinterestedness was again evident in his staunch support of the nonimportation agreement at the same time he was opening his new wharf. The sacrifice of a considerable amount of business from a boycott made his appeals much more effective. But Gadsden again allowed his zeal and temper to influence his judgment when he engaged in the bitter and personal newspaper feud with William Henry Drayton and William Wragg. It was unfortunate that this discussion was not tied more closely to the issues for, when he defended the Association, Gadsden's arguments were reasonable and effective. Yet, even here, Gadsden was in danger of assuming a position too far in advance of the community. This was certainly true of his suggestion that independence was a possible solution if the British ministry did not reform itself. Though

Gadsden realized that such a threat was premature and never mentioned it except as a last resort, the word independence took an increasingly prominent position in his vocabulary. Gadsden did express a willingness to overthrow British authority in the economic sphere when he advocated the importation of goods from Holland at the Liberty Tree meeting of December 13, 1770. Such a policy was a direct challenge to the Navigation system and, if the colonies were allowed to become economically independent, political independence would some day follow. Though Gadsden continued to deny any desire for independence and still expressed hopes for reconciliation, he clearly doubted that harmony could be restored in the foreseeable future. Thus, as Henry Laurens entered the protest movement, Christopher Gadsden set out upon the road to independence.

7

The Wilkes Fund Crisis, 1770–1774

Even as the argument over nonimportation intensified, a new and more bitter controversy broke out in South Carolina, one that created a legislative stalemate that would remain unresolved during the remainder of the colonial period. This dispute centered around the decision of the Commons House to send ten thousand five hundred pounds currency (fifteen hundred pounds sterling) to the Society of the Gentlemen Supporters of the Bill of Rights, a London club engaged in raising funds for the defense and support of the English radical, John Wilkes. A well-educated man, Wilkes had entered Parliament in 1757 and had been appointed to several responsible positions through the influence of his friend, William Pitt. Yet Wilkes was something of a scoundrel and began criticizing George III shortly after the king ascended the throne in 1760. In 1762, Wilkes and some friends launched *The North Briton* and used it as a vehicle to ridicule the ministry headed by the Scot, John Stuart, the earl of Bute. Wilkes took great liberties with Bute, to the extent of accusing Bute of having seduced the king's mother. His legal problems began, however, when, in the *North Briton No. 45* of April 1763, he strongly denounced a speech that the king had delivered from the throne. George III lost both his temper and his patience and ordered Wilkes deposited in the Tower of London on a charge of criminal libel. Wilkes's problems intensified when an obscene parody he had written on Alexander Pope's *Essay on Man* fell into the hands of his enemies. Under indictment for libel and blasphemy, Wilkes fled to France in 1764 and was promptly declared an outlaw by the ministry.

His finances depleted, Wilkes returned to England in 1768 and stood for election to Parliament. After being defeated for a London seat, Wilkes was able to win election from Middlesex county. This did not save him from the consequences of his past actions, however, as Wilkes was fined one thousand pounds and sentenced to twenty-two months in prison on the libel and blasphemy charges. At the same time, the king was determined that a rogue like Wilkes was unfit to sit in Parliament and ordered his expulsion. Unwilling to submit to such dictation, the Middlesex electorate repeatedly re-elected the imprisoned Wilkes by overwhelming majorities. Each time Wilkes was promptly expelled. The ministry finally tired of this game and, in February 1769, passed a resolution through Parliament that declared Wilkes "incapable" of sitting in Parliament. Then, to add insult to injury, they anointed Henry Luttrell—who had recently been trounced by Wilkes by a vote of 1143 to 296—as the duly elected representative for Middlesex. These developments stirred up a considerable amount of bitterness and controversy in England, resulting in riots and several deaths. Regardless of Wilkes's private character, such persecution made him the hero of English and American radicals alike. Christopher Gadsden was among the staunchest supporters of Wilkes and repeatedly honored him as a defender of British liberty. In 1763, Gadsden had decided to develop some land he owned near Charles Town into a new subdivision. Now, he used the occasion to honor the friends of American liberty, naming the subdivision Middlesex, and the first four streets Virginia, Pitt, Wilkes, and Massachusetts. During the Stamp Act crisis, Gadsden had joined the mechanics in founding the John Wilkes Club, also known as the Club No. 45. Adopting the number forty-five as a symbol, this club filled the air with cries of "Wilkes and Liberty!"[1]

In 1769, Wilkes's friends and supporters formed the Society of Gentlemen Supporters of the Bill of Rights and appealed to British and American supporters to contribute to the rights of Englishmen and to help defray Wilkes's legal expenses. While several American groups sent good wishes and small gifts, the South Carolina Commons House was the only official body to respond. In December 1769, Gadsden laid the letter from the society before the Commons House. After minimal debate, the assembly, without the approval of either the council or Lieutenant Governor Bull, voted to send ten thousand five hundred pounds currency to Wilkes's support. It was ordered that the public treasurer, Jacob Motte, should withdraw the sum from the treasury and give it to a committee consisting of Speaker Peter Manigault, Gadsden, John Rutledge, James Parsons, Thomas Ferguson, Benjamin Dart, and Thomas Lynch. These men would send the money to England and an item would be included in the next tax bill for repayment of the sum to the treasury. This was, apparently, a popular measure, for Peter Timothy reported in the *Gazette* that only seven members in "the fullest House ever Known" voted against the measure and that these would have approved if the grant had been for only one thousand pounds sterling.[2] The assembly could hardly have expected a contribution to the king's most persistent and notorious enemy to have gone unnoticed. Among those who expected a severe reaction was Henry Laurens, who had been away on business and was not present for the vote. Years later, while a prisoner in the Tower of London, Laurens recalled that his initial reaction to the news had been the startled declaration that "these Chaps will get a rap o' the Knuckles for this."[3]

William Henry Drayton, in a parting shot before sailing to England after losing his battle against the nonimportation Association, sarcastically congratulated the province on being in such a position of economic strength that it could afford to "defray the bills of a certain club of patriots at the *London* tavern." Drayton also offered the insightful observation that the authors had taken such a bold step in order to defend the province "from the reproach of having always remained in a state of inactivity, till in the northern hemisphere a light appeared to shew the political course we were to steer." There was some truth to this statement, as Gadsden and his associates had always smarted under the sneers that they were incapable of independent action and always looked to Boston and the northern colonies for guidance. As the delay in adopting a nonimportation agreement seemed to confirm that South Carolina was lagging in the common cause, a bold move was desired to boost the confidence of the opposition movement. As Peter Timothy proudly pointed out in the *Gazette*, such a brash step as the grant to Wilkes was a clear indication that South Carolinians were capable of independent and creative measures.[4]

Official reaction was slower in coming. Lieutenant Governor Bull immediately informed Hillsborough of the proceedings, explaining that the letter from the Bill of Rights Society had been carefully concealed until its introduction in the House. He explained that he had been powerless to prevent the resolution, for "from the great religious and civil indulgences granted by the Crown to encourage Adventurers to settle in America, the Government of the Colonies has gradually inclined more to the democratical than regal scale." Hillsborough was shocked to learn that the assembly had been unilaterally borrowing money from the treasury for years and that the only check available upon this practice was a veto of the tax bill. Since this was a serious step that would leave the government without funds, Bull explained, the council had never resorted to this option and the practice had become generally accepted. Bull admitted that he might have expressed his dissatisfaction with an immediate dissolution, but there was little hope that a new House would provide much change in either men or temperament and, thus, a dissolution would only give the assembly a new sense of grievance. Advising caution, Bull also relayed the information that a new tax bill would probably be ready in May and requested instructions in the likelihood that an item for the repayment of the grant to Wilkes appeared in the bill.[5]

The surprised ministry turned at once to Attorney General William de Grey for legal advice. In February 1770, de Grey reported that all three branches of the legislature—governor, council, and assembly—had to approve of any appropriation of public funds from the treasury. The fact that the Commons House had been exercising this power for several years was irrelevant, for the House could not unilaterally alter the constitution and this action was contrary to both the governor's commission and to royal instructions. Therefore, de Grey concluded, the gift to the Bill of Rights Society was illegal and he advised the ministry to take steps to prevent the future repetition of such an action. The Privy Council agreed with this recommendation and the Board of Trade prepared an additional instruction that Hillsborough transmitted to Bull on April 14, 1770. Under this instruction, Bull and all future executives were ordered to refuse their consent to any bill that appropriated money for any purpose in which South Carolina was not directly concerned. In addition, it was ordered that no bill be passed that did not explicitly limit the use of the money to the declared purpose. The governor and lieutenant governor were threatened with immediate removal and the public treasurer with triple damages and lifetime ineligibility for any office if they violated these instructions. Along with the additional instruction, Hillsborough ordered Bull to veto any tax bill that contained an appropriation for repayment of the sum sent to Wilkes. Thus, the assemblymen responsible for the measure might learn a lesson by being forced to personally reimburse the treasury.[6] Hillsborough hoped that such a strong stance would solve this problem forever, but quickly found that it only aggravated the situation.

Even as the Board of Trade was preparing the additional instruction, the Commons House attempted, in April 1770, to pass a tax bill that included an item for the repayment of the Wilkes fund. The council absolutely refused to consider this proposal and asserted that the grant to Wilkes was in no way "honourable, fit, or decent," as it represented a blatant insult to a king who was "in our opinion, Gracious, Mild, and Good to all of his faithful people."[7] The assembly immediately appointed a committee, which included Laurens and Gadsden, to prepare a reply. This committee denied the "unjust imputations" of the council and insisted that, as the representatives of the people, the assembly had the right to grant the public money for any purpose whatsoever. The committee felt that it was ridiculous for the council to feign amazement that the assembly had unilaterally ordered money from the treasury, for this had been a common occurrence for years and had never been questioned by either the governor or the council. This touched upon the crux of the constitutional argument that would paralyze the colony for the next four years: whether or not local action, precedent, or custom could alter the nature of the constitution. The position of the Commons House was that local precedents could alter the constitution if accepted by all three branches of the provincial government. Attorney General de Grey took the opposite position, insisting that royal statements and proclamations always took precedence and that illegal local action could not be legitimized through common practice. Finally, the committee pointed out the absurdity of a small board of placemen sitting as both advisors to the governor and as an upper house of the legislature. They denied that the council was an upper house and asked that the Crown appoint some men of property who had some stake in the colony to a true upper house. In conclusion, the committee insisted that a contribution for the Support of the Just and Constitutional Rights and Liberties of the people of Great Britain and America, can not be construed to be disrespectful or Affrontive to His Majesty, the great patron of the Liberty and Rights of all his Subjects.[8]

The assembly would maintain this position throughout the controversy.

The timing of this exchange served to intensify the celebration that greeted the release of John Wilkes from prison on April 18. This event was marked by the ringing of bells, the display of colors, and several celebrations at which the number forty-five figured prominently. The Club No. 45 took the leading role in this festival, when ninety-two members met at 6:45 P.M. at Dillon's Tavern. An hour later a procession led by twenty-six candles moved to another room to enjoy an elegant entertainment. After dinner, "45 loyal and patriotic Toasts" were drunk before the gathering finally broke up at 12:45. Peter Timothy noted in the *Gazette* that over one hundred fifty houses were illuminated, many with forty-five lights, despite the fact that illumination had been discouraged for fear of attacks upon those who did not illuminate. Had this not been discouraged, Timothy wrote, over four hundred homes would have been illuminated as evidence of the regard of South Carolinians for "those who suffer in the Cause of Liberty, by a resolute and steady Opposition, to the arbitrary and tyrannical Attempts, of such wicked and corrupt Ministers as would overturn the English Constitution."[9]

A similar celebration was held on July 5, when the statue of William Pitt, commissioned to honor his services in gaining the repeal of the Stamp Act, was raised in Charles Town. The mood of the people was unmistakably revealed in between these parties when the birthday of the king was greeted, in early June, in a much more subdued manner. Timothy reported in the *Gazette* that few illuminated for the king's birthday because "the People are not Hypocrites. They will not dissemble Joy, while they feel themselves unkindly treated, and oppressed."[10] While Christopher Gadsden was in the forefront of these festivities, Henry Laurens viewed them with distaste. While Laurens supported the right of the Commons House to dispose of the public money as it saw fit, he could not bring himself to honor a man of Wilkes's character. Nor did he care much for the loud and boisterous parties of the Club No. 45, informing a friend in 1771 that "I have always disliked those stupid Garnishings of No. 45, Wilkes and Liberty, and drinking 45 Toasts to the Cause of true Liberty 450 Times unnecessarily."[11]

The additional instruction arrived in Charles Town during August 1770 and Bull laid it before the Commons House with little hope that it would have any modifying effect. The assembly confirmed his pessimism and appointed a committee, chaired by John Rutledge and including Gadsden and Laurens, to consider the matter. This committee reaffirmed the earlier declaration of the House that the assembly had the right to solely grant the public money to any purpose it deemed proper. It again denied that the practice was unconstitutional, insisting that the practice had been commonly exercised for years with the knowledge and approval of the governor, lieutenant governor, and council. Thus, it was boldly asserted, the grant was neither unprecedented nor dangerous and would have been overlooked entirely "if the Money borrowed had not been applied towards frustrating the unjust and unconstitutional measures of an arbitrary and oppressive Ministry." The committee expressed surprise that the ministry had referred to the grant as an innovation on the part of the House. This could only have been the result of "a false, partial, and insidious" misrepresentation of the true facts by a small group of mischief-makers who were "guilty of high misdemeanours and are Enemies to his Majesty and the Province." The committee then turned to the additional instruction, denouncing it as a blatantly unconstitutional attempt by the ministry to dictate how money bills should be framed. In light of these circumstances, the committee suggested that Charles Garth, the provincial agent in London, be directed to relate the true facts of the situation to the king and obtain the repeal of the additional instruction.[12]

After the Commons House accepted these resolutions, the council again denied that the assembly had the right to unilaterally allocate public funds "for any specious pretences whatsoever." It ridiculed the assembly's contention that the money had been offered to benefit the interests of the king, observing that George III needed no assistance from it and had asked for none. Rather, the assembly had placed public money "into the hands of a set of People, who have been daily disturbing the repose, and Embarassing the Councils of the best of Princes." While admitting that the assembly had borrowed money from the treasury in the past, the council denied that this made the practice legal. Just because a law was abused and dormant, the council members insisted, did not make it any less of a law. The Council suggested that the assembly now stop playing games, admit its error, and start applying money to legitimate provincial concerns. They concluded with the promise that if the provision for the repayment of the ten thousand five hundred pounds was not withdrawn, the tax bill would be vetoed. When the Commons refused to budge, the council carried out its threat and vetoed the tax bill, blaming the assembly for the disruption in the public business. At this point, Lieutenant Governor Bull, displeased that no compromise could be reached and realizing that it was useless to continue the assembly in session, prorogued the House until January.[13]

Bull felt that many of the moderate members of the House were embarrassed by the grant to Wilkes and were sorry for their action. Yet, he observed that assemblies could be quite stubborn and asked Hillsborough if some compromise might be reached that could forestall the serious political and economic dislocations that could result from a long stalemate. After proroguing the House, Bull informed Hillsborough of the proceedings and sent a copy of the resolutions passed by the assembly in response to the additional instruction. He warned Hillsborough that these resolutions were "the result not of precipitate warmth, but of three weeks deliberation" and that the assembly would "very tenaciously" maintain their position. Hillsborough was upset by the resolutions, writing that they were "as ill-founded as they are unbecoming." After ordering Bull to adhere strictly to the additional instruction, Hillsborough directed the vacationing governor, Lord Charles Greville Montagu, to return to America as soon as possible. The strong stance of the ministry was confirmed by Charles Garth, who informed the assembly in March 1771 that the Board of Trade stood firmly behind the additional instruction.[14]

When the assembly met again in January 1771, Bull urged it to pass a tax bill without the appropriation for Wilkes. The assembly refused, but came up with a new ploy by which it hoped to win acceptance of its right to unilaterally allocate funds. In late January, Bull asked the assembly for money to help support some poor Irish Protestants who had recently arrived in the province. The Commons House eagerly complied, but ordered the public treasurer to pay seven pounds currency per head and stated that an item would be placed in the next tax bill for the repayment of the sum. Bull was not a fool and angrily vetoed the bill "as an insult to my understanding, or to my Integrity in the discharge of my duty."[15] As a result, the situation lapsed into a deadlock.

This was the situation when Laurens, to supervise the education of his sons, left Charles Town for England in July 1771. Though Laurens disapproved of the grant to Wilkes as an unwise act that was likely to bring a harsh response, he was certain that such a step was well within the authority of the House. Thus, Laurens staunchly supported the position of the assembly and repeatedly urged it to stand firm, even in the face of constant dissolutions and prorogations. Upon his arrival in England, he set out to present the true facts of the situation to his English friends. In a letter to his brother in Charles Town in December 1771, Laurens expressed astonishment that so few people on both sides of the ocean really understood what was at stake in this contest. He then insightfully presented the nature of the stalemate as he saw it:

> If the Governor passes a Bill without such Clauses (even admitting the Council would put it in his Power) he will disobey a Royal and very absolute Instruction and will incur very severe penalties. If the House of Assembly ever submit to insert such Clauses, they will sell the Birth Right and dearest Privilege of their Constituents, and will incur the Hatred and Detestation of the present Age, and their names will be branded in all future Ages with the infamous

Characters of Betrayers of the Trust reposed in them by the People. I would rather forfeit my whole Estate and be reduced to the necessity of working for my Bread, than to have those Clauses in Consequence of *Ministerial Dictate*, made part of our Tax Bills. The Gift was an unlucky Act. Those who prompted it, I am sure must now be sorry for it. But he who mischieviously and insidiously misrepresented the Act on this Side, and from hence draw those Instructions which now are, and must continue to be for some time a Bar to our Public Happiness and Welfare in Carolina, on him let the Curses of the present and future Generations be fix'd.

Laurens continued that many advised him to personally present these conclusions to Hillsborough. This he declined to do, noting that, as Charles Garth was the official agent of the colony, he should play the leading role. He was willing, however, to provide any support that Garth might find necessary or desirable.[16]

Laurens's continuing development as a leader of the protest movement is apparent in the letters he wrote at this time. The rhetoric of these letters was unusual for Laurens, and seems much more likely to have come from the pen of Christopher Gadsden. Indeed, Laurens's views on the nonimportation Association and the Wilkes fund crisis seem to have worked a truce between these two old friends turned bitter rivals. Though the warm and personal relations and their personal correspondence were not restored, Laurens did perform several services for Gadsden while in England. These improved relations are clear in a letter Laurens wrote to his brother in late 1771, which concluded: "My good wishes to my Neighbor Gadsden. The Year has been propitious to him. May every Year be so to him and to his Children."[17]

As the controversy over the Wilkes fund heated up, support for Wilkes began to decline on both sides of the ocean. Laurens predicted that Wilkes was fast slipping into political oblivion and expressed amazement that he had so long remained the center of attention, stating that

The Man is almost universally detested, but the Cause retains all of its true Friends. Men join now in one Sentence. A wretched miscreant Wilkes, a Wayward mad County of MiddleSex, for returning him one of their Members. And a venal, corrupt, and impolitic House of Commons for refusing him a Seat to which he had an undoubted Right.[18]

Regardless of the fate of Wilkes, the controversy continued in South Carolina. Governor Montagu returned to the province in September 1771 and asked the assembly to break the deadlock and return to business. Instead of surrendering, the assembly made another effort to circumvent the additional instruction. The death of Public Treasurer Jacob Motte in June 1770 had caused a new argument between the assembly and the council, this time over Motte's successor. The assembly favored Benjamin

Dart, a member of the assembly and of the committee that had transmitted the money to Wilkes, while the council favored Henry Peronneau. When neither side would back down, Lieutenant Governor Bull solved the problem by commissioning both men as joint treasurers. In November 1771, the assembly ordered the public treasurers to advance three thousand pounds currency to the silk manufacturing commissioners to purchase South Carolina silk for sale in Great Britain. The Commons was disappointed by Dart's refusal to comply and ordered him and Peronneau to explain their conduct. The two pointed out that they were under strict orders to refuse to release any funds except with the agreement of all three branches of the legislature. They added that disobedience to these directives would result in removal from office, legal action, and heavy fines. The frustrated assembly found this explanation unsatisfactory and ordered the two officials sent to prison for contempt. At this point, Montagu intervened and dissolved the House before the commitment could be carried out.[19] This incident destroyed any flickering illusions Montagu might have entertained about an early end to the crisis.

The stalemate continued throughout 1772 as both sides repeated the same arguments and neither gave any indication of a willingness to surrender. While this was transpiring in South Carolina, the year 1772 witnessed a deepening of the estrangement of Henry Laurens from the mother country. By nature a religious and highly moral man, Laurens had been extremely disappointed by the serious decline in English moral standards, which he perceived had occurred since his residence during the 1740s. His extreme disappointment in the quality and discipline of the English schools was one factor in this estrangement, as was his increasing disillusionment with English politics. Laurens still considered himself a devoted British subject and could still become excited by the prospect of a visit to the House of Lords to view the king upon his throne. Still, he could not and would not conceal his revulsion at the decadence of English politics and informed friends in South Carolina that, if anything, reports of English corruption had been understated. He reported that one English friend had laughed at his problems with Daniel Moore and Egerton Leigh as mere trifles compared with what Englishmen had to put up with every day in every ministerial department. Laurens agreed with this assessment and grew even more disgusted by the king's handling of his brother's seemingly endless problems with women. Unaware of the complexity of the king's relations with his brothers, Laurens was deeply offended and clearly hoped that the filth of the English atmosphere would not pollute Carolina virtue.[20]

As Laurens considered the personal lives of the royal family, South Carolina faced an intensification of the crisis. Governor Montagu, against the advice of Lieutenant Governor Bull, hoped to break the deadlock by calling the assembly to meet at Beaufort, rather than Charles Town. Montagu was convinced that the present assembly would never surrender on the Wilkes fund issue and hoped the distance (seventy-one miles) to Beaufort might keep some of the radical Charles Town members away, at least long enough to pass some necessary legislation. He further hoped that the implied threat of a permanent removal of the capital might serve to intimidate the Charles Town members into assuming a more conciliatory position. This blundering policy was ruined even before the assembly convened at Beaufort, when Montagu received orders not to take any action that might be considered provocative. Indeed, the ministry was shocked when it learned of Montagu's action and reproved him for pursuing a measure that would only "increase that ill humour which has already too unfortunately prevailed."[21]

This proved to be an accurate prediction of what was to come. The *South Carolina Gazette* counseled firmness in this unusual situation and reported that the voters were determined to consider only those candidates who could be relied upon to make the trip to Beaufort. On October 8, the *Gazette* reported that, despite the hazards of a long journey, Gadsden and all the other Charles Town members had set out for Beaufort. The *Gazette* then reflected the anger of the people at this unusual proceeding by declaring that "no Measure of any Governor was ever more freely and generally condemned."[22] The condemnation would get even louder as the Beaufort assembly adjourned almost as quickly as it opened. The failure of Montagu's policy was immediately evident when the generally slow-to-assemble Commons House met on October 8 with thirty-seven members, far more than the necessary nineteen, present. The assembly quickly chose Peter Manigault as its speaker and informed the governor that it was ready to do business. The bewildered Montagu refused to receive the legislators for two days and then, after a short speech, prorogued them back to Charles Town. The legislators returned to the capital to the ringing of bells and with a renewed sense of grievance.[23]

The assembly was in very bad humor when it met again on October 22 and immediately appointed a committee on grievances. The mood of the House was evident by the selection of Christopher Gadsden to chair the committee, which included many prominent members. Gadsden quickly drew up a petition demanding that the governor explain his reasons for moving the assembly to Beaufort. Montagu replied that he had already given his reasons for the move and, since no one disputed his right to call the assembly into session whenever and wherever he pleased, refused to discuss the matter any further. Unsatisfied, Gadsden reported from the committee, on October 29, that the conduct of the governor would justify a resolution to suspend all business with him. Yet, the public business would not allow such a course and, instead, Gadsden suggested four resolutions, including one to instruct the agent in London to secure the removal of the

governor. By the time Gadsden finished reading the report of the committee, the hour was late and the House adjourned before voting on the
resolutions.[24]

Aware of the anger of the Commons House, Montagu hoped to prevent
any complaints to London by inspecting the Commons House journals
every night. On this evening, however, he was informed that Speaker
Rawlins Lowndes (who had replaced the ill Peter Manigault[25]) had taken
the books home with him. The annoyed governor sent a note to Lowndes
requesting the books. Lowndes, however, did not return until late and did
not send the books until the following morning. After reading the committee report, Montagu at once sent for the assembly, in order to prorogue
them before they could adopt it. To Montagu's anger, the Commons House
continued its session after receiving the summons and adopted the report
before attending the governor. Montagu became even more enraged, however, when he discovered that the committee of correspondence had met
after the prorogation and prepared a letter directing Charles Garth to secure his removal from the governorship. Montagu responded to this
provocation by dissolving the House.[26] When the new assembly met in
early January 1773 and again chose Lowndes as Speaker, Montagu refused
to recognize this choice and ordered it to choose someone else. When the
House again chose Lowndes, it was again dissolved. Many were losing
patience with the governor, observing that this was the fourth dissolution
since Montagu had returned to the province in September 1771. Peter
Timothy reflected this popular sentiment when he wrote in the *Gazette* that

> By an unparalleled Succession of Prorogations and Dissolutions, the Inhabi-
> tants of this Province have been unrepresented in Assembly about three
> Years—*A Correspondent asks, Whether this is a Grievance?* And, if it is,
> Whether *it* is one of *the least Magnitude?*[27]

Gadsden, as usual, was more blunt. Josiah Quincy, visiting the Commons
House at the time, noted that Gadsden was "plain, blunt, hot and
incorrect—though very sensible." As the debate progressed, Quincy continued, Gadsden "used these very singular expressions for a member of
parliament: 'And Mr. Speaker, if the Governor and Council don't see fit to
fall in with us, I say let the General duty law and all *go to the Devil*, Sir. And
we go about our business.'" Finding himself increasingly isolated, Montagu
sailed for England in March 1773, the second straight governor forced from
the colony by the determination and persistence of the Commons House.
Upon arriving in England, Montagu was pressured to resign his position
and his place was filled by Lord William Campbell. Through all of this,
Laurens and Garth continued to work for the retraction of the additional
instruction. Though Laurens held out hope that this might be accomplished
during 1773, both sides continued intransigent through the year.[28]

In August and September 1773, a new controversy developed that ended in another humiliation for the council. The humiliation began when the council, determined to force compliance with the additional instruction, attempted to raise a public clamor against the Commons House by portraying the financial position of the colony as desperate. It asserted that the treasury was almost bare, due to the intransigence of the assembly on the Wilkes fund issue, and claimed that the situation would worsen when the general duty law, which was almost the sole source of revenue during the crisis, expired at the end of the session. The council hoped to force the assembly to revive the duty law by refusing to pass any other legislation until this was accomplished. Two counselors, John Drayton and William Henry Drayton, refused to agree, arguing that this strategy placed unfair pressure upon the assembly. William Henry Drayton, in his first act of resistance, exposed the plan by requesting that Thomas Powell, who had temporarily replaced Peter Timothy as printer of the *Gazette*, publish the relevant portions of the council journal in his newspaper. When Powell complied, the furious council delivered a stern reprimand to Drayton and imprisoned Powell for violating its legislative privileges.[29]

This action hit the Commons House like a bolt of lightning. Powell was released almost immediately when his lawyer, Edward Rutledge, convinced two justices of the peace, Rawlins Lowndes and George Gabriel Powell, that the council was not a legislative body and, thus, was not entitled to the privileges of one. Such a result might have been expected, for all three of these men were leading members of the Commons House, and each had consistently denied that the council had any claim to legislative functions. The next move was determined by the council, and it responded with an action that almost seemed calculated to draw a torrent of abuse upon itself. The council asked the assembly to waive the privilege of immunity from arrest for Speaker Lowndes and for George Gabriel Powell, so that legal action could be taken against the two justices. This the assembly refused to do. Instead, it approved the conduct of the two justices, denounced the arrest of Thomas Powell as "unconstitutional and Oppressive," and requested that Lieutenant Governor Bull suspend the counselors responsible for Powell's imprisonment. When Bull refused the latter request, Edward Rutledge and Thomas Powell sued Egerton Leigh, who had signed the commitment warrant, for damages. This campaign was only thwarted when Chief Justice Thomas Knox Gordon, himself a member of the council, dismissed the suit, ruling that the council was an upper house of assembly and thus possessed the power of commitment.[30]

Lieutenant Governor Bull was dismayed by the stupidity of the council and sadly informed the ministry that the episode had further "degraded" the council, which had already become "humiliated and obnoxious."[31] After being practically expelled from Charles Town for his role in the Molly

Bremar scandal, Egerton Leigh was determined to defend the council before the London public. Thus, in January 1774, Leigh published a pamphlet entitled *Considerations on Certain Political Transactions of the Province of South Carolina*, in which he attacked the original grant to Wilkes and defended the additional instruction and the legislative role of the council.[32] The mere fact of Leigh's participation in this controversy sparked the interest of Henry Laurens, who was already enraged at Leigh for his immoral conduct with Molly Bremar. By now, Laurens was convinced that Leigh was a wicked man who was bent upon the destruction of his country and he promised that "these Specious, partial, fallacious Considerations Shall not pass unnoticed." After informing John Lewis Gervais of the latest adventures of John Wilkes, Laurens presented an unflattering comparison of Leigh with the English radical:

> I wish He [Wilkes] & your Baronet [Leigh] were better Men. However, he, bad as he is, & whatever his Motives may be, pretends to be fighting up Hill for his Country. The other is a Villain & a Traitor on both sides of the Question, Cheats His King, betrays his Country & Revels in the destruction of the Orphan.[33]

Aware that he did not personally possess the literary skill to effectively refute Leigh, Laurens teamed up with Ralph Izard to secure a reply. Laurens took the lead and assumed the financial burden of commissioning the Virginian, Arthur Lee, to respond to Leigh. Laurens had an active interest in this project and obtained materials from Charles Garth and the Board of Trade to aid Lee in the preparation of his pamphlet, *Answer to Considerations on Certain Political Transactions of the Province of South Carolina*, which appeared in April 1774. Laurens also performed some editorial work on the pamphlet, though he remained disappointed that Lee did not act upon his recommendation that all personal abuse should be carefully avoided. Laurens was further disappointed when Lee's pamphlet sold only forty-two copies in six weeks. Yet, he could draw some comfort from the fact that Leigh's pamphlet sold no better, circumstances he attributed to the increasing weariness of the English public with American disputes.[34]

As there seemed to be no hope of solving the financial problems created by the Wilkes fund crisis through traditional measures, the assembly prepared to try an unprecedented step. In March 1774, the House audited the accounts of the public creditors to January 1, 1773, and ordered the clerk to issue certificates of indebtedness to the creditors. These certificates were to be signed by the clerk and five members of the assembly and, as they were acceptable as payment for taxes, circulated like any other form of money. Bull informed the ministry that the public accepted these certificates, but was anxious to get rid of them in order to avoid suffering losses if the experiment should prove unsuccessful. He also registered his disappointment that he was the only Crown official who refused to accept the certificates.[35] The cautious Henry Laurens was among those who initially distrusted the plan, as he warned John Lewis Gervais that the certificates represented "another very dangerous & delusive project in Trade, & I would recommend to you to be concerned in none of it." A month later, however, as the success of the program was more evident, Laurens modified his opinion and he declared that the certificates "may answer a very good end if the business is discreetly confined & faithfully transacted."[36]

The success of this program relieved the financial distress of the colony and reduced the pressure on the assembly to pass an acceptable tax bill. As a new crisis over tea and the Coercive Acts moved to center stage in late 1773 and 1774, the Wilkes fund crisis and the stalemate in South Carolina politics occupied a less prominent position in the minds of imperial officials. In several conversations with Lord William Campbell, Laurens and Garth convinced the new governor that the withdrawal of the additional instruction was absolutely necessary to the resumption of legislative affairs in South Carolina. Thus, Campbell used his influence to obtain a set of instructions that did not include the additional instruction of April 1770. Yet, the ministry made it clear to Bull that it had not surrendered on the main issue. Citing the fact that Bull had demanded and secured high bonds that would prevent the public treasurers from issuing money from the treasury without the consent of all three branches of the legislature, the earl of Dartmouth felt that the main question in dispute had been adequately safeguarded. Thus, he was willing to drop the additional instruction, as long as there was no attempt to repay the grant to Wilkes.[37] While the hated additional instruction had been withdrawn, the Commons House could hardly claim a victory, since neither side had backed down on the main issue of the right of the assembly to order money from the treasury on its own authority.

The Wilkes fund crisis was an extremely important factor in the development of the revolutionary movement in South Carolina. While other colonies enjoyed a brief relaxation of tension with Britain between 1770 and 1773, this was not true of South Carolina. Here, there was no interlude of tranquility, and the opposition gained, rather than lost, momentum during these years. This crisis also saw some of the more moderate members of the movement, such as Henry Laurens and Rawlins Lowndes, increase their commitment to the cause and grow closer to Gadsden and the radicals. Though Laurens disapproved of the original grant to Wilkes as a policy blunder, he felt that the action itself was well within the rights of the assembly. He firmly believed that the crisis was provoked by the ministry and that the additional instruction was an oppressive and unacceptable attempt to dictate how the assembly could appropriate the public money. Looking back over the controversy in 1774, Laurens angrily asked what Shall we Say of the Injury done to a Province by a Ministerial Mandate held over that province & totally Stagnating public business for four Years, & then withdrawn from Conviction that it was founded upon Misrepresentation & in its nature unconstitutional?[38]

Though Laurens was incorrect in his reasons for the withdrawal of the additional instruction, his statement reflected the thoughts of many in South Carolina.

The legislative stalemate did prove harmful to the province, though it was even more detrimental to British authority in the colony. Five years of intense political controversy created a great deal of bitterness against imperial authorities among leading Carolinians. The journals of the Commons House show that Christopher Gadsden was again in the forefront of the opposition. He served on every committee—often as chairman— appointed to deal with this issue. While the sparsity of his private papers leaves the historian frustrated in searching for Gadsden's inner thoughts during this important period, his public commentary, reflected in his committee reports, provide evidence of an increasingly frustrated and impatient patriot. While the ministry never surrendered on the major issues in dispute, Gadsden could still claim another victory over British authority in South Carolina. Though Lieutenant Governor Bull continued to enjoy the affection of the people, the protest movement succeeded in practically expelling Governor Montagu (the second governor to suffer this fate in a decade) and in annihilating what was left of the prestige of the council. Furthermore, the success of the certificates of indebtedness provided a clear indication that British authority was in retreat in South Carolina. A new crisis would bring it to the brink of collapse.

8

The Breakdown of British Authority, 1774–1775

THE NEW CRISIS ARRIVED WITH THE PASSAGE OF THE TEA ACT IN MAY 1773. THE Tea Act was designed to relieve the difficulties of the East India Company that, because of restrictive British policy and continued American opposition to the Townshend tea tax, was faced with warehouses full of unsold tea. By this act, the ministry, led by Lord North, agreed to allow the East India Company to ship tea directly to America, exempting the company from the taxes required for reshipment of goods to America. That the Townshend tea tax was not similarly suspended encouraged the fear that this was merely an underhanded method of gaining tacit consent to the principle of parliamentary taxation through the bribe of cheap tea. Radical leaders in all of the seaports, including Charles Town, encouraged this fear and insisted that the people take steps to prevent the tea from being landed. From London, Henry Laurens agreed that there should be opposition to the Tea Act, but hoped that his friends would act with "an uncensurable propriety." Still, he feared that they might allow the influence of the Boston zealots to lead them into more violent tactics.[1]

Laurens had reason to be concerned, for as early as November 15, 1773, Peter Timothy was sounding the alarm in the *Gazette* that three hundred chests of tea were on their way to Charles Town. Timothy expressed the hope that the citizens would band together to take the necessary steps to prevent the landing of the expected cargo.[2] When the ship *London* arrived in Charles Town on December 2, a new wave of excitement buzzed through the town. Gadsden and the radicals immediately organized a meeting for the following evening to discuss the measures of opposition to be employed. The complete absence of the merchants infuriated Gadsden, and the outraged patriot greatly offended some of them through a torrent of abuse. Nevertheless, Gadsden was appointed, along with Thomas Ferguson, Charles Pinckney, Charles Cotesworth Pinckney, and the prosperous mechanic Daniel Cannon, to a committee charged with circulating an agreement among the merchants that would reaffirm the tea boycott. The meeting also directed the chairman, George Gabriel Powell, to inform the consignees of the tea that the reception of a product that carried an unconstitutional tax would be "exceedingly disagreeable" to the people of the province. Powell was instructed to request that they not only refuse to accept the tea, but that they should return it to England on the same ship upon which it had arrived.[3]

Though Gadsden was able to obtain fifty signatures to the agreement, he found that many of the merchants were adamantly opposed to another agreement that would adversely affect their economic interests. The consignees yielded to popular pressure and refused to accept the tea, but the law required the collector of customs to seize the cargo if the duties were not paid within twenty-one days. This left Lieutenant Governor Bull with another dilemma, for it was clear that the duties would not be paid, but an effort to confiscate and land the tea was likely to meet with violence. Bull once again maintained his composure and formulated a plan that would prevent trouble. Early on the morning of December 21, under the cover of darkness, Bull had the tea secretly landed and locked in the cellar of the exchange. When the people awoke and realized what had happened, Bull warned them that the tea would remain in the cellar and that any attempt to remove it would be resisted by force. Thus, Bull was able to land the tea and avoid the disturbances that rocked Boston, Philadelphia, and other northern ports. Lord Dartmouth congratulated Bull on his tactful handling of the situation, but observed that the Charles Town events "altho not equal in criminality to the Proceedings in other Colonies, can yet be considered in no other light than that of a most unwarrantable Insult to the authority of this Kingdom." At the same time, Dartmouth informed Bull that measures were being prepared that would "be effectual for securing the Dependence of the Colonies upon this Kingdom."[4]

The news of more spirited acts of defiance by the northern colonies embarrassed Gadsden and the Sons of Liberty, as Charles Town was the only seaport at which the tea had been landed. Determined to prove their patriotism, the radicals resurrected the General Committee of the nonimportation Association and appointed Gadsden as chairman during January 1774. This new General Committee numbered forty-five members and slowly fulfilled the prediction of William Henry Drayton that popular committees would usurp the reigns of government in South Carolina. With the Commons House reduced to helplessness by the Wilkes fund crisis, the General Committee steadily increased its power as the effective representative of the people. Yet, even as it was decided within another general meeting to boycott anyone who had any concern with British tea until the duty was removed, Gadsden remained frustrated by the recalcitrance of the merchants. He assured Samuel Adams that the people of Charles Town were still devoted to American liberty, but were prevented from providing stronger evidence of their devotion by the efforts of a considerable number of "Ministerial men." Though these traitors were tireless in their efforts to undermine the cause of liberty, Gadsden assured Adams that their plans would be thwarted by the intervention of the liberty-loving backcountry-men. Awake now to the political potential of the frontier, Gadsden clearly hoped to use the back settlers to overcome the opposition of the merchants to stronger measures.[5]

In contrast to Gadsden's embarrassment, Henry Laurens applauded the actions of his fellow South Carolinians. He was not surprised by the violence of the "Wily Cromwellians" of Boston, but felt that the proceedings at Charles Town "were certainly the most prudent" and least offensive.[6] Laurens continued to support the measures of the South Carolina protest movement until he learned of the resolutions against buying and selling tea. In a stance that might be seen as a contradiction of his support for the non-importation Association of 1769 and 1770, Laurens denounced these resolutions as an "attempt to lay violent & illegall [sic] prohibitions on our fellow Subjects." He felt that such resolutions must have been the work of some "Judas" who wished to separate South Carolina from its remaining English friends. Already, he warned, the actions of the Bostonians had led many members of Parliament to insist that Lord North was proceeding "with the tenderness of an Indulgent Father" and that "any thing short of hanging us and battering down our Towns is perfect Lenity." He begged his Carolina friends to avoid any provocative actions, stating that

> I believe no Man in Carolina will do more for his Country than I will do. I feel a willingness to sacrifice my Life & fortune in support & defence of its true Liberties. But I am not a Mock Patriot, I will not rush into measures which are at the same time Unconstitutional, & obstructive to our wishes. I take it for granted that we do not wish to be unconnected with or independant of the Mother Country, not to involve our selves in Contests which must prove fruitless & disgraceful while our opponents can preface their own unconstitutional measures with a recital of our Popular Illegal Resolutions.[7]

As Laurens advised moderation to his friends, he also kept them informed of developments while the ministry considered the situation. He saw little reason for optimism as "the King is very angry—the whole Ministerial Board Inimical to the Liberties of America." Laurens was certain that the government would respond with severe measures, perhaps even a new stamp act, and warned his Charles Town friends to prepare for another crisis. Still, he continued to counsel moderation to his English friends and predicted that "an Independance will be accelerated which might be kept far off" if a hostile policy were prosecuted.[8] When several members asked him for advice shortly before Parliament was to consider American affairs, Laurens replied

Slumber on the supposed opposition to Government & before the Rising of your House, Repeal all those Laws which are calculated for raising a Revenue on the Colonists without their own Consent. They are Galling to the Americans, Yield no benefit to the Mother Country, You disagree among yourselves concerning the *Right* & every man sees & acknowledges the *inexpediency* of such Taxation. What then are we Contending for, Imaginary emolument, at the risque of Thousands of Lives & Millions of Pounds, possibly of the Dignity of the British Empire.[9]

When Parliament finally passed the Coercive Acts, Laurens was shocked by the severity of the measures and denounced them as "Violent, Arbitrary, & unjust." As familiar as he was with the American temperament, Laurens saw little chance that the Bostonians would tamely submit to these outrages and predicted a violent clash. When this occurred, he felt that the other colonies must rush to the assistance of Boston, for "common Sense informs me that in Boston all the Colonies are to Stand or fall." The situation in England was steadily deteriorating, Laurens reported, as the ministry was planning an attack upon the assemblies in which an oath acknowledging parliamentary supremacy would be the prerequisite for continued existence.[10]

Laurens quickly discovered that there was very little the Americans in London could do to reverse the situation. The measures were popular among the public and it would be useless to appeal to George III, for Laurens was now convinced that the king was dictating policy and that Lord North was merely his puppet. The American cause had lost its most influential voice with the humiliation and disgrace of Benjamin Franklin over the Hutchinson letters scandal. With the influence of Franklin gone, "we have lost our principal Advocate, & American Rebel or Enemy to the Interests of Great Britain are now Synonyma." Under these circumstances, Laurens advised his friends to adopt a more conciliatory attitude and encouraged the raising of an intercolonial subscription to pay for the tea destroyed in Boston. Still, he doubted if even this action would have any appreciable effect and suggested that Americans consider another economic boycott as a measure that might moderate ministerial policy.[11] In the meantime, Laurens assisted in the preparation and presentation of petitions to the king and both Houses of Parliament during late March 1774. In these petitions it was argued that it was unfair to punish the entire town of Boston, indeed the whole colony of Massachusetts, for the criminal actions of a misguided few. The petitioners also declared that punishment should have been withheld until Boston had the opportunity to defend itself against the charges.[12] Laurens had little faith that petitions would have any effect and grew even less confident when word arrived that the Americans were determined to resist the acts, which they called intolerable. He was clearly losing hope by June 1774, when he informed his former partner George Appleby that

> I am more of opinion now, than ever, that there will be Bloodshed. God avert it. Innocent persons will fall a Sacrifice to the knavery & bad policy of wrong Heads on each Side & these will escape with the plunder.[13]

Still, pessimistic as he was, Laurens continued to search for a peaceful solution to the crisis.

Among the South Carolina "wrong heads," Laurens undoubtedly numbered Christopher Gadsden who, while Laurens worked to calm tempers in London, was attempting to heat them up in Charles Town. The passage of the Coercive Acts played directly into the hands of Gadsden and other American radicals. American opinion had been divided over the actions of the Bostonians, but the Coercive Acts represented such an extreme overreaction that Americans discovered a surprising degree of unity. Many Americans, particularly those in the seaports, worried about their own security, as they remembered that their behavior had not been beyond reproach. As David Ramsay recalled, "they believed that vengeance, though delayed, was not remitted, and that the only favour the least culpable could expect was to be the last that would be devoured." Americans also wondered that, if the ministry was allowed to reorganize the Massachusetts government without their consent and in violation of the charter, what was to prevent this same fate from befalling other colonies? In addition, there was the simple moral outrage expressed against the closure of the port of a town whose citizens depended upon trade for their very existence.[14] Gadsden and other radical leaders immediately utilized such fears to raise anti-British sentiment to a fever pitch. Though Gadsden's suggestion of an immediate boycott of all British goods was rejected, South Carolinians were determined to demonstrate their support for Boston. Gadsden took the lead in collecting donations for the relief of the stricken town, and South Carolinians could proudly boast that they contributed more to this purpose than any other colony, including Massachusetts. The Charles Town General Committee reported that, by the end of April 1775, South Carolinians had contributed thirty-three hundred pounds and eighty barrels of rice. In transmitting part of this to Boston, Gadsden left Samuel Adams with no doubt as to his position, exclaiming that "We depend on your Firmness, and that you will not pay for an ounce of the damn'd Tea."[15]

Gadsden assured Adams that South Carolina, which had been the last to desert the nonimportation agreement in 1770, would now act in a similar manner and that his colony would support the northern colonies, even if events proceeded to extremities. In this case, Gadsden insisted that "for my part I would rather see my own family reduced to the utmost Extremity and half cut to pieces than to submit to their damned Machinations." After proudly describing his impressive new wharf, Gadsden declared that he would rather see it, and thus his entire fortune, destroyed than to neglect the cause of liberty at this critical junction. He could no longer refer to Great Britain as the mother country for, he explained, it acted more like "our mother *in law*," constantly treating Americans with contempt.[16] Yet, angry as he was, Gadsden still depended upon Boston for the formulation of policy. He again wrote to Adams to inform him that the General Committee had called a general meeting of the inhabitants of the province for early July. The Charles Town radical community was waiting "with the utmost Impatience" to learn what measures had been adopted by the northern colonies, so that they could implement a similar program.[17]

Two weeks later, Gadsden again wrote to Adams, this time to inform him that the people of Charles Town were prepared to support an intercolonial congress. Also, wrote Gadsden, the people could be depended upon to agree to an immediate nonimportation agreement and would support a nonexportation agreement after the rice crop was shipped in October.[18] Though Gadsden exaggerated the patriotism of his fellow Carolinians, he now placed himself at the forefront of a movement to ban trade with Britain until all American grievances were redressed. Such a policy could prove ruinous to his personal fortune, but Gadsden was a steady and devoted patriot who placed the interests of his country above those of himself. Gadsden's position in 1774 was well described by David Ramsay, the future son-in-law of Henry Laurens, who observed that

> He had about this time completed the largest wharf in Charlestown, which was just beginning to yield an interest on an immense capital expended in building it. His whole prospect of reimbursement was founded on the continuance of trade, and especially on the exportation of rice. He nevertheless urged the adoption of a non-importation and non-exportation agreement; and that the colonists should retire within themselves and live on their domestic resources till Great Britain redressed their grievances, most heartily concurred in these measures when adopted in the latter end of the year 1774 by Congress, which he was a member, and was uncommonly active in afterwards enforcing their strict execution, though few men lost more by them than he did.[19]

On July 6, 104 delegates selected to represent the entire province met in general meeting at the Exchange in Charles Town. This was an extremely important gathering for two reasons. First, these 104 delegates were truly representative of the entire province and, as Gadsden had promised Adams, this included the backcountry. The frontier was finally invited to play a significant role in provincial politics, as Gadsden intended to depend upon their support to defeat the opposition of the merchants to any plan that restricted trade. Even more important, however, this meeting marked the fulfillment of William Henry Drayton's prediction that the legislative functions of the province would be transferred from the Commons House to extralegal meetings of the people. Gadsden and his colleagues would have preferred to work through the Commons House, but suspension of business in the Wilkes fund stalemate, not to mention the very nature of the new business, made this impossible. The necessity of obtaining popular approval of resistance measures forced these men to find alternative methods, and the general meetings proved adequate to the purpose.

As the general meeting turned to business, the radicals scored a quick victory when the radical planter, George Gabriel Powell, was elected to chair the meeting. The importance of this choice was evident when Powell imposed rules upon the meeting that left the radicals with a distinct advantage in the coming deliberations. Of these rules, the most significant was one that allowed any man in attendance, regardless of whether or not he was an elected delegate, to vote. Gadsden and other radical leaders took advantage of this situation to pack the Exchange with mechanics in an effort to sweep the radical program through the meeting. As a result, the Exchange was crowded to capacity, at times with more than four hundred people, in what was the largest gathering ever held in the colony until this time. With the rules established, Powell announced the major questions to be considered—whether to declare an immediate suspension of trade with Great Britain, whether to send delegates to the proposed Continental Congress, and, if so, how many and with how much authority. Both radicals and moderates agreed that South Carolina should be represented in the Congress and that the delegation should consist of five men. The issues of the ban on trade, and the membership and powers of the delegation, were more controversial and were put off until the following day.[20]

The resumption of the meeting on July 7 occurred amid great excitement as both radicals and moderates were active in gathering support. Gadsden and the radicals were stunned when the moderates were able to defeat the proposal that the colony join Boston in an immediate suspension of trade with Britain. This was not a complete defeat, however, as it was decided that the subject would be reconsidered after the Continental Congress addressed it. The meeting then turned to the composition of the delegation that would represent the colony in Philadelphia. Both sides could agree upon Henry Middleton and John Rutledge, but there was disagreement over the other three delegates. The moderates had already decided among themselves to support Charles Pinckney, Rawlins Lowndes, and Miles Brewton: men who could be relied upon to oppose the expected radicalism of the New Englanders. The radicals were prepared to endorse more severe measures and supported Gadsden, Thomas Lynch, and Edward Rutledge, the younger brother of John Rutledge. This latter choice was somewhat surprising for, though young Rutledge was a firm supporter of the assembly

during the Wilkes fund controversy, he did not possess the radical credentials of Gadsden or Lynch. Indeed, Edward Rutledge would often vote
against his radical colleagues, leaving the moderates with a majority in the
delegation. Here, Powell's decision to allow anyone present in the hall to
vote was critical, as the mechanics crowded into the Exchange and, according to Edward Rutledge, elected the radical ticket by a majority of 397
votes. The meeting then moved to the question of instructions to the delegates. The radicals wished to place no limitations upon the delegation,
believing that the radical majority would align South Carolina with the New
Englanders. This was absolutely unacceptable to the moderates who, led
by Lowndes, argued that it was well known that the Bostonians completely
denied the authority of Parliament, while few in South Carolina were willing to go this far. Lowndes was afraid that the delegation might bind the
colony to support positions that the overwhelming majority of the population denied. A compromise was finally agreed upon in which the delegation
was given unlimited power to agree to any *legal* measures. While this
instruction could be construed in many different ways, it was generally
understood to preclude a vote for independence and, in the minds of some,
another boycott.[21]

While the meeting was explicitly opposed to following Boston into revolution against the British government, it was just as clearly involved in the
early stages of a revolution against the government of South Carolina. On
July 8, the last day of the meeting, a new General Committee of ninety-nine
members (fifteen merchants, fifteen mechanics, and sixty-nine planters)
was appointed to correspond with the committees of other colonies and to
oversee the execution of the resolutions adopted by the meeting. This
General Committee would serve until the next general meeting was held in
January 1775, when the resolutions of the Continental Congress would be
discussed. This General Committee, acting as a committee of correspondence, was clearly exercising functions reserved for the Commons House.
The mere size of the General Committee bore a much more striking resemblance to a legislative body than to the mere executive board it was
supposed to have been. Indeed, when the next general meeting was held in
January 1775, it immediately confirmed this transfer of power by transforming itself into the First Provincial Congress and moving its meetings
from Pike's Tavern to the assembly room of the State House.[22]

While the July general meeting demonstrated the support of the people
for a Continental Congress, Gadsden and other protest leaders also hoped
to provide the Congress with an endorsement from the Commons House.
They realized, however, that Lieutenant Governor Bull would never allow
the assembly to give official support to a meeting that the ministry was
likely to denounce as an illegal assembly. Thus, Gadsden and the Commons

House members engineered a creative plan that allowed them to circumvent the opposition of the wary lieutenant governor. As Bull described the situation to Lord Dartmouth, the assembly was scheduled to meet at 10:00 in the morning on August 2. But, expecting to be immediately prorogued, the assembly had secretly agreed to meet at 8:00 and had already constructed an agenda. Bull wrote that he was informed of the situation within five minutes of the meeting of the House. He quickly went to the Council chamber, summoned the assembly, and prorogued it. He reported that he was back at home by 8:20, yet the assembly had made such careful plans that it was able to accomplish its purpose within this brief period of time. Thus, the Commons House approved of the delegation chosen to represent South Carolina at the Philadelphia Congress and, perhaps as a reminder of the Wilkes fund controversy, resolved to provide fifteen hundred pounds sterling to defray the delegation's expenses.[23]

The departure of Gadsden and Lynch on Sunday, August 14, created a considerable stir in Charles Town. The morning began with the assistant rector of St. Michael's, the Reverend John Bullman, delivering a vitriolic sermon in which he denounced both Gadsden and Lynch as traitors. This produced a storm of protest, including demands for Bullman's resignation, creating a new dispute that would continue unresolved until Bullman left the province in 1775. As Gadsden left Charles Town aboard the *Sea Nymph*, with his son Thomas and Lynch and his wife, the travelers were saluted by the discharge of seventeen cannon. The festive event turned tragic, however, when some of the powder exploded, burning three men terribly, with one of these men subsequently losing his life.[24]

The *Sea Nymph* arrived at Philadelphia on August 22, two weeks before the Congress was scheduled to open. This left Gadsden with the opportunity to reacquaint himself with the city in which he had lived thirty years before. More importantly, just as with the Stamp Act Congress, it allowed him the chance to meet and assess the other delegates before settling down to business. Gadsden's closest contact came with the Connecticut delegates Silas Deane and Eliphalet Dyer, with whom he and his son shared lodgings during the Congress.[25] Still, he was particularly anxious to meet and discuss strategy with the Massachusetts delegation, which arrived on August 29. He had already established a correspondence with Samuel Adams and looked forward to a personal relationship with him and his cousin John, who was also a member of the Congress. Gadsden had several opportunities to converse with the Massachusetts delegates between their arrival and the opening of the Congress on September 5, and must have been impressed by his observations. John Adams kept a diary of his impressions of the Congress and its members and, though not impressed by the South Carolina delegation as a whole, and particularly the Rutledge brothers, he was impressed by Gadsden. Indeed, after paying a visit to

Gadsden, Adams was surprised to find that the South Carolinian was even more radical than he was. Adams wrote that

> Gadsden is violent against allowing Parliament any Power of regulating Trade, or allowing that they have any Thing to do with Us. —Power of regulating Trade he says, is Power of ruining us—as bad as acknowledging them a Supream Legislature, and a Right of Legislation in one Case, is a Right in all. — This I deny.[26]

As the Continental Congress opened on September 5, Gadsden could be heartened by a larger, more well-organized, radical presence than that which had graced the Stamp Act Congress nine years earlier. In 1765, he had joined with James Otis as the (almost) lone voices of the radical position. Times had changed, however, and persistent British innovations and mistakes had caused American sentiment to move steadily closer to the radicals. Thus, Gadsden found that the Continental Congress contained a strong radical contingent. In addition to Gadsden and Lynch, Patrick Henry and Richard Henry Lee of Virginia, John and Samuel Adams of Massachusetts, Thomas Mifflin of Pennsylvania, and Stephen Hopkins and Samuel Ward of Rhode Island were all prominent spokesmen of the radical viewpoint. Realizing the suspicion with which the Massachusetts delegation was viewed in the more conservative quarters, the radicals decided that others should present the radical position. Thus, to the surprise of many, the Massachusetts members were relatively quiet and the most radical pronouncements came from Virginia and South Carolina. This confused the conservatives, who were prepared to refute the arguments of the Massachusetts radicals as the crazy exclamations of low-born levelers. But how could such arguments be used against the southern aristocrats? The strength of the radicals was quickly evident when the Congress accepted Lynch's suggestion that the group meet at Carpenter's Hall, the seat of the Philadelphia mechanics, rather than at the Pennsylvania State House. It was also Lynch who nominated Peyton Randolph of Virginia to preside over the Congress and Charles Thomson, the "Sam Adams of Philadelphia," as secretary.[27]

Gadsden expected to play a role similar to that he had adopted during the Stamp Act Congress: to support a broader view in order to achieve a unified America, rather than merely looking out for narrow provincial interests. He agreed with Laurens that the fate of all America was tied to Boston and worked to bring others to this realization. When a rumor reached Philadelphia at the outset of the Congress that British ships had bombarded Boston and killed several inhabitants, Gadsden suggested that an attack should be launched upon General Gage before he could receive reinforcements. Hearing this, Silas Deane informed his wife that

> Mr. Gadsden leaves all N. England Sons of Liberty far behind, for he is for taking up his Firelock, & marching direct to Boston, nay he affirmed this Morning, that were his wife, and all his Children in Boston, & they were there to perish, by the sword, it would not alter his Sentiment or proceeding, for American Liberty, by which You may judge of the Man, when I add that he is one of the most regularly religious Men I ever met with.

Though tempers would cool when this rumor was proven false, Gadsden would make a similar appeal during the discussion over the Suffolk Resolves.[28] His urgent desire for unity would also be indicated by his willingness to risk splitting his own delegation over the crucial question of a suspension of trade with Britain.

On September 7, the Congress decided to appoint two major committees. The first was a committee on rights and grievances, which would include two delegates from each of the twelve colonies (Georgia was not represented at the Congress). The second was a committee on trade and manufacturing, consisting of one delegate from each colony. Gadsden was selected to represent South Carolina on the latter committee, which meant that his energies would be channeled largely into the economic sphere. Gadsden had left no one in doubt as to his stance upon economic questions. For years he had been flirting with a complete disavowal of the Navigation system, and he made it clear throughout the Congress that he was now prepared to endorse such a drastic step. Since the beginning of the tea crisis, Gadsden had been advocating a continental nonimportation and nonexportation agreement. In the Continental Congress, he staunchly supported Richard Henry Lee's motion for a Continental Association that would ban all trade with Britain and the West Indies until all American grievances were redressed. He had little patience with those who, like John Rutledge, urged caution in dealing with the mother country. To these men, Gadsden replied that "Our seaport towns are composed of brick and wood. If they are destroyed we have clay and lumber enough to rebuild them. But if the liberties of our country are destroyed where shall we find the materials to replace them?"[29] Gadsden denied any intention of starting a fight with Great Britain, but insisted that American liberty was in such a precarious state that strong measures were absolutely necessary. As the debate over the Continental Association continued, Gadsden pleaded that

> I am for being ready, but I am not for the sword. The only way to prevent the Sword from being used is to have it ready. . . . Boston and New England cant hold out - the Country will be deluged in Blood, if we don't Act with Spirit. Don't let America look at this Mountain, and let it bring forth a Mouse.[30]

Gadsden was satisfied with the Continental Association, which finally passed the Congress, though he would have preferred that the ban on imports be instituted before the December 1 starting date. The ministry would be given until September 20, 1775 to repeal all of the objectionable acts. If not, then a ban upon exports would also go into effect. Gadsden felt that this agreement represented an acceptable compromise, but a new problem developed when the South Carolina delegation suddenly denounced the Association as unfair to its colony. Pointing out that New England had few direct exports to England while two-thirds of Carolina rice and almost all of its indigo went to the mother country, the South Carolinians insisted that they would carry the burden of any nonexportation agreement. Thus, they demanded the exclusion of rice and indigo as the price of their consent. Gadsden refused to support this position and pleaded with his colleagues to subordinate their local interests to the foremost issue of a unified defense of American liberty. When his efforts appeared fruitless, the enraged Gadsden announced that he would sign the Association, even if his colleagues refused to do so. Finally, a compromise was reached in which the South Carolinians agreed to the Association, but with the exemption of rice alone. Gadsden was extremely disappointed with the stance of his colleagues, as it again gave the appearance that South Carolina lacked the patriotism of the other colonies. And, as usual, Gadsden was not shy about making his position absolutely clear to the South Carolina delegates. His actions were resented by Edward Rutledge, who wrote that Gadsden was "if possible, worse than ever; more violent, more wrong-headed." Yet, Gadsden was confident that South Carolina patriotism would triumph and the decision to exempt rice would be reversed when the resolutions were presented to the people.[31]

With the exception of the controversy over the Continental Association, Gadsden was satisfied with the results of the Continental Congress. While the resolutions of the Congress were presented in much more moderate language than Gadsden might have liked, the radicals had made a clear impression upon them. Though the Congress was careful to recognize the supremacy of the Crown and made clear its desire for reconciliation, the machinery was in place to proceed with more drastic measures if redress was not forthcoming. Though Gadsden was unable to achieve a complete renunciation of parliamentary authority, it is unlikely that he considered this a realistic possibility. What had been obtained was a complete renunciation of Parliamentary authority in American internal affairs. Gadsden had always insisted that he did not desire independence, but, in effect, home rule within the empire. This was largely the position endorsed by the Continental Congress. The choice now lay with the ministry to either grant home rule or take steps that would ultimately lead to American independence.

Gadsden and the other delegates returned to Charles Town on November 6 and, that evening, presented the reports of the Congress to the general committee at the State House. Gadsden also read copies of an address that was sent to Canada and the petition to the king, neither of which were included in the official records of the Congress. Then, Thomas Lynch explained the reasons why rice alone was exempted from the Continental Association and offered a plan that would place rice and indigo planters upon an equal footing. Though Lynch's speech was "highly approved and gave entire satisfaction," Gadsden stepped forward and courageously proclaimed his opposition to the exemption of rice. What response there was to his speech went unrecorded, but the General Committee decided to call a general meeting to discuss the recommendations of the Continental Congress. The meeting, to be held on January 11, would also select a delegation to represent South Carolina at another meeting of the Continental Congress scheduled for May, as well as a new General Committee. Afraid that royal officials would attempt to break up the general meeting, it was quickly resolved that no man could be arrested or detained while engaged in the public business. Clearly, royal government was on the brink of collapse in South Carolina.[32]

As tensions increased during 1774, Henry Laurens grew more determined to return to South Carolina and share the fate of his countrymen. In addition to his concern over political affairs, Laurens was also worried about his private interests, as his brother had been advising him since late 1773 that these were in need of his personal attention.[33] Thus, Laurens began to make preparations for his return to America. In early July 1774, unsure of future events, he recalled his sons from Geneva, placing John in the Middle Temple to study law, and Harry in another English school.[34] Laurens expressed surprise at the unity of the colonies behind the Continental Congress and pledged his support so long as the Congress pursued constitutional claims. Yet he remained pessimistic about the effects that any such Congress could have. Convinced that Lord North was "as perverse and obstinate as his Master," Laurens predicted that neither the king nor the ministry would pay any attention to the resolutions, regardless of how they were presented. Thus, as Laurens prepared to sail, he placed his hopes for a peaceful settlement not in the king of England, but in the "King of Kings." Leaving his three sons behind, he sailed for Charles Town in early November and arrived there on December 11. After receiving visits of welcome from many, including Christopher Gadsden, Laurens settled down to the business of finding some means of settlement before his beloved empire was irretrievably split in two.[35]

As Henry Laurens sailed to South Carolina, he found himself faced with the choice he had worked so hard to avoid since 1765: that between American liberty and the probability of armed opposition to British authority. His sojourn in England had played a crucial role in his development as a revolutionary. Arriving in England in 1771 as a loyal subject who wished to educate his sons in the same virtuous atmosphere that he remembered from his youth, Laurens soon became so disillusioned that he removed two of his sons to the purer, more republican environment of Geneva. Similarly, Laurens grew increasingly alarmed at the degree of corruption that he perceived to be present in the British political system. Already suspecting a ministerial plot against American liberty, Laurens had arrived with a confidence in the benevolence of the king. His observations during his stay in London not only confirmed his suspicions of the ministry, but significantly altered his faith in the king. Indeed, Laurens grew convinced that George III was not only a participant in the assault upon American liberty, but served as its main strategist. Thus, Laurens had arrived at the same conclusion that Gadsden had reached in 1765: that the survival of American freedom depended solely on the unity and resolve of the American people. While continuing to hope for a peaceable resolution that would leave the empire intact, Laurens had made his choice and would defend the rights of America, regardless of the cost.

Though he was not present in South Carolina during the critical years from 1771 through 1774, Laurens's contributions to the protest movement should not be ignored. Acting as an unofficial agent, Laurens's letters to South Carolina served as insightful commentary on British attitudes and helped to convince South Carolina moderates of the necessity for stronger action. Many of the moderates suspected any proposition emanating from Gadsden as the jaundiced ideas of an insane radical bent upon the dissolution of the empire. But how could the same be said of Henry Laurens, whom no one could identify as either crazy or subversive? Thus, the reports of Laurens provided South Carolinians with strong evidence that the fears and suspicions propagated by Gadsden and the radicals were not unfounded.

Christopher Gadsden was the dominant figure in taking South Carolina to the brink of revolution in 1773 and 1774. Not only was Gadsden a leading figure in the Commons House as it destroyed the influence of Governor Montagu and the council during the Wilkes fund crisis, but he also engineered the resistance that brought royal authority near the point of collapse after the passage of the Tea Act. Realizing that the assembly was inadequate to their purposes, Gadsden and other radical leaders searched for some extralegal means of conferring a sense of legitimacy upon measures of resistance. This was achieved through general meetings of the inhabitants, which, in turn, resurrected the old General Committee of non-importation days. The General Committee steadily increased its power until, by 1775—without the consent of the legitimate authorities—it had usurped much of the power of the Commons House. While this was transpiring, Gadsden attended the Continental Congress and surprised even the Massachusetts delegates with his radicalism. On the question of parliamentary authority, Gadsden far surpassed many of his contemporaries when he advocated a complete denial of parliamentary authority in America. While the Congress was unwilling to assume such a drastic position, Gadsden could take satisfaction in the fact that the Congress had made the demand for what was, in effect, home rule. If this was rejected, as all but the most optimistic thought likely, the Congress had committed itself to stronger action. Gadsden could well be satisfied with his efforts, for a united America had left the ministry with the choice between home rule or revolution. While Gadsden had earlier advocated the former, he was already embarked upon the latter.

9

The Collapse of British Rule, 1775

As the year 1775 opened, South Carolinians found themselves in an extremely difficult political situation. To a man they denied any desire for independence, but their actions during the previous year had already placed them in a revolutionary position. Throughout 1774, effective political power had gradually, though steadily, shifted from legitimate royal institutions to general meetings of the people and their creation, the General Committee. Royal officials such as Lieutenant Governor Bull disapproved of this situation, but found themselves helpless to intervene. Christopher Gadsden had been an enthusiastic promoter and supporter of these measures and would continue to occupy a position in the forefront of the radical movement. Though it would be another year before he publicly declared himself in favor of independence, Gadsden was already talking and acting like a man who desired far more than mere home rule within the empire. During 1775, Gadsden consistently supported policies that would have the effect, if not the intention, of destroying the hope of reconciliation. Though Gadsden had appeared to have constructed a truce with Henry Laurens as the latter drew closer to the protest movement during the early 1770s, the battle was renewed in 1775. Like Gadsden, Laurens saw independence as a very real possibility by early 1775. Yet, unlike Gadsden, he viewed separation as undesirable and worked hard to prevent any reckless adventures that might cause an irrevocable break with the mother country. Thus, Laurens disapproved of Gadsden's activities and continued to pursue a moderate agenda that, it was hoped, would prevent any irredeemable act before the ministry could be brought to its senses. As his worst fears became realities, Laurens was disappointed, but not surprised. He was reluctant to accept independence, but favored separation over reconciliation on terms dictated by the ministry.

The general meeting, set for January 11, 1775, to discuss the recommendations of the Continental Congress promised to be a tense and interesting session. As the meeting approached, Laurens assured his British friend Richard Oswald that Americans were inclined to peace, but only if the rights and privileges that they had enjoyed before 1763 were restored. If concessions were not forthcoming, Laurens told Oswald that he could count upon the resistance of a unified America. Yet Laurens noted that there was some disagreement over the mode of opposition:

> Some are Red-hot & foolishly talk of Arms & there is another extreme who Say that implicit obedience is the Surest Road to a redress of Grievances—the great majority of numbers lie between, & are Men of Wealth & consideration.

Laurens further explained to John Laurens that a major problem was expected to arise from dissension over the exemption of rice from the Continental Association. Tensions were high over this issue and there was some talk of censuring the delegates who had supported this policy and changing the delegation for the next meeting of the Continental Congress. Laurens opposed this idea, as he feared that it would create a split within the South Carolina patriot movement.[1]

The general meeting, which opened on January 11, was the most democratic representative assembly that had yet met in South Carolina. The meeting was to consist of 184 delegates chosen from every part of the colony. While forty of the forty-eight members of the Commons House were to sit as delegates, and care was taken to assure the dominance of the low-country elite, there was a genuine effort to open the meeting to a wider spectrum of the population. The mechanics, none of whom held seats in the Commons House, possessed thirteen of the thirty seats allocated to Charles Town. The backcountry, with only token representation in the regular assembly, was allowed fifty-five seats in the general meeting. Of course, the increased representation of two groups that had been largely ignored in the past was not due to a sudden transformation of the political principles of the Charles Town elite. Rather, this was another in a series of maneuvers by Gadsden and his radical associates who controlled the General Committee to gain approval for stronger measures of resistance. The mechanics had always been the nucleus of the radical movement, and Gadsden and the radicals understood that the backcountry, uninvolved in rice production, might be relied upon to provide significant support for their policies. With their participation, Gadsden was confident that the exemption of rice could be stricken from the Continental Association along with other measures that would be more demonstrative of South Carolina patriotism. This confidence appeared justified as the meeting began by transforming itself into the First Provincial Congress and, in an appropriate and symbolic move, holding its meeting in the assembly room of the State House.[2]

The meeting of the First Provincial Congress lasted for a tumultuous week (January 11–17) and featured, in Gadsden's words, "some long Disputes and Heats." The sharpest and most important argument came, as expected, over the exclusion of rice from the Continental Association. Gadsden introduced the matter, defending his own conduct and insisting that the stance of the South Carolina delegation had almost resulted in the breakup of the Continental Congress. He had refused to support the article at Philadelphia and now hoped that the Provincial Congress would reverse this decision that reflected so poorly upon South Carolina patriotism. This provoked a heated debate that lasted for the better part of three days. John Rutledge immediately answered Gadsden's criticism with the reflection that the only sufferers from a complete ban on trade with Britain would be the south, particularly South Carolina. The northern colonies, Rutledge noted, would suffer little, as a relatively small portion of their trade went to the mother country. He sarcastically congratulated the northerners on their magnanimity in demonstrating their patriotism by ruining the economies of the southern colonies. Pointing out that almost all of the South Carolina indigo and two-thirds of its rice went directly to Britain, he saw no reason why South Carolina commerce should be ruined while that of the north continued almost uninterrupted. Rutledge refused to allow his colony to become the dupe of the north and insisted that if hardships were to be assumed, they should be assumed equally.[3]

Rutledge's arguments appealed to many in the Provincial Congress. Yet, he still faced the anger of the indigo planters who were upset that rice had been excluded from the trade ban and their crop was not. Rutledge and his supporters had expected this opposition and had already prepared a plan to combat it. Assisted by Thomas Lynch, Rutledge explained why rice had been exempted and indigo had not: rice was a perishable commodity, it did not serve as an aid to British manufacturing, and indigo fields could be converted to other crops while rice lands could not. Still, Rutledge and Lynch insisted that they had no intention of giving special advantages to the rice planters and suggested a plan by which the indigo producers would be compensated for their losses. In pursuit of this plan, Rutledge and Lynch received valuable support from Edward Rutledge, Thomas Lynch, Jr., and William Henry Drayton. On the other side stood Gadsden, who, with Rawlins Lowndes and the Reverend William Tennent, saw an opportunity to defeat the rice exemption by portraying it as an unfair advantage to special interests and by denouncing any compensation scheme as impractical. In addition, Gadsden pointed out that, though the compensation plan would satisfy the rice and indigo planters, it held no benefit for those, primarily westerners, who relied upon other crops. These arguments were effective, but not effective enough to carry the day. The Continental Association, with rice excluded, was passed by the narrow vote of eighty-seven to seventy-five. It was understood, however, that a compensation plan would be adopted to satisfy the interests of all producers. The plan that was finally agreed upon contained a complicated schedule of compensation that would allow indigo and other producers to receive payments from the profits of the rice planters.[4]

The debate over the Continental Association would prove costly to Christopher Gadsden. His performance left him censured by many, including Henry Laurens, who portrayed him as an "uncouth figure." More serious was the split this issue caused between Gadsden and the Rutledge brothers. Though John Rutledge could never have been identified as a radical, he had been willing to cooperate with Gadsden and the radicals throughout the controversy with the mother country. Indeed, their political ties had been strengthened by the marriage of Gadsden's eldest daughter Elizabeth to Rutledge's younger brother, Andrew. John Rutledge, however, was unwilling to entertain any thoughts of separation from the British Empire, and his experiences during the Continental Congress had led him to believe that Gadsden was determined to press the issue until all ties were completely dissolved. He was unwilling to follow Boston blindly into revolution, particularly if the main burdens were to fall upon the south and South Carolina in particular. Thus, the debate over the Continental Association marked the split between Gadsden and the Rutledge brothers. John Rutledge would steadily increase his influence as a leader among the moderates, while Gadsden found himself increasingly isolated among the less influential radicals. During the next few years, Rutledge would emerge as Gadsden's strongest rival in South Carolina politics.[5]

Though Henry Laurens was disturbed by Gadsden's position on the Continental Association, he was positively shocked by several other proposals made by his neighbor in the Provincial Congress. Laurens informed his son that

> in the course of his debates, he made & repeated certain declarations which whatever might have been his private Sentiments, discretion Should have locked up in his own breast—in full Congress in the hearing of a Crowd of Spectators, he insisted that from the beginning his opinion was to prohibit the Merchants from paying their debts to Great Britain by any Remittances in Bills of Exchange, Gold & Silver or other Merchandize—& if his advice had been followed General Gage & his Soldiers would have been Sent back to England immediately upon their landing at Boston—I heard the first Scheme with abhorence & did not fail to declare my Sentiments accordingly & for the latter I knew how easy it was for that Gentleman to March through the Cherokee Mountains kill every Indian & return to Charles Town without moving one Step from his Fire Side—Shipping off a veteran British General & three Thousand regular Troops with less trouble than he could Ship a Cargo of Rice was an enterprizing Reverie fit only to be laughed at.[6]

Laurens was appalled by Gadsden's suggestion that all payments to British creditors be suspended. He argued that any such scheme, particularly as it affected debts owed the Crown, would be inconsistent with the assurances of loyalty that figured prominently in the petitions against British policy. Surprised that his objection was seconded only by John Rutledge, Laurens was distressed by the decision to place a moratorium on all debt payments except those approved by a committee appointed for this purpose. Certain that the patriots were moving too fast, Laurens expressed dismay at the refusal of Rawlins Lowndes and other moderates to heed his warnings about the implications of their actions. Laurens grew even more dissatisfied when he discovered that the Charles Town committee on debt payments contained a sizable bloc of debtors who held little property. Clearly no democrat, Laurens firmly believed that the leaders should be recruited from the propertied classes, as these were the men with the keenest interest in the welfare of the state.[7]

This was not, however, the extent of the revolutionary activity engaged in by the first session of the Provincial Congress. The Congress recommended that all citizens begin military training and become proficient in the use of arms. It also authorized its president, Charles Pinckney, to nominate a Secret Committee of five men who would be charged with securing and distributing the materials necessary for the defense of the colony. The committee, consisting of William Henry Drayton, Arthur Middleton, Charles Cotesworth Pinckney, William Gibbes, and Edward Weyman, was enthusiastic in the performance of its duty. Finally, the Congress set February 17 as a day of fasting, humiliation, and prayer. In a show of unity, the Congress decided to return the same delegation to the second meeting of the Continental Congress scheduled for May. Before adjournment, it was decided that the Charles Town General Committee should act as a board of enforcement until the Provincial Congress met again on June 1. Then, the First Provincial Congress adjourned.[8]

Thus, the Provincial Congress placed South Carolina firmly on the revolutionary path. Despite their inability to defeat the exemption of rice from the Continental Association, Gadsden and the radicals had achieved measures that served to widen the breach between South Carolina and the mother country. Laurens, on the other hand, shed tears over unwise policies, particularly the suspension of debt payments, and saw himself as part of a minority who "perceive Errors on both Sides & am for conciliatory measures, recommending Strongly on our Side the Innocence of the Dove with the Wisdom of the Serpent." Laurens would remain steady in his support for American rights, but would continue to oppose excesses that could diminish the deteriorating chances of reconciliation.[9]

As his fears of violence increased, Laurens began to worry about the future of his family. His three sons had remained in England, and his two daughters would join them there after James Laurens and his wife sailed to England because of his health in June 1775. Laurens grew more concerned when he received a letter from his eldest son John, who was now twenty years old and anxious to return to America and fight for his country. Such enthusiasm distressed Laurens for, unsure of future events, he was depending on John to assume the reins of family leadership in the event of his own death. Thus, Laurens refused to allow his son to return home and insisted that he reflect longer on his desire to risk his life in battle. Laurens had seen battle and saw nothing glorious or romantic about war. He tried to convey these sentiments to his son and observed that "Life is the Gift of God & we are accountable to him not only for, but for the improvement of, it— Reserve your Life for your Country's call, but wait for the Call." He denied his son permission to return to America and suggested that he spend less time arguing politics and more on his legal studies.[10]

When the Commons House met again in late January, it quickly adopted the resolutions of both the Continental and Provincial Congresses and expressed its appreciation for the services of the delegates to the Philadelphia Congress. This was to have been expected, as the nucleus of the Provincial Congress consisted of members of the Commons House: forty-three of the forty-eight members also sat in the Provincial Congress, and three of the remaining five would sit in the Second Provincial Congress.[11] The continuing transfer of power was demonstrated by the increasing influence of the General Committee, even as the assembly remained in session. Significantly, when South Carolinians again became concerned with Georgian affairs, it was the General Committee, rather than the Commons House, that dealt with the problem. Georgians had not been represented in the Continental Congress and gave no indication that they planned to abide by the Continental Association. Thus, in February 1775, the General Committee resolved to have no further trade with the neighboring colony; it would "hold them as unworthy of the rights of freemen, and as inimical to the liberties of their country." The committee made it clear, however, that this prohibition would not apply to residents of South Carolina who, like Laurens, owned plantations in Georgia or had debts outstanding from that colony.[12]

The Continental Association proved to be even more successful in halting imports than the nonimportation agreements of 1769 and 1770 had been. Trade with Britain declined by 97 percent in 1775 and, in South Carolina, imports fell from £378,116 in 1774 to £6245 in 1775.[13] Exports were a different story, however, as many South Carolinians, including Henry Laurens, took advantage of the rice exemption to continue shipping their product to England. Indeed, South Carolinians exported more to Britain, worth £579,549, in 1775 than in any previous year. Still, there was nothing illegal about this trade, and few seemed to view such actions as unpatriotic. Yet the people were determined to enforce the letter of the Continental Association and provided evidence of their seriousness when three ships arrived from Britain during February 1775. One of these ships was turned back, while the contents of the other two, which included 3844 bushels of salt, thirty-five caldrons of coal, 45,500 tiles, and two tons of potatoes, were cast into the sea. More vessels were turned away during March.[14]

The real test of the Continental Association came in late March when Robert Smythe, a resident of South Carolina, returned from a visit to England and requested permission to land some furniture and two English horses. Only by the deciding vote of the chairman did a bare majority of the General Committee agree that landing these items would not violate the Association. This decision raised a great uproar among the mechanics, many of whom disagreed with the judgment and insisted that the case provided solid evidence that the Association would be unevenly enforced to benefit the wealthy. The mechanics raised a petition, demanding that the matter be reconsidered and threatening to kill the horses if they were landed. The General Committee quickly retreated and agreed to reconsider. Before the large and excited audience that gathered to observe the proceedings, Gadsden moved that the decision be reversed on the grounds that it would violate the Association and signal the northern colonies that South Carolina had deserted the cause. More importantly, he argued that the General Committee was supposed to be the instrument of the people and, thus, should be responsive to public opinion. This plea alarmed moderate opinion, including John and Edward Rutledge, Thomas Lynch, Rawlins Lowndes, and Thomas Bee. These men were unwilling to surrender to popular demand and insisted that a reversal would undermine the authority of the General Committee and bring it into contempt. In response, William Henry Drayton rose and asked that if the committee refused to change a decision for fear of becoming contemptible, why could the king not use a similar justification for his course of action? Drayton, in a stunning reversal of his earlier position, now joined with Gadsden to demand that the popular voice be heeded. This marked the conversion of Drayton to the radical cause and the beginning of an unlikely political alliance between him and his old antagonist Gadsden.[15] For now, the arguments of Gadsden and, more particularly, Drayton, proved convincing and the General Committee, in a close vote of thirty-five to thirty-four, reversed the decision and prevented the landing of the horses. Though a seemingly minor affair, the Smythe horses affair was actually a very significant event. With his usual insight, Lieutenant Governor Bull explained the importance of this reversal to the ministry. Had the original decision remained unchanged, Bull reported, the merchants would have considered the Association breached and sent to England for goods. Such an event might well have led to a similar course by merchants in New York and elsewhere, destroying the Association. Even more insightfully, Bull observed that the victory was not without its costs for the patriot leaders, for the people had discovered their power and, he predicted, they would not be so easily controlled in the future.[16] While this prophecy was not immediately fulfilled, Gadsden would be among the most prominent losers when Bull's prediction later came true.

Events moved quickly and excitement mounted during the spring of 1775. A martial spirit prevailed as the capital prepared for war and, according to William Moultrie, Charles Town bore "the appearance of a garrison town." The festival atmosphere was sobered somewhat in April when word was received that Parliament had rejected the petitions of the Continental Congress and had instead opted to send troops to enforce British authority in America. This news, along with resulting rumors that British officials were plotting insurrections among the slaves and the frontier Indians, jolted the Secret Committee into action. On April 21, three different bodies of men, which included Henry Laurens and other influential patriots, seized the weapons and powder stored at the State House and several other magazines at or near Charles Town. These materials were then received by Christopher Gadsden and stored at his wharf. Though the mission had been conducted at night in an effort to avoid insulting the lieutenant governor, Bull was furious at such effrontery and angrily demanded that the Commons House investigate the disappearance of the supplies. The assemblymen, many of whom had actively participated in the bold adventure, replied that they were unable to discover the whereabouts of the missing materials. Nor did they confess to any knowledge of the perpetrators of this event, though they insolently informed Bull that "there is reason to suppose that some of the Inhabitants of this Colony may have been induced to take so extraordinary and uncommon a step in consequence of the late alarming Accounts from Great Britain." Understanding the meaning of this message, Bull threw up his hands and dropped the matter.[17]

By May, royal government was in a desperate position in South Carolina. Alexander Innes, who had arrived in Charles Town on April 19 to serve as secretary to the new governor and to provide the ministry with confidential accounts of the political situation within the colony, observed that "this Province hardly falls short of the Massachusetts in every Indecency, violence, and contempt to Government." Yet, even though he felt that the South Carolina leaders were united in a conspiracy to overthrow British rule, Innes felt that they could agree on nothing else.[18] This disunity was short-lived, however, for, on the day of Innes's arrival, the long-expected clash between British troops and patriot militia occurred at Lexington. When this news reached Charles Town, Lieutenant Governor Bull observed that it produced "effects here very different from intimidation." Innes reported that the reports did much to unify opinion and that "nothing less is talked of than storming Boston, and totally destroying the British Troops." Though action was delayed until the Provincial Congress met again on June 1, Innes accurately predicted that, unless news of a successful blow by General Gage was soon received, "there will be a total change of Government here, and the very slight mask they now condescend to wear entirely thrown off." Innes warned that the situation in South Carolina was dangerous and he pleaded with the ministry to send troops.[19]

As tempers grew warmer after Lexington, Henry Laurens noted that his fellow citizens were in arms and universally resolved to resist any further British aggression. The unanimity of American opinion surprised Laurens, and he hoped that the ministry would finally see the futility of a repressive policy. Expressing his belief that further violence would only disrupt the empire, Laurens insisted that even conquest "will prove an effectual defeat of the true Interest of England in America." Still, Laurens hoped that the blood shed at Lexington would finally bring both sides to their senses. He was certain that the critical interim, while Gage awaited instructions from London and the New Englanders solicited the advice of the Continental Congress, presented a valuable, and perhaps final, opportunity for both sides to retreat from the abyss of civil war:

> now the immense danger of proceeding by violence will be Seen by both parties, now is the Critical moment & now I flatter my Self the friends to both will be roused from their Slumbers & be attended to, by both—a Treaty will be offered, the consequence of which I am Sure will be peace & a good understanding—in the mean time nothing appears on the Continent from Georgia to New Hampshire but preparations for defence & resistance.[20]

In the midst of this excitement, the Provincial Congress met again on June 1. Henry Laurens was elevated to the presidency of the Congress after the conservative Charles Pinckney resigned the chair as a gesture of his disapproval of the progress of the revolutionary movement. The choice of Laurens was a good one, for two reasons. First, Laurens's stance was similar to that of most South Carolinians at this time: a staunch supporter of American rights, he also hoped to restrain any excesses which would hamper the work of reconciliation. Second, his industriousness would be useful to a Congress that faced a large amount of business. Aware of the amount of work and frustration involved, Laurens was not anxious to assume the chair. The first week confirmed his anxiety, as Laurens informed his brother that the Congress was sitting between eight and thirteen hours every day, including Sunday.[21] Though the sessions were conducted behind closed doors and the members were asked to observe secrecy, the reports of Alexander Innes demonstrate that the public was well informed of the proceedings. The Congress had three major subjects to discuss: a new provincial Association, plans for placing the colony upon a defensive position, and arrangements for providing for an effective means of government while the crisis continued. Laurens himself was not entirely happy with the results of the Congress, and observed that the boundaries of prudence had been overstepped in each of these areas. After one session, Laurens remarked to some nearby delegates that

> If I was an Enemy to your Cause I would transmit a Short word of advice to Lord North—"You need not My Lord be at expence or trouble to humble the Carolinians they are effectually ruining their own Country".[22]

The Association, which was placed before the Provincial Congress, had been prepared and unanimously adopted by the General Committee on May 12. The document placed the blame for the current predicament squarely upon British provocations. Signers were pledged to resist force with force and to be prepared to sacrifice their lives and fortunes for the cause of American liberty. This obligation was to continue until all matters in dispute were settled "upon constitutional principles—an event, which we most ardently desire." The Association concluded with a promise to hold all those who refused to sign as inimical to American liberty. This document produced heated debate, as it appeared to many of the moderates as a veritable declaration of war upon the mother country. As the president of the Congress, Laurens felt constrained from joining the debate and offering his sentiments. But his chance came on June 4, when, after the Association had passed the Congress, it was submitted to Laurens, who, as president, had the honor and responsibility of being the first to sign.[23]

When the paper was presented, Laurens requested and was granted permission to state his views. He drew the attention of the gathering to the grave importance of this document, declaring that it might be

> the most important of any to which my signature has been annexed, I compare it to my last Will & Testament but with these awful distinctions—the former is signed by my hand & sealed with a bit of common black Wax—this is to be signed by my hand & may be Sealed with my Blood by the former I transmit my Estate to my Children according to my own Will—by signing this I may forfeit my Estate into the hands of my Enemies.

Laurens insisted that he was willing to assume the risks involved in the defense of American liberty, but objected to the Association on two major grounds. The first concerned the omission of any declaration of loyalty to the king. He reminded his listeners that they had all sworn repeated oaths to the British Crown and to George III in particular. Though he had earlier expressed reservations about the innocence of the king, he now declared himself to be "one of His Majesty's most dutiful and Loyal subjects," and insisted that it was the evil and ignorant advisors who had provoked the crisis. Against such men, he would gladly take up arms and repel any hostile assault upon his country. Yet he remained unwilling to participate in the overthrow of royal authority and asked, unsuccessfully, that a declaration of allegiance to George III be inserted into the Association.[24]

Even more troubling was the clause that labeled all who refused to sign as inimical to American liberty. Laurens informed his son that he had not planned to speak on this issue. He decided to do so, however, after Daniel Legare publicly denounced several of his friends (most probably Gabriel Manigault, Dr. Alexander Garden and Elias Ball) that Laurens knew to be sympathetic to American liberty. Thus, he told the Congress that he personally knew of several men (in the margin he named Ball and Manigault) who, for various reasons, were likely to withhold their signatures from the Association. Yet he knew for a fact that these men wished the American cause well and had spent much of their lives in unselfish public service. Did these men now deserve to be denounced as traitors? And what of the Quakers and other pacifist sects, such as the Moravians? What of those who were prepared to die for the cause but thought such a step premature before discovering the advice of the Continental Congress on the subject? Such questions bothered Laurens, and he wondered how he could "anathematize good Men—& declare those to be Enemies whom I beleive [sic] & know to be freinds [sic]? I cannot be such a Fool I dare not be such a Villain." This said, the tolerant and open-minded Laurens went on to express his hatred for "all Dogmatic & arbitrary dictates over Men's Consciences," whether they be in the religious or political spheres. As he continued, he was "very rudely interrupted" by the Reverend William Tennent, who, fearing that Laurens's speech might turn the Congress against the Association, insisted that the president was out of order. Observing that the Congress had granted him permission to speak, Laurens threatened to refuse his signature if he were not allowed to finish his remarks. When the Congress demanded that he be heard, Laurens concluded with a plea for tolerance and generosity, counseling that no man should be stigmatized for the mere act of refusing to sign such a document. Then, to the relief of his audience, Laurens affixed his signature to the Association.[25]

After adopting the Association, the Congress turned to the question of a military establishment. Viewing the regular militia as insufficient, the Congress voted to raise two regiments of foot to consist of seven hundred fifty men apiece and a regiment of four hundred fifty rangers. The Congress, having assumed the powers of the Commons House, agreed to raise, pay, and commission the officers for these regiments and later appropriated one million pounds currency for this purpose. Turning to the selection of officers, the Congress appointed Christopher Gadsden, currently absent while attending the Continental Congress, to be colonel of the First Regiment, making him the highest ranking military officer in the province. William Moultrie was appointed colonel of the Second Regiment. In addition, the Congress acted to prevent food shortages by banning the exportation of rice and corn for a three-month period and establishing several granaries throughout the colony.[26] Though Laurens supported defensive measures, he "uniformly declared my opposition to every disloyal uncon-stitutional & inexpedient Act." But what constituted disloyal, inexpedient, or unconstitutional acts? Certainly Laurens felt that the members had al-lowed their zeal to interfere with their judgment when they reorganized the military. He saw the act to establish a standing military force, under the authority of the Congress rather than the king, as a premature and un-necessarily expensive, not to mention treasonous, program that should not have been undertaken without instructions from the Continental Congress. Similarly, he saw little to be gained from ordering the militia officers to exchange their royal commissions for those issued by the Provincial Con-gress. This, he felt, provided no practical gain and would not go unnoticed in London.[27]

While Laurens and the moderates were unable to carry the militia issue, they were more successful in blocking the more extreme adventures pro-posed by the radicals. Among these was the suggestion that the Congress should outfit a warship that would seize the *Tamar*, a British warship anchored in Charles Town harbor, and then keep the bay clear of all other British ships. Laurens thought this a ludicrous proposition and was not surprised when it was defeated by an overwhelming vote. More formidable, but still defeated, was a plan that had been under discussion for several months: the obstruction of the harbor through the sinking of several ves-sels at advantageous points. Laurens bitterly opposed such a plan as the height of folly, predicting that it would be economic suicide, irreparably destroying at least nine-tenths of Charles Town's commerce. Laurens might well have breathed a deep sigh of relief at the defeat of this and other radical proposals, for he was convinced that these

> would have cost this Province half a Million of our Currency . . . ruined Charles Town & the adjacent Country, run counter to the advice (since re-ceived) of the Continental Congress, drawn the heaviest degree of Great Brit-ain's resentment against us & have remained objects of the derision of all the world.[28]

Such propositions surprised and frightened many of the moderate leaders who, like Rawlins Lowndes, had not fully understood the implications of the actions they had been taking for the past eighteen months. Laurens pitied these men and observed that Lowndes, who "could see nothing to cry about" in January, now sat indignant and bewildered at the proceedings of the Congress. The radical program came as no surprise to more prescient men such as Laurens, who now gently chided his old friend Lowndes that he had warned him during the early days of 1775 that it would come to this if the radicals were allowed to proceed virtually unhindered.[29]

Yet, unlike Lowndes, Laurens was unwilling to sit stupefied as the radi-cals plunged South Carolina into a bloody civil war. When the radicals suggested that the landing of the new governor, Lord William Campbell, be forcibly resisted, Laurens figured prominently in the opposition that blocked the measure.[30] Still, Laurens agreed that it was necessary to provide for a temporary body of patriots to oversee defensive preparations during the long adjournments of the Provincial Congress. To this purpose, the Congress established a thirteen-member Council of Safety and granted it sweeping powers to strengthen, secure, and take every "expedient and necessary" measure to place the colony on a firm defensive footing. Laurens was unanimously elected to a seat on the Council of Safety, which also included Charles Pinckney, Rawlins Lowndes, Thomas Ferguson, Miles Brewton, Arthur Middleton, Thomas Heyward, Jr., Thomas Bee, John Huger, James Parsons, William Henry Drayton, Benjamin Elliott, and William Williamson. At the first meeting of the council on June 16, Laurens, against his objections, was chosen to act as president. He was quite dissatisfied with this appointment and attributed it to the desire of his fellows to take advantage of his strong work habits while keeping themselves out of "the post of danger."[31] With the Council of Safety established and left in capable hands, the Provincial Congress prepared to adjourn. Before doing so, however, the Congress decided on one more act of defiance. They resolved that anyone who violated or refused to accept the authority of the Provincial Congress should be tried by the local General Committee, and, if convicted, be advertised as an enemy to American liberty. Then, the Congress adjourned on June 22, leaving the province in the hands of the Council of Safety.[32]

Into this situation walked Lord William Campbell, the last royal governor of South Carolina, when he landed at Charles Town on June 18, 1775. Campbell was unsurprised at the quiet of his reception, a strong contrast to the joyful demonstrations that usually accompanied the arrival of a new governor. He was dismayed, however, by the progress of the revolutionary movement and his discovery that his authority had been almost completely annihilated. For this situation, Campbell joined other officials in placing the blame squarely upon the shoulders of Lieutenant Governor Bull. Prominent officials, including Attorney General James Simpson, Indian Superintendent John Stuart, and private secretary Alexander Innes, wasted no time in denouncing Bull to the new governor. These men suspected that the lieutenant governor had betrayed secret information to patriot leaders and held him responsible for the deteriorating military situation. They cited Bull's refusal to call for British troops following the seizure of the public military stores and the calling of the militia as further evidence of his disaffection. Bull's uncharacteristic behavior grew even stranger following the arrival of Campbell, as his lethargy lapsed into complete inactivity. His failure to attend any subsequent meeting of the council, as well as the official welcome of the governor, added to the doubts concerning Bull's loyalty. Campbell quickly shared these concerns and, lacking the evidence to prosecute the lieutenant governor, he secretly appointed Simpson as deputy governor, thus bypassing Bull in the government.[33] Meanwhile, Governor Campbell faced more pressing problems than the breakdown of Lieutenant Governor Bull. On June 20, the Provincial Congress, over Laurens's signature, presented an address to the governor in which they professed loyalty to the Crown and asked the governor's help in procuring a reconciliation on constitutional principles. Campbell made his position perfectly clear when he curtly informed the Congress that he would recognize no legitimate representatives of the people except those convened in the Commons House.[34]

When the Commons House assembled on July 10, Campbell elaborated further on his position. Refusing to enter into a debate over the issues in dispute, Campbell observed that the legal government had been virtually abolished and "the most dangerous measures adopted—and acts, of the most outrageous and illegal nature, publicly committed with impunity." He warned the assembly that the colony was on dangerous ground, and that persistence in the present illegal measures could only draw "inevitable ruin on this flourishing Colony." When the assembly defended the conduct of the patriots, Campbell lamented that "I cannot prevent the ruin I foresee." This reply made it painfully obvious to the patriots that they could expect neither assistance nor sympathy from the governor and, on July 21, they requested permission to adjourn. Campbell refused this request, hoping that the continued meeting of the House would hamper the revolutionary activity of its members. This was a vain hope, however, as the assembly simply refused to muster a quorum, causing quick adjournments on a daily basis. For all practical purposes, the South Carolina Commons House was dead.[35]

With hopes of an understanding between Governor Campbell and local leaders dashed, the crisis escalated. Fears were rampant that an invasion was imminent and that efforts were being made by royal officials to turn the backcountry and the Indians, as well as the slaves, against the Charles Town patriots. Prior to these developments, the Council of Safety was divided as the dominant moderates repeatedly frustrated the radical propositions of William Henry Drayton and Arthur Middleton. Laurens, while consulting his own conscience, clearly fell within the moderate camp, as he thought that General Gage had enough problems in Boston without planning an invasion of South Carolina.[36]

The break with the governor caused even the most moderate of South Carolinians to reevaluate their positions. It also led to a flurry of activity in the Council of Safety. After discovering that a significant quantity of powder had been shipped aboard the British ship *Betsey*, the council ordered Clement Lempriere to cruise off the coast of St. Augustine and seize the powder. Explaining that this decision had been reached late at night when the council was tired and had not fully considered the matter, Laurens took the liberty of altering the order. Always a moderate, Laurens told Lempriere to purchase, rather than seize, the powder and authorized him to draw a note upon the Council of Safety for this purpose. Realizing that the council might disapprove of this action, Laurens assured Lempriere that he would personally assume the debt if the council refused.[37] The Council of Safety also demonstrated considerable craftiness in its efforts to ward off an invasion. During this period, several letters from Governor James Wright of Georgia to General Gage were intercepted and found to contain requests for troops. The council ingeniously replaced the original contents with forgeries that assured the general that the south was peaceful and would remain so unless troops were sent to the area. These forgeries may well have fooled Gage, for no troops were sent at this time. However, as Laurens had assured his friends, Gage was in no position to be sending troops from Boston, even if he were so inclined.[38]

As rumors intensified, both sides competed for the allegiance of the backcountry. To the ministry, Campbell privately ridiculed the preparations of the province, asserting that the vain and ambitious provincial officers were recruiting such a collection of "vagrants" and other rabble that he would not be surprised if they "destroy their Officers and plunder the Country" at the first sign of discipline. In addition, while assuring provincial leaders that he was not in contact with pro-British elements on the frontier, Campbell was active in the promotion of the royal interest, promising protection and rewards to loyal elements in the backcountry.[39]

Suspecting that royal officials were in contact with dissatisfied elements along the frontier, the Council of Safety launched its own campaign to win over the backcountry leaders. In mid-July, Laurens wrote to Thomas Fletchall, a prominent westerner, and urged him to lend his support to the forces of freedom. Do not be tempted by British offers of rewards and offices, Laurens warned, for "the time is approaching too fast, when Such Commissions & Such appointments will not be productive either of honour or profit to the holder."[40] When such encouragement failed to achieve the desired result, the Council of Safety, on July 23, appointed a commission to visit the backcountry and explain the issues in dispute. Hoping to utilize Laurens's reputation with the back settlers, the council asked him to serve on the commission. When Laurens declined, the council appointed William Henry Drayton, the Reverends William Tennent and Oliver Hart, Colonel Richard Richardson, and Joseph Kershaw. This commission was well chosen, as the latter two gentlemen were prominent westerners, while the two ministers represented dissenting sects, a move calculated to appeal to the popular hostility to the Church of England in the backcountry. The choice of Drayton is interesting: among the most capable and energetic of patriot leaders, he was also among the most fiery and least diplomatic. This leaves the strong suspicion that the Council of Safety, dominated by moderates, selected Drayton as much to remove a leading radical voice from Charles Town during this critical period as to take advantage of his talents.[41]

The resulting mission, which lasted from August 2 through late September 1775, exemplified the best and worst in Drayton's character. Drayton began negotiations with backcountry Loyalists, but when these stalled, he responded by raising a military force. This only encouraged Thomas Fletchall and other Loyalist leaders to raise a similar force of their own. Similar in numbers, the two sides avoided a bloody battle only when Drayton reopened negotiations. He then skillfully produced an agreement in which the Loyalists agreed to remain militarily neutral during the dispute with Britain. Though this was the best agreement that could reasonably have been expected, many of Drayton's colleagues on the Council of Safety were uneasy with a solution that promised only neutrality. When a new threat arose in November 1775, the council ordered the arrest of all of the leading backcountry Loyalists and sent a military force under Colonel Richard Richardson to deal with the situation. This expedition proved successful and the Loyalists, by the end of 1775, had been temporarily crushed.[42]

Even more threatening than the backcountry Loyalists was the danger of slave insurrection. As residents of the only mainland colony in which whites were outnumbered by blacks, white South Carolinians were acutely aware of the vulnerability of their position. Concerns were particularly sharp in the low country, a region that featured a black majority of five to one, with areas that reached twenty to one or even higher.[43] These figures are important in explaining the general moderation that, Gadsden and a few radical colleagues excepted, characterized the low-country elite during the conflict with Britain. The large numbers of slaves forced most South Carolinians to adopt a more cautious tone than their northern counterparts in their exclamations concerning liberty and their denunciations of British efforts to "enslave" America.[44]

While the problem of slavery had served as a moderating influence on some of the South Carolina hotheads, uncertainty concerning the allegiance of the heavy slave population contributed to a growing hysteria in Charles Town during the spring and summer of 1775. Even those most generously inclined to the mother country realized that the slaves might serve as an attractive source of support for the British if matters degenerated into open warfare. These fears seemed confirmed when, on May 3, a letter was received from Arthur Lee in London in which the Virginian asserted that the ministry was giving serious thought to the promotion of slave revolts and Indian disturbances on the frontier. Such rumors had been floating around Charles Town for months, but none had possessed the aura of authority of this one. Henry Laurens certainly took the report seriously, as he had worked closely with Lee during the Wilkes fund crisis and had developed considerable respect for Lee's judgment and his contacts within the ministry. The Lee letter, arriving at the same time as the news of the fighting around Boston, raised the sense of crisis in the capital to a new level.

Matters quickly soared to an hysterical climax. Spurred by rumors, the Charles Town General Committee, on May 12, called out the militia to deal with any prospective foe, internal or external. The authorities turned wary eyes to the slaves and, not surprisingly, quickly discovered several purported plots. Henry Laurens was extremely skeptical of these charges and reported that most were quickly dismissed and the implicated blacks released. One case that was not dismissed, however, was that of Thomas Jeremiah (known locally as Jerry), a free black pilot who owned a considerable amount of property and was himself a slaveowner. Jeremiah had achieved a certain prominence around Charles Town as a proud man whose independence had alternately won him the praise and the condemnation of local authorities. Now, he stood accused of plotting to use his piloting skill to guide a convoy of British warships into the harbor to lead a slave revolt.

The evidence against Jeremiah was, and remains to this day, contradictory and inconclusive. Laurens, at first, associated the Jeremiah case with the others and believed the pilot to be guilty of little more than having a quick tongue and an overactive imagination. However, the powerful combination of the mounting hysteria and apparent perjury by Jeremiah served to change his mind. Jeremiah's testimony contained several important inconsistencies, not the least of which was his insistence that he did not know a leading prosecution witness, a man who later turned out to be his brother-in-law. Thus, Laurens approved of the resulting conviction and death sentence. Governor Campbell, however, remained unconvinced and expressed outrage at a verdict that he considered to be nothing more than a case of judicial murder. In recognition of the transformation of the political situation in South Carolina, Campbell appealed to Laurens to use his influence as president of the Council of Safety to spare Jeremiah's life. The governor assured Laurens that there was no British naval squadron poised to attack Charles Town and pointed out that several of the key prosecution witnesses had recanted their testimony. In his report to the ministry, Campbell noted that he sent appeals for clemency to both Laurens and the judge who had presided over the trial. While the latter wavered and attempted to raise a petition to spare the pilot, Laurens could not be persuaded to intervene. Indeed, Campbell wrote, Laurens warned against a royal pardon and assured the governor that any intervention on his part would likely result in a renewal of mob violence. The bitter governor held Laurens personally responsible for the execution of Jeremiah and he vowed to save the correspondence from this incident, implying that it might be used as the basis for a future criminal prosecution.[45]

The Jeremiah case further undermined the position of Governor Campbell, as many wondered why the governor was so interested in saving the life of a man convicted of plotting the ruin of the colony. At the same time, there were strong suspicions that the governor was conducting clandestine negotiations with the backcountry Loyalists and that he was plotting with John Stuart, the Indian Superintendent, to unleash the Indians upon the frontier.[46] By late summer, the position of the governor had become practically untenable. In early September, the radicals launched a direct assault upon the governor, as Arthur Middleton proposed that the General Committee take Campbell into custody as a menace to the peace. Laurens and the moderates did not feel that the evidence warranted such a harsh step and defeated the motion by a wide margin. The events of the next few weeks, however, would change the minds of many, including Laurens. The critical evidence against Campbell was supplied by a local spy who, masquerading as a confidential messenger from the backcountry Loyalists, had gained the confidence of the governor. According to this spy, Campbell had offered the "severest reflections" upon the local patriot governing bodies and had assured him that troops were on the way to crush the rebellion. As a result, the General Committee, of which Laurens was chairman, demanded that the governor submit for inspection his correspondence with the ministry and the backcountry. When he refused, another vote on whether or not the governor should be taken into custody was held in the General Committee. Once again, the motion was defeated, but this time by the narrower margin of twenty-three to sixteen. By this time the capital was rife with invasion rumors, and the Council of Safety, roused to action, ordered Colonel William Moultrie to seize Fort Johnson. This post, hastily abandoned by the meager British force, was taken on September 15. Now convinced that matters had progressed far beyond his control, Lord William Campbell, on September 15, dissolved the Commons House, took the seals of government, and retreated to the warship *Tamar*, anchored in the harbor.[47]

The retirement of the governor only increased tensions, as many in Charles Town feared that it signaled an impending British attack. The Council of Safety took feverish measures to defend the town and harbor. Among the many proposals was a revival of the plan to obstruct the harbor by sinking ships in the channel. Laurens had not changed his mind about the potentially disastrous effects of such a policy and spoke against it in the council. When the vote ended in a tie, Laurens, as president, was left to cast the deciding ballot. After requesting and receiving leave to consider the issue overnight, Laurens decided in favor of the proposal. He explained that he voted this way not because he approved of the idea, but because he felt that it was necessary to maintain the ardor of the people. Also, he realized that obstruction was impossible while the British warships (the *Tamar* had been joined by two other ships) remained in the harbor, and hoped that wiser heads would prevail in the meantime. Whether Laurens foresaw such a possibility, this was precisely what happened. In early October, Thomas Bee circulated a petition that convinced the Council of Safety to reverse its decision and prevent this drastic step.[48]

By mid-September, Laurens was certain that the revolutionary movement had gone too far. Though he would continue to stand with his country, even if he disagreed with some of its actions, he feared that the time of trial was drawing near. He informed his son that

> Our people here are proceeding by hasty Steps to attempts too mighty for their abilities, & every day convinces me that I was not wrong when I endeavoured to dissuade them from taking the Reins of Government into their hands. . . . You think the people in England are acting madly, & I am Sure we may Safely compare Notes with them in this Country—I am ready to cry out, a pox on both their Houses; we are all Mad; all wrong; but if I am to die it Shall be on the right Side, I honestly mean this Side.

Convinced that "the imprudent mad conduct of some of our Contemporary Politicians will no doubt draw a burst upon our heads," Laurens was more anxious than ever that John Laurens resist the temptation to return to America. Observing that he might not survive the impending bloodletting that seemed increasingly likely, and that his brother, James Laurens, was unlikely to ever regain his health, Laurens ordered his son to remain in London, to concentrate on his studies, and to prepare to assume the mantle of family leadership.[49]

Laurens did not enjoy his service as president of the Council of Safety, as the public business dominated his days and, often, his nights as well. Noting the adverse effects that public service had upon his private affairs, Laurens eagerly anticipated surrendering his position when the Provincial Congress reconvened on November 1.[50] Laurens did not expect to miss the Council of Safety and its endless disputes between the moderate and radical members, which often left the committee paralyzed and unable to act. Though Laurens pursued an independent course, he almost always found himself in agreement with the moderates. Laurens thought that his refusal to endorse the radical program was responsible for a serious dispute with young John Faucheraud Grimke, which ended in a duel that almost cost Laurens his life. More specifically, Laurens was convinced that his opposition to the radical proposal that private correspondences be opened and inspected led Arthur Middleton and Peter Timothy to put the hot-tempered Grimke up to his challenge. According to Laurens, Middleton and Timothy had opened and read several private letters in the possession of Grimke's father and, when discovered, attempted to cover their behavior by claiming that such conduct had been sanctioned by the Council of Safety. When Laurens denied the charge, a brief newspaper battle ensued, followed by Grimke's challenge. The duel was a tense affair, but one that again demonstrated Laurens's character. Though he personally engaged in several duels during his lifetime, Laurens had always denounced the practice, stating that he was brave enough to receive the fire, but too much of a coward to kill another man unless it was absolutely necessary. Certain that young Grimke was familiar with his position, Laurens was shocked when the young firebrand took deliberate aim as if to kill him. When the gun misfired, Laurens and his second, John Lewis Gervais, angrily stalked off the field, insisting that Grimke had not acted as a gentleman.[51]

When the Provincial Congress met again on November 1, Laurens' wish to resign the chair was granted and the honor was bestowed upon Drayton. While this may have been a move by the moderates to silence the most effective voice of the radicals, the move backfired. Abandoning the idea that the president should serve as a mere moderator, Drayton actively engaged in debate and used his position to further radical aims. For his part, Laurens unhappily found that the elevation of Drayton had not released him from the public service. On November 16, Laurens was reappointed to the Council of Safety and, two weeks later, was again unanimously elected council president. Though gratified by the expression of approval from his peers, Laurens found it difficult to hide his disappointment that his private affairs would have to suffer further disruption.[52]

With Drayton in the chair, the Provincial Congress, which sat from November 1 to 29, experienced a great surge in activity. On November 20, after shots were exchanged between provincial ships and the British warships, the favorite scheme of the radicals was brought to fruition when two schooner hulks were sunk in the bay to prevent any further penetration by British vessels. A few days later, orders from the Continental Congress to detain all royal officials were received and implemented. Defensive preparations were also stepped up upon the receipt of orders from Philadelphia to defend the capital "to the last extremity." While these orders were welcomed by many, they were distressing to Henry Laurens, who observed that the Philadelphia Congress might have issued such orders, but they had provided no means for effecting them. Laurens considered the province to be on the verge of serious trouble, but if destruction were to be the fate of his beloved Charles Town, he was prepared to share it, for he was certain that his cause was just, and he would "prefer poverty & Death to a tame Submission" to the "diabolical Measures" of the British ministry.[53]

While Laurens spent the year 1775 exerting his influence to restrain any unnecessary provocations, Christopher Gadsden was doing just the opposite in Philadelphia. He had arrived in this city on May 8, 1775, and found the town in near hysteria from the news of the action at Lexington. While there is no record of Gadsden's immediate reaction to these reports, it can be safely assumed that he shared the excitement and the anti-British feeling that swept through Philadelphia. It was under these circumstances that the Second Continental Congress opened on May 10. This assembly was an even more respectable gathering of prominent Americans than the first Congress. Most of the men who sat in the first Congress were back and were now joined by such prominent names as Benjamin Franklin, John Hancock, and, six weeks later, Thomas Jefferson. In addition, Lyman Hall appeared to take his seat as the first representative of Georgia in an intercolonial Congress. Though events would force the Congress into more active measures than many of the delegates would have liked, the radical element was still in the minority. Thus, as in South Carolina, the radicals could proceed only slowly. Indeed, the temper of the Congress can be gauged by the fact that it was an entire month before the Congress organized the Continental Army, and another five days before George Washington was appointed commander in chief on June 15.[54]

Such languor no doubt galled the energetic Gadsden. Nevertheless, he was prepared to be practical and signed the Olive Branch Petition in which the colonies made a final plea for autonomy within the empire. Gadsden, of course, was certain that this plea would have no more effect than countless previous efforts, but he recognized the psychological value of a final publicized attempt. With this step out of the way, Gadsden joined with John and Samuel Adams, Roger Sherman of Connecticut, and Richard Henry Lee to form the nucleus of a minority movement for independence. John Adams never forgot the support that Gadsden gave to the independence movement during 1775 and 1776. Even in 1818, while addressing another issue in his remarkable correspondence with Thomas Jefferson, Adams remembered that "Independence of Church and Parliament was a fixed Principle of our Predecessors in 1620 as it was of Sam. Adams and Chris. Gadsden in 1776."[55] While writing his autobiography in 1804, Adams recalled that as early as May 1775 he had proposed a sweeping program that would dissolve traditional ties with Britain. Included in this plan, according to Adams, were provisions to seize all royal officials and hold them as hostages against the citizens of Boston, formation and control of a Continental Army, and an immediate declaration of independence. Adams suggested that once independence was declared, the new nation should use the threat of alliances with France, Spain, and other European powers to force Great Britain to negotiate a peace settlement. Adams could count on the support of his South Carolina colleague, as Gadsden was prepared to go even further, suggesting that the Congress should open American ports to the trade of all nations except Britain.[56]

Though Adams sometimes remembered his own role as being much more heroic than it really was, it is clear that such ideas were being discussed in the Continental Congress during 1775. Adams wrote that it was John Dickinson of Pennsylvania who provided the main opposition to these plans. He recalled that South Carolina held the balance and that even John Rutledge made a speech in favor of the program. On this point, however, Adams was almost surely mistaken, for John Rutledge was to prove an extremely determined opponent of independence, and did not support the idea wholeheartedly even after 1776. It was the Pennsylvanians, Adams asserted, who went to work upon Lynch and the Rutledge brothers and finally persuaded them to swing their votes against the plan. Significantly, Adams noted that Gadsden was considered such a hopeless case that the Pennsylvanians did not even attempt to convert him. Gadsden continued to be a staunch supporter of the independence movement throughout his stay in Philadelphia. While congratulating himself for his repeated efforts toward independence and the formation of a confederation, Adams named Gadsden, Richard Henry Lee, and Roger Sherman as his most dependable supporters. Adams was very much drawn to Gadsden and used the disinterested patriotism of the South Carolinian as the standard by which he measured his other colleagues. Finding most of these wanting, Adams lamented that Gadsden lacked the influence that should have been accorded to such a pure heart.[57]

As an enthusiastic supporter of strong military action, Gadsden was involved in military preparations from the start. His prominence was recognized when he was appointed to serve, along with Silas Deane, Benjamin Franklin, John Jay, and Richard Henry Lee, on a committee to secure military supplies for the colonies. Gadsden was tireless in this position and worked hard to supply the force that was gathered around Boston with powder and weapons. For this purpose, Gadsden joined his fellow delegates from South Carolina in sending a message to the South Carolina secret committee asking for as much powder as could be spared. The response was generous, as the Council of Safety sent five thousand pounds of gunpowder to Philadelphia, a supply that not only helped the patriots at Boston, but also assisted in the invasion of Canada.[58] Perhaps Gadsden's most important immediate contribution during the Continental Congress was his assistance in the founding of the United States Navy. In light of his ideas on free trade, it was only a matter of time before Gadsden began exploring the possibilities for the creation of a navy. He realized that if Americans were going to establish more direct trade connections with continental Europe, some provision would have to be made for the protection of American vessels. His earlier service in the Royal Navy led Gadsden to conclude that British ships were not nearly as formidable as most Americans feared. In fact, Gadsden assured John Adams, the colonies might obtain a fleet very inexpensively if they took advantage of the discontent he thought existed in the British navy. Gadsden asserted that many of the British sailors had been impressed into service and were only looking for the opportunity to escape the low pay and rigid discipline of their current situation. He assured Adams that the most loyal and experienced British seamen served aboard the smaller sloops, schooners, and cutters, vessels that could be taken easily and then used against the larger warships. Assuring Adams that most of the sailors serving aboard the warships were unhappy, Gadsden was certain that these men would not fight against their American brethren. Instead, he predicted that they would appreciate the opportunity to "obtain their Liberty and Happiness" and deliver their ships to the waiting Americans.[59]

Though this plan was too impractical to appeal to the Congress, it did contribute to the growing awareness of the importance of a navy. On October 7, the delegates from Rhode Island submitted a plan for the development of a navy. Confronted by opposition from delegates outside New England who were unwilling to assume the expense involved in an enterprise from which they expected to gain little, the motion underwent a lively debate. In the end, however, the Continental Congress agreed, by a narrow margin, to establish a navy. On October 13, Gadsden replaced John Adams and joined Silas Deane and John Langdon on a committee appointed to estimate the cost of outfitting two ships to be used to intercept British supply ships. By November, John Adams had returned to the committee, along with Stephen Hopkins, Joseph Hewes, and Richard Henry Lee, and the committee adopted the title of the Naval Committee, soon changed again to the Marine Committee. By the end of the year, four ships had been commissioned and launched, with the Continental Congress slated to receive a two-thirds share of all prizes seized.[60] At the same time, Gadsden decided that the new American navy required a distinctive flag of its own and set out to develop such a banner. He came up with the famous gray coiled rattlesnake poised upon a bright yellow background with the phrase "DON'T TREAD ON ME" displayed underneath. This flag was unfurled from the mast of the *Alfred* on December 20, 1775, and quickly became popular among the American public.[61]

The end of 1774 saw South Carolina poised upon the precipice of rebellion, and the following year witnessed the dismantling of the royal government and a gradual move toward independence. Once again, Gadsden and Laurens found themselves locked in opposition: Gadsden pressed for strong measures, which both men realized could block the decreasing chances for reconciliation, while Laurens hoped to avoid any provocative action. The voice of moderation, Laurens supported preparedness, but urged his colleagues to act prudently, economically, and with regard for the consequences of their actions. By 1775, Laurens understood that South Carolina was already embarked upon a revolutionary course and had taken the early steps toward independence. Unlike Gadsden, he did not welcome these developments and grew increasingly frustrated as Rawlins Lowndes and other moderate leaders unwittingly facilitated the designs of the radicals. Yet, while maintaining his belief that mistakes were made on both sides, Laurens was certain that the major responsibility lay with a wicked ministry that was conspiring against American liberty. Thus, he accepted the highest positions in the revolutionary organizations: chairman of the Charles Town General Committee, president of the Provincial Congress, and president of the Council of Safety. Though Laurens used these positions to block or delay policies that could close the door to a settlement, he realized, by late 1775, that time was running short.

So, too, did Christopher Gadsden. As 1775 opened, no one in South Carolina, including Gadsden, was prepared to openly advocate independence. This changed quickly after the fighting at Lexington, and John Adams recalled Gadsden as advocating independence as early as May 1775 in the Continental Congress. Gadsden had likely decided on the necessity of independence before 1775, but not until he returned to Philadelphia did he begin to pursue this course openly. When not advocating independence, Gadsden was proposing or supporting policies such as free trade, the construction of a navy, and the replacement of royal officials with the local patriot elites, policies that clearly facilitated separation. By 1776, Christopher Gadsden was prepared for the final break with Great Britain.

10

Independence Proclaimed, 1776

As THE CRITICAL YEAR OF 1776 DAWNED, BOTH HENRY LAURENS AND CHRISTO-
pher Gadsden were faced with important changes in their lives. For Laurens, the change was personal and painful, as he learned that young James
Laurens, not yet ten years old, had died from a fall in London on September
5, 1775. Henry Laurens admitted that the unfortunate event had shaken him
and, through his tears, he expressed the wish that he could join his son in
the hereafter. Quickly regaining his composure, however, Laurens assured
his son John, who apparently felt guilty over the death of his brother, that
he held John blameless for the sad event. To his own brother, James, Henry
expressed his faith in God and wrote sorrowfully that "I will dwell no
longer on the melancholy topic of the Dead. I shall go to him—it is decreed
that he shall not return to me—thy Will be done—I have reason to be
thankful—All is not lost."[1]

For Christopher Gadsden, the changes were more exhilarating and excit-
ing. As South Carolina leaders grew increasingly anxious about the threat
of invasion, orders were dispatched to Gadsden to return home and assume
command of the provincial military. Eager to demonstrate his military talents, Gadsden left Philadelphia on January 18, 1776.[2] Thus, Gadsden was
not present in Philadelphia as the Continental Congress progressed steadily toward the Declaration of Independence. Though Gadsden was not
present to vote for and sign the Declaration, his role in laying the groundwork for it must not be ignored. That Gadsden has not been given more
credit for his part in the early stages of the independence movement is due
largely to the almost total loss of his writings for this period and to the
incomplete nature of congressional records. Gadsden's role in the Congress, therefore, must be pieced together from the fragmentary records and
scattered recollections of his fellow delegates. It is almost entirely on the
diary and memoirs of John Adams that our knowledge of Gadsden's congressional activities is based. Adams made it clear that Gadsden was at the
center of a small group of radicals who were moving toward independence
from the start of the Second Continental Congress. Exactly when Gadsden
became convinced of the necessity of independence is unclear, but he was
definitely arguing in this direction after the conflict at Lexington. While
Paine, the Adamses, Jefferson, and others have monopolized the glory of

171

prodding the Congress toward the final break, the contributions of delegates who, like Gadsden, set the foundation on which the patriots of 1776 built, must not be forgotten.

The departure of the blunt and fiery Gadsden brought a great sigh of relief from several of the delegates, particularly those of the more conservative persuasion. His fellow South Carolinian, Thomas Lynch, exclaimed that "My Colleague Gadsden is gone home to Command our Troops, God Save them," while, a few weeks later, another delegate marveled at how much business the Congress was able to accomplish since the departure of Gadsden.[3] Sailing with his son Thomas aboard the small boat *Hawke*, the trip home provided much more excitement than Gadsden would have liked. He spent much of the voyage immersed in the freshly published *Common Sense*, copies of which he had purchased for himself and the South Carolina and Georgia Provincial Congresses. Gadsden's fascination with this pamphlet can be seen by the large number of underlined passages in his personal copy.[4] The trip was a risky enterprise, as British warships and cruisers were patrolling the American coast and, despite the efforts of Gadsden and the Marine Committee, the American navy could provide little protection from the British. Gadsden discovered just how dangerous such a voyage could be when the *Hawke* was spotted by the British warship *Syren* and chased along the coast of North Carolina. The *Hawke* was finally forced ashore, and the passengers, including Gadsden, who carried his copies of *Common Sense* and a copy of the journal of the Continental Congress, hurried inland to safety. Though this had been a close call, all that was left to the British was the damaged vessel. Afterwards, Gadsden and his son completed their journey by land, arriving in Charles Town on February 8.[5]

While Gadsden was concluding his service in the Continental Congress, the heavyhearted Laurens returned to the Council of Safety after an absence of only one day. His presence was clearly necessary for, on January 11, Charles Cotesworth Pinckney notified Laurens that several British warships had again appeared off the bar. Another wave of excitement swept Charles Town as the Council of Safety called out the militia and prepared to meet an attack. This, too, turned out to be a false alarm as the squadron remained off the bar for a few weeks before sailing south to raid the coasts of South Carolina and Georgia. While this reduced the pressure on the capital, it did not relieve the pressure on the colony or the Council of Safety. When the British raiding parties began seizing slaves and rice, local officers requested instructions as to what countermeasures should be taken. From Laurens's reply, it is clear that no one wished to take the responsibility of issuing the order to fire upon vessels of the Royal Navy. Thus, the Council of Safety left it to the discretion of the local commanders to decide whether or not to fire upon the British ships. However, the council did suggest that, since the British were stealing valuable property, any attempted landing should be forcibly resisted.[6]

It was this situation into which Gadsden stepped upon his return. He was more than prepared to meet the challenge. Gadsden received an enthusiastic welcome when he took his seat in the Provincial Congress on February 9. As he entered the assembly room of the State House, Gadsden carried his "DON'T TREAD ON ME" banner and presented the flag to the Congress. The members were delighted by this gesture, and Gadsden's new ally, William Henry Drayton, the president of the Congress, ordered the flag to be displayed prominently in the assembly room. Gadsden's arrival coincided with a crucial period in the deliberations of the Provincial Congress. The Continental Congress had recommended that the colonies formally provide for temporary governments to remain in effect until the dispute with Britain was settled. The day before Gadsden's arrival, the Congress had appointed a committee, to consist of the members of the Council of Safety and a few others, to consider this proposal. Immediately upon his return, Gadsden was added to this committee and to another on defense.[7]

On February 10, Laurens presented the recommendation of this committee that a temporary constitution was necessary and should be immediately prepared. Then, Gadsden threw the Congress into chaos when he introduced a copy of *Common Sense* to the meeting. After reading several passages from the pamphlet, Gadsden declared that he not only favored the preparation of a new government, but also the "absolute Independence of America." This unexpected pronouncement struck the Congress like "an explosion of thunder," as few were ready to entertain such a radical idea. Gadsden's speech brought violent abuse upon both himself and Paine by several of the most prominent members of the Congress. His old friend Rawlins Lowndes, who had seethed for months at the progressively radical proposals he heard, now offered such a profane rebuttal that John Drayton recorded the passage by leaving it blank. John Rutledge thought the idea treasonous and declared that he would ride day and night to Philadelphia to prevent any separation from the mother country. Even the few members who, like William Henry Drayton and Arthur Middleton, might have agreed with Gadsden's sentiments, were shocked and dumbfounded at his indiscretion in making such an ill-timed proposal.[8]

Henry Laurens was among those who disapproved of Gadsden's performance, and he again shook his head at the seeming madness of his former friend. To his son, Laurens made clear his thoughts on *Common Sense* and Gadsden's patronage of it:

> I know not how the Doctrines contained in it are relished in the Northern Colonies, nothing less than repeated & continued persecution by Great Britain can make the People in this Country subscribe to them, I have already borne

my testimony against them in open Congress & more against those indecent
expressions with which the Pages abound—however the Author's reasoning,
tho not all original is strong & captivating & will make many converts to
Republican principles, if, I have said above the present scene of Kingly persecution is much longer continued—Mr. Gadsden introduced the Book into
this Colony, he is wrapped up in the thought of seperation & independence &
will hear nothing in opposition when I told him his freind [*sic*, Paine] had
stolen from an "Apology for the Revolt of the Low Countries", "I don't dislike it
on that account" was his reply, although the discovery cast a little shade upon
the Credit which had been given to the supposed Author, a young Gentleman at
Philadelphia.

Though Gadsden's declaration for independence was immediately shouted
down, Laurens realized that time was running short if a reconciliation with
Britain was to be effected. While he still held out hope for an understanding, he was sure that "a few steps further & Adieu dependance—Adieu the
connexion between the Colonies & the Mother Country."[9]

To his old friend, the London merchant William Manning, Laurens affirmed that he still loved Great Britain, but that a wicked and wrongheaded
ministry had brought matters to such a state that "I perceive that I am to be
Seperated from her & that my Children are to be called by Some new
name." He insisted that the mere thought of independence caused tears to
trickle down his cheeks and that a firm reconciliation was his greatest
wish, "but I own the work which would have been easy twelve aye Six
Months ago, will now be uphill." He freely admitted that his colony was by
no means impregnable to attack, but he was sure that such an attempt
would be extremely bloody work, for the population was firmly united in
support of their liberties. Even the back settlers, Laurens asserted, had
"only wanted information in order to become as violent Liberty-Boys as
Hancock or Adams." Once the true issues in dispute were explained to the
Loyalists taken prisoner during Richardson's expedition, Laurens wrote,
they quickly repudiated their past and declared their allegiance to the
patriot forces. Thus, Laurens remained convinced that Britain might conquer his colony, but "her Conquest will be her defeat," as it would be
extremely difficult to rule such an alienated people. Laurens continued to
hope that it would not come to violence, but he was beginning to despair
and noted that only a sudden and dramatic change in British policy could
avert the horrors of civil war.[10]

On February 11, the shaken Provincial Congress agreed to the preparation of a temporary government. As a reaction against Gadsden's speech of
the previous day, the Congress expressly rejected the idea of independence
and underscored the temporary nature of the new government. A committee of eleven was selected to prepare the constitution, and care was taken
to ensure that the committee was dominated by moderates. Thus, the chair-

man, Charles Cotesworth Pinckney, was a staunch moderate, as were seven other members: Laurens, John Rutledge, Charles Pinckney, Rawlins Lowndes, Henry Middleton, Thomas Bee, and Thomas Heyward, Jr. The radical element consisted of only three members: Gadsden, Arthur Middleton, and Thomas Lynch, Jr. Of these, only Gadsden had given evidence that he would favor any significant constitutional changes. Thus, it was evident that the members of the Provincial Congress had no intention of making any major alterations in the government, with the exception of the replacement of the royal officials by themselves.[11]

While some have criticized the South Carolina constitution of 1776 as being an exact replica of the old British government under new leadership, some significant revision did occur. The most important change came in the area of representation. Henry Laurens, with occasional support from Gadsden, had long been a champion of more equitable representation for the backcountry. Opposition from royal officials, who refused to allow an enlargement of the Commons House, and of low-country leaders, who refused to sanction the erosion of their influence, had prevented a more equitable distribution of power during British rule. Efforts were made to increase backcountry representation in the Provincial Congress, and further concessions were offered in the constitution of 1776. Though representation was still unevenly apportioned, the backcountry emerged with a far greater percentage of seats than it had held during royal rule. Under the constitution of 1776, Charles Town and the surrounding area received 96 of the 202 seats and, thus, was no longer able to unilaterally dominate the politics of the province. Still, other low-country districts were allocated thirty more seats, giving the low country a majority of 126 of the 202 seats. The role of the backcountry had been increased, however, as they were allowed seventy-six seats, an increase of eighteen over the fifty-eight they held in the Provincial Congress. While it is true that the west, which contained about 60 percent of the population, was still woefully underrepresented, this area was steadily increasing its influence. This trend would continue in the future. Though there was no provision for reapportionment in this constitution, the backcountry continued to gain power through the adoption of successive constitutions. Finally, in 1808, the west achieved a majority of seats in both houses of the legislature.[12]

Other than representation, there were few other changes in the government besides the replacement of the British officials with the local elite. The constitution was submitted to the Provincial Congress on March 5, and the next three weeks were spent debating the document. Considerable opposition on several grounds threatened ratification of the constitution. Most important was the role of the executive, since the South Carolina constitution was the only one of the new American constitutions that did not severely limit, if not destroy, the power of the executive. The new "president" of South Carolina was to be a formidable figure. Whereas other colonies sought to prevent abuses of power by holding annual elections and mandating rotation in office, the president of South Carolina would be elected by the General Assembly for a two-year term and would always be eligible for reelection. In addition, a fixed salary was provided for the president, taking from the assembly a weapon that had proven useful against the royal governors. But the greatest dissatisfaction came from the provision for a presidential veto, a point that created the fear that this executive would be even more powerful than his royal predecessors. Equally important was the objection raised to the manner in which the constitution had been written and adopted. Looking for any grounds that might contribute to the defeat of the constitution, Lowndes and others argued that the document had been prepared without a popular referendum. Not only this, but by March 21, only 52 of the 184 members were present in the Provincial Congress. By March 26, attendance was so poor that the Congress had to order the attendance of twenty-two absent delegates who lived near the capital. Even with these men present, opponents observed that the remaining members were almost exclusively representative of low-country districts. Thus, Lowndes hoped to block acceptance of the constitution under the pretext that ratification should be delayed until a more representative sample of the population could be obtained. This was the last thing Gadsden wished to consider, for an indefinite delay in ratifying the constitution could interrupt the momentum of the independence movement. But despite Gadsden's efforts, it appeared that the opposition might make passage difficult, if not impossible. This situation changed dramatically, however, when news was received that the British Parliament had declared the colonies to be in a state of rebellion and had placed American lives and property outside the protection of the empire. Thereupon, the opposition collapsed and, on March 26, 1776, South Carolina became only the second colony to adopt a new constitution.[13]

While the debate continued, Laurens eagerly awaited the adoption of the new government and the opportunity to relinquish his duties as president of the Council of Safety. Hoping to be allowed to retire to his private affairs, Laurens expected Henry Middleton to be elected to the presidency and John Rutledge, or perhaps Christopher Gadsden, to receive the vice presidency. It came as an unpleasant surprise, then, when John Rutledge was elected president and Laurens himself was elevated to the vice presidency. Laurens was so upset by his nomination that he immediately declared that he would not serve if elected and left the room. He again attempted to decline after his election, but when the General Assembly insisted, Laurens reluctantly accepted the position, explaining that no man could reject the call of his fellow citizens. Assessing the new constitution, Laurens stressed the temporary nature of the document and concluded that "in our present situation with England, it is certainly a good Act, it can work no Evil & will be productive of much good."[14]

Neither Laurens nor Gadsden was blind to the new situation created by the British proclamation of an American rebellion. Both men could see that, besides serving as an important impetus for quick adoption of the constitution, the parliamentary action placed another difficult barrier in the path of reconciliation. This brought sorrow to Laurens, who declared that he would gladly sacrifice his life for a lasting settlement, "but I now begin to fear not only that Peace is at a distance but that reconciliation including filial dependance will never be effected."[15] Gadsden's evaluation of the situation brought similar conclusions, but, where Laurens saw looming catastrophe, Gadsden saw opportunity. Thus, on March 23, Gadsden took a leading role in the preparation of a new set of instructions for the South Carolina delegates to the Continental Congress. According to these new instructions, the delegates would be authorized to

> concert, agree to, and execute, every measure which they or he, together with a majority of the Continental Congress, shall judge necessary, for the defense, security, interest and welfare of this colony in particular, and of America in general.[16]

Whether the Congress realized, as Gadsden surely did, the implications of these instructions is unclear. Nowhere in these orders was there any restraint against a vote for a motion for independence, a clause that had been carefully inserted into all previous instructions. Thus, while the new constitution emphasized the continued desire for reconciliation, the instructions to the delegates at Philadelphia opened the door for separation.

As this political drama was being played out, South Carolina leaders also had to worry about a developing military crisis. During mid-March, British warships again appeared off the coast of the Carolinas, and it was feared that the long-awaited invasion was at hand. The British had developed plans to reduce the Carolinas through a coordinated attack from several sides during 1776. According to the original plan, a naval force under Sir Peter Parker was to rendezvous off the coast of Cape Fear during February 1776 with a military force under Sir Henry Clinton. This combination would land on the Carolina coast, while backcountry Loyalists and Indians were to rise simultaneously on the frontier. These plans were upset from the start, and by the time the mission was ended all involved on the British side wished they had stayed at home. For one thing, the operation was poorly coordinated, as both Clinton and Parker fell far behind schedule. Clinton did not arrive at the rendezvous site until mid-March, and most of Parker's fleet did not filter in until late May. Not until June were the British forces prepared to attack and, by then, they had learned that the Loyalists had already been routed. Yet, determined that some use must be made of the fleet and the over three thousand men, Parker and Clinton decided to move against Charles Town in early June.[17]

With the long-expected attack now imminent, the South Carolina leaders prepared to meet it. Gadsden was now upon the scene to assume command of the South Carolina forces. He must have been disappointed by what he found, for in February, his regiment consisted of only 263 men, while that of Moultrie contained only 207. That these men were drawn almost entirely from the lower orders and appeared unresponsive to discipline made Gadsden's task seem even more difficult. His efforts were further hampered by his own lack of command and military experience. As David Ramsay pointed out, it was Gadsden's prominence in the patriot movement, rather than his military background, that was responsible for his appointment:

> For personal courage he was inferior to no man. In knowledge of the military art he had several equals and some superiors; but from the great confidence reposed in his patriotism and the popularity of his name, he was put at the head of the new military establishment.[18]

The delay in assembling their forces probably cost the British an easy victory for, had they attacked in April as Laurens expected, they would have moved against a poorly defended capital. Their delay allowed the patriots, who now dropped their personal antagonisms and worked together to defend their homes, time to turn Charles Town into a formidable defensive position.

When the patriots discovered Clinton's presence, shortly after his arrival off the North Carolina coast, they immediately called in the militia and began making serious defensive preparations. The military men, Gadsden and Moultrie, oversaw the preparations in the harbor, while Rutledge, Laurens, and the civil officials fortified the town itself. Despite having suffered several painful attacks of gout, Laurens undertook his task with his accustomed determination. He proudly informed his son that

> I, who you know had resolved never again to Mount a Horse, I, who thought it impossible for me to Gallop five Miles in a day, was seen for a Month & more every day on the back of a Lively Nag at 1/2 past 4 in the Morning sometimes Galloping 20 Miles before Breakfast & sometimes sitting the Horse 14 Hours in 18.

On June 4, General Charles Lee arrived to assume command, bringing with him reinforcements that brought the number of defenders to 6722, including about 3400 Continentals. By this time, Charles Town resembled an armed camp with barricaded streets, entrenchments throughout the town, and wharves cleared of buildings to facilitate batteries.[19]

Even more important was the work that Gadsden and Moultrie were doing in the harbor, for these fortifications would be the first line of defense against the invading British. There were two major posts in the harbor, Fort Johnson and Sullivan's Island, and both were in need of improvements. As the senior officer, Gadsden chose to defend Fort Johnson, as it was here that he felt the main attack would fall. While Gadsden improved the defenses of Fort Johnson, Moultrie was left with the more difficult task of finishing an incomplete fort on Sullivan's Island. Despite the frenzied efforts of the defenders, however, the palmetto-log fort was still incomplete when the British crossed the bar. With the arrival of General Lee, the regular South Carolina forces were taken into the Continental service, and Gadsden and Moultrie both received commissions as colonels in the Continental Army. Lee was not pleased with the harbor defenses, particularly those on Sullivan's Island. After surveying the palmetto fort, Lee observed that there was no avenue of escape, declared the fort to be a "slaughter-pen," and proposed that the island be abandoned. Rutledge, however, on the advice of Moultrie, overruled this proposal, and Lee bowed to the wishes of the president.[20]

On June 10 the British forces, joined now by the royal governor, Lord William Campbell, appeared at the bar and demanded that the South Carolinians surrender their arms and return to their allegiance to the Crown. When this request was refused, both sides prepared for battle. After reconnoitering the scene, Clinton and Parker decided that the works on Sullivan's Island were more susceptible to attack and, to Gadsden's frustration, took care to avoid the guns of Fort Johnson. Thus, when the attack finally came on June 28, Gadsden could do little more than watch as the British cannonballs lodged harmlessly in the spongy palmetto logs of the fort on Sullivan's Island. Moultrie's forces, on the other hand, launched a devastating fire upon the British ships that left Parker and Campbell wounded (Campbell later died of his wounds) and the British fleet crippled, with heavy casualties. Anxious to strike a blow, Gadsden fired three cannon shots, but, as expected, these fell well short of their targets. While the British ships remained in the harbor for another month, licking their wounds, Gadsden proposed that the crippled ships be attacked and destroyed. Lee, however, was content with the victory that had already been achieved and quickly rejected the rash suggestions of the zealous colonel.[21]

If this campaign ended in humiliation for the British, it ended in catastrophe for the Indians, particularly the Cherokee. Patriot leaders, including Henry Laurens, had long feared that the efforts of British Indian agents John Stuart and Alexander Cameron would lead to an attack by those "treacherous Devils," the Cherokee. In another poorly timed adventure, the Cherokee fell upon the frontier two days after the repulse of the

British fleet. The response was quick and furious, as each of the southern colonies launched an expedition against the Indians. The South Carolina militia under Colonel Andrew Williamson was particularly effective and, by October 1776, the Cherokee threat to South Carolina had been destroyed forever. This decisive victory was recognized by the treaty that followed, in which the Cherokee ceded all the lands east of the Unacaye Mountains to the South Carolina authorities.[22] The military threats faced and defeated by South Carolinians during the summer of 1776 left them both angry and confident. There was reason to be proud, for the repulse of the British fleet marked the first time that American forces had been able to inflict a defeat upon the British in open combat. They also did more than the arguments of Gadsden and all of his radical associates combined to prepare the colony for the final break with the mother country. The combination of bloodshed and a successful defense against attacks on several fronts led many to embrace a policy that they had been previously unwilling to consider.

While Charles Town was dealing with the British warships, the Continental Congress was discussing the question of independence. Though the South Carolina delegates had been relieved from the compulsion of voting against independence, they, unaware of recent developments, did not think that their colony was prepared to support such a measure. By July 1, only South Carolina and Pennsylvania were holding out against independence, while New York and Delaware remained divided. That night, Edward Rutledge convinced his fellow delegates Arthur Middleton, Thomas Lynch, Jr., and Thomas Heyward, Jr., that American sentiment was now in favor of independence. As it would be increasingly difficult to oppose this movement, Rutledge felt that the South Carolinians should change their vote in order to preserve American unity. Thus, on July 2, South Carolina joined the other colonies (excepting New York, which abstained) in the unanimous vote for independence. However, the delegates clearly feared that their action would not be popular at home. It took them until July 9 to finally report this important news to President Rutledge and, even then, they mentioned it only casually in the midst of other Congressional resolutions.[23]

This apprehension proved unnecessary, as the news of the Declaration of Independence was greeted with joyful celebrations when it reached Charles Town on August 2. The Declaration was proclaimed "with great Solemnity" on August 5 and a grand procession, which included all of the civil and military officers, moved to the Liberty Tree, where the document was read to an enthusiastic crowd of thousands. While Christopher Gadsden must have observed this culmination of his efforts with great pride and joy, not everyone could muster the same satisfaction. Among these was Henry Laurens. Though he accepted independence as a necessity after the failure of repeated efforts at reconciliation, Laurens could not help but feel sorrow that he was no longer a member of his beloved British Empire. To his son, he observed that

> the scene was Serious Important & Awful.—even at this Moment I feel a Tear of affection for the good old Country & for the People in it whom in general I dearly Love.—there I saw that Sword of State which I had before seen four several Times unsheathed in Declarations of War against France & Spain by the Georges now unsheathed & borne in a Declaration of War against George the third—I say even at this Moment my heart is full of the lively sensations of a dutiful Son, thrust by the hand of violence out of a Father's House into the wide World. what I have often with truth averred in London & Westminster I dare still aver, not a Sober Man & scarcely a single Man in America wished for seperation from Great Britain. Your King too, I feel for, he has been greatly deceived & abused.[24]

As hard as Laurens had worked to postpone or prevent this event, he would never, from then on, consider any peace that did not recognize American independence. For Laurens, the time for reconciliation was past. The British had had their chance to retain the allegiance of their American children, but had provoked their own ruin through the unwise policy of a wicked ministry.[25]

In addition to all of his other problems during 1776, Laurens was faced with the repeated pleas of his eldest son to return to America and take up arms in the service of his country. Since the beginning of the fighting, John Laurens had been anxious to participate in the struggle and, in the face of his father's repeated refusals, had even considered attaching himself to the Prussian army in an effort to learn the military art.[26] This sort of talk upset Laurens to no end. After the death of young James, Laurens became even more insistent that John drop his enthusiasm for the military and devote his undivided attention to his studies. In January 1776, he offered the sage advice to "be not ambitious of being half a Soldier half a Lawyer & good for nothing—aim at Character, which you could not expect in any high style if you were to commence Soldier tomorrow." Besides, continued Laurens, if young John returned at this point he would be so disgusted that, within a week, he would wish that he had never left London. Thus, Laurens felt that both his son and his country would be better served if John Laurens remained in England and completed his legal studies.[27] As long as Laurens retained hopes for reconciliation, he was determined to prevent his son, whom he knew to be fearless and something of a firebrand, from recklessly throwing away a promising future. After the Declaration of Independence finally crushed his hopes for a settlement, Laurens at last granted his son permission to return to America.[28] Even then, John Laurens's departure was delayed by his hastily arranged marriage to Martha Manning, daughter of his father's close friend William Manning, and the birth of a daughter.

Though the exact date of the marriage of John and Martha Laurens is unknown, the fact that their daughter was baptized on February 18, 1777, strongly suggests that Martha Manning was pregnant when she married John Laurens. Shortly after the birth of his first and only child, John Laurens left his new family and landed at Charles Town on April 15, 1777.[29]

The question of independence permeated the atmosphere during 1776. The appearance of *Common Sense* intensified Gadsden's feelings concerning independence and led him to expound his views publicly before the Provincial Congress. Though Gadsden's (and Paine's) arguments surely converted some to the independence movement, it was continued British blundering that provided the main propulsion toward independence. The majority prayed fruitlessly for British concessions. When positive news from London might have blocked ratification of the constitution of 1776, the only news was a proclamation of rebellion placing the Americans outside the royal protection. Even then, some South Carolinians, including Henry Laurens, continued to hope for a change of policy that might save the empire at the eleventh hour. Instead, they were faced with a strong naval and military assault upon Charles Town, accompanied by the uprising of the Cherokee on the frontier.

Under these circumstances, even moderates such as Henry Laurens were converted to the independence movement. For Laurens, the years since 1765 had been tortuous, as his hopes of more conciliatory attitudes on both sides were repeatedly disappointed. By 1776, Laurens understood that he was fighting a losing battle. When news of the Declaration of Independence arrived on August 2, Laurens could comfort himself with the knowledge that he had done everything within his power to avoid the final break. The day he had long feared was upon him and Laurens tearfully exchanged his British citizenship for a new identity. Convinced of the justice of his cause, Laurens looked to the future and joined Gadsden in unwavering support for the new nation.

11

The Eclipse of Christopher Gadsden, 1776–1778

THE ADOPTION OF THE DECLARATION OF INDEPENDENCE MARKED A TURNING point in the career of Christopher Gadsden. For more than a decade he had enjoyed the prestige of being foremost in the resistance to British policy in South Carolina. In these years a premium had been placed on his ability to create and maintain suspicions against the actions and motivations of British officials. Events had moved quickly during the last few years and culminated in triumph as the colony of South Carolina was transformed into the state of South Carolina. For these developments, no man could claim a greater share of the responsibility than Christopher Gadsden. Yet, even as he proudly surveyed this accomplishment, a new and greater challenge had presented itself. Having annihilated British rule, South Carolinians were now faced with the problem of building and defending a new government and society. For Gadsden, this was truly a problem, as many of the traits that had made him so successful as a revolutionary—his singleness of purpose, his suspiciousness, his zeal, his rashness, and his daring—were not particularly desirable in a statesman.

Though Gadsden looked forward to playing a leading role in the government of the newly independent state, a sober look at the political situation during 1776 would have provided reason for concern. The moderate element, which included the Rutledge brothers, Henry Laurens, and Rawlins Lowndes, was clearly in the dominant political position. This group had never approached the idea of independence with any enthusiasm. Indeed, they had opposed Gadsden and the radicals on almost every issue, including that of independence. They held out until invasion, bloodshed, and action by the Continental Congress forced their hand. And, as future events would demonstrate, some of them were still not wholehearted in support of independence. Under these circumstances, a less-confident and secure man than Gadsden might well have been anxious about his political future. The next few years would in fact bring great disappointment to Gadsden. He would become increasingly isolated as his old allies, the mechanics, found him too conservative for their emerging social and political demands, while he remained anathema to the moderates. Thus, by the end of

183

1778, it seemed that Christopher Gadsden retained only that influence that could be commanded by his forceful personality and the prestige of his patriotic name.

For Gadsden, the first half of 1776 had been extremely busy, personally as well as professionally. In addition to his public services, Gadsden had also found time to marry his third and final wife. On April 14, 1776, he had married Ann Wragg, a first cousin of his old nemesis William Wragg, and a member of one of the wealthiest and most prominent Tory families in South Carolina. Despite this background, however, Ann Gadsden always stood firmly behind her husband, even during the darkest days, and the couple enjoyed a happy marriage until his death in 1805.[1] The successful defense against the British fleet brought great prestige to both Moultrie and Gadsden, and both men were promoted to the rank of brigadier general in the Continental Army on September 17, 1776.[2] After the battle, Gadsden assumed command at Sullivan's Island and began to make improvements to guard against the event of another British attack. The most significant and time-consuming project of late 1776 and early 1777 was the construction of a bridge that would connect the island with the mainland. General Lee had ordered the construction of a bridge that would allow the escape of the garrison if, as Lee expected, the fort could not withstand an attack. The fragile structure that emerged was practically worthless, one that Moultrie laughed at as being more useful to the British than to his own men.[3]

When Gadsden assumed command on Sullivan's Island, he made the construction of a permanent bridge his first priority. This project commenced during September 1776 and was not completed until the following June. Gadsden devoted much of his time to the bridge and was quite proud of the finished product. The completed bridge was a rather curious object, as it covered nearly three-fourths of a mile, but was zigzagged rather than straight. Realizing that the bridge must be sturdy enough to support the weight of cannons and large numbers of men, Gadsden took care to ensure that the bridge was well built. The bridge was constructed of wood, overlaid with sheets of iron, and was high enough that boats could pass below and wide enough to allow ten to twelve men to march abreast upon it. Gadsden was convinced that his efforts had greatly strengthened the defenses of Charles Town, and declared that the harbor was now "almost as strong as Gibraltar." He continued to take pride in this accomplishment and, in 1778, proudly observed that the bridge, named in his honor, was so solid that it had emerged virtually unscathed from a damaging hurricane.[4]

Gadsden was also proud of his rank in the Continental Army and enjoyed the prestige of being the highest-ranking South Carolinian in the service. Unfortunately, his pride would shortly combine with his temper to cost him his rank and cause another embarrassing public controversy. After the defeat of the British fleet, General Charles Lee remained in Charles Town until the early fall of 1776, when he embarked upon a campaign against St. Augustine. Thereupon, Brigadier General Robert Howe, a North Carolinian who had arrived with Lee in June, assumed command in South Carolina. In November 1776, Howe left for a campaign in Georgia and, noting that Gadsden was occupied with the construction of his bridge, turned the command over to Moultrie. When Moultrie also joined the Georgia campaign, the command devolved onto Gadsden. Apparently this position was agreeable to Gadsden, for he was reluctant to return the command to Howe when the latter returned to Charles Town in 1777. Howe saw no reason why this should be a problem, as he had been a brigadier general six months longer than Gadsden and, thus, outranked him. But major problems did develop and Gadsden was not the only one in South Carolina who was dissatisfied with Howe. The general was an unpopular figure in Charles Town, a sentiment reflected in the resignations submitted by several officers when he resumed command. Many in South Carolina questioned Howe's competence after his failure to take St. Augustine, while others were unhappy that he had ordered many of the South Carolina troops to remain in Georgia, whereas most of the North Carolinians were allowed to return home. In addition, many were offended by Howe's personal conduct, as he was separated from his wife and had attained quite a reputation as a womanizer. The situation intensified when Howe asked Moultrie and Gadsden for an explanation as to why so many officers were resigning their commissions. The answer of these two generals is unknown, but the resulting hostility between Howe and Gadsden suggests that Gadsden bluntly challenged Howe's competence.[5]

As the situation developed, Gadsden took steps to challenge Howe's right to command in South Carolina. Hoping that Howe's commission did not date before his and that Howe had received no orders to leave Georgia and return to South Carolina, Gadsden requested that President John Rutledge obtain a list of the Continental officers and their dates of commission. Gadsden knew that Rutledge was unlikely to do him any favors and, when the president seemed unresponsive, he turned to the General Assembly. In August 1777, William Henry Drayton, seconded by Rawlins Lowndes and Gadsden himself, moved that an inquiry be launched into Howe's right to command. With the assembly dominated by moderates who had no love for either Gadsden or Drayton, the resolution seemed doomed to failure. Still, Gadsden's defeat cannot be attributed entirely, as Gadsden himself asserted, to his personal unpopularity among the moderates, as Howe was not a popular figure either. Most of the members agreed with John Lewis Gervais, who observed to Laurens that Drayton's request was "an extraordinary motion," for "I don't know What can be said on the Subject it seems a plain Case he [Howe] is a Senior Officer. I am not blinded by partiality, you know Genl. How is no favourite of mine."[6]

While Gadsden understood that the motion had little chance of success, he did not expect it to be rejected out-of-hand. When the assembly refused to even consider the matter, Gadsden angrily and impulsively resigned his commission. Henry Laurens, serving as a delegate to the Continental Congress, was kept abreast of developments in South Carolina by Gervais and Rutledge, among others. Laurens described the scene of Gadsden's resignation in a letter to his son:

> Gen. Gadsden moved by means of the Chief Justice [Drayton] in August the House of Assembly to enquire into the nature of Gen. Howe's appointment the House by a large majority rejected the proposition, the humble General immediately stripped off the Bauble as he called it, the Ribband, in the House, tendered his Commission to G.H.—who politely declining to receive it abruptly—he threw it as politely into the General's Hat, next day he appeared in plain habit & the day following it was signified in Public orders that General Gadsden had resigned—what follies spring from a sensible Man.[7]

Though Howe had not desired Gadsden's resignation, he had little choice but to accept it when offered in this manner. In submitting the resignation to Congress, Howe sent a report describing the situation and explaining that the assembly had rejected Gadsden's arguments concerning the command. He informed the Congress that he had tried to refuse the resignation, but was forced by Gadsden's insistence to accept it. While this letter contained a balanced account of the dispute and no personal criticism of Gadsden's conduct, the same cannot be said of a private letter Howe sent to Laurens on the same date. Howe was clearly familiar with the hostility between Gadsden and Laurens and hoped to take advantage of it to convince Laurens to use his influence in Philadelphia on his behalf. Howe begged Laurens to obtain for him a promotion to the rank of major general. Such an effect, he argued, would settle the current dispute and prevent him from being "persecuted by the Malevolence of that Party to whose views you cannot be a Stranger, & from whose principles You cannot be averse." He also requested that a firmer separation be placed between the civil and military authorities so that "designing Men may not have room to Cavil or have an opportunity of promoting their own private views under the cover of publick confusion."[8]

Gadsden was not disappointed that the matter was referred to the Continental Congress, as he was confident of a sympathetic hearing from former friends and colleagues. Thus, he was surprised and disappointed when the Continental Congress, already disgusted by several other resignations submitted after similarly petty disputes, accepted his resignation without debate. For this development, Gadsden placed the blame squarely on his "greatest and most inveterate Enemy," Henry Laurens.[9] Realizing that he had no friends among the current South Carolina delegation, Gadsden bided his time, waiting for an opportunity to place his case before Congress. In the meantime, the Continental Congress decided to solve the problem within South Carolina by promoting Howe to major general and transferring him to Washington's headquarters. Shortly afterwards, however, Congress reversed its decision to transfer Howe, and the general remained in South Carolina.[10]

Gadsden had a long time to wait before he could set his side of the story before Congress. But, with the arrival of William Henry Drayton in Philadelphia during late March 1778, Gadsden was ready to proceed. On June 1, he wrote to Drayton that he had not received a fair hearing before Congress because "my Arch Enemy by some dextrous Movement took to time it so when they had just before thought themselves indelicately treated by 2 or 3 Officers who seemed to threaten them with a resignation." This arch enemy was Henry Laurens, who, Gadsden mistakenly believed, was serving as president of the Continental Congress when his resignation was received. Gadsden was careful to insist that none of his actions had been motivated by disrespect for Congress. Indeed, he reminded Drayton, no man had done more than he to establish a Congress in 1765 and to respect and support it since that time. Rather, he was convinced that General Howe had no authority to resume command in South Carolina and explained that all he desired was that if such orders did exist, that Howe produce them. His resignation proceeded from "as *you know* the Indelicate Treatment of a thin House" when he tried to explain his position to the assembly. Thus, "as I think I now have a fairer Opportunity from having some Friends among our Delegates which was *not* the case before," Gadsden asked Drayton to show his letter to Richard Henry Lee and other delegates, who might then join together to justify his conduct.[11]

On July 4, Gadsden again took up his pen and wrote to Drayton about this affair. He repeated that the sole question in dispute was by what authority Howe had left Georgia and returned to the South Carolina command. When Gadsden found that Howe based his command solely upon the verbal orders of General Lee, he felt within his rights to request a Congressional investigation. He was genuinely hurt that Congress had refused to grant him a hearing, particularly after they had listened to Howe. He confessed that he was not surprised that the South Carolina delegates had said nothing in his support, but was hurt that the New Englanders, whom he had always defended against attack, made no effort to help him.[12]

After again complimenting himself upon his patriotism and insisting that he meant no disrespect to the Congress, Gadsden turned to Howe's report of August 28, 1777, which he had only recently seen. He launched a lengthy attack upon Howe, accusing the general of using misrepresentations, half-truths, and even outright lies in an effort to blur the real issues. Though Gadsden thought that the events that had occurred before Howe left

Georgia were irrelevant to this dispute, he nevertheless denied that Howe had exercised any command over him, even before he left Charles Town. Rather, Gadsden insisted, he had received his orders and directions from General Lee and President Rutledge. Yet the main question concerned Howe's resumption of command when he returned from Georgia. Gadsden again declared that Howe had no orders to return to South Carolina and thus his conduct could only be seen as

> a mere subterfuge, a piece of downright low cunning, Jockeying and sharping, and none but a Man determined at any rate to wedge himself into Command would stoop to it, the effect of low ambition indeed.

What it all came down to, from Gadsden's perspective, was that Howe had left one command for another without orders. Such an action was ridiculous, for no army allowed its officers to move from one command to another at their own personal whim. Gadsden explained that it was the customary procedure that when an officer assumed command from a brother officer, he present his authorization for doing so. This was only common sense and Howe had refused to comply with it. Again, Gadsden insisted that if Howe had shown him any legitimate authorization, he would have gladly relinquished the command, regardless of his personal doubts about Howe's competence. But Howe had not done this, and Congressional approval of his conduct would only confirm Howe's apparent belief that he was the "light, Itinerant Brigadier General Knight Errant to General Lee's whole Department."[13]

Gadsden then proceeded to take another look at the refusal of the South Carolina assembly to consider Drayton's motion to discover Howe's authority for assuming command in the state. Declaring that "no man has shewn himself more dextrous in the Political intriguing way than General Howe," Gadsden asserted that the general had joined together with his political enemies to misrepresent the motion to the assembly. These enemies had succeeded in convincing the thin House (only 89 of the 202 members were present) that the motion was an insult to the Continental Congress. Once the members discovered the true nature of the motion, Gadsden insisted, they regretted voting against it. Stating that Howe's letter had falsely portrayed his conduct in a poor light, Gadsden accused Laurens of placing the letter before Congress at an inopportune moment:

> If it had not been *necessarily* laid before Congress by the greatest and most inveterate Enemy I have in the world. I might then have thought the *Contretemps* owing to my ill luck only, and that Howe's immediate promotion was not set on foot by, and made part of a gratification to an individual for his outing me.

Finally, Gadsden directed his friend to circulate this letter in and out of Congress, emphasizing that it be shown to South Carolina delegates Thomas Heyward, Jr., John Mathews, and Richard Hutson. No mention was made of the remaining South Carolina delegate, Henry Laurens.[14]

Gadsden was naive if he thought that the contents of his letter could be kept from Laurens. When Laurens learned of the letter he was absolutely furious and he denounced Gadsden's charges as groundless. He insisted that he had played no role in the acceptance of the resignation and described the incident in a letter to John Lewis Gervais:

> His resignation was tendered to Congress the 2nd of October by Mr. Hancock. I was order'd in the Chair the 1st of November. It is true I said nothing upon the occasion: neither did any Member in the house, except those who said, "accept it," "accept it," I was not one of them. I should have been very cautious should it have been put to a vote, even of giving my voice against it. 'Tis probable I should have withdrawn upon such an occasion—the risk of offending would have been equal on either side. When Mr. Gadsden was in the service I now am in, he knows, I endeavoured to assist and serve him & God knows I never attempted to undervalue or depreciate him—if he had any foundation for censuring me, he should have communicated his complaints directly to myself or have reserv'd them to be communicated at my return, instead of such generous procedure, he has, according to his custom, stabb'd me in conversations and private letters.

Laurens then instructed Gervais to read this passage to Gadsden, for "it will keep up a consistency in all my conduct toward that Gentleman."[15]

Though Laurens hoped that this explanation would put an end to the conflict, or at least to his part in it, he was soon surprised by the contents of Gadsden's letter of July 4. Gadsden had sent copies of this letter to several individuals in Philadelphia, one of which fell into Laurens's hands. Laurens was enraged by this latest effort "to ruin me among the People with whom I live in the strictest harmony, and from whom I have the honor of receiving daily marks of friendship and respect." To Gervais, Laurens made it clear that he was losing patience with these secret attacks and that if an immediate end were not put to them, Gadsden might find himself faced with more serious trouble than an angry letter:

> and as he must feel conviction of his error, I expect from him an immediate and ample acknowledgement to each of the Persons to whom he has written, and to as many as possible to whom he has related such Articles contained in that Letter as respect my Character, even this will fall far short of that justice which a vindictive Mind would demand, and which a generous Heart would, without prompting, express immediately upon discovery of so great a fault. I am willing to sacrifice at the Shrine of Peace all that I might further with strict propriety exact from him.[16]

This letter did have some effect, as Gervais shortly reported that he had been informed by Rawlins Lowndes that Gadsden was prepared to offer apologies.[17]

The apology offered by Gadsden could hardly have satisfied Laurens, however:

> I thought Col. Laurens was President when my Affair happened. I am therefore sorry I mentioned that Circumstance, which and which alone I shall be obliged to you to expunge out of my Letter of the 4th July; no Person knows me better than he does and he can't mention an Instance of any Publick Matter (or I believe indeed private either) that ever I undertook, I did not go through with; therefore he above all others must think I must have had some extraordinary Reasons for my Acting so suddenly in the matter I did, and had he or any one of our Members only moved the Congress to give me an Opportunity to give my Reasons before my Commission was accepted it was all I wanted for. I had no Intention of taking it back. Tho' there is no love lost between him and I, yet I wou'd have done it for him. To go out upon any Question unless I really did not understand it, or that it related merely to myself, I ever looked upon as cowardly, and I never did and never will I hope in my life.[18]

While this was not exactly the apology Laurens was looking for, he realized that it was about the best he could expect and allowed the matter to drop here. This marked the end of the most heated dispute that had occurred between the two men since their friendship was destroyed over the Cherokee War sixteen years before. It was also to be the last major altercation between the two men. Each was now completely disenchanted with the other, and both seemed determined to avoid future conflict by avoiding contact whenever possible.

While Gadsden managed to avoid a violent confrontation with Henry Laurens, he was not to be so fortunate in his dealings with Robert Howe. Gadsden could not have been surprised when Howe called upon him to either publicly apologize or meet him on the field of honor, as the violent abuse of the July 4 letter seemed almost calculated to draw such a challenge. When Gadsden received the challenge on August 17, he readily agreed to meet under any conditions named by the general. Indeed, Gadsden accused Howe of being the aggressor in sending Congress a biased report that completely ignored Gadsden's side of the story. The duel was arranged for August 30 at the Liberty Tree. Unfortunately, word of this event leaked and a large crowd gathered to observe the proceedings, with some even sitting in the tree itself. It was then decided that, in the interests of safety, the duel should be moved to the empty lot near the home of Mr. Percy. Upon reaching this location, the principals "paid each other the usual compliment of hat and hand" and declared that they were meeting to settle a point of honor. After each man charged his second not to prosecute the other if he should be killed, "eight very small paces" were marked off. The two men then stood looking at each other, neither anxious to fire first. After each offered and declined the first shot, they agreed to fire together. Still, neither fired. Howe then smiled and asked, "Why won't you fire, General Gadsden?" Gadsden replied, "You brought me out General Howe to this ball play and ought to begin the entertainment." Howe fired and missed. Gadsden took careful aim and fired deliberately wide of his target. When Gadsden invited Howe to fire again, the general refused, stating, "No! General Gadsden, I cannot after this." Colonel Barnard Elliott, acting as second for Gadsden, then exclaimed that both men had conducted themselves honorably and that Gadsden could not have made "a handsomer apology." Gadsden then told Howe that, though he might speak of this matter again in the future, he would henceforth refrain from using any harsh expressions concerning the general. This satisfied Howe and the two men shook hands and left the field.[19]

Thus ended the dispute between Gadsden and Howe over the command in South Carolina. Gadsden gained little and lost much by this affair. Once again, he had allowed his pride and temper to lead him into an inflexible stand that might have been avoided by sounder judgment. Questions of competence and personality aside, Howe had pursued the logical military course in returning to Charles Town after the completion of his Georgia expedition. This fact hurt Gadsden's case, leaving him with only the technicality of whether or not Howe had obtained direct orders from General Lee for his return. Though Gadsden would have been wise to accept the situation, he was a proud man of principle and felt that he had a right to the command. While Gadsden did retain his honor, he retained little else. His stance cost him his treasured military rank and led to a publicized duel that might have cost him his life. In addition, this dispute caused another serious altercation with Henry Laurens, opening old wounds and ensuring that no reconciliation could ever be achieved.

Even while Gadsden was engaged in this dispute, he saw his political fortunes eroding during the years between 1776 and 1778. Indeed, as he very well recognized, his declining political influence was a factor in the refusal of the General Assembly to support him in the controversy with Howe. Though Gadsden was deeply involved with the construction of his bridge during late 1776 and early 1777, he could always find time for politics. Here, his main attention was focused upon constitutional revision, as the Declaration of Independence had rendered the temporary constitution of 1776 obsolete. A new constitution that specifically affirmed independence was now Gadsden's driving passion and, according to David Ramsay, he "considered nothing done while this remained undone."[20]

Constitutional revision was no small problem in South Carolina, for the constitution of 1776 contained no provision for either amendment or replacement. Still, this did not prevent the General Assembly from appointing a committee of revision during October 1776. The origins of the new constitution lay among the committee recommendations of October 1776. David Ramsay and John Lewis Gervais both wrote that the elections held at this time were clearly intended to elect a new assembly that would draw up a new constitution.[21] Gadsden played a major role in the adoption of the new constitution. Though he certainly hoped to establish a more popular government, Gadsden also had a strong personal and political stake in the issue: he saw the new constitution as an opportunity to settle old scores with, and reduce the power of, the Rutledge brothers and the moderates who surrounded them. Gadsden had neither forgiven nor forgotten the refusal of his political foes in the assembly to allow him even the opportunity of stating his case in the Howe affair. Nor was he happy with the persistence of John Rutledge and his associates in delaying independence and blocking radical programs both before and after the break with Britain. Thus, Gadsden was an eager participant in any program that would curtail the power of the Rutledge element. Nevertheless, Rutledge and his allies presented formidable opposition and might have delayed the passage of the constitution even further if Gadsden and his supporters had not resorted to the familiar threat of refusing to pass any legislation until the document was ratified.[22]

A look at the constitution of 1778 explains why the moderates fought so hard against it. The document contained several major changes and marked another step on the road to democracy. Of these revisions, perhaps the most significant concerned the area of religion. The Church of England received the support of such formidable champions as Charles Pinckney and Rawlins Lowndes, but Gadsden and the dissenters finally carried the vote in favor of disestablishment. The "Christian Protestant Religion" was the official religion of the state and all of its various denominations would enjoy equal privileges under the law. Any fifteen adult white males could petition the legislature for incorporation as a congregation, and, when approved, receive the right to own and control their own religious property. Yet complete religious freedom was reserved only for Protestants. For one thing, the oath that would be required for incorporation would be impossible for Jews, and difficult for Catholics to take. The Jews would be eliminated by the requirement that the congregations accept both the Old and New Testaments as being of divine inspiration, while Catholics might object to the requirement that the Scriptures be the only basis of religious faith and practice. Moreover, while non-Protestants were allowed to vote if they acknowledged the existence of God and "a future State of Rewards and Punishments," they were excluded from holding office. Despite these inequities, however, freedom of religion in South Carolina was by and large enhanced by the constitution of 1778.[23]

The new constitution also included important political changes that would have the effect—if not the actual intention—of weakening the influence of the Rutledge faction. These liberal changes received support not only from Gadsden and Drayton, but also from a surprising new source: Rawlins Lowndes. While Lowndes and Gadsden had always been on friendly personal terms, Lowndes had never shown any inclination to support any policy that even hinted in the direction of democracy. It remains unclear why Lowndes chose to do so at this time, though it seems likely that he experienced some sort of falling out with John Rutledge. Regardless of motivation, it was Gadsden, Drayton, and Lowndes who led a direct assault upon the presidency, severely slashing the authority of the office. By the time they were through, even the title of the office had been changed, from "president" back to "governor." Under the new constitution, the legislature would still be empowered to elect the governor, and it would also gain the power to remove him for misconduct through impeachment. The executive veto, an issue that had been controversial in 1776, was now stripped from the governor, as was his fixed salary. The constitution did allow the governor a salary, but the amount was unspecified, leaving it to the annual discretion of the legislature. The principle of rotation in office was also extended to the governor, as he would be ineligible to serve again for four years after the expiration of his two-year term. As a final slap at Rutledge, a clause was inserted that would exclude the son, father, or brother of the Governor from a seat on the Privy Council. Thus, Gadsden and his colleagues had seriously reduced the power of the executive, bringing the governorship closer into line with the weak governorships being created by the other American states. In the process, to Gadsden's satisfaction, the personal power of John Rutledge was considerably decreased.[24]

The executive was not the only department to be transformed in a more democratic direction. The Legislative Council was abolished altogether and replaced by a Senate to be elected by the voters, rather than by the lower house of the assembly. This Senate would act as a true upper house, for, with the exception of introducing, altering, or amending money bills, the Senate would now possess all of the rights and privileges of the lower house. Meanwhile, the distribution of representation in the legislature produced mixed results. The west gained nothing in the assembly, as the proportion of seats between the low and backcountry remained the same. But the story was different in the Senate, where Charles Town and the surrounding area was allowed thirteen seats, the backcountry received eleven, and Beaufort and Georgetown garnered a combined total of five. Thus, Charles Town would not be able to dictate policy in the Senate. Though the backcountry still did not enjoy equitable representation in the legislature, backcountry settlers could be encouraged by a provision for reapportionment. The constitution called for a reapportionment in 1785, and then at fourteen-year intervals, to establish a fair representation based on white population and taxable property. Thus, while the government remained firmly in the hands of the low-country elite, the machinery was in place to eventually establish a more fair distribution of power.[25]

The constitution of 1778 also slightly extended the suffrage. The property requirement was largely unchanged, as any adult white male could vote if he possessed fifty acres of land free of debt or a town lot, or if he paid taxes equal to that of a fifty-acre holding. There would be no religious requirement other than a basic belief in God and an afterlife. This represented a slight liberalization of the colonial constitution, which required voters to be Christian. The elite, however, compensated for the extended suffrage by raising the property qualifications for office holding.[26] Thus, while a democratic victory was achieved by bringing the government closer to the people, the elite ensured their continued dominance with higher office-holding requirements. Finally, the constitution of 1778 provided a bill of rights, an item that had been missing from the document of 1776. Included among these rights was freedom of worship for all Protestants, freedom of the press, and the right to due process in legal matters. In addition, the military was formally subordinated to the civil power within the state.[27]

The constitution of 1778 represented a victory for Gadsden and the radicals over John Rutledge and the moderates who had kept the radicals largely in check for the past few years. Rutledge was not about to accept this defeat without a defiant gesture of his own. When the constitution was laid before him on March 5, 1778, Rutledge, to the dismay of all present, refused his approval. Instead, he delivered a speech outlining his objections to the document and then submitted his resignation from the presidency. In his speech, Rutledge presented three major reasons for his disapproval of the constitution: first, he asserted that the power to write a constitution resided solely with the people, not the legislature; second, he noted that he had taken an oath to enforce the constitution of 1776 until an accommodation could be reached with Britain, and he still viewed this as "an Event as desireable now as it ever was"; third, he found the new constitution to be too democratic, and he distrusted democracy as "its Effects have been found arbitrarily severe & destructive." To emphasize the latter point, Rutledge commented on the replacement of the appointed Legislative Council with the popularly elected Senate. He argued that this revision "annihilates one Branch of the Legislature" and was a far more democratic provision than the people desired. Thus, Rutledge refused to consent to a constitution that violated both his oath of office and his principles.[28]

Gadsden was among those who were stunned and angered by this speech, and an assessment of it indicates that, except for his denunciation of democracy, Rutledge's objections were in fact inconsistent with his past statements and actions. His insistence that he had sworn to uphold the constitution of 1776, which contained no provision for revision (until an accommodation was reached with Britain) conflicted with the changed political situation and with his own past actions. The 1776 constitution was, after all, an explicitly temporary measure, the purpose of which was rendered obsolete by the Declaration of Independence. Rutledge's assertion that an accommodation with Britain was still desirable conflicted with the previous acceptance of independence both by himself and by the state. If Rutledge had been uncompromising in his opposition to independence, then it would have been proper to resign his office immediately after independence was declared. Not only had he refrained from doing that, but he had also approved several alterations in the constitution that would recognize the new political situation. Nor was his objection to the manner in which the new constitution was written and approved consistent with either the facts or his own actions. If Rutledge was convinced that a constitution had to be written by the people, then how could he explain his conduct concerning the constitution of 1776? Rutledge was a prominent member of the committee that had written that document, and he had urged its adoption despite the fact that the legislature had no popular mandate to perform such a function. Indeed, the constitution of 1776 had been adopted in a far less democratic manner than the new one. John Lewis Gervais, certainly no friend to Gadsden and the radicals, informed Laurens that the recent elections had been held with the understanding that the assembly would replace or alter the constitution.[29] Thus, Rutledge's arguments against the legality of the constitution lacked credibility. While his expressed desire for an accommodation might be accepted as genuine, the main reasons for his conduct appear to have been his fear of democracy and his anger at the reduction of his own power.

It has been suggested that Rutledge used his resignation as a political weapon designed to throw the legislature into chaos and force the removal of some of the more democratic provisions from the constitution. If so, he nearly succeeded, as the assembly was shocked by the unexpected occurrence and, as related by Gervais, "stood amazed looking at one another." Rutledge had certainly created confusion, and he was arguably the most popular man in South Carolina. Yet, if he hoped that his popularity would carry the day, he was to be disappointed, as Gadsden and Lowndes quickly joined forces to restore order. After the initial shock, Lowndes rose and, though disapproving of Rutledge's reasons for rejecting the constitution, congratulated him on having the courage to act upon his conscience regardless of personal consequences. He then proposed that a committee should be established to decide what should be done in this situation. Gadsden seconded the motion, though he was not so charitable toward Rutledge and severely censured his conduct. The motion was accepted and a committee selected from both Houses reported the next day that Rutledge had the right to resign, that his resignation should be accepted, and that a successor should be chosen the following day.[30]

This election did little to stabilize the situation, for when Arthur Middleton was elected to succeed Rutledge, he declined the honor, declaring that he, too, disapproved of the new constitution. Another vote was taken amid further confusion. While no one could muster a majority of votes, Lowndes and Gadsden, with fifty-four and forty-eight votes respectively, were the only candidates to receive significant support. Thereupon, Lowndes attempted to withdraw and, in a generous gesture, asked that his votes be given to Gadsden, the more capable candidate. The thought of Christopher Gadsden exercising even the weakened powers of the governor was a nightmare that few among the moderates wished to see transformed into reality. Thus, they banded together to elect Lowndes. Citing the precarious political situation of the state, Lowndes accepted the office. Yet, perhaps in an effort to give the impression of continuity, he decided to retain the title of president.[31] Shortly afterward, Gadsden was selected to serve as vice president. He was unhappy with this development, as he understood it to be a tricky political move by the Rutledge element "to get rid of me at the next meeting and to make me ineligible at next Election." The unhappy Gadsden informed Drayton that he had been elected by a poorly attended House at the end of a session and only accepted to avoid "throwing the State into Confusion."[32]

The resignation of John Rutledge was a political event of great importance in South Carolina. His conduct had thrown the assembly into confusion and threatened to reverse the approval given to the new constitution. Gadsden and Lowndes had managed to stabilize the situation, but now found themselves faced with the unenviable task of running the government with the powerful and hostile Rutledge faction in opposition. Few could approve of Rutledge's conduct in resigning the presidency. Even Henry Laurens, now in Philadelphia, could not sanction the action of his friend. Laurens informed Rutledge that, though he shared his views on the constitution, "you ought to have done every thing you did, the last act excepted." Yet, even then, it was not Rutledge, but Gadsden, whom he blamed for this unfortunate situation, informing John Laurens that "That Restless Spirit continues like the troubled element in which he has been so long dabling. I mean an old Neighbor of ours. I see he has been at the bottom of this untoward event."[33]

While Laurens was willing to excuse Rutledge's behavior, Gadsden was not. When a motion was introduced into the assembly to thank Rutledge for his services, Gadsden led a challenge that resulted in a floor debate on the question. When the motion finally passed by the vote of sixty-eight to fifteen, Gadsden seconded the motion of Charles Pinckney that the thanks of the assembly should specifically exempt Rutledge's speech rejecting the constitution. This motion was accepted, though in a modified form, and the final resolution thanked Rutledge for his services "from the commencement of his administration to the time of his resignation."[34] Though Gadsden must have savored this victory over his most powerful rival, he had little time to enjoy it. Lowndes, who was now disowned by the moderates as a turncoat, and Gadsden, who had never been a favorite of the moderates, were placed in a very difficult political situation. They had to implement and support a new government in the face of determined opposition from the Rutledge faction, which represented a significant bloc in the legislature.

Gadsden was about to get another taste of just how quickly political fortunes could change in South Carolina. Within months of his greatest victory over John Rutledge, he was to be dealt his most crushing defeat. When the adoption of the constitution of 1778 formally ended all hope of reconciliation, the South Carolina assembly passed an act requiring every free adult male inhabitant to swear allegiance to the state and to help defend it against George III and his minions. Failure to comply would be accompanied by severe penalties, including the loss of legal and political rights, as well as the right to buy and sell property and to engage in any profession or trade. Those individuals who left the state rather than take the oath were to be banished and subject to treason trials and the death penalty if they should ever return. This program led many of the Tories and even some of the moderate patriots to begin making plans for departure. The situation changed dramatically, however, when, in late May 1778, news arrived that the French had recognized American independence and were preparing to enter the war. This stiffened the resolve of many who had formerly doubted whether the American states could successfully defend their independence. As men rushed to sign the loyalty oaths, feelings grew high against the Tories and others in Charles Town who still refused to sign. Into this situation, in another case of incredibly poor timing, came two new recommendations from the Continental Congress: a suggestion that the states extend the time allotted for the swearing of the loyalty oaths, and that amnesty be extended to those who had not yet signed, but were willing to do so by June 10.[35]

President Lowndes understood the difficulty of this situation. Noting that they had received the approval of both the Continental Congress and General Washington, he thought the recommendations to be benevolent and reasonable. Yet he also realized that, with anti-Tory feelings running so high, such a proclamation could spark another round of violence in Charles Town. The mechanics had long felt that the government was too indulgent toward the Tories and the lukewarm supporters of America. With news of the French alliance, the mechanics were determined to prevent any more coddling of the Tories. To add to his problems, Lowndes was dealing with the recent death of one son and the imminent death of another. Thus, he remained undecided for several days, during which Gadsden repeatedly urged him to issue the proclamation. While it might seem surprising that Gadsden would support such a moderate measure, Gadsden had a strong sense of justice, and he considered this proclamation a fair and reasonable policy. Gadsden believed that just and responsive governments had been established at both the national and state levels and that their authority must be respected. Lowndes finally issued the proclamation on June 5 and, as feared, Charles Town erupted in violence. Lowndes reported to Laurens that "the Bells of St. Michael's were set ringing, the people collected and my Conduct reprehended in the severest terms" and that "the People were in such a ferment that fatal consequences were to be apprehended if I did not recall the Proclamation."[36]

This unhappy crowd included many of the same mechanics with whom Gadsden had been closely allied since the outbreak of the conflict with Britain. Nevertheless, Gadsden stormed into the midst of the new crisis with his customary courage and zeal, determined that the law be enforced. Gadsden wrote that the proclamation had "hardly got into the Sherrif's Hands before some Myrmidons Alarm'd the Town." The mob then sent a delegation to meet the president, and according to Gadsden,

> His Proclamation was returned to him in my presence which of itself was Insult enough but besides that the spokesman Mr. Ward told the President He thought the people were right and he would lose the last Drop of Blood to support them. This I thought so high an Insult that I immediately began with Ward, sarcastically applauded his Heroism and great Exertions for the publick Good. In return he told me I was a Madman, but first took Care to sneak out of my reach, however, had he not, I should have done nothing more, as I was prepared, than what I did, laugh in his Face.

When a public meeting was called that evening to discuss the matter, Gadsden boldly attended in an effort to calm the people. But he "found them chiefly a Mere Mob" and, according to John Lewis Gervais, "was used pretty ruffly by some of them." Yet Gadsden was not one to be intimidated and

> told them I advised the Measure, and that they should put a Halter about my Neck and hang me at once if they thought it wrong. That they had a Constitutional Remedy; they might impeach the President and Council if they had acted improperly and that they had better do that.

Gadsden promised the crowd that he would perform his duty and personally administer the oath to any who cared to take it, and he and Lowndes did precisely this during the next few days.[37]

Gadsden was determined to have the proclamation printed, but found this to be a difficult proposition. While Peter Timothy was recovering from the effects of a major fire on January 15, 1778, the only press in operation was that of John Wells, a conservative who was unwilling to do any favors for either Gadsden or Lowndes. Noting the unpopularity of both men, Wells declared that he "had not the Smallest idea of being a *Scape Goat.*"[38] Thus rejected, Gadsden turned to his old friend Timothy, reminded him of their old friendship and the great amounts of public business that had always been conferred upon him, and asked his friend to print the proclamation. His plea struck a chord: Timothy declared that he would not desert an old friend, and he managed to print several copies of the document.[39]

In analyzing this problem, Gadsden was certain that the mob had been incited by the Rutledge faction. His suspicions were enhanced by the public meeting on June 5, during which several men asserted that nothing like this would have happened if John Rutledge was still president. That Edward Rutledge was present at another public meeting held on June 10, and was even rumored to have authored one of the resolutions of the meeting, further confirmed Gadsden in this opinion.[40] While it would be ridiculous to blame this entire incident upon the Rutledges, they clearly enjoyed the discomfort of Lowndes and Gadsden and did little to relieve the pressure on their rivals. They had suffered a serious defeat a few months before, but had now turned the tables and could enjoy the crippling blow suffered by Lowndes and Gadsden.

Lowndes had never been a popular figure among the mechanics, and this incident served to intensify their low opinion of him. For Gadsden, however, the incident was a watershed, for it caused him to lose the support of the group upon which he had long depended. The alliance between Gadsden and the mechanics had never been one based on complete agreement. Later in life, Gadsden presented an insightful evaluation of himself:

> In his political principles he was an excellent representative of the liberal portion of the South Carolina aristocracy—insistent on the rights of self-government, but with standards of public order and official responsibility practically precluding anything more democratic than popular rights with aristocratic leadership. Despite impetuosity to the point of rashness, and a temper he controlled with the greatest difficulty, his integrity and religious zeal, his courage, optimism, and energy made him an invaluable champion.[41]

Such a champion had indeed proven invaluable to the mechanics in the years before 1778. During the political crises of the 1760s and 1770s, Gadsden and the mechanics could heartily join together in organizing resistance to British authority. But, though they pursued similar policies, they did so for different reasons. For Gadsden, the struggle was largely constitutional, and the anti-British measures were pursued to force changes in

British policy. For the mechanics, however, the conflict was primarily economic, and they embraced the boycotts and emphasis upon domestic manufactures as a means of mere survival. Even after independence, the mechanics and Gadsden could still cooperate, as the artisans supported Gadsden's efforts to obtain a constitution that guaranteed popular rights. He felt that this goal had been achieved in 1778 and was content to maintain a government controlled by the elite, but that governed in the interests of the people. While this philosophy was liberal, it was hardly democratic. What Gadsden considered to be a conclusion, the mechanics looked upon as a beginning. With the mechanics determined to continue in the democratic direction, the final split with Gadsden was only a matter of time.[42]

Gadsden realized that his new unpopularity had crippled him politically. Yet he was determined that the riot of June 1778 should be investigated and hoped that an inquiry would connect the disorder to the Rutledge faction. A committee was appointed by the assembly, but the membership, which included Edward Rutledge, virtually guaranteed that the investigation would not be serious. Even John Lewis Gervais was disgusted with this travesty and declared that "never was a business carried with more partiality, the whole aim is to censure the president & to let the people get clear." Gervais expected the report to be so hostile to Lowndes that the president would have little choice but to resign. He sighed that "we shall make a pretty figure in the eyes of the World that we can't agree 6 months with a Governor of our Own chusing."[43] Though Lowndes did not attempt to resign when the committee refused to support him, Gadsden did. Citing the long and meritorious service performed by Rawlins Lowndes, Gadsden angrily denounced the refusal of the assembly to support him now. He emphasized the fact that he was not accustomed to quitting offices designed for the public service, but felt that he must give up this "station in which much insult has been experienced, more may be expected and little probability thro' want of *undelayed* support and countenance of being any use." He warned the assembly that if they allowed justice to be defeated by "an artful and indefatigable Cabal" that "none but dastardly Trimmers, ambitious Caballers, interested Jobbers will serve in a Department rendered so low, suspicious, and despicable." Gadsden was surprised when the assembly refused to accept his resignation and suspected that the refusal was motivated by a desire to keep him ineligible for the next legislative elections. Nevertheless, he agreed to continue as vice president.[44]

Gadsden might have retained the vice presidency, but he had no illusions about his own political future. While his famous name and patriotic reputation would continue to make him a force to be reckoned with, he had lost the main body of his support. Independence and the creation of the new state marked the culmination of his career, as Gadsden lacked the qualities necessary for effective leadership in the new political structure. He had achieved many of his goals and was too independent a personality to be a good party man. In August 1776 Gadsden had been at the height of his influence: the highest ranking local officer in an army that had just won an important military victory, and honored as the earliest and foremost proponent of the independence movement. Two years later he had lost almost everything, due, at least in part, to his own personality. His pride and temper had led him into an unnecessary dispute with General Howe that cost him his rank and ended in a duel.

Politically, Gadsden's decline was not so rapid, but equally disastrous. He had continued to represent the mechanics and other dissatisfied groups in the fight for constitutional revision during the period between 1776 and 1778. Here he achieved concrete results, creating a more democratic constitution in both the political and religious spheres. Coincidentally, he had achieved a satisfying political victory over his most prominent and powerful rival, John Rutledge. But here he was content to stop. As Gadsden himself noted, he was a champion of benevolent and liberal government, but under the leadership of the elite. He felt that these goals had largely been achieved by the constitution of 1778. For Gadsden, the revolution was now largely complete, and the work to be done was that of consolidation. Unfortunately, the nucleus of his support, the mechanics, had a larger agenda. When Gadsden found himself unable to support these new demands, the final and inevitable break occurred. The political position that Gadsden found himself in at the end of 1778 was hardly enviable: politically isolated in a powerless office. Still, Christopher Gadsden was neither a brooder nor a quitter, and he would continue to provide important service to the state. By this time, Gadsden might have consoled himself with the hope that things could only improve. If so, he was again mistaken, for his life would get far worse before it would turn for the better.

12

A Nationalist at Philadelphia: Henry Laurens in the Continental Congress, 1777–1778

W<small>HILE</small> G<small>ADSDEN WAS BEING ECLIPSED BETWEEN</small> 1776 <small>AND</small> 1779, H<small>ENRY</small> L<small>AU</small>-rens was developing into a respected and powerful national figure. After the victory at Sullivan's Island and the proclamation of independence, Laurens was finally allowed that respite he had so eagerly desired during 1775 and 1776. As his position as vice president was largely a position of honor that demanded little exertion on his part, Laurens was able to devote much of his time between August 1776 and June 1777 to his private affairs. In June 1777, however, he answered the call of his fellow citizens and jour-neyed to Philadelphia to represent his state in the Continental Congress. Though he hoped that this assignment would be brief, Laurens continued to serve in Congress until November 1779. He quickly became a prominent member of this body and even served as its president for over a year in 1777 and 1778. As president, Laurens presided over and played a leading role in several critical events in the history of the Congress. Though he was gener-ally careful to guard the interests of South Carolina, Laurens developed into a staunch nationalist during his service in Philadelphia.

Relieved from his most burdensome political duties by his election to the vice presidency, Laurens plunged into the difficult business of straighten-ing out the disordered affairs of his plantations. Though he made several visits to his various plantations during these months and even purchased new lands, Laurens was still dissatisfied with the state of his affairs when he set out for Philadelphia. In addition to the difficulty of repairing planta-tions in the midst of a war, Laurens was frustrated by his agreement to look after the disordered affairs of absent friends such as Ralph Izard. A severe attack of gout, which incapacitated Laurens during much of October 1776, took further time from his affairs.[1] Laurens's brief respite ended, however, on January 10, 1777, when the South Carolina legislature elected him to represent the state in the Continental Congress. Unhappy with this development, Laurens attempted to refuse, explaining that his private af-fairs would make departure impossible before May. When this delay was accepted, Laurens reluctantly agreed to the appointment, considering it a command from his fellow citizens that could not be refused. He arrived in

Philadelphia on July 21 and took his seat in Congress the following day.[2] The arrival of such a prominent figure as Henry Laurens was applauded by many delegates who could already observe that Congress had lost the services of many of its most capable members. Among the happiest at this new addition was John Adams, who informed his wife that Laurens

> is a great acquisition—one of the first Rank in his State, Lt. Governor, of ample Fortune, of great Experience, having been 20 Years in their assembly, of a clear Head and a firm Temper, of extensive knowledge, and much Travel. He has hitherto appeared as good a Member, as any We ever had in Congress. I wish that all the States would imitate this Example and send their best Men.[3]

Though Laurens had hoped to spend his first few weeks in Philadelphia as an observer, educating himself on the issues and sizing up his fellow delegates, his new colleagues had other ideas. Within three weeks, he was assigned to several major committees, including the Commerce Committee, the Treasury Board, and committees to assess the state of affairs in the northern department and the deep southern states, respectively.[4] Nor could he remain quiet for long, as Congress had adopted "vague & indigested plans" for an expedition against West Florida. Though Laurens agreed that it was necessary to expel the British from the Floridas, particularly "that Pestiferous Nest" St. Augustine, he considered the present plan to be hastily adopted and almost guaranteed to fail. His interference played a crucial role in leading Congress to reconsider and reverse the decision.[5]

Thus began the service of Henry Laurens in the Continental Congress. His early observations show him to be impressed by neither the Congress nor the ardor of the middle states. In fact, he detected so little patriotism in the middle states that he wished "ten thousand time [sic] more I had never come as a delegate."[6] Particularly disillusioning were the antics of what he termed "property men": men who had vigorously supported resistance to British policy until they discovered that such opposition could cost them their lives and property. Such men, insisted Laurens, could not be trusted, as they were interested only in personal gain and would place their allegiance accordingly. He feared that there were many such men in New York and Pennsylvania and warned John Lewis Gervais that there were also some in South Carolina. As British generals John Burgoyne and Sir William Howe led their armies against American targets, Laurens predicted that "if we were united & would act with vigour only three Months no British Troops would remain on this side the Lakes but such as were protected by Men of War or confined by prison Walls." He denounced the lack of patriotism of the property men and declared that if the American cause was lost "it will be the effect of their timidity & their pernicious examples."[7]

If Laurens was surprised by the activities of the property men, he was shocked by the procedures of Congress. From the beginning of his service, he was displeased by the manner in which Congress handled the Continental Army. In August 1777, he, like Gadsden before him, supported the request of Brigadier General Benedict Arnold for promotion. Arnold's request was denied, according to Laurens, "not because he was deficient in merit or that his demand was not well founded but because he asked for it & that granting at such instance would be derogatory to the honour of Congress."[8] Laurens was upset that Congress wasted so much time on small matters such as these (and his belief that they often decided such questions wrongly did not make him any happier) while there was so much real work to be done. In early September 1777, he complained that the "House of Idleness" wasted so much time that it often took six hours to transact business that could easily have been completed in half an hour. Never one to waste time, Laurens was outraged by the thought of squandering eight to ten hours a day in Congress, particularly at a time when his private affairs were in such a disordered state. He angrily told Gervais that

> it is extremely unreasonable in my Country Men to compel me to this useless Service, if they had only considered how much of my time had been devoted to theirs & how very little to my own affairs, I think common gratitude would have induced them to give me a moments respite—did they know how their delegates are now mis Spending time I am sure they would recall them or give them very Special orders—Congress is not the respectable body which I expected to have found.

A month later he informed his son that the situation had changed little and that he was tempted to return to South Carolina, with or without permission.[9]

Laurens's discomfort at this time was intensified by two other unrelated factors. In early September 1777, he received the alarming news that the Georgia assembly had recently passed a law to vacate the land titles of all absentees as of December 12, 1777. Realizing that his vast and profitable Georgia plantations fell under the letter of this act, Laurens quickly asked Joseph Clay, a Savannah resident who held power of attorney over his Georgia lands during his absence, to obtain a repeal, or at least an exemption, from this law. Adding that he would gladly leave Congress if he could obtain permission, Laurens insisted that he was looking after the interests of Georgia as well as those of South Carolina. Thus, he felt that he deserved the gratitude of Georgia, not the the confiscation of his lands. To his relief, the efforts of Clay and others were successful and the act was repealed.[10]

Laurens was also faced with the disagreeable necessity of consenting to the decision of his eldest son to enter the military. As John Laurens had reached his majority, there was little that his father could do to prevent his enlistment. Still, Laurens did not have to like this decision, and he made it perfectly clear to his son and to several of his friends that he felt that the young man could be more useful in another field. Yet, Laurens realized that his son was set upon his course and he approved of the position that John obtained on the staff of General Washington.[11] While this position was not as dangerous as some others, Laurens well knew that the zeal and recklessness of John Laurens could easily lead him into the middle of some fierce fighting. Though he often counseled his impetuous son to be cautious, Laurens worried that he might receive a report at any time of the death of young John Laurens. When this news finally did arrive, it proved almost as destructive to the father as the event itself had been to his son.

Laurens had ample reason for concern, not only for his son, but for his country as well. By the end of July 1777, Laurens reported that the British fleet had sailed from New York to an unknown destination. A month later, he was convinced that the fleet was bound for Charles Town, the capture of which would "ruin our United Cause, for in the capture of Charles Town I see the destruction of the confederacy."[12] By late August, however, it had become clear that Sir William Howe had targeted Philadelphia, rather than Charles Town. As the crisis neared, Laurens was hopeful that the impending battles against Howe in Pennsylvania and against John Burgoyne in New York might bring final victory:

> We are now at the Eve of a grand Crisis. Much blood will be spilled & possibly the fate of American Independence suspended or confirmed in the course of this Month. I feel confident of success persuaded that our Cause is good & that it cannot fail. Indeed the many false steps which have been taken by the mighty omnipotent British Generals, are enough to make every man on this side confident. However the event of War is uncertain.[13]

These hopes were dashed, however, by the British victory at the Battle of Brandywine on September 11. As the British approached Philadelphia, Congress agreed on Lancaster, some sixty miles to the west, as the new capital, should evacuation be necessary. On September 18, Washington warned Congress to depart at once. With no sign of panic, Laurens left Philadelphia early the next morning. Marking the beginning of a strong friendship, Laurens picked up the wounded Marquis de Lafayette and transported him to the military hospital at Bethlehem. From there he proceeded to Lancaster where, after a brief meeting, Congress adjourned to York, where they resumed business on October 1.[14]

As Congress settled into its new quarters, John Hancock announced his intention to resign the presidency. Laurens presented a motion that the House request Hancock to reconsider, but, to his surprise, his motion received no more than a second. When the customary motion of thanks was offered, however, Laurens joined the New England delegations in opposing it on the grounds that it was inappropriate to thank an official for the discharge of his official duties. When the vote ended in a tie, Laurens was the only delegate to change his vote and the motion was carried. Then, on November 1, Congress turned to the choice of a new president and elected Henry Laurens.[15]

Laurens took his new office seriously and applied himself with his customary vigor. The job of the president was not an easy one, as he was the official source of communication between Congress and the states, military leaders, and American commissioners in Europe. In addition, it was the president who was forced to deal with the Frenchmen and others who solicited military commissions and other favors from the new government. Laurens worked long hours as president, and was often at work when other delegates had retired to bed and before they rose in the morning. Little wonder that Laurens, observing that it had been twelve or thirteen years since he had retired from the strain of business, at one point exclaimed that "if this be retirement, I most devoutly wish to go to work again." Laurens performed a tremendous amount of work as president, and he often accomplished it without benefit of a private secretary. This was largely due to his own exacting standards, as he explained that he sometimes went for long periods without a secretary because he could not find a good one and would rather do without than employ a lesser man. It was just as well, however, that Laurens had much work to keep him occupied at York, for, outside of Congress, there was little to do. York lacked all of the comforts and conveniences of Philadelphia, a fact that contributed to the poor attendance while Congress met at this location. There were few dining and lodging establishments in York, and those that did exist took full advantage of the situation to charge the highest possible prices for their services. Laurens was disappointed in York and he complained that, while he lived expensively, his lifestyle was far below his usual standards and he compared his lodgings unfavorably with those of the overseers employed on his plantations.[16]

The gloom of York was temporarily broken in late October by news that the British army under General John Burgoyne had surrendered to General Horatio Gates at Saratoga in upstate New York. The joy at this event was quickly tempered, however, by an examination of the convention that Gates had reached with Burgoyne. Fearing that Sir Henry Clinton was approaching with a force that would relieve the pressure and allow Burgoyne to escape, Gates granted generous terms in the Saratoga Convention. Instead of demanding a surrender at discretion, as Laurens and Congress felt he should have done, Gates allowed Burgoyne the prospect of transporting his army back to England, under the condition that he and his army would not serve again in North America during the war. This alarmed

Congress as it would allow Burgoyne's army to serve as garrison troops in England, thereby freeing other troops for service in America. Such a course would surrender much of the military benefit of the victory at Saratoga. The convention placed Congress in a difficult position, as they were unwilling to allow Burgoyne's army to be transported back to England. Yet they wished to avoid publicly insulting the popular Gates by repudiating the convention. Thus, Congress decided to delay Burgoyne's departure while considering a course of action. On November 8, Laurens instructed General William Heath, who commanded at Boston, the port from which the British army was to depart, to take a complete census of the British army. Two weeks later, Congress ordered Gates to investigate rumors that the British had violated the convention by refusing to surrender all of the arms, colors, and other materials required by the agreement. Though the British had clearly violated the convention, Congress still felt that they possessed inadequate cause to abrogate the agreement.[17]

It was Burgoyne himself who unwittingly provided the solution to this dilemma. On November 14, 1777, the British general addressed an angry letter to Gates in which he complained of the treatment of his men at Boston, concluding with the unfortunate observation that "the publick faith is broke and we are the immediate sufferers."[18] With Laurens in the lead, Congress seized upon this passage to suspend the embarkation of Burgoyne's army. Years later, in 1782, Laurens justified the suspension on the grounds that the British were planning to ignore the convention and that Burgoyne's letter to Gates was merely a crafty effort to lay the blame on the United States when they did so. Laurens insisted that the ships sent by the British to transport the army were clearly inadequate to an ocean voyage. He combined this with the oft-stated views of Burgoyne, Howe, and Clinton that they did not consider themselves bound by any agreements reached with rebels to argue that the British were secretly planning to break the Convention. Subsequent information, unavailable to Congress at the time, demonstrates that these suspicions were not entirely unfounded, as Sir William Howe had directed Burgoyne to send his British troops to New York, rather than England.[19]

Henry Laurens played a prominent role in this affair, and his importance is indicated by his personal circumstances at the time. Since 1768, Laurens had suffered periodic attacks of gout, some of which had been severe enough to disable him for several weeks at a time.[20] Now, as Congress prepared to consider the Saratoga Convention, Laurens was felled by another attack of gout, one that prevented his attendance in Congress between December 9 and 25. Realizing that he was likely to be incapacitated for some time, Laurens offered to resign the presidency. He was flattered by the refusal of the House to accept his resignation, and for two weeks he conducted the business of the government from his bed. On Christmas Day, however, he was visited by a member of Congress who told him that the question of the Saratoga Convention was to be debated the next day and that his influence would be crucial. Realizing the importance of his presence, particularly because of the fact that he was the only delegate present from South Carolina and his state would have no vote without him, Laurens resolved to attend, even if he had to be carried physically into the chamber.[21] This was precisely what occurred and Laurens was present for the entire debate, which lasted for two long days. Finally, on December 27, Congress took note of Burgoyne's letter to Gates and decided that it was necessary to suspend the embarkation of the British army until the British government formally ratified the convention. The final report, in which Congress justified its position, was not adopted until January 8, 1778.[22]

It was left to Laurens to relay the wishes of Congress to General William Heath at Boston. As Laurens was writing on December 27, before the formal resolution had been prepared, he warned Heath not to release the contents of his letter to anyone, particularly Burgoyne. Laurens instructed Heath to refuse to allow the departure of the British army and supplied the general with several pretexts for delay. Heath was ordered to complete his census and then to ensure that the British ships possessed the tonnage necessary to carry the entire army to Britain. On the outside chance that these conditions could be met, Laurens instructed Heath to demand that all outstanding British accounts be liquidated in gold or silver before departure. Of course, neither Laurens nor Congress felt that there was any possibility that all of these conditions could be met before the Congressional resolution was adopted and sent to Boston. If this did occur, Laurens provided Heath with another letter that outlined Congress's reasons for suspending the convention. This letter was postdated "January 1778" and Heath was instructed to fill in the proper date and present it to Burgoyne.[23] This policy was definitely devious, but Laurens felt it necessary to prevent the British from repudiating the convention and utilizing Burgoyne's army in the upcoming campaign. Laurens was proud of his role in the suspension of the Saratoga Convention and he informed his son that he would rather have lost half his estate than be defeated on this issue. In addition to his satisfaction that Burgoyne's army was to remain in America, Laurens also took pleasure in the uncomfortable political position into which the British had been placed. Congress would not allow the release of Burgoyne's army until the British government formally ratified the convention. Such a step would be a tacit acknowledgment of the right of Congress to treat as a nation—and thus of American independence. Either way, Laurens felt that the United States would come out ahead. As matters turned out, Burgoyne's army remained as prisoners, many of them loosely confined in Virginia, until the end of the war. Even then, some of the prisoners were so attracted to America that they chose to remain in the new country.[24]

While Congress was dealing with the problem of the Saratoga Convention, the army was in squalor and upheaval at Valley Forge. In addition to the physical discomforts produced by the winter, the officers were alarmed and upset by the alleged conspiracy to supplant General Washington, known as the Conway Cabal. Criticism of Washington's performance might have been expected during the winter of 1777–1778, as it was easy to contrast his failure to hold Philadelphia with Gates's great victory at Saratoga. Yet, as Laurens informed his son on Washington's staff, "I have never been at a loss for argument to convince reasonable Men, there was no ground for censure in one Case, & that in the other we had been *fortunate.*" He was certain that it had been circumstance, rather than ability, that was responsible for the contrasting conclusions to the two campaigns. Still, as Laurens admitted, not all men were so reasonable and some stubbornly refused to listen to this argument.[25] Always a supporter of the commander in chief, Laurens reported, as early as mid-October 1777, serious concerns about Washington's competence and charges that he was dominated by a set of designing and incompetent officers. Though Laurens denounced the efforts of gossips and other "loose tongues," he was "afraid there may be some ground for some of these remarks, a good Heart may be too diffident, too apprehensive of doing right righteous proper Acts, lest such should be interpreted arbitrary." At the same time, Laurens expressed the wish that he was better acquainted with "the Man whom I think, all in all, the first of the Age, & that he would follow my advice. He accepted the opinion of some who have no superior claim all vanity apart."[26]

Though these sentiments indicate that Laurens, shortly after the loss of Philadelphia, was not prepared to summarily reject all criticism of Washington, his comments of a month later place him firmly behind the general. On November 15, he assured his fellow South Carolinian Benjamin Huger that rumors that Washington was under the "pernicious influence" of two generals (probably Nathanael Greene and Henry Knox) were entirely groundless.[27] While Laurens was solidly behind Washington, several others, both in Congress and in the army, were not. Though accusations of a genuine conspiracy against Washington were exaggerated, there certainly were individuals, including Generals Horatio Gates, Thomas Conway, and Thomas Mifflin in the army, along with James Lovell, Benjamin Rush, Richard Henry Lee, the Adamses, and perhaps a few others in Congress, who were highly critical of the commander in chief and exercised little caution in expressing their sentiments. Washington was painfully aware of the discrepancy between his military record and that of Gates during 1777. Yet, he agreed with Laurens that such comparisons were unfair, for Gates's army had greatly outnumbered Burgoyne's, while Washington had been at a disadvantage before Howe. Washington suspected that he was the subject of a considerable amount of criticism. Always a sensitive man, Washington became convinced of a movement against him when he was informed that Conway had sent a letter to Gates that supposedly contained the passage "Heaven has been determined to save your Country, or a weak General and bad Counsellors would have ruined it." Washington responded by sending this passage, without further comment, in a note to Conway on November 9, causing a considerable amount of disarray in the anti-Washington camp.[28]

Washington's suspicions were intensified when Congress provided for a new Board of War, which would be presided over by Gates and that would also include Mifflin and others suspected by the commander in chief. At the same time, and against the expressed wishes of the commander in chief, Conway was appointed inspector general and promoted over deserving American-born officers to the rank of major general. Not without reason, Washington suspected that a maneuver was underway to force his resignation. The crisis reached a climax in late December when Conway visited the camp at Valley Forge and was received icily by Washington. Unnerved by his reception, Conway wrote Washington an insulting letter in which he sarcastically compared the commander in chief to Frederick the Great, under whom he had earlier served in Europe.[29] In response, the officers of the Continental Army rose in a demonstration of rage that sent the Gates faction reeling in confusion.

Laurens became aware of the situation when he received a letter from John Laurens of January 1, 1778, criticizing the promotion of Conway as an act that "has given almost universal disgust" and was viewed as an insult by the entire line of brigadier generals. John Laurens also observed that "the influence of a certain general officer at Reading [Mifflin] is productive of great mischief." Two days later, John Laurens submitted a more detailed account to his father. Here, John Laurens explicitly identified Mifflin, Conway, and others as the leaders of a conspiracy against Washington. He denied that Conway had been treated poorly in camp and insisted that, though the commander in chief was cool toward Conway, such conduct was much friendlier than the inspector general had any right to expect. John Laurens felt that Conway had taken an ungenerous advantage over Washington, since the position of the latter made it impossible for him to settle the matter on the field of honor. Blocked in this regard, John Laurens told his father, Washington had decided to place the matter before Congress and "they will determine whether Genl. W. is to be sacrificed to Genl. C. for the former can never consent to be concern'd in any transaction with the latter, from whom he has received such unpardonable insults." Finally, young Laurens hoped that his father and "some virtuous and patriotic men, will form a countermine to blow up the pernicious junto spoken of above."[30]

Meanwhile, Washington himself sprang into action. First, on January 2,

Washington laid his dispute with Conway before Congress. Though he denied any improper behavior toward Conway, Washington readily admitted the cool reception, explaining that "my feelings will not permit me to make professions of friendship to the man I deem my Enemy." Turning to Gates, Washington angrily informed him that he was aware of the correspondence that had passed between Gates and Conway and that these letters had included disparaging remarks about him (Washington). He made it clear that he was not happy about being the subject of a secret correspondence and warned Gates against further association with the "secret enemy" and "dangerous incendiary" Conway.[31]

Alarmed at the letters from Valley Forge, Henry Laurens stepped in to ease tensions. Knowing that his son had grown close to Washington during his service on the general's staff, Laurens was confident that his comments to his son would reach the ears of the commander in chief. Thus, he agreed that there appeared to be a party gathered around Mifflin that was actively hostile toward Washington. Yet, he denied that there was any widespread conspiracy against the general. He confirmed that there had been criticism of Washington in Congress, even among Washington's declared friends, but insisted that few, if any, in Congress would even consider entering a cabal against the commander in chief. Rather, Laurens contemptuously dismissed the anti-Washington junto as a group of "prompters & Actors, accomodators, Candle Snuffers, Shifters of Scenes & Mutes." He declared himself "uniformly opposed" to this group, as he recognized that the "motives of your friend [Washington] are pure, he has nothing in view but the happiness of his Country." This view was in strong contrast to his opinion of Mifflin and the anti-Washington faction who "make patriotism the stalking horse to their private Interests." As for Conway, Laurens was outraged by his conduct. He wrote that Conway had visited him while he was bedridden with gout and had denied that he had written the sentence that had been quoted from his letter to Gates. Rather, Conway had asserted that he had always spoken of Washington in respectful terms. Yet, Laurens felt that

there was *something* in the manner of his representation which raised doubt in my mind, the correspondence even under favour of his own narrative appeared to me to have been indiscrete & dangerous.

The conduct of Conway toward Washington since this meeting, Laurens continued, had been "very reprehensible, but the taunts & sarcasm contained under the 31st December are unbecoming his Character & unpardonable." Thus, Laurens made it quite clear that the commander in chief could rely on the affection and support of the President of Congress, and Laurens felt that his sentiments represented the opinion of the great majority of the House.[32]

A few days later, Laurens similarly assured the Marquis de Lafayette, who had also expressed his concern in a letter to the president. While admitting that there had been criticism of Washington in Congress, Laurens assured Lafayette that "the whole amounts to little more than tittle tattle" and again insisted that there was no design or offense intended on the part "of so large a majority as 9 in 10."[33] Laurens hoped that his letters would reassure the general and put an end to this distasteful incident. While the support of Laurens did relieve some of Washington's anxiety, it had little effect on his officers, who continued to appear at York to argue the cause of their general. Laurens grew increasingly impatient with the wanderings of the officers and finally observed disapprovingly to his son that "By the continual passing of Officers from your Camp One would think you had all broke up for the holy days."[34]

The anti-Washington faction was busy as well, though their efforts were almost comical in their ineptitude. On January 26, a member handed Laurens a letter addressed to the president, which he claimed to have found upon the stairs. Suspecting the origins of the letter, Laurens decided to read the contents before reading it aloud in Congress, as was the usual custom. Glancing through the letter, Laurens found it to be an anonymous attack upon Washington and informed the House "that it was an anonymous production containing stuff which I must be content with as perquisites of office—that the hearth was the proper depository for such records." Laurens was upset by the contents of the letter, which blamed all of the shortcomings of the Continental Army and the precariousness of its current existence upon Washington and his advisors. After a long series of abusive charges, the author declared that "the people of America have been guilty of Idolatry, by making a man their god" and concluded that "no good may be expected from the standing Army until Baal & his Worshipers are banished from the Camp." Insulted by the clumsiness with which the anti-Washington faction had hoped to introduce such poison into the Congressional record, Laurens did not burn the letter. Instead, he sent it to Washington. The commander in chief, if he had ever doubted the affection of the president, was now convinced that he had a friend in Henry Laurens and warmly thanked him for his support. Thus, the Conway Cabal marked the beginning of an increasingly friendly relationship between Henry Laurens and George Washington.[35]

The support of the president mollified Washington, and the reassured general now turned his attention to the upcoming campaign. For Laurens, however, the headache was not yet over, as a new crisis developed in late January 1778 when Congress appointed Lafayette to command a projected expedition against Canada, but selected Conway to serve as second-in-command. Laurens clearly expected trouble over this arrangement and even doubted if Lafayette would accept the command under these circumstances. Still, he assured his son that there was "nothing else intended but honour to the Marquis & benefit to the Public."[36] Laurens's fears were confirmed when Lafayette absolutely refused to serve with Conway, who, with William Duer (who was also assigned to the expedition), he considered "the two greatest ennemys and most insolent calumniators of my friend [Washington]." Lafayette was convinced that such rascals as Conway and Duer would doom any expedition to failure and insisted that "if my endeavourings to do well are attended with such impassable obstacles, my hating cabals and cabalors will send me back to france [sic]." Not only this, but Lafayette also observed that Conway was extremely unpopular among the French officers. He warned that if Congress and the Board of War persisted in patronizing Conway over more deserving and honorable officers, the entire group of French officers would follow him back to France. Realizing that such action would display the break between Washington and Gates before the entire world, and aware that they possessed neither the men nor the supplies for such an expedition, Congress decided to abandon the Canadian expedition altogether.[37]

The Conway Cabal had exactly the opposite results from those that the anti-Washington faction had intended. Rather than being eclipsed, Washington had emerged in a stronger, almost impregnable, position. The crisis served as an important testimonial of the confidence and devotion that the great majority in Congress and the army felt for the commander in chief. The anti-Washington faction was thoroughly routed, and those in the army were left to patch things up with the commander in chief and his allies as best they could. Gates managed to obtain at least a superficial truce with Washington, and Laurens hoped that "he will hereafter be aware of designing flatterers."[38] Conway, however, was not so fortunate. He twice threatened to resign his commission and was shocked when, at the end of April 1778, Congress accepted his offer. The startled general then turned on Laurens and roughly insisted that his letter had been private and had not been intended to be made public. Laurens was so offended by Conway's language that he resolved to have no further contact with him. Matters went from bad to worse for Conway, however, when, on July 4, 1778, he was seriously wounded in a duel with General John Cadwalader. In a curious end to this story, the injured Conway, fearing that he was on his deathbed, became the only one of the anti-Washington faction to formally apologize to the commander in chief.[39]

While the final acts of this drama were being played out, a new source of conflict arose between Congress and the army, and this time Laurens and Washington were on opposite sides. This new problem concerned retirement pensions for the officers of the Continental Army. Washington supported a plan that would grant half-pay to the officers for the remainder of their lives. In arguing his position before Congress, Washington was careful to point out that he would not benefit personally from such a proposal, since he received no salary from Congress. Yet, he considered such a plan to be essential to the survival of his army, as many of his best officers were leaving the army in order to save their personal affairs from complete collapse. He pointed out that the training of an effective officer corps had been a long and difficult process and he did not wish to see his efforts undermined as they were finally beginning to show results.[40]

Henry Laurens was among the most bitter opponents of any pension plan. A staunch republican, Laurens outlined his opposition in several letters. To Washington, he declared himself an irreconcilable opponent of the plan:

> I view the scheme as altogether unjust & unconstitutional in its nature & full of dangerous consequences. Tis an unhappy dilemma to which we seem to be reduced—provide for your Officers in terms dictated to you or lose all the valuable Soldiers among them—establish a Pension for Officers, make them a seperate Body to be provided for by the honest Yeomenry & others of their fellow Citizens many thousands of whom have equal claims upon every ground of Loss of Estate, health, &c &c &c lose your Army & your Cause.

He pointed out that many people, including himself, were sacrificing for the war effort, but these did not expect, nor would they receive, any special compensation for their services. Patriotism had its own rewards and Laurens hoped that the officers would follow the example of their commander in chief and be motivated by love of country rather than the prospect of gain. He reminded Washington that the war had created many orphans and widows, and he felt that these poor individuals had contributed enough without being called upon to give from what little they had left to the future comfort of the officers.[41] To Governor William Livingston of New Jersey, Laurens was even more direct. He would give half of his estate, he asserted, to defeat such an "unjust, unconstitutional, unreasonable" scheme as this. He pointed out that commissions had been eagerly sought and, as the officers knew the terms of service when they accepted their ranks, they should now honor them. Among other things, Laurens insisted, the idea of half-pay for life would tax the people without their consent, and lay the foundations for an American aristocracy, as well as for a standing army. Thus, Laurens remained unalterably opposed to the half-pay program. His stance, particularly the fear of a permanent standing army, was widely shared in Congress and these fears were reflected in the passage of a compromise agreement on May 15, 1778. By this plan, officers who served for the duration of the war would receive half-pay for seven years after the conclusion of the war, while noncommissioned officers and enlisted men would receive a single bonus of eighty dollars.[42]

This issue of pensions for the officers of the Continental Army emphasized the matter that most distressed Laurens during early 1778: the evident decline of patriotic fervor in America. Laurens was extremely disappointed as he surveyed the American scene. He saw an army in chaos, with an officer corps riven by factionalism and self-interest; he saw a rank and file that suffered and starved while the men responsible for their survival subordinated the public interest to their own private concerns; he saw a shameful lethargy among the states and the American people that not only allowed such conditions to persist, but seemed to actively promote them. To Laurens, nothing was more symbolic of the bankruptcy of American patriotism than the deplorable condition of Congress. He noted that Congress was so poorly attended that it often lacked the necessary delegates to perform even basic committee work. By late January, he observed that Congress could rarely even muster twenty-one delegates, often only fifteen, and sometimes "barely 9 states on the floor represented by as many persons." It was a depressed Laurens who wrote that "we want genius, Insight, foresight, fortitude & all the virtuous powers of the human Mind. O shameful, shameless Sons of Liberty—versatile boasting Americans!" Convinced that the winter of 1777 and 1778 represented the nadir of the American cause, Laurens expressed his despair to Governor William Livingston of New Jersey: "If there be not speedily a Resurrection of able Men and of that Virtue which I thought had been genuine in 1775—We are Gone—We shall undo ourselves—We must flee to the Mountains."[43]

He was particularly distressed by the lethargy of his own state, observing that he was the lone representative of South Carolina and that, during his illness, his state had no vote in Congress. There was no excuse for such a situation, Laurens insisted, and he suggested that he be relieved and replaced by a full delegation of capable individuals. To his disappointment, however, the South Carolina assembly reelected him on January 21, 1778. At the same time, they filled the delegation by also electing Christopher Gadsden, Arthur Middleton, and William Henry Drayton. Fortunately, Congress was spared the spectacle of watching Gadsden and Laurens struggle to work together, as Gadsden declined the appointment. Of these three individuals, only Drayton took his seat in Congress, and he did not arrive until March 30. It was just as well that Gadsden and Middleton declined their appointments, as their presence would have done little to calm Laurens's temper. While it might have been interesting to observe the interaction between Laurens and Gadsden, the strained relationship that developed between Laurens and the Gadsden-ally Drayton suggests that it would not have been a pleasant situation. When Drayton finally arrived, he brought news that Laurens would have welcomed earlier: leave to return to South Carolina. By this time, however, the situation had brightened considerably, as new and capable delegates were arriving and rumors were rife that the French had entered the war. Thus, Laurens chose to remain in Congress a while longer.[44]

While rumors of French assistance were welcome, many American leaders, including Laurens, remained wary. To these, it seemed ironic that the nation that they had learned to hate and fear above all others was now the great friend to America, while the mother country had become hated and despised. Though Laurens had long disliked the French, the Declaration of Independence inspired a more charitable attitude, and he worked hard to establish trade contacts with the leading French firms.[45] Still, he performed these tasks with a heavy heart. He informed his brother that

> I cannot, however Ill we have been treated by a wicked or misinformed British Administration, see this extraordinary change, without some affecting reflections—I cannot easily forget my old friends, I could more easily forgive them.[46]

Laurens found it difficult to trust the French, and his letters of 1777 and 1778 demonstrate this suspicion. He was certain that the French cared nothing for the cause of America, but were merely pursuing their own interests in their American policy. With this in mind, Laurens advised caution, particularly when it came to the subject of loans. He was a bitter opponent of reliance upon French loans and he sharply opposed the idea when it came before Congress in September 1777. Fearing that the French would insist upon the mortgage of American territory in exchange for loans, Laurens felt that Congress should instead tighten its belt, cut all unnecessary expenditures, recommend taxes to the states, borrow at home on the best available terms, sell vacant and forfeited lands, and "a Thousand other things." Insisting that only such steps would make the United States truly independent, Laurens joined John Adams and a small bloc of delegates in an effort to defeat the motion for the negotiation of a French loan. Their opposition was doomed to failure, however, and the motion was passed by a wide margin.[47]

Though he continued to suspect the motives of the French, Laurens was heartened when the French finally recognized American independence and entered the war as an ally of the United States. When the treaty arrived in early May 1778, Laurens declared that while it was not "altogether unexceptionable," it was very good under the circumstances. At the same time, Laurens hoped that Americans would resist the temptation to accept the treaty as a sign that peace and independence were imminent. On the contrary, he wrote, "there is blood much blood in our prospect," as he realized that the war would now take on a greater significance for Great Britain. He pointed out that the entrance of the hated French would cause the British to grow more determined to fight even harder. Thus, Americans must resist the temptation to relax their efforts, for the treaty, while cause for celebration, was also cause for concern.[48]

The French alliance brought new headaches to Laurens who, as president of Congress, was now bombarded with even more requests from French adventurers for commissions in the Continental Army. Both Laurens and Washington suspected that the Frenchmen were taking advantage of the popular Marquis de Lafayette in order to wedge themselves into the high command of the Continental Army and, perhaps, for more insidious purposes. The suspicions of both men flared when Lafayette suggested that the Canadian expedition be resurrected and implemented with the main reliance placed upon French troops commanded by French officers. While neither suspected Lafayette, both feared that he was an unsuspecting pawn of a French government interested in the conquest of Canada not for the United States, but for themselves. Neither man was interested in pursuing such a plan under these circumstances, and nothing further came of the idea. Thus, while Laurens welcomed French assistance, he continued to distrust their motives and was under no illusion that the French had entered the war to fight for American liberty.[49]

When the British government realized that the French were about to enter the war, they frantically resolved to make an effort to satisfy the Americans and reach a settlement that would preserve the empire. Thus, a commission consisting of Lord Carlisle, William Eden, and George Johnstone arrived in Philadelphia on June 7, 1778, prepared to offer concessions on all issues except independence. A week later, Laurens informed the British commissioners that Congress would not consent to any peace negotiations until the British removed their armies and fleets and formally recognized American independence. As the commissioners had neither the inclination nor the authority to agree to such demands, it appeared that all hope of a settlement was gone.[50] The desperate commissioners, however, had not traveled such a great distance to be rebuffed without even a meeting. Suspicions had already been raised against the British trio, when, shortly after their arrival, they brought letters to individual members of Congress from their personal friends in Britain. These letters invariably contained pleas to accept British concessions and return to their British allegiance. Laurens received letters from his old friends William Manning and Richard Oswald, but refused to allow their pleas to sway his devotion to American independence. When these letters were discovered, a motion was presented in Congress demanding that all such letters be presented for inspection by the House. Just as he had done in South Carolina in 1775, Laurens absolutely opposed this effort to allow public inspection of private letters. He refused to present his letters under compulsion, though he added that he had shown them to several members and would be happy to show them to others. Though Congress did not insist upon inspecting the letters, this episode only increased suspicions concerning the commissioners.[51]

When the letters failed to soften the stance of Congress, George Johnstone turned to other tactics. He was soon accused of trying to bribe several members of Congress, most particularly Joseph Reed and Robert Morris. Reed was reportedly offered ten thousand pounds sterling and any office in North America if he could convince Congress to reverse its position and return to the empire. These efforts failed miserably, however, when the recipients of the offers turned them over to Congress. Laurens was incensed by this "highest possible affront to the Representatives of a virtuous Independent People" and adamantly insisted that this outrage justified a resolution to refuse any further contact with the British commissioners. Furthermore, the furious president demanded that a resolution to this extent be adopted and delivered to the commissioners under a white flag, so that they could be the bearers of their own disgrace. Such a position was judged too harsh by Congress and it was finally decided to exclude only Johnstone from future negotiations, while leaving the door open to further talks with the other commissioners.[52] This door was quickly slammed shut when the commissioners defended Johnstone's conduct and took their case over the head of Congress and to the states and people. They published a proclamation promising desolation to the American states if they persisted in fighting the mother country and aligning themselves with Britain's mortal enemy, France. Such a proclamation was hardly diplomatic and had no effect upon the states. It did bring a rousing response from Congress, however. On October 30, the House answered with the promise "that if our enemies presume to execute their threats, or persist in their present career of barbarity, we will take such exemplary vengeance as shall deter others from a like conduct."[53] Thus, the British peace offensive of 1778 ended not with embraces, but with renewed threats.

Even as the British were preparing their peace offensive, Sir Henry Clinton, finding that possession of the American capital provided little in the way of either military or political advantage, was planning to evacuate Philadelphia. As early as May 17, 1778, Laurens was reporting that evacuation was imminent. Yet the British continually delayed their departure and it was not until June 23 that Laurens reported that they had left the capital. Congress happily adjourned to Philadelphia on June 27. They met again on June 30, but were unable to use the State House for another week because the British had used the building as a hospital and "left it in a condition disgraceful to the Character of civility."[54]

The return to Philadelphia marked an important break in the Congressional service of Henry Laurens. Certainly, his first year had seen its trials: the loss of Philadelphia; the retreat to the less-appealing York; and the physical and moral suffering of the army at Valley Forge. Yet, there were successes as well. Elected to the presidency shortly after Congress arrived in York, Laurens presided over some of the most important events that occurred in the Continental Congress. He occupied the chair during the Conway Cabal, providing unwavering and appreciated support and reassurance to George Washington during his hour of need. Almost simultaneously, he played a critical role in the suspension of the Saratoga Convention, an unpleasant but necessary action that allowed the United States to retain the fruits of the great victory at Saratoga. On a happier note, Laurens presided over the news of the French alliance and the return to Philadelphia. As Congress reoccupied the capital, Laurens might have been excused for thinking that the most difficult period had passed. Yet, with the immediate danger past, Congress in general, and Laurens in particular, were about to embark upon a series of frustrating and disillusioning controversies.

13

Contention in Congress: Henry Laurens and the Continental Congress, 1778–1779

By the time Congress returned to Philadelphia, it had already entered into the conflict that would produce the sharpest party battle in the history of the Continental Congress. At the heart of the matter were the sharp disagreements among the American commissioners in Europe, a disputatious lot who seemed unable to agree upon anything. The main combatants in this sordid duel were Silas Deane and Arthur Lee, and members of Congress divided into factions supporting one or the other. Laurens had always denounced the existence of parties, and from his earliest days in Congress declared that he would refuse to associate with any of the Congressional factions.[1] Until mid-1778, Laurens had been successful in this quest. Afterwards, however, and particularly during 1779, he found it increasingly difficult to avoid such a characterization. Though he continued to describe himself as free from all party considerations, Laurens was often found taking positions similar to those of the Lees of Virginia and the Adamses of Massachusetts. This was particularly true during the battle between the partisans of Deane and Lee, when Laurens placed his support squarely behind the latter.

In 1776, Congress had selected Silas Deane, Benjamin Franklin, and Thomas Jefferson to represent American interests in France. When Jefferson declined the honor, Congress appointed another Virginian, Arthur Lee, to take his place. Trouble began almost immediately, as a personality conflict developed between the sanctimonious Lee and the gregarious duo of Deane and Franklin. As the relationship deteriorated, the latter two commissioners increasingly ignored the former, which rankled the jealous and egotistical Virginian. Nursing his bruised ego, Lee suspected that Deane and Franklin were mixing private and public business in an effort to enrich themselves. Thus, Lee began sending sharply critical reports to his brother, Richard Henry Lee, in Congress. As ambitious as he was self-righteous, Arthur Lee suggested to his brother that he secure an arrangement by which Deane would be sent to The Hague, Franklin to Vienna, and the plum of Versailles would be reserved for himself.[2]

As reports of problems among the commissioners in France reached Congress, Laurens had a strong tendency to side with Lee. He had never been satisfied with the performance of Silas Deane, and within a month of his arrival in Congress had declared that Deane was incompetent and would have to be recalled.[3] By contrast, Laurens entertained a high opinion of the abilities of Arthur Lee. He had met Lee during his residence in England before the war and had respected him as a disinterested, if abrasive, patriot. His confidence in Lee was demonstrated when he commissioned the Virginian to pen the response to the attack of Egerton Leigh on the South Carolina Commons House during the Wilkes fund crisis in 1774. Thus, his instincts told him to trust Lee. His sentiments were reinforced by Lee's complaints of financial misconduct on the part of Deane, charges precisely of the sort that most infuriated Laurens, who strongly denounced those who used public business for private profit.

Laurens's pro-Lee leanings were enhanced by reports received from his friend and fellow South Carolinian Ralph Izard. Delayed in Paris awaiting reception as commissioner to Tuscany, Izard was shocked by the conduct of Deane and Franklin, who

> had they been in politics as infallible as the Pope intends to be in matters of religion, they could not have acted in a greater degree of confidence; and upon every occasion they consider themselves as the only persons interested in the fate of America.

Izard remarked that, considering the obnoxious personality of the Virginian, he had at first assumed that Lee must be at fault for the quarreling among the commissioners. He was surprised, then, to discover that, while Lee was not entirely blameless, "the conduct of the other gentlemen towards him has been unjustifiable, and such as could not fail to provoke any man not dead to all sense of injury."[4] As time progressed, Izard grew increasingly hostile towards Franklin and Deane. By April 1778, he had concluded that "it would have been impossible to have found one on every account more unfit" for his office than Deane.[5] As for Franklin, Izard called him "a crafty old knave" and declared that "he has neither honour nor honesty; he has abilities it is true, but so much the worse when they are not under the restraint of virtue and integrity; and I declare before God, he is under the restraint of neither."[6] In support of Lee's charges of corruption, Izard asserted that Deane and Franklin had involved themselves in such shady business activity that only the news of the victory at Saratoga prevented the French government from expelling the entire American commission.[7]

These were serious accusations and, in December 1777, Congress recalled Deane to answer them.[8] After Deane landed in America in July 1778, Laurens expressed regret that the "scandalous" disagreements and "School

Boy jarrings" among the commissioners had become public. He observed that errors had been made on both sides, but felt that the commissioners "are all good Men, but I know there are in some of them vile tempers which alloy their general goodness."[9] When Deane appeared before Congress to defend his conduct in mid-August 1778, Laurens was disappointed that he was not required to submit a written report. He felt that the latter method would have been less time-consuming and more exact and complete than an oral report. He also registered disappointment that so many of the delegates had already taken sides in the dispute, and he took "the liberty to recommend the fillet and scales of Justice to one of my worthy Colleagues who appears strongly attached to one of the parties." Though he was already leaning toward Lee, Laurens was clearly making a determined effort, at this point, to remain objective. After Deane concluded his defense, Laurens informed him that his account appeared to be candid, but he would hear the other side before making up his mind on the subject. Nevertheless, Laurens admonished Deane for leaving his accounts and records in France, adding that he would never have a better opportunity of presenting them than at this time.[10]

No decision was reached on Deane during August 1778 and the issue quickly descended into a party fight between the supporters of Deane and those of Lee. Claiming that he had understood that the summons had been for the purpose of reporting on conditions in Europe, Deane expressed anxiety that the investigation be completed so that he could return to his post. To his intense frustration, however, Congress repeatedly postponed consideration of the question and refused to allow him another opportunity for defending himself in the House. Bitter at such treatment, Deane defended himself and attacked Arthur Lee in the December 5, 1778 issue of the *Pennsylvania Packet*. This effort drew the attention of Congress. Convinced that Deane had intentionally insulted the honor of the House, Laurens moved that a committee be appointed to consider this publication and that Deane be denied a further hearing until the report was received. When Congress refused this request, Laurens abruptly resigned the presidency.[11]

Laurens's resignation was sudden, but it was hardly a surprise. He had been seeking permission to return to South Carolina almost from the day he arrived in Philadelphia, and he had received this permission when William Henry Drayton took his seat in March 1778. Though Laurens decided to remain to oversee the important business of the spring and summer of 1778, by the middle of July he was again declaring his intention to retire from Congress. He set November 1 as his target date for retirement, for this would mark the completion of one year in the presidency, and the not yet ratified Articles of Confederation required that the president could only serve for one year in every three.[12] His plans were upset when John Mathews announced that it was absolutely necessary for him to return to South Carolina in November, forcing Laurens to remain in order to ensure that his state maintained adequate representation.[13] Unable to return home, Laurens remained determined to at least vacate the presidency on November 1. True to his word, Laurens appeared upon the floor of Congress on November 2, but refused to take the Chair. He reluctantly agreed to continue as president, however, after the unanimous voice of the House appealed to him to remain "until the Articles of Confederation should be acceded to by all of the States, or at least, for some time longer."[14]

When Laurens read Deane's article in the *Pennsylvania Packet*, he was shocked by a production that "had created anxieties in the minds of the good People of this City, and excited tumults amongst them." He denounced the article as "highly derogatory to the honor and interests of the United States" and insisted that it was sufficient cause to deny Deane a further hearing before Congress. In his resignation speech, Laurens pointed out that Deane had never produced a written account of his adventures in France, nor had he submitted any accounts or vouchers for his vast public expenditures. He insisted that there was no justification for Deane's placing his case before the public, particularly if his true reason for doing so was that Congress had denied him a hearing. He reported that he had personally informed Deane that Congress would take up the question of foreign affairs on December 3 and that his case would be included in this discussion. In response, Deane sent a note thanking Congress for its consideration, but stating that he had made arrangements to leave the city and could not change them. Nevertheless, he still had time to print his article of December 5, accusing Congress of denying him a hearing. Laurens also noted that Deane had chosen to make public the disputes between the commissioners in Europe and that he had levied a public attack upon Arthur Lee. Thus, Laurens considered the paper

a sacrafice of the Peace and good Order of these States to personal resentments, and so far as it regards Congress, it is groundless and unwarrantable; wherefore, be the remainder false or true, it is, in my humble opinion, a pernicious and unprovoked Libel, affrontive to the Majesty of the People.

He expressed outrage that Congress not only refused to proceed against Deane for this work, but now offered him time to prepare a written report on his conduct in Europe, a project he felt Deane should have completed before he even landed in America. Laurens concluded that "from the consideration abovementioned, as I cannot consistently with my own honor, nor with utility to my Country, considering the manner in which Business is transacted here, remain any longer in the Chair, I now resign it."[15]

If Laurens had earlier worked to maintain an open mind in the Deane-Lee Affair, he was now firmly placed within the anti-Deane camp. The pro-

Deane faction disliked his resignation speech, and when a motion was presented on December 10 to present the thanks of the House to Laurens, they managed to delay passage for five days. Finally, on December 15, Laurens "in modest terms demanded a testimonial of my Conduct," and Congress directed the new president, John Jay, to convey the thanks of the House to his predecessor. Though Laurens expressed no regret over either his decision to resign or the manner in which he had accomplished this, he realized that others might use his words as evidence that he had become a party man. He strenuously denied this allegation and, in the same letter in which he notified President Rawlins Lowndes of his resignation, he also found it necessary to deny to the president of his state "that I have any improper attachment to the Lees."[16] Yet, outside of the Lees, one would have been hard pressed to find a more determined opponent of Silas Deane than Henry Laurens.

After Deane read his defense in Congress during late 1778, the main question concerned whether to recall Arthur Lee to substantiate his charges and, if so, whether Deane should be detained until this time. The pro-Deane faction charged that Lee held the respect and confidence of neither the French nor the Spanish courts and, thus, he should be recalled and replaced. In response, Laurens informed Congress that, shortly after these reports began to circulate, both he and Samuel Adams had questioned Conrad Alexandre Gerard, the French minister to the United States, about the truth of the rumors. Gerard replied that reports had reached the ears of the king and his leading ministers that Lee was strongly attached to England and disliked the French. The king personally insisted upon an investigation, which found the charges to be groundless. Yet, Laurens was forced to admit that while Gerard confirmed that the French regarded the charges to be groundless, they also found Lee to be obnoxious and would prefer that he be recalled.[17] As the debate dragged into the summer, Laurens, by now the foremost champion of Lee in Congress, declared himself prepared to vote for recall, but only if Deane was detained in America until Lee could present his case. Convinced of Deane's baseness, Laurens was certain that a face-to-face confrontation in Congress would expose Deane as a dishonest scoundrel. Such a dramatic debate was not to occur, however, as Lee was eventually recalled, but only after Deane was allowed freedom to leave the country. Congress did reorganize the foreign service, however, deciding that commissioners were needed only at Versailles, Madrid, and The Hague. All former commissions were invalidated and Franklin was chosen to continue at Versailles, John Jay to succeed Lee at Madrid, and Laurens himself to proceed to the Netherlands.[18]

The Deane-Lee affair marked a turning point in the Congressional career of Henry Laurens. Previously, he had scrupulously avoided participation in the factional squabbles and, as a result, was highly respected in the House.

Though he would continue to truthfully assert that he belonged to no party or faction, Laurens would henceforth be involved in several bitter controversies, most of which stemmed from the Deane-Lee conflict, which tainted his record in Congress. He had become what he had claimed to despise: a disputatious member who hindered the work of Congress and contributed to the decline of the reputation of this body.

Laurens held very strong views about the separation of public and private business, and his self-righteousness was to lead him into a new dispute, this time with Robert Morris. His problems with Morris had their roots in the Deane Affair, as Morris was a friend, supporter, and business associate of the embattled Deane. This alone would have been enough to arouse suspicion in the mind of Henry Laurens. Yet, Laurens later informed Morris that he had suspected Morris's motives and conduct long before any charges were leveled against Deane. He explained that even before he had come to Congress, he had heard complaints about the manner in which the Secret Committee, "in which you had been always viewed as the ostensible Actor," had conducted its business and kept its accounts.[19] These suspicions were increased by the notorious misconduct of Thomas Morris, a half-brother of Robert Morris, who represented the United States as a commercial agent in France before his death in early 1778. Not only was Thomas Morris involved in numerous questionable business transactions in France, but Robert Morris continued to defend his brother until the evidence grew so overwhelming that he was forced to distance himself from this agent. Such conduct only increased the suspicion Laurens felt for Morris and when, in November 1778, Laurens denounced war profiteers in a letter to Washington, it is likely that his allusions were to Morris.[20]

The trouble between Laurens and Morris grew serious when Laurens was added to the Commercial, or Secret, Committee following his resignation of the Presidency in December 1778. Convinced that Deane, Morris, and their cronies were carrying on a lucrative private trade at the public expense, Laurens studied the books of the committee to discover the actual state of affairs. To his dismay, the books were in such disorder that no clear understanding could be gained from them. Laurens's frustration was fueled by the recollection that Morris had been granted leave by Congress during November 1777 with the understanding that he would adjust the books during his absence. Though he had estimated that this task would take about two months, the books were still in his possession during February 1778. Congress was unhappy with the delay, and Laurens saw no reason why the adjustments should take such a long time. Despite Laurens's frustrated pronouncement that he could post the books in nine days if the entries were properly made, the books remained in Morris's hands until September 1778. After this long delay, Laurens now recalled, the latter declared "that they were in such confusion you could make nothing of them" and sent them back to Congress, as "you did not know you had any more to do with them than any body else." Upon appointment to the committee, Laurens took up the books, hoping that his own business experience could be useful in making sense of them. No sooner had he taken the books than he was visited by a messenger from Morris who requested that the books be returned to him, since only Morris could straighten them out. Surprised by this request, Laurens reminded the messenger that Morris had already declared that he "could make nothing of" the books. He also pointed out that it would be improper to release the books to someone who was not a member of Congress. Finally, Laurens concluded that Morris had already had his chance to adjust the books, and now he himself would give it a try.[21]

Laurens later assured Morris that, at least at this stage, he had no intention of accusing him of dishonesty. Still, he was critical of Morris's conduct and thought him "a little faulty for keeping the Books upwards of ten Months & them returning them in their present disorderly state." Laurens had little sympathy with Morris's plea that he was a busy man and did not have as much time for the books as he would have liked. This was no excuse, replied Laurens, as he asked:

> Why did you engage in so much more business than you were competent to? If private affairs would not admit of close attention to your Public duties for the due execution of which in the particular case before us Congress had altogether depended upon you you should have relinquished in time & delivered up the Books in good order.

Rather disingenuously, Laurens insisted that he was not combing the records for evidence of impropriety; rather, he was merely interested in straightening out the business affairs of Congress. He expressed the hope that at the conclusion of his work, he could declare that Morris merited no censure and, indeed, "that you deserve the thanks of your fellow Citizens."[22]

Yet, having observed the manner in which Morris conducted his business, Laurens thought it extremely unlikely that he would be recommending the latter course. Indeed, Laurens was not entirely candid in his assurances that he had not been scouring the books for evidence of financial impropriety. He was likely investigating a story he had heard from Francis Lewis, a delegate from New York, that Morris had placed 470 hogsheads of tobacco on board a ship bound for Europe upon the account of his company, Willing, Morris, and Co. When the ship was captured, less than thirty hogsheads appeared upon private account, with the remainder charged to the public. Thus, according to this story, Morris had shipped a cargo that would have benefitted his private account if it arrived safely, but that he charged to the public when it was seized. Persuaded of the accuracy of the charge, but unable to prove it through the committee books, Laurens provided secret information to Thomas Paine, who used it in an attack upon Deane and Morris, published during early January 1779 in the *Pennsylvania Packet*.[23] After Morris publicly refuted Paine's charges, insinuating that Laurens was the source of the charges, Laurens raised the issue on the floor of Congress. Explaining himself after the fact to Morris, Laurens denied making any accusations. Rather, he insisted that rumors were rampant and "if the account which I have received be true, the Public ought to be informed, if it be groundless, Justice forbids that Mr. Morris be kept in ignorance."[24]

Morris was extremely upset when he learned that these charges had been aired in Congress and he bitterly protested the fact that Laurens had gone to the public before first allowing him the opportunity of defending his conduct in private. He again denied that he had done anything illegal or improper.[25] When Congress ordered an investigation, it quickly became clear that Morris was indeed innocent. It was found that the Secret Committee, in an effort to avoid the inflated prices charged by profiteers for purchases upon the public account, had authorized Morris to purchase tobacco for the public under the appearance of private transactions. This explanation satisfied Laurens and he moved in Congress on February 11, 1779 that Morris be cleared of all suspicion under this incident. The House unanimously agreed and the matter was dropped.[26]

Even this conclusion did not restore the personal relationship between Laurens and Morris. Morris might well be excused for his anger, for the entire episode might have been avoided if Laurens had asked for a private explanation before he aired his charges in public. Nor was Laurens reconciled to the business practices of Robert Morris. While he was satisfied that Morris had not defrauded the government in this case, he could not condone the mixture of private and public business, and Morris had admitted to this. To Laurens, Morris's conduct might not have been dishonest, but it certainly created the opportunity for dishonesty. In a later letter, Laurens warned Morris not to deceive himself into thinking that Congress had approved of his methods, as

> there appeared 'tis true no proof against you of criminality but there were nevertheless more persons than my own clearly of opinion that the manner in which the business had been transacted, was, to speak in the mildest terms, highly improper.

While those unfamiliar with business proceedings might see nothing wrong with the methods employed by Morris, Laurens insisted that "Men of business & discernment will more greatly declare—'This is a very extraordinary & a very dangerous mode of disposing of the Public Money.'" To conclude his role in this affair, Laurens told Morris that

If you rank me among your Enemies, you do me great injustice, I acknow. that I have not approved of your general conduct in public business, it has in every instance within my knowledge been ambiguous—always wanting your own explication.[27]

After delivery of this sermon, Laurens turned from Robert Morris to other matters.

It took little time for Laurens to become embroiled in an even more heated dispute, this time with the North Carolina delegation and his colleague William Henry Drayton, over the consideration of peace terms. As Congress considered this question, a strong sectional dispute arose over the use of the Newfoundland fisheries. The New England delegations, representing an area that depended upon fisheries for its livelihood, demanded that this right be included in the instructions to the American negotiators. The southern delegates, having nothing to gain from such a condition and desperate for peace in the face of a British invasion that had already resulted in the conquest of Georgia and a serious threat to the Carolinas, opposed making this a condition of peace. The cause of the southerners was enhanced when the French minister, Conrad Alexandre Gerard, declared that the French government would not consider itself bound to prolong the war in a dispute over the fisheries. Henry Laurens quickly found himself in a great deal of trouble when he and Richard Henry Lee became the only southern delegates to break with their sectional peers and support the New Englanders. Laurens, in an admirable display of broadminded nationalism, thought the fisheries necessary not only to the New England economy, but also as training grounds for the sailors upon which the infant United States Navy would depend. This position, along with the refusal of the two to join their southern colleagues in an insistence on free navigation of the Mississippi River, was very unpopular among the southern delegations.[28]

The stance of Laurens was much more critical than that of Lee, since Laurens and Drayton were the only two South Carolina delegates present. When these two disagreed upon an issue, as they often did, South Carolina would have no vote. This was the case on the issue of the fisheries. Virginia, on the other hand, had a fuller representation, and Lee's vote could be cancelled by those of the other delegates. Thus, the southerners concentrated their efforts on changing the vote of Laurens. Numerous methods were applied to this purpose, including the use of reason, and, later, the recruitment of Alexander Hamilton to try to convince his close friend John Laurens to use his influence with his father in behalf of the southern viewpoint.[29] When subtle measures failed, the North Carolina delegates (Thomas Burke, Whitmill Hill, and John Penn[30]) implemented more forceful tactics.

On April 2, the North Carolina delegates addressed a sarcastic note to Laurens and Drayton in which they claimed to have misunderstood the ability of South Carolina to withstand a British attack. From the anxious calls for assistance that South Carolina had sent to both North Carolina and Congress, they had received the impression that South Carolina was weak and practically defenseless. Thus, they expressed surprise that Laurens would vote to continue the war until the British agreed to concessions on the fisheries, an issue of little to no importance to the Carolinas. But, they wrote, Laurens surely understood the military condition of South Carolina. Since Laurens, through his vote on the fisheries, did not seem too apprehensive of the possible consequences of a continuation of the war, they informed the South Carolinians that they had sent a letter to their governor, Richard Caswell, informing him of this situation and advising him to discontinue all military aid to South Carolina. In the event that Laurens might have placed too much confidence in the ability of South Carolina to withstand attack, the North Carolinians took the liberty of explaining what might be expected if the war continued much longer:

> your Country will probably experience all the calamities which can be apprehended from an Insolent, Relentless, Iritated, and Rapacious enemy, from your own Slaves armed against their former Masters, from the Savages excited to more bloody and merciless dispositions and conducted by leaders who have Inclination and Abilities to make their force and ferocity as effectual against you as possible.[31]

Laurens was infuriated by such a blatant attempt to pressure his vote. He grew even angrier when he discovered that Drayton had sent an individual answer to the North Carolinians in which he apologized for Laurens's vote and asserted that it did not represent the interests and opinions of his constituents. Laurens quickly shot off a note to this colleague, accusing him of having prior knowledge of, and encouraging, the intentions of the North Carolinians. He declared himself open to reasonable arguments and invited Drayton to provide him with "an explicit and candid" opinion of the conduct of the North Carolinians, in a private conference. When Drayton refused to meet on this issue, the enraged Laurens lost his temper and wrote a furious letter to his fellow South Carolinian:

> In my address of last Night I requested you would honor me with explicitude and candour in your answer. You are pleased to give a preference to illusion and ambiguity. You have declined giving an opinion, or holding a conference, which evinces that you not only "vote" but *act* "systematically," here you have drawn a line between us—henceforward I will neither receive from you, nor trouble you with a Letter of controversy but I will never with hold my voice in confirmation of any motion of yours in Congress nor my utmost support to

your Measures out of doors where we may be jointly concerned, which shall appear conducive to Public good.[32]

Laurens then launched an attack upon Drayton's conduct in this matter, asking

Did you not feel a little for the breach of plighted faith and honor to keep secret deliberations upon a point, the disclosure of which may dash our infant Independence against the Stones? Or did you think me blind? Think, speak and act Sir, as you shall judge most convenient. I shall persevere in acting in all respects with propriety towards you, with diligence and fidelity in the common Cause of America, and with the most inviolable attachment to that State whose particular Servant I am.

Even the conclusion to this letter dripped with venom, as Laurens withheld the customary "Your obedient and humble servant," instead substituting "Comprehending all proper Ceremonies."[33]

Then, Laurens turned his rage away from Drayton and launched a stinging counterattack on the North Carolinians. First, he wrote a letter of his own to Governor Caswell, in which he bitterly condemned the conduct of the North Carolina delegation:

It is possible I may have erred in judgement, the Gentlemen in their attempt to correct the supposed error, have committed Acts, which appear to me in the glare of heinos Crimes. They have attacked the freedom of debate & suffrage. They have menaced a free Citizen in order to bias his Vote. They have advised the abandonment of an Innocent people to the rage of a powerful & merciless Enemy. They have recommended measures which if adopted will endanger the safety of the United States. And have they not sacrificed their sacred faith & honor to pique & resentment?

Laurens then directed his fire onto the North Carolinians themselves. After denouncing them for conspiring with Drayton against him, Laurens sent them a copy of his letter to Caswell "in order to anticipate the Poison by the antidote."[34] The North Carolinians had not expected such a strong and direct response and they nervously beat a hasty retreat. Laurens's letter had so rattled the North Carolinians that it took them four days to construct a reply. Finally, they weakly explained to the angry South Carolinian that they had never intended to pressure his vote, but had only wished to ensure that he understood the seriousness of the political and military situation. Laurens then informed the North Carolinians that he would accept this letter as an apology, and was willing to drop the matter, as he now considered himself "once more a free Agent." Still, this apology had arrived too late to prevent Laurens from sending his letter to Governor Caswell.[35]

Laurens was satisfied with his triumph and he hoped that it would secure his reputation as an independent man of honor who avoided party entanglements. At the same time, he realized that he had made some enemies among the southern delegates who saw him as a pawn of the Lees and Adamses. This, he vehemently denied:

> It has been falsely transmitted to Charles Town that I was too closely connected with the Eastern States, you now have proof of the contrary & I glory in the reproach of being with no Man, with no party longer than he or they steers or steer by the Pole Star of reason, Justice, reciprocity. When Men diverge into the Road of self Interestedness, I walk no further with them. In a word, I fear I have given offence to some of my friends. If it be so, I can't help it, I would rather offend my Father than meanly or wittingly transgress against those principles.[36]

Yet Laurens did violate these principles, and only a month after his dispute with the North Carolinians. As the debate over peace terms continued, Laurens noted that the credentials of Edward Langworthy, the lone delegate from Georgia and an opponent of Laurens on both the fisheries and Arthur Lee, had expired on February 26, 1779. Noting that Langworthy had continued to vote in Congress until his departure on April 13, Laurens motioned that all of his votes for this period be voided. He realized that if his motion was carried, Georgia would have no vote on either the peace terms or on the recall of Lee. He was not appeased by the response that his position was a technicality, as the military situation made it difficult for Georgia to update Langworthy's credentials or send a new delegation. It was further pointed out that it would be a difficult problem to rummage through all of the votes during this period in order to recall all of the votes cast by Langworthy. Though Laurens remained unconvinced, he did withdraw his motion, largely due to a change of tactics on the part of the New Englanders and their allies. Realizing the divisive nature of the fishery question, they decided to relax their insistence on use of the fisheries as a condition of peace, but, instead, pressed for the appointment of peace commissioners who would be sympathetic to their interests.[37]

While the surrender of the North Carolina delegation repaired its relations with Laurens, the same cannot be said of the relationship between Laurens and his colleague William Henry Drayton. Laurens had never really trusted Drayton and always viewed him as an erratic personality. He could never forget that, during the early 1770s, Drayton had transformed himself from one of the most conservative opponents of the South Carolina protest movement into one of its most radical supporters. Nor could he applaud Drayton's alliance with Christopher Gadsden and his support for the radical movement during 1775 and 1776. Yet, he had not experienced any of the bitter disputes with Drayton that he had with Gadsden, and he warmly welcomed his fellow South Carolinian to Congress in March 1778. When Drayton visited the camp at Valley Forge a short while later, Laurens provided him with cordial letters of introduction to Washington and several other friends in the army.[38] Still, there was friction between Laurens and Drayton almost from the start, and the two men developed into the least congenial delegation in the Congress. The relationship began to deteriorate after Laurens hired a young man, Moses Young, to serve as secretary to the South Carolina delegation. Laurens became upset when he learned that Drayton was monopolizing Young's time and his irritation turned to anger when he discovered that much of this work concerned private correspondence. Laurens expressed surprise that Drayton would use Young in this manner when he knew the purpose for which the secretary had been employed. He then directed Young to refuse any business that was not directly related to the official business of the delegation. Laurens was clearly losing patience with Drayton, and his anger was demonstrated shortly afterwards when he spoke sharply to his younger colleague in the presence of Samuel Adams. Though Laurens apologized for this incident, the relationship between the two men continued to deteriorate during 1778.[39]

Still, the two South Carolinians managed to work together with a minimum of bickering until they took opposite sides in the Deane-Lee controversy in 1778 and 1779. Thus, relations between the two men were strained before the dispute over the peace terms served to break them altogether. After this, several disputes of varying severity kept the conflict raging for the remainder of their service together. Perhaps the most serious of these clashes occurred in early June 1779 over the case of Dr. John Morgan, who had been removed for misconduct from his position as chief physician and director-general of United States hospitals. Morgan's replacement by Dr. William Shippen, Jr. of Philadelphia, a brother-in-law of the Lees, caused this dispute to merge into the wider Deane-Lee conflict. When Dr. Morgan submitted a memorial to Congress that cast severe reflections upon several members of the Lee faction, Laurens and Drayton again squared off on opposite sides in the ensuing battle. Almost two weeks after the memorial was submitted, Laurens watched with amazement as Drayton approached the table in Congress and crossed out parts of the document. When Congress began to consider the matter, Laurens brought this action to their attention. Drayton admitted removing several phrases and then, according to Laurens, foolishly explained "that there were severe epithets which had been struck out (or expunged) *in order to make it go down the better.*" The surprised president, John Jay, rebuked Drayton with a brief but sharp lecture.[40]

The final confrontation between Laurens and Drayton came in early July 1779, when the latter suggested that Congress celebrate the Fourth of July with a fireworks display. He observed that all nations, modern and ancient, set aside certain days for festivals and pointed to the Olympic games of ancient Greece as an example. Laurens immediately rose and expressed "his astonishment at the conduct of his Honorable Colleague, who seemed to be altogether joyous at a time when he thought he was loudly called on to serious reflection." He reminded Drayton that his own state was currently faced with the prospect of an imminent British invasion and, after listing several other serious problems confronting the United States, declared that "the Olympic Games of Greece and other fooleries brought on the dissolution of Greece—my Colleague may think this a day for joy and mirth, I am of a different opinion. I rather think it is a day of fasting and mourning." To Laurens's dismay, Congress agreed to provide for an expensive entertainment and fireworks show on July 5, which, Laurens proudly wrote, he took care to miss.[41]

By this time, Laurens was prepared to ridicule just about any idea that emanated from his colleague, and Drayton's zeal supplied his rival with good material for comment. On July 17, Laurens informed his son that Drayton had seconded the motion of John Dickinson that Congress should adjourn and fight with the army. Laurens sneered at such an idea, writing that "this shews more of valour in those Gentlemen than of the wisdom & reflection of grave Senators, but who can restrain the ardor of fighting Men when an opportunity offers?"[42] The conflict came to an abrupt halt, however, when, in August 1778, Drayton was taken seriously ill and, after suffering for almost a month, died on September 4, 1779 at the age of thirty-seven. The poor relationship between the two men was again demonstrated when Laurens remained unaware that Drayton was seriously ill until the latter had been bedridden for three weeks. At this point, however, Laurens applied for, and received, permission to visit the dying man at his bedside. It was only at this late date that the two men were reconciled to each other. After Drayton's death, Laurens and John Mathews were chosen by Congress to administer his affairs in Philadelphia. In an unfortunate decision, Laurens, according to Drayton's son, John Drayton, ordered the destruction of a considerable number of papers that Drayton had collected in anticipation of writing a history of the Revolution.[43]

The death of Drayton might have served as an opportunity for Laurens to pause, reflect, and finally resolve to avoid future disputes of this nature. Yet, even while Drayton still lived, Laurens was locked in another controversy, this time with Charles Thomson, the secretary of Congress. Thomson was efficient, but he could also be irritable and became involved in several heated disputes with members of Congress. The relationship between Laurens and Thomson had always been somewhat tense, though the two men were able to maintain a working relationship during Laurens's presidency.[44] Matters deteriorated thereafter until, on August 31, 1779, inspired by "an unprovoked repetition of insults which the Secretary had at divers preceding times offered to Delegates of Congress and to myself in particular," Laurens filed a formal complaint against the behavior of the secretary. In his written statement, submitted the next day, Laurens complained that Thomson had, on several occasions during his presidency, treated him rudely and had missed no opportunity to inconvenience him. He noted several examples of such conduct. Most prominent among these examples was the commission that John Adams carried as commissioner to the court of Versailles, which Laurens thought sloppy and poorly done. Noting that the commission would be presented to the king of France, he asked Thomson to make a better copy. When the secretary abruptly refused, Laurens replied that he would then have it copied by his own secretary and that all Thomson would have to do was attest it. Thomson "imperiously" refused. Such conduct continued after Laurens's presidency until the two nearly exchanged blows on the floor on Congress. This latter incident, Laurens recalled, began when he requested two copies of the Journal of Congress for his state. Thomson refused, though there clearly were extra copies available. Thus, Laurens remembered,

> I reached out my hand to take another Copy, he snatched from me and said, you shan't have it—this repeated insult brought instantly to my mind his former conduct & provoked me to say, he was a most impudent fellow, that I had a good mind to kick him; he turned about, doubled his fist and said you dare not, I recollected the time and place and let him pass on. When he had humoured himself he returned with many spare Journals in his hands and gave me one, I barely asked him if he might not as well have done this at first.[45]

In his response, Thomson confirmed that he had not been on good terms with Laurens. He also demonstrated, however, little understanding of either the personality or the character of the former president. Thomson began with the declaration that of the five presidents he had served, only Laurens did not respect and befriend him. He asserted that conflict began shortly after Laurens assumed the presidency, when Thomson defended the character of the late Thomas Lynch, whom he accused Laurens of repeatedly attempting to vilify. In addition, Thomson felt that Laurens was angry that he had not been more successful in his efforts "to persuade Me that Moses the man of God and deliverer of Israel was an imposter and that he had deceived the Israelites at Mount Sinai by having had a knowledge of the use of gunpowder." In light of Laurens's deeply held religious views, this charge is inexplicable unless, as the editors of the *Letters of the Delegates to Congress* point out, Thomson had been fooled by Laurens's dry humor and sarcasm.[46] On a more serious note, Thomson accused Laurens of acting in an undignified and unpresidential manner while he occupied the chair. He accused Laurens of complaining of his conduct to other delegates in his absence, of engaging in debate from the chair, and of taunting several members, including John Penn of North Carolina. Finally, he complained that Laurens repeatedly and intentionally harassed him by purposely sending his messages to coincide with his meals or rest periods. Rather than attributing this to Laurens's own work ethic and willingness to sacrifice, Thomson was convinced that "he carefully attended to my hours of refreshment and rest and wished me to enjoy as little of either as possible." In searching for an explanation for such conduct, Thomson decided, in a note to his report, that

> This outrageous language & insolent behaviour may be attributed to his want of education and to his having been bred among negro slaves over whom he had been accustomed to tyrannize & against whom he could vent his ill humours & turbulent passions not only with impunity but to effect.[47]

This unpleasant subject was submitted to a committee and, under a compromise, probably devised by John Dickinson, both men expressed regret that the matter had arisen and promised to henceforth treat the other more respectfully. The subject was then dropped without the necessity of a committee report or a floor debate.[48]

By this time Laurens was again anxiously expressing his desire to return to South Carolina. Again he was frustrated, this time by the death of Drayton, which forced him to remain in Philadelphia to ensure that his state would have a vote in Congress. This delay would hold important consequences for Laurens: on October 21, 1779, he was elected to travel to The Hague to negotiate a loan not to exceed ten million dollars. On November 1, he received additional instructions to negotiate a treaty of amity and commerce with the Netherlands. For his services, he would receive a salary of fifteen hundred pounds sterling and would be allowed to appoint a secretary who would be paid no more than five hundred pounds sterling.[49] In accepting this commission, Laurens made it a condition that he first be allowed to pay a visit to Charles Town. When this request was granted, Laurens finally left Congress on November 9, 1779. After an overland journey that lasted an entire month, Laurens arrived at home in Charles Town on December 10 and began making preparations for the most perilous and fateful trip of his life.[50]

Thus ended the service of Henry Laurens in the Continental Congress. Though he had hoped that his service would be brief, Laurens spent over two uninterrupted years in Congress. This marked a degree of selflessness that was unparalleled among South Carolinians: indeed, other delegates, such as John Mathews, took advantage of Laurens's known devotion to the cause to shorten their own service in Congress at his expense. Laurens's record in Congress is mixed, as the accomplishments of his presidency are sometimes overshadowed by the tumultuous nature of his final year in Congress.

Laurens played an increasingly prominent role in the Deane-Lee Affair, a controversy that poisoned the atmosphere of Congress and aggravated the already distressing factional squabbles in the House. The dispute, in Laurens's eyes, was increasingly a battle between the true patriots and the war profiteers. Identifying himself with the former, Laurens embarked on a crusade against corruption that not only led to attacks on Deane, but also to charges against Robert Morris. As he descended from the presidency into the rampant political strife of Congress, Laurens insisted that he would continue to act independently as his conscience directed him. Like Christopher Gadsden before him, however, his conscience often led him to support the policies advocated by Richard Henry Lee and the Adamses. Though readily admitting that his views were similar to those of the Lees and the Adamses, Laurens steadfastly denied that either his voice or his vote was controlled by considerations of party.

Again repeating the course followed by Gadsden, Laurens assumed a strongly nationalistic stance in Congress. This stance, rather than any attachment to the Adamses and the Lees, was responsible for his position on the Newfoundland fisheries, a stance that brought a torrent of abuse from his fellow southerners in Congress. His performance in the resulting dispute with the North Carolina delegation marked perhaps his finest hour in Congress, as he courageously and successfully refused to allow his vote to be influenced by such strong external pressure. In the other controversies that marred his last year in Congress, however, Laurens did not show up so well. Had he been able to relax his strong sense of self-righteousness and his exaggerated sense of honor, he probably could have avoided, or at least moderated, the other conflicts he was engaged in during 1779. By November 1779, Laurens was more than ready to leave Congress and wished only that his release had come earlier. His only regret was that he would be unable to remain in South Carolina and defend his country against the imminent British onslaught. Yet, Laurens recognized the importance of his diplomatic mission to the Netherlands. As Laurens prepared for the honor and responsibility of representing his country abroad, little did he realize that he was about to be faced with the most dangerous crisis of his life.

14

Tribulation and Triumph, 1780–1785

HENRY LAURENS RETURNED TO A CHARLES TOWN THAT WAS MARKEDLY DIF-
ferent, both physically and psychologically, from the city he had left in
1777. The confidence and exuberance that had sprung from the defeat of
the British at Sullivan's Island and the Declaration of Independence had
lasted into 1777. Yet, not long after Laurens left for Philadelphia, the spirits
of the South Carolinians had begun to sag under the weight of several bitter
personal and political conflicts. As usual, Christopher Gadsden was in the
middle of these contests. It was his struggle with General Robert Howe
over the command of the military in South Carolina that produced the first
of these new controversies. It was the constant bickering between the
political faction led by Gadsden and Rawlins Lowndes and the one led by
the Rutledges that did the most to divide the people. This continual fighting, in addition to dealing a serious political blow to Gadsden, destroyed
the brief era of good feelings that had existed in Charles Town during 1776
and 1777. The new restlessness was reflected in the renewal of mob activity
during 1778, as the former Sons of Liberty rose against Lowndes and
Gadsden in June, and then engaged in a deadly brawl with French sailors in
September. Matters went from bad to worse in 1778, as the year opened
with a destructive fire in Charles Town in January and closed with the fall
of Georgia to the British. Though Charles Town defiantly held out throughout 1779, Laurens could not have been heartened by what he saw upon his
return. Gone was the cheerful confidence and brashness of the past. Instead, he saw a grim determination that masked a growing fear that
catastrophe was looming on the horizon. Even the normally optimistic
Gadsden feared that disaster was imminent if considerable assistance was
not received from Congress. Little did either Gadsden or Laurens know, as
they considered the situation at the end of 1779, that their names were
about to be closely joined again. This time, after the fall of Charles Town,
these two patriots would serve as the most prominent examples of British
vengeance.

Other than the curious bridge that Gadsden had constructed to connect
Sullivan's Island to the mainland, little was done to improve the Charles
Town defenses during 1777 and 1778. To add to this problem, the great fire

of January 15, 1778 destroyed a considerable amount of valuable property in the city. Both Gadsden and Laurens emerged from this disaster virtually unscathed, but many others were not so lucky. Gadsden estimated that there were 1434 nonbrick houses in Charles Town and that 252 of these, with a value (excluding contents) of over five hundred thousand pounds were destroyed by the fire. The most serious damage had occurred in the fashionable and mercantile districts near the bay and along Elliott, Tradd, Union, and Broad streets. John Wells, the conservative printer, informed Laurens that considerable quantities of indigo, rice, tobacco, and other products were lost in the warehouses along the bay. All told, Wells estimated the total damages to be in excess of one million pounds sterling. Among the greatest sufferers were the absent James Laurens, whose house was destroyed; Peter Timothy, who lost his press to the blaze; and the Charles Town Library Society, which suffered an almost total loss.[1]

While Gadsden and others in Charles Town were clearing the damage from the great fire, Laurens was in Congress nervously watching the movements of the British in New York. He was certain that the British had not forgotten about the South, and he warned Rawlins Lowndes that it would not hurt to be prepared, even if no British attack materialized. In mid-September 1778, however, Laurens received the alarming rumor that, after the end of the hurricane season, the British would launch an expedition of ten thousand men and a strong fleet against the southern states. Knowing that General James Grant, his old friend from the Cherokee War, favored such a plan and that Sir Henry Clinton might "be glad of an opportunity to recover the honor he left in the Sands of Long Island," Laurens tended to believe the report. General Washington, however, discounted such rumors with the observation that it would be "an Act of insanity" for the British to divide their fleet and army while the intentions of the French fleet remained unclear. Nevertheless, Laurens relayed the reports to South Carolina, along with urgent warnings to prepare for an attack. His alarm was shared by Congress, as this body, on September 25, 1778, ordered four thousand troops, both continentals and militia, to proceed from Virginia and North Carolina into South Carolina and Georgia.[2]

Laurens's alarm, though somewhat exaggerated, proved to be accurate when a small British force landed in Georgia during December 1778 and quickly conquered the weak and almost defenseless state. The fall of Georgia led South Carolinians to finally break their lethargy and prepare to meet the imminent attack. As Lowndes begged Congress for more aid, all Laurens could do was sadly shake his head and observe that he was "reduced to the state of many an old Man to content myself with saying 'I told you so.'"[3] Assessing the strength of his state, Laurens found little reason for encouragement. He calculated that, with a month's warning and no Indian problems, South Carolina could probably raise ten thousand men for the defense of the seacoast, though half of these would be poorly armed and clad. An Indian threat, however, would reduce these numbers to four to five thousand, precluding any effective defense of the entire coast.[4] As matters developed, even these figures would prove optimistic.

As the British fleet sailed toward Georgia, South Carolina was holding elections during November 1778. Though Gadsden won a seat in the General Assembly, the Rutledge faction scored a great victory, as John Rutledge was returned to the governorship and Thomas Bee was elected to succeed Gadsden as lieutenant governor. Despite his declining popularity, Gadsden was elected to a seat on the eight-man Privy Council, an advisory body to the governor. Still, Gadsden would be held firmly in check, as only he, Thomas Ferguson, and John Edwards could be labeled radicals, while the other five counselors were firmly in the moderate camp.[5] Just as political authority was changing hands, so, too, were changes coming to the military. The command of the Continental Army in South Carolina was transferred from Robert Howe to General Benjamin Lincoln, a solid and respectable, though hardly outstanding, officer from Massachusetts. Lincoln and Rutledge faced a difficult task as they attempted to coordinate military operations in South Carolina. The main problem came from the militia, as many of its leaders distrusted the Continentals and refused to cooperate with them, despite orders from Rutledge to do so. This caused the military strength of South Carolina to be dispersed throughout the state, with no guarantee that these forces would join together against the British.[6]

In April 1779, Lincoln decided to take four thousand of his Continentals and march into Georgia in an effort to protect the Georgia legislature in Augusta and prevent a British thrust into the backcountry. Such a course was frightening to the inhabitants of Charles Town, as it left the capital defended by a meager force of twelve hundred men under the command of General William Moultrie. Under these circumstances, Gadsden scribbled an urgent plea for help to his friend Samuel Adams in the Continental Congress. Gadsden reminded Adams that South Carolina had always been a firm supporter of Massachusetts when British efforts were aimed at that state. Yet now, when the roles were reversed and South Carolina was dependent upon Massachusetts and the other states, "we seem to be entirely deserted." No one was more disappointed with this state of affairs than Gadsden, as he continued:

And what must we think here, but that we are intended to be sacrificed to make a better Bargain for the other States? Such Taunts as these my Friend I *particularly* frequently receive who have been always a strong advocate for the New England States as especially so, as a Friend in need is a Friend indeed, in the Day of their Distress and Calamity. Now I am *seriously* told, *did we not tell you so*. When their turn was served we might go to the Devil.

Gadsden asked Adams to secure more aid for South Carolina before it was too late, insisting that if South Carolina fell, the entire South was likely to follow. If such an event were allowed to occur, Gadsden predicted that New England would again feel the wrath of the British and, this time, with no prospect of aid from the South.[7]

The desperation of Gadsden and other leaders turned to near panic in early May when a British force of twenty-four hundred men under General Augustine Prevost left Georgia and set out for Charles Town. This movement surprised the South Carolinians, who had expected the assault to come from the sea and had made few preparations against a land assault. Thus, while Moultrie moved out to slow Prevost's advance, the townsmen worked feverishly to prepare the capital against a land attack. The houses in the suburbs were razed for defense, while cannon and other fortifications were quickly thrown up upon the neck. Though messages were sent summoning the various military forces to assist in the defense of the capital, it was clear that Lincoln, who was marching on Savannah, would not be able to beat Prevost to Charles Town.[8] Even worse, as Moultrie retreated before the British, his force was reduced by half due to casualties and desertions. For many of these losses Moultrie blamed Lieutenant Colonel John Laurens, who had obtained leave from Washington's headquarters to assist in the defense of his home state. The rash young colonel led a near-disastrous rearguard action that threatened the destruction of a quarter of Moultrie's entire force before the Americans could extricate themselves. After this narrow escape, Moultrie distrusted the temperament of John Laurens, and later assessed him as "a young man of great merit and a brave soldier, but an imprudent officer; he was too rash and impetuous." By the time that Moultrie reached the capital, his force had dwindled to only six hundred, and the entire number of defenders probably did not exceed two thousand, most of these being militia.[9]

When Prevost arrived in front of the capital on May 11, Governor Rutledge sent a messenger to inquire into the terms of surrender. Prevost offered protection to all of those who returned to their allegiance to the Crown, though all others would be regarded as prisoners of war. Rutledge raised a white flag over the capital and summoned the Privy Council for consultation. Gadsden was shocked by the sight of the white flag, and was outraged when Rutledge proposed that the town be surrendered on condition that none of the citizens be held as prisoners, that Charles Town be declared a neutral port, and that the ultimate fate of South Carolina be decided at the final peace conference. To Gadsden, this proposition confirmed all of his worst fears about Rutledge, as it would not only result in surrender, but also in the retraction of the Declaration of Independence and the destruction of American unity. When the council voted along factional lines, five to three, to adopt Rutledge's proposal, Gadsden refused to accept the decision. Ignoring Rutledge's order of secrecy, Gadsden stormed out and rallied his friends in the assembly and the militia against the proposition. Reappearing a short time later, Gadsden declared that the militia had agreed that the authors of a surrender along these lines would pay with their lives.[10]

In addition to his problems with Gadsden, the governor had a difficult time finding a messenger willing to take his proposal to Prevost. Among those who refused this task was John Laurens, who declared that "he would do anything to serve his country; but he would not think of carrying such a message as that." After Rutledge finally found a messenger, Prevost refused his terms and insisted that he would negotiate only with Moultrie and only upon terms of immediate surrender, with everyone in arms as prisoners of war. Moultrie, who had only reluctantly acquiesced to Rutledge's proposal, then declared that if Prevost wanted the town he would have to take it, for there would be no more talk of surrender. As he lowered the white flag and prepared to withstand an attack, Moultrie was enthusiastically supported by Gadsden, Ferguson, and John Laurens. Yet no attack came. Instead, responding to rumors that Lincoln was approaching with his Continentals, Prevost withdrew from his lines to await reinforcements. For the moment, Charles Town was saved.[11]

The defenders of Charles Town had some breathing room, but not very much, as units of the British army were still close enough to threaten the capital. Indeed, the advance troops were so close that their movements were constantly monitored from the steeple of St. Michael's. Within a few weeks, however, Prevost recalled these units and set up camp near Beaufort, sixty miles to the south. Though Prevost had been stopped short of his goal, his expedition proved costly to South Carolina, as his army plundered the countryside at every opportunity. Most of the plantations in his path (including that of Lieutenant Governor William Bull) were looted, regardless of whether they belonged to patriots or Tories. Prevost's army carried off whatever valuables they could, including millions of pounds worth of indigo and approximately three thousand slaves, many of whom were later resold in the West Indies.[12]

The Prevost expedition had brought the horrors of war to South Carolina, and few were naive enough to think that the danger was over. In July 1779, Gadsden sent another appeal for help to Adams, noting, perhaps as a reflection upon Rutledge, that "we have had a narrow, very narrow, escape indeed, more from the treacherous Whispers and Insinuations of *internal* Enemies than from what our own external and open Tories were able to do against us here." Observing that the British were still within a few days' march of Charles Town and would surely renew the offensive, Gadsden again chided Congress for not offering more assistance. Noting that the only recent aid from Philadelphia was the unpopular advice to arm the slaves for defensive purposes, Gadsden rejected the proposal as one that was "received with great resentment, as a dangerous and impolitic Step." Instead, Gadsden repeated his earlier request that Congress send several frigates for the defense of the harbor. At the same time, he again displayed a suspicion, shared by many in South Carolina, that Congress was sacrificing his state to the British, when he asked, "but why do I say *our* Frigates, when by the Whole proceedings of the Congress, we begin to think, they imagine We have no right or pretensions to any share in them."[13]

The situation appeared to brighten when the combination of Lincoln's Continentals and a French fleet and army under the Count d'Estaing forced Prevost to retreat into Savannah. The siege, however, was broken off after the attempt to storm the town was bloodily repulsed. By fall, the French had departed and Lincoln returned to Charles Town to await future events.[14] By the time Henry Laurens returned to Charles Town in early December 1779, the morale of the inhabitants was at a low point. As the people nervously awaited the future, little had been done to repair the damage from either the fire of January 1778 or from the Prevost raid. Profiteers were charging excessive prices for even the bare necessities, and a raging smallpox epidemic discouraged the country militia from remaining in Charles Town. Even the Continentals were anxious to escape the capital and, by the end of 1779, the continental regiments had declined in strength from twenty-four hundred to only eight hundred men. Thus, by the end of the year, Charles Town was again almost defenseless against attack.[15]

Matters went from bad to worse when Sir Henry Clinton, after receiving the news of the British victory at Savannah, decided to launch a major offensive against Charles Town. Thus, on December 26, 1779, Clinton and Admiral Marriott Arbuthnot sailed from New York with a powerful fleet and a military force of eighty-five hundred men. Clinton landed at Edisto Island, about thirty miles south of Charles Town, on February 11, 1780. Had he moved quickly against the poorly defended capital, he could have captured it with little difficulty. But Clinton was a cautious soldier, and he spent several weeks organizing and augmenting his army to over ten thousand men before he finally moved against Charles Town in late March.[16]

Clinton's delay gave the South Carolinians precious time to prepare for defense. Aware of the British approach, the General Assembly gathered on January 26, 1780 and immediately set to work. Both Gadsden and Henry Laurens, who qualified as a member on January 31, were appointed to important committees.[17] As Clinton prepared his forces at Edisto Island, the patriots worked frantically to gather more troops and repair the defenses of the capital. A desperate Governor Rutledge issued a proclamation threatening to confiscate the property of any citizen who did not join the garrison at Charles Town. These efforts brought some men into the city, but not enough to give the patriots a realistic chance of holding out against the British. By the time that Clinton appeared before the capital, Lincoln commanded approximately fifty-five hundred men, as well as a few frigates sent by Congress to assist in the defense of the harbor. That Clinton had an army of over ten thousand men and a sizable fleet made the prospects for success dismal.[18] With this in mind, several South Carolina leaders began making plans for escape. Henry Laurens, in light of his diplomatic mission to the Netherlands, was among the first to go. Laurens had hoped to sail from Charles Town to France, but, as he prepared to sail at the end of February, thirteen of Arbuthnot's men-of-war dropped anchor outside the harbor, forcing him to seek out a departure site further to the north.[19] As Clinton approached, it was agreed that Governor Rutledge, along with counselors Charles Pinckney, Daniel Huger, and John Lewis Gervais, would leave the capital and set up a government in exile in the hills to the northwest of Charles Town. It was also agreed that Gadsden and the other counselors—Thomas Ferguson, David Ramsay, Richard Hutson, and Benjamin Catell—would remain in the capital to act as the civil authority and to encourage the people. In addition, since Lieutenant Governor Thomas Bee was serving in the Continental Congress, Rutledge, in accordance with a clause in the constitution, appointed Gadsden to serve in Bee's stead. Thus, after Rutledge left the capital on April 12, Gadsden was the highest ranking civil official in Charles Town. It would be difficult to imagine a worse choice, as this situation demanded a flexible and pragmatic statesman, rather than a determined, single-minded zealot.[20]

While Gadsden's decision to remain in the capital was certainly among the most courageous of his life, it was not among the most prudent. By the middle of April it was clear that time was running out and that escape would soon be impossible. Though Gadsden refused to give up and was still sending urgent messages as far away as the Spanish authorities at Havana, the situation was approaching the critical point. Clinton crossed the Ashley River on March 28 and began construction of his works before Charles Town on April 1. Six days later, British warships sailed past Fort Moultrie and settled in the harbor below Fort Johnson. With the sea exit blocked and the land works nearing completion, Clinton and Arbuthnot, on April 10, called upon the town to surrender. Three days later, after the summons had been rejected, the British opened fire on the American lines. As the British extended their lines to within three hundred yards of the capital and British guns began firing into the city, Lincoln was faced with massive desertion among the militia, and even several units of Continentals. Lincoln was now in an extremely uncomfortable position, as the sea escape was blocked and Clinton was close to blocking all other avenues of escape. Only quick and decisive action could save the remnants of the army.[21]

As Lincoln discussed his diminishing alternatives with his officers on April 20, Gadsden arrived and joined the conversation. No law or custom required Gadsden's attendance at this meeting and, as the subject was military tactics, Lincoln had no obligation to allow him to remain. Nevertheless, in what was perhaps his most critical mistake of the entire campaign, Lincoln not only allowed Gadsden to remain, but he also allowed the lieutenant governor to dominate the proceedings by the strength of his personality. Though the situation was clearly becoming hopeless, Gadsden absolutely refused to consider evacuation or surrender, declaring that he would rather die than do the latter. The Continental officers curtly dismissed such bravado and urged Lincoln to ignore the lieutenant governor and take the steps necessary to save his army. But Gadsden refused to be ignored and wrung from the general the promise that no action would be taken without the consent of him and his council. Thus, when the meeting reconvened that evening at Lincoln's headquarters, Gadsden was again present, this time with the entire council. When Lincoln leaned toward evacuation, Gadsden angrily denounced it as unacceptable to the inhabitants. Thomas Ferguson went further, crying that if any attempt at evacuation was made, the gates would be opened and the people would fall upon the Continentals themselves. The shaken Lincoln was then confronted by an irate Colonel Charles Cotesworth Pinckney, who stormed into the meeting and demanded that the struggle be continued. Under these assaults, Lincoln wilted and allowed himself to be bullied by the belligerent South Carolinians. To the dismay of his officers, he ignored the military realities and agreed to hold out. This weak decision sealed the fate of over two thousand badly needed Continentals and virtually guaranteed the worst catastrophe that was to befall the United States during the Revolutionary War.[22]

Within days Clinton had blocked all of the escape routes, leaving the defenders with only the choice between capitulation and annihilation. Within one hundred yards of the American lines, the British lobbed shells into Charles Town. Lincoln finally decided to ignore Gadsden and to surrender the garrison on the best available terms. After the failure of initial negotiations, Clinton, on May 8, offered Lincoln a choice between surrendering the inhabitants of the town as prisoners of war or submitting to an assault that could result in heavy civilian casualties. By this time, even Gadsden was prepared to admit that the capital was doomed, and he prepared his proposals for surrender. His suggestions bore little resemblance to the realities of the situation. Gadsden demanded that the persons and property of all of the citizens, as well as the Frenchmen and Spaniards in the town, be protected as inviolable and that the citizens be allowed one year to decide whether they wished to continue under British rule or move to a new location. Though Lincoln had already been refused similar terms, he again yielded to Gadsden and incorporated the proposals into a new offer.[23]

It is hardly surprising that neither Clinton nor Arbuthnot even considered such terms. Instead, they demanded that all of the inhabitants of the town, including the militia, be surrendered as prisoners of war on parole. The citizens would be free from molestation in their property as long as they observed their paroles. The garrison would be refused the honors of war and would be required to march out of the town at a designated time and place, but would not be allowed to beat a British march or have their colors uncased. Lincoln was unwilling to accept such harsh terms and, without the knowledge of Gadsden, countered with a new offer. When Gadsden discovered that Lincoln was negotiating independently, he flew into a rage and wrote a bitter letter to the general, which the council prevailed upon him not to send.[24]

Realizing that negotiations were getting them nowhere, Clinton and Arbuthnot notified the Americans that, unless their terms were accepted, they would commence firing at 8:00 P.M. on May 9. When the hour arrived, both sides waited to see what the other would do. Finally, the American artillery opened up, followed by the British in response. The resulting bombardment did considerable damage inside Charles Town and, by morning, the town was ready to surrender. Even Gadsden had had enough and, as Clinton prepared the final assault, Lincoln ran up the white flag and agreed to the terms offered earlier by the British. When Clinton agreed, the garrison marched out and, without the honors of war, laid down their arms on May 12, 1780. Under the terms of capitulation, signed by Gadsden in his capacity as lieutenant governor, all the inhabitants of Charles Town, as well as the militia and continental soldiers, were prisoners of war. Thus, Clinton could boast that he had taken over five thousand prisoners.[25]

The surrender of Charles Town was the worst defeat suffered by the United States during the Revolutionary War, a disaster that might have been avoided had Lincoln been bolder and Gadsden less so. When Clinton arrived before Charles Town, it was clear that the fall of the capital was imminent, particularly after Arbuthnot's fleet entered the harbor. As there was little hope of a successful defense, it was Lincoln's duty to see to the welfare of his Continentals and the citizens of the town. Yet, despite the hopelessness of the cause, he allowed Gadsden to bully him into defending the doomed capital, subjecting the inhabitants to the hardships of a siege and assuring his continentals the rigors of British prison camps and ships. The conduct of Gadsden during this episode also calls for some severe criticism. While he again exhibited his tremendous determination, this quality was disastrous, as it was not tempered by discretion. Once it was clear that Charles Town was doomed, Gadsden should have directed his efforts to helping Lincoln salvage whatever he could from the loss of the capital. Instead, he placed every obstacle he could devise in the path of the Continental officers as they tried to save their army. Gadsden possessed no authority in military affairs that Lincoln was bound to respect, and he should not have been allowed to dominate the military conferences. Lincoln should have possessed the backbone to ignore the interference of the lieutenant governor and his council and, if necessary, to arrest them when they threatened mutiny. Instead, Lincoln surrendered to Gadsden's browbeating and thereby multiplied the costs of an already serious defeat.[26]

Regardless of where the blame lay, Christopher Gadsden was now a prisoner of the British. He was allowed to return to his home as a prisoner on parole, and was assured that he would not be molested as long as he did nothing injurious to the British interest. As Gadsden surveyed the situation, there was little room for optimism. The bombardment had caused a considerable amount of damage to the town, though there is no exact record of how much Gadsden's property suffered. It is clear, however, that he was more fortunate than some of his neighbors. Gadsden could at least live in his Ansonborough home, while others, such as Henry Laurens, suffered severe losses. John Laurens, who also became a prisoner at the surrender, informed his father that his Charles Town property had "been rudely handled by the Enemy." His house was uninhabitable and his gardens and fences, like those of Gadsden and his other neighbors, had been completely destroyed. Still, Laurens had saved his papers and many other possessions through the foresight of transfering them to Mepkin before the commencement of the siege.[27]

For the inhabitants of Charles Town, the outlook was even bleaker. Clinton and Arbuthnot disagreed on how the defeated rebels should be governed. Though Arbuthnot proposed a lenient policy, hoping that the reopening of the port and the early reestablishment of civil government might win the people over to the British side, Clinton was not in such a charitable mood. Assuming that the surrender of Charles Town had represented the capitulation of the entire state, particularly since Lieutenant Governor Gadsden had signed the articles of capitulation, Clinton was angry to discover that Governor John Rutledge was organizing opposition in the northern part of the state. Thus, Clinton felt the need for a clear distinction between loyalists and rebels. It was this policy that was implemented by Lord Cornwallis, who took command when Clinton returned to New York in July 1780.[28]

The British were extremely frustrated by their inability to restore the allegiance of many South Carolinians. Cornwallis quickly found that patriot resistance in the backcountry was much stronger than he had anticipated. Even after he routed an army under General Horatio Gates at Camden, it was apparent that the patriots would not quit. Instead, a vicious civil war erupted in the backcountry, which lasted for the duration of the war and included patriots, Tories, and British regulars. As outrage followed outrage on the frontier, Cornwallis decided that greater pressure was necessary to bring the bulk of the patriots to return to their British allegiance. Thus, he destroyed the estates of some patriot leaders, confiscated those of others, and placed economic pressure on those who refused to swear loyalty to the king. Particularly strong pressure was placed upon the capital, as Cornwallis decreed that any man who refused to take the oath would be denied permission to engage in any trade, sue in court (though he could be sued), or even leave the city limits. To implement these plans while he was away on campaign, Cornwallis appointed Lieutenant Colonel Nisbet Balfour to serve as commandant of Charles Town. Balfour rigorously and effectively enforced Cornwallis's edicts. By refusing to allow the mechanics to practice their trades unless they took the oath of allegiance, Balfour forced many patriots to take the oath in order to feed their families. For those who managed to hold out, the example of Gadsden and other leaders was quite important. While careful to obey the constraints of his parole, Gadsden realized that his refusal, and that of other leaders, to accept British protection contributed to patriot morale and encouraged further resistance.[29]

Cornwallis also recognized the importance of these examples, and was determined to take action against the patriot leaders. This was a problem, however, as the South Carolinians were not actively working against British interests and, thus, the British could not revoke their paroles and order sterner punishments. Still, the paroles expressly stated that the prisoners could be ordered to surrender themselves at any place and time demanded by the British. Thus, Cornwallis decided that it was too dangerous to allow Gadsden and other leaders to continue their residence in Charles Town and ordered them sent into exile. Early on the morning of Sunday, August 27, 1780, armed soldiers appeared at the Gadsden residence. He was taken, "felon like," to the upper part of the exchange building where he met twenty-eight other prominent patriot leaders who had been likewise arrested on the order of Lord Cornwallis. Among those detained with Gadsden were Thomas Ferguson, David Ramsay, Richard Hutson, Edward and Hugh Rutledge, Thomas Heyward, Jr., and Peter Timothy. The prisoners remained at the exchange for only a few hours before they were taken to the warship *Sandwich*, anchored in the harbor.[30]

As the surprised patriots gathered aboard the *Sandwich*, they prepared a memorial to Balfour complaining of their treatment and requesting an explanation. They asserted that Sir Henry Clinton had agreed to respect their persons and property, as long as they observed their paroles. But Clinton had done no such thing. Indeed, he had explicitly refused to guarantee either the persons or the property of the civil officials. The actions taken by Cornwallis were unduly harsh and poor policy, but they were within his rights under the terms of the paroles.[31] Even while the inquiry of the prisoners was being delivered, a British officer appeared and presented a note to Gadsden. This note, bearing neither signature nor date, read as follows:

> Gentlemen—In obedience to the order of the Commandant, I am to inform you that my Lord Cornwallis being highly incensed at the late perfidious Revolt of many of the Inhabitants of this province and being well informed by papers that have fallen into his hands since the defeat of the Rebel Army, of the means that have been taken by several People on Parole in Charles Town to promote and foment this Spirit of Rebellion. His Lordship in order to secure the quiet of the province, finds himself under the necessity to direct the Commandant to order several Persons to change their Place of Residence on Parole from Charles Town to St. Augustine; His Lordship has further directed that a proper Vessell be provided to carry their Baggage with them.[32]

While this note suggests that the relocation was ordered as punishment for parole violations, the evidence indicates that the action was taken as a policy, rather than a punitive, measure. No further charge appeared that the patriot leaders had broken their paroles, and no concrete evidence was ever presented proving that this had occurred. Indeed, both Balfour and Cornwallis hanged Americans for violating their paroles, and there is no reason to believe that such punishment would have been withheld from Christopher Gadsden or other leaders if it could be established that they had broken their paroles. The matter was quickly settled, however, when, later that same day, another message was received that explicitly stated that the relocation was for policy reasons.[33]

While such an explanation was unsatisfactory and of little comfort to the prisoners, there was nothing they could do about it. During the next week, the British collected several more prisoners and transferred the entire company, which now numbered thirty-seven, to the *Fidelity* for the voyage to St. Augustine. After being allowed a final visit from friends and family on September 3, the prisoners on the *Fidelity* sailed the next day. Conditions aboard the vessel, a small transport ship, were crowded, as 106 people, including servants and soldiers sent to protect the ship, were aboard. Additionally, the ship carried a considerable number of livestock; their purpose was to support the prisoners, but they added to the unpleasantness of the journey. Just before the *Fidelity* sailed, the captain gathered the prisoners together and insisted that they take a new parole for their conduct aboard the ship and at St. Augustine. Thirty-six of the patriots agreed to give the new parole. Only Christopher Gadsden defiantly refused, stating that he had already given his parole and, as his word was still good, would not do so again. Apparently, the captain was satisfied with this, for there is no record of any disciplinary action taken against Gadsden at this time. Then, the *Fidelity* sailed, arriving at St. Augustine on September 8, after a three-day voyage.[34]

The next day, the prisoners landed at St. Augustine and were presented with yet a new parole. This one would be more severe than the parole taken at Charles Town for, in addition to promising not to work against the British interest, the prisoners would be restricted to certain areas of the town. Governor Patrick Tonyn and Lieutenant Colonel Glazier, the military commandant, appeared and asked the prisoners if they were prepared to give their paroles. Tonyn added that those who agreed would be granted the liberty of the town, while those who refused would be sent to the dungeon. Gadsden defiantly complained that the treatment of the patriots was illegal under the articles of capitulation. Tonyn interrupted, declaring that he had not come to enter into an argument, and demanded that Gadsden give his parole. Gadsden courageously answered that

> With men who have once deceived me, I can enter into no new contract. Had the British commanders regarded the terms of the capitulation of Charles Town, I might now, although a prisoner, under my own roof, have enjoyed the smiles and consolations of my surrounding family; but even without a shadow of accusation proferred against me, for any act inconsistent with my plighted faith, I am torn from them, and here, in a distant land, invited to enter into new engagements, I will give no parole.

"Think better of it, Sir," replied the officer, "a second refusal of it will fix your destiny—a dungeon will be your future habitation." Gadsden boldly answered, "Prepare it then. I will give no parole, so help me God!" Gadsden was immediately taken and conducted to the Castillo de San Marcos, where he was placed in the damp, and dark dungeon that would be his residence for the next forty-two weeks. None of the other South Carolinians followed this example, as each gave his parole.[35]

While Gadsden was adjusting to life as a prisoner of war, Henry Laurens was frustrated by other problems. Though he had escaped Charles Town in pursuit of his diplomatic mission to the Netherlands, he was unable to find transportation to Europe and, by the end of June, was back in Philadelphia.[36] The fall of Charles Town, Laurens's own disordered private affairs, and Congress's commissioning of John Adams to negotiate the Dutch loan in his absence led Laurens to question the necessity of his trip. Yet, when transport suddenly became available, Laurens left Philadelphia aboard the brigantine *Mercury* on August 13, 1780. In an interesting sidelight, John Laurens, who had been exchanged shortly after the fall of Charles Town, rushed to Philadelphia in time to accompany his father on the first leg of his journey. This would be the last meeting between these two devoted friends, as Laurens would not return to America until 1784, almost two years after the death of his beloved son.[37]

Though the *Mercury* was highly regarded as one of the fastest American ships, its small size placed it at the mercy of any British warship it might encounter. Thus, the ship was accompanied by the sixteen-gun warship *Saratoga*, and orders were dispatched to two other warships to join the convoy. After several days of waiting, Laurens feared that further delay would lose the advantages of a favorable wind and decided to sail without the delinquent warships. Six days later, tired of being slowed by the larger and clumsier *Saratoga*, Laurens ordered the vessel to return to America. This represented a serious risk, for it left the *Mercury* alone and unprotected. The gamble was quickly lost when, on September 3, the British frigate *Vestal* appeared to threaten the smaller American ship. Aware of the danger, Laurens destroyed all of the papers that he deemed important, though he saved other papers that he considered inconsequential. Recalling that there were some private papers among the latter papers, Laurens submitted to the urgings of his secretary, Moses Young, and threw them overboard in a weighted bag. The alert British retrieved this bag and found that it contained the draft of a proposed treaty with the Dutch, a text that the British government would later use as the pretext for a declaration of war against the Netherlands. When the *Mercury* surrendered, Laurens and his secretary were conducted to the *Vestal*. Noting that Young appeared downcast, Laurens told him to cheer up, as his capture would place him in England "where I shall be of more real service to my country than I could possibly be in any other part of Europe." Had Laurens been able to foresee the future, he might have been less enthusiastic. In any event, the evening of September 3, 1780 found Henry Laurens and Christopher Gadsden in similarly precarious situations: as prisoners aboard British warships, awaiting transportation to an unpleasant new life.[38]

Laurens was satisfied with his treatment aboard the *Vestal*, as it anchored off the coast of Newfoundland. He reported that the officers were friendly and hospitable and that he never heard the term "rebel" during his stay among them. He was often invited to dine at the table of the admiral of the fleet. The conversation was pleasant, though politics were not avoided and Laurens did not hesitate to make his position clear when such subjects arose. At one dinner, the admiral proposed a toast to the king. Laurens drank the toast and then raised another to General Washington, which his hosts likewise drank. When the conversation turned to the war, the admiral, according to Laurens, "observed that I had been pretty active among my countrymen." Laurens replied that

> I had once been a good British subject, but after Great Britain had refused to hear our petitions, and had thrown us out of her protection, I had endeavoured to do my duty. The Americans, I added, had not set up an independence. Great Britain had made them independent by throwing them out of her protection, and committing hostilities upon them by sea and land. Nothing remained for Congress but to declare to the world that the United Colonies were independent.

The admiral replied that the British were now prepared for peace upon any terms, providing that the French alliance was renounced. This was unfortunate, responded Laurens, for the treaty was a sine qua non that could not and would not be violated.[39] Even these political discussions were friendly and, by the time the fleet reached England, the officers were advising Laurens on which hotels to stay in when he reached London. When one suggested the New Hotel, Laurens asked if there was not a hotel called Newgate. The shocked officers hastened to assure him that the ministry would not dare confine him in the notorious prison. Laurens remained unconvinced.[40]

On landing at Dartmouth, Laurens was taken by coach to London. He thought this a peculiar journey, for not only did it last several days, but he was given repeated opportunities for escape. Yet Laurens refused to attempt escape and he arrived in London late on the evening of October 5. Ominously, his treatment now changed, as he was taken to Scotland Yard and placed under heavy guard, despite the fact that he was seriously ill and unable to get in or out of a carriage or to climb stairs without assistance. The next morning he was taken to Whitehall, where he appeared before several of the ministers, including Lords Hillsborough, Stormont, and George Germain, as well as Mr. Justice Addington. After formal identification and a few brief questions, Laurens was informed by Lord Stormont that he was to be immediately committed to the Tower of London for "suspicion of high treason."[41]

Laurens was received by Major Gore, the governor in residence of the Tower, and a man determined to treat his new prisoner as rigorously as possible. Thus, he assigned Laurens to a two-room apartment that measured barely twenty square feet and was located in the most conspicuous part of the Tower. This was no accident, for it was Gore's intention to expose his prisoner to the view of passersby, as if he were a beast confined in a zoo. Laurens, however, managed to arrange some nearby vines in a way that concealed him from view, but allowed him a view of the outside. As if this were not enough, Laurens must have read with concern the orders issued by the ministry concerning his confinement. In Laurens's words these orders were

> To confine me as a close prisoner; to be locked up every night; to be in the custody of two wardens, who were not to suffer me to be out of their sight *one moment* day or night; to allow me no liberty of speaking to any person, nor to permit any person to speak to me; to deprive me of the use of pen and ink; to suffer no letter to be brought to me, nor any to go from me, &c.

To add insult to injury, the next day wardens appeared in Laurens's rooms and attached iron bars to the windows.[42]

To make matters worse, Laurens quickly found that the ministry was prepared to make no provision for his support. He learned that he was responsible for rent, food, bedding, and other supplies. When he received no reply to his query of how he was expected to obtain these materials without the use of pen and ink, Laurens bitterly proclaimed that "Whenever I caught a bird in America I found a cage and victuals for it." Yet, the thing that left him with the deepest sense of bitterness was the failure of the ministry to offer medical assistance, despite its awareness of his poor health. Laurens found this conduct completely unacceptable and resolved that he would survive his ordeal, if for no other reason than to spite his captors. On October 14, he was allowed his first visit, a half hour conversation with his son Henry Laurens, Jr. and his old friend William Manning. He spent much of this visit bitterly denouncing his treatment and finally declared that since he landed in England, "he was treated with a barbarity which he could never expect from Englishmen."[43] The other American commissioners in Europe did what little they could to relieve the severity of Laurens's treatment. His old friend John Adams urged Benjamin Franklin to use whatever influence he still retained in England to secure better treatment for Laurens. Though Franklin complied and wrote a letter to a friend in the British government, his efforts were fruitless.[44]

Though denied the use of pen and ink, Laurens was a resourceful man and was determined to find a means of serving his country, even in his disadvantaged state. Shortly after his arrival in the Tower, a woman approached him and offered to smuggle any of his writings from the prison.[45] At first, he suspected that the offer was arranged by the ministry in an effort to entrap him. Yet, he soon decided that he had little to lose and began making anonymous contributions to the "rebel newspapers" of London. These writings baffled and infuriated the ministry, as Laurens contributed many articles defending the American cause, including one defending the conduct of Congress in suspending the Saratoga Convention and another concerning "the history of the apostate Arnold." Laurens was pleased that his writings were so frustrating to the ministry and pleasurably recorded that, at one point, one of the ministers exclaimed that the writings "smelt strong of the Tower."[46] Besides writing, there was not a great deal for Laurens to do in the Tower. When he was not lame from gout, he often enjoyed walking in the Tower grounds. Even this exercise, however, could be used by Governor Gore to harass his prisoner. It was required that Laurens always be accompanied by a warden with a sword, and Gore insisted that Laurens walk along paths that would expose him to public view. Even after General Vernon, Gore's superior and a man respected by Laurens for his civility, ordered that Laurens be allowed to walk a more private route, Gore still found a way to make trouble for the prisoner. In early December, when out on his walk, Laurens met Lord George Gordon, imprisoned on the suspicion that he had sponsored the serious anti-Catholic rioting in London in 1780. Though Laurens declined Gordon's invitation to walk with him and immediately returned to his quarters, Gore still ordered him locked up and closely confined for the next forty-seven days. While Laurens was thus deprived of his exercise, no punishment was assessed to Gordon.[47]

By early 1781, it was apparent that the ministry had failed in its effort to break Laurens through severity. Thus, at the end of February 1781, they decided to employ new measures. Laurens received a message from his old friend, the Scottish merchant Richard Oswald, that he had petitioned the ministry for Laurens's release and had pledged his entire fortune for the good conduct of his friend. The ministers had agreed to Laurens's release if he would make a public statement acknowledging British authority. Laurens was gratified by Oswald's gesture, but insulted by the response of the ministry. Noting that he could regain his freedom if he were a rascal, Laurens refused to dishonor either himself or Oswald by gaining release on these terms. Several days later, in early March, Oswald visited Laurens and again raised the possibility of a pardon if Laurens would apologize for his past actions. Laurens felt he had nothing to apologize for and replied without hesitation that "I will never subscribe to my own infamy, and to the dishonor of my children." When Oswald alluded to the possible consequences of a refusal, Laurens replied that the only consequences he feared were those that would result from dishonorable acts. Oswald then took his leave, but "with such expressions of regard and such a squeeze of the hand, as induced me to believe, he was not displeased with my determination."[48]

This was not the last effort to convince Laurens to regain his freedom through a renunciation of the American cause. A week after the rebuff of Oswald, Laurens was visited by another old friend, General James Grant. The "queer" questions offered by Grant led Laurens to quickly suspect that his visit was more than a courtesy call. His suspicions were confirmed when Grant announced that he had brought paper and pencil and was prepared to relay any propositions to the ministry. Laurens replied that his only proposition was for release upon parole, an indulgence that he considered only fair when one considered his generosity toward British prisoners in America. As for personal hardship, "I had well weighed what consequences might follow before I entered into the present dispute. I took the path of justice and honor, and no personal evils will cause me to shrink." Grant appeared chagrined at this answer and soon departed, promising to visit again, though he never did. A similar visit from Manning a few days later brought similar results.[49]

Matters grew more dangerous, however, when, in April 1781, it was learned that John Laurens had arrived in Paris on a special mission from Congress. Both Manning and Oswald informed Laurens that this mission was greatly resented by the ministry and could result in even harsher treatment for Laurens himself. Manning pleaded with his old friend to ask his son (and Manning's son-in-law) to withdraw, adding that such a course would gratify the ministry. Always mindful of questions of honor, Laurens replied that

> my son is of age, and has a will of his own; if I should write to him in the terms you request, it would have no effect; he would only conclude that confinement and persuasion of my old friends had softened me. I know him to be a man of honor; he loves me dearly, and would lay down his life to save mine; but I am sure, he would not sacrifice his honor to save my life, and I applaud him.[50]

While in France, John Laurens appealed to the French government for assistance in obtaining the release, or, at least, better treatment for his father. He received little satisfaction, as the French observed that the British were no more inclined to gratify the court of France than the United States. Instead, they suggested that the British might moderate their position if Congress practiced similar treatment on a prominent British prisoner or two. This proposal appealed to John Laurens and he endorsed it in a letter to Congress.[51] This body had already reached a similar conclusion and threatened to recall Burgoyne before finally authorizing Franklin to exchange Burgoyne for Laurens. Franklin thought such an exchange unlikely since the current ministry had little love for Burgoyne and "would have no objection to Americans recalling and hanging" him. Thus, despite the efforts of Congress, Laurens continued as a prisoner in the Tower and his treatment remained severe.[52]

By the middle of June 1781, Laurens was beginning to suffer the effects of rigid imprisonment. His funds were nearly exhausted and he was allowed few visits. In addition, he was hearing reports, which he seemed to blame upon Lieutenant Governor William Bull, that distorted his record and portrayed him as a violent revolutionary and as a leading contributor to the outbreak of hostilities. Thus, on June 23, 1781, Laurens constructed an address to the secretaries of state, in which he pursued three purposes. First, he applied for pen and ink so that he could draw a bill for his support on John Nutt, a London merchant who owed him a debt in excess of eight hundred fifty pounds. Second, he applied for permission for his son Henry, Jr. to visit him so that the future education of the youth might be planned. Finally, he hoped to clarify the record concerning his role in the protest movement, while at the same time gaining release upon his parole. Laurens clearly saw nothing objectionable or dishonorable in his petition, as he mentioned it in a matter-of-fact manner in his "Narrative" and added little more than that the ministry had taken no notice of the paper.[53]

The representation, addressed to Hillsborough, Stormont, and Lord George Germain, was written in respectful terms and definitely downplayed his role in the protest movement. This might be expected, as Laurens had been in the Tower for over eight months, and had received no hint that anyone had taken any measures for his relief. Thus, he may be excused for seeking to alleviate the rigidity of his treatment. Laurens denied the charges against him: that he was a born republican, naturally opposed to royal government; that he was among the greatest smugglers and had been in constant conflict with the Navigation Acts; that he was among the most prominent promoters of the disturbances in America in 1765 and afterwards; that he was a staunch persecutor of the Loyalists; and that he had proposed and effected the resolution for suspending payment of British debts in 1775. A glance at these charges explains Laurens's anger and disappointment with Lieutenant Governor Bull, as these charges were all patently false and Bull was in a position to know it. Yet, Laurens was convinced that Bull had done nothing to refute the accusations, if he had not actively assisted in spreading them.[54]

Nothing in the representation was new, as Laurens denied the charges in terms that he had often used in the past. Yet, while Laurens could truthfully refute the charges, he did so in a way that could have been considered unpatriotic to some Americans during the early 1780s. As he had done so many times before, Laurens proclaimed that he had always revered Great Britain and the king and viewed the prospects of separation with extreme displeasure and distaste. He insisted that he had always opposed any radical or illegal schemes and had always demanded that opposition be based on firm constitutional grounds. He continued to operate under such a policy until repeated British oppression had forced the separation of the two countries. Even at this point, he felt sorrow at the event and continued to treat British prisoners and sympathizers with a respect and benevolence that was now denied to him. Finally, Laurens wrote that

> In a word the Represular never acted the Demagogue or Incendiary of the People, never suggested or promoted any measure which could possibly be affrontive to His Majesty or tend to disturb the order of good Government & he cannot forbear contrasting the present circumstances of persons who did act in such Characters & persecuted him as described above who are now treated as Prisoners of War & also in possession of their Estates—with his own.

In this appeal, as might be expected, Laurens had little to say about his services as president of the South Carolina revolutionary bodies during 1775 and 1776 and as president of the Continental Congress. None of these statements were false, nor did they betray any sympathy for the British cause. Yet, they might easily be seen as unpatriotic by those enjoying the comforts of Philadelphia. Perhaps Laurens himself would have seen them in such a light if he were in the American capital. Still, from the vantage point of the Tower, such a representation appeared to be reasonable, unobjectionable, and calculated to achieve his limited objectives. In this, Laurens was disappointed, as he received no indication that the ministry ever saw his appeal, much less responded to it.[55]

As Laurens dealt with life in the Tower, Gadsden languished in the dungeon in St. Augustine. He could boast of few of the meager privileges possessed by Laurens in London: his quarters were more spacious than those occupied by Laurens, but the dirt floors, sparse furnishings, and total absence of windows or other sources of light made his residence even more depressing. The treatment accorded to Gadsden seems to have been at least as rigorous as that offered to Laurens. He was never allowed to leave the dungeon, even for meals or exercise. He, too, was denied the privilege of sending and receiving letters and, in contrast to Laurens, seems never to have discovered a means for circumventing this order. The guards were under orders to have no conversation with their prisoner, though, as Gadsden later informed Washington, they frequently ignored this command. Gadsden found his guards much friendlier than did Laurens, and he wrote that they generally behaved decently and did not insult him. Gadsden was allowed to have a candle so that he could read, and he took advantage of the situation to take up the study of Hebrew. Yet, the guards could be arbitrary and, upon one occasion, they took away his candle for several days.[56]

The treatment of the other exiles was much better. With the exception of Jacob Read, who was sent to a dungeon separate from Gadsden after his correspondence ran afoul of the censor, the exiles were allowed a limited degree of freedom. They were allowed to receive food and drink from their families, and thus, could live at whatever standard their families could afford to support them. Meanwhile, they were subjected to twice-daily roll calls, censorship of their correspondence, and a ban on fraternization with the townspeople. At first, they were allowed to hold their own private church services, but an abrupt end was put to this practice after Governor Tonyn found one of their sermons to be offensive. Henceforth, they were required to attend the local parish church and to pray for the king. They complied with the first demand, but refused the second. Psychologically, the treatment was more severe, as the British controlled all of the sources of information and were very selective about the news released to the South Carolinians. The exiles were told that the British had won several key battles and that the rebellion was about to collapse. Then, they were told, the prisoners might expect the fate of defeated rebels. Such threats grew more serious in October 1780 after the treason of Benedict Arnold and the capture of Major John André. Retribution on the South Carolinians at St. Augustine was promised if André were executed. Colonel Glazier sent word to Gadsden to prepare himself, for, if André were executed, he was the likely candidate for retaliation. Undaunted, Gadsden bravely answered that "he would not shrink from the sacrifice, and would rather ascend the scaffold than purchase with his life the dishonor of his country."[57]

Though there were no executions in retaliation for the hanging of André, the British continued to hold the South Carolina exiles as hostages against the good behavior of the patriot militia. The physical treatment of all the exiles, including Gadsden, worsened as the British employed harsher measures to defeat the rebellion in South Carolina. The most significant of these measures was the confiscation of the estates of those who refused to return to their British allegiance. On November 18, 1780, Cornwallis issued a proclamation that he was seizing all of the real and personal property of the South Carolina patriot leaders, including Henry Laurens, Christopher Gadsden, and the remainder of the exiles at St. Augustine. This policy created new hardships for the exiles, as their families were faced with a struggle for mere survival and found it difficult to send food or other materials to the exiles. As supplies dissipated, the British relented somewhat and allowed small groups to go fishing in the river for food. This prevented the South Carolinians from starving, but it hardly allowed them the lifestyle to which they were accustomed.[58]

As conditions deteriorated, good news finally came on July 9, 1781, when the exiles were notified that they were to be included in a general exchange of prisoners. Their joy quickly turned to anger and concern, however, when they learned that, three days after the ratification of the exchange, Balfour published an order expelling from South Carolina the families of all exchanged prisoners of war. At the same time, he refused to permit the exiles to stop at Charles Town to assist in the departure of their families. The exiles were given the choice of being released at either Philadelphia or Virginia, but not at Charles Town. While such an edict was unnecessary and cruel, there was nothing to be done but to make preparations for meeting their families at Philadelphia.[59]

Gadsden was finally released from the dungeon and, reunited with his fellow exiles, sailed for Philadelphia on July 17, arriving there thirteen days later. It is unknown how many members of the Gadsden family were among the 670 people who left Charles Town under the orders of Balfour. Ann Gadsden was certainly among this number, and she landed at Philadelphia shortly after August 10. Perhaps she was also accompanied by Gadsden's sons, Thomas and Philip, who had been held as prisoners aboard a British prison ship before being exchanged. Regardless of which family members joined him in Philadelphia, it is clear that Gadsden did not intend to stay there long. He was determined to settle his family into temporary quarters and then return to South Carolina to join Governor Rutledge and avenge himself on Cornwallis and the British. Yet, this was a more difficult problem than he had supposed, as Philadelphia was an expensive city, and the South Carolinians, due to the sequestration of their estates, were poor. Thus,

Gadsden and the members of the council who were present submitted a petition to Congress for financial assistance during their residence and for the trip home. Though Congress agreed to raise thirty thousand dollars for support, less than twenty-five thousand dollars was subscribed and it appears that only a small part of this, less than seventy-six hundred dollars, was actually received by the exiles. While the financial situation concerned Gadsden, he remained anxious to return to South Carolina and take part in the final victory, which he believed to be imminent. Thus, Gadsden spent only six weeks in Philadelphia and, in early September, he set out with a group of exiles to join John Rutledge in the hills of South Carolina.[60]

While Gadsden was regaining his freedom, Laurens remained in the Tower with his funds virtually exhausted. In early October 1781, one of Laurens's jailors appeared and presented him with a bill for £97.10, to cover the expenses of two wardens for the past year. Laurens laughed at this effort, declaring that it was the most ridiculous thing he had ever heard. He pointed out that he had been in a distressed financial state since his petition to draw on John Nutt for funds had been denied. Yet, even if he could pay, Laurens insisted that he would not, for he had not employed the wardens and would be happy to be without them. Laurens was so upset by this incident that he wrote an account of it for the London newspapers. This report brought a flood of gifts of food from friends and assorted well-wishers. It also caused considerable embarrassment for Gore, who finally allowed Laurens to draw upon Nutt for funds. The episode also led to renewed activity in France, as John Adams and Benjamin Franklin each ordered one hundred pounds to be placed at Laurens's disposal.[61] With Laurens assured of financial support, one final effort was made in November 1781 to convince him to renounce the American cause. When William Manning visited on November 8, he informed Laurens that the patriot cause in South Carolina looked bleak, and that friends such as Gabriel Manigault and Henry Middleton had returned to their British allegiance. Though sorry to learn this news, Laurens was not surprised. He noted that Manigault was old and ill and wished only to be left in peace during his last years, while Middleton "loves his rice fields." Laurens then, once again, refused to "subscribe to my own infamy."[62]

Laurens remained staunch in his support for the American cause, but he grew bitter at the seeming neglect of Congress. He was extremely upset with a letter from Franklin, in which the latter commented that he was pleased to hear that Laurens was satisfied with his treatment in the Tower. Laurens wondered where Franklin could have received his information, for he thought that it was common knowledge that he was extremely dissatisfied, not only with his treatment in the Tower, but with the lack of effort by Congress to gain his release.[63] Yet, unknown to Laurens, the wheels were already in motion to secure his freedom. Edmund Burke expressed interest in Laurens's case, due, in part, to his desire to secure the release of his friend, John Burgoyne, from his parole. Burke began exploring the possibility of an agreement between Franklin and the ministry that might result in an exchange of Laurens for Burgoyne. By the beginning of December, the prospects for such a deal appeared bright. Matters were complicated, however, when Lord Hillsborough intervened to observe that Laurens was not a prisoner of war, but a state prisoner, and his status could only be changed by a pardon. When Laurens learned that Burke was working to obtain a pardon, he objected, refusing to apply for or accept pardon, since this carried the imputation of guilt. Instead, Laurens decided to submit a petition for better treatment to the House of Commons. He again downplayed his role in the patriot movement and emphasized his generosity and consideration for British prisoners and the Tories. That he did not view this address as in any way dishonorable is indicated by his direction that a copy be sent to Congress. Fortunately, this direction was ignored, as several members of Congress reacted violently when they later saw a copy of the petition. At the same time Laurens scribbled a bitter note to be smuggled from the Tower and sent to Congress:

> Almost fifteen months I have been closely confined and inhumanly treated, and even now I have not a prospect of relief. The treaty for exchange is abortive. There has been languor, and there is neglect somewhere. If I merit your attention, you will not longer delay speedy and efficacious means for my deliverance. Enter this and what it may produce on the secret journal, and pardon the omission of ceremony.[64]

By December, it was clear that Laurens would soon leave the Tower. With the surrender of Cornwallis at Yorktown, even the ministry recognized the futility of continuing the war in America. Thus, there was little to be gained by continuing to hold Laurens. By the time the ministry could agree upon the conditions of his release, Laurens was so consumed by gout that he could no longer walk. Thus, he was placed in a sedan chair and carried to the Inns of Court to appear before Lord Mansfield on December 31, 1781. As he awaited the arrival of Mansfield, Laurens boldly declared that he was a citizen of the United States and would enter into no obligation that insinuated any allegiance to Great Britain. To Laurens's surprise, this statement was overlooked and Mansfield proceeded to accept Richard Oswald and his nephew, John Anderson, as bail. The only requirements from Laurens were that he agree to appear at the court of King's Bench during the Easter term and that he not leave the country without the permission of the court. The promise given, Laurens was released to the care of his friends, putting an end to "a long, and to me an expensive and painful farce."[65]

Imprisonment in the Tower had been a difficult experience for Laurens and he complained that it had "broken one of the best constitutions in the world." Fortunately, he had seen the end of British prisons. By April 1782, when he was scheduled to appear in court, Laurens was involved in the peace negotiations. Lord Shelburne, realizing that Laurens was more valuable in this role than as a prisoner in the Tower, told him that he could consider himself at full liberty, with no consideration required from America. Laurens appreciated this gesture, but insisted that there be some compensation for his release. Thus, he suggested that since Congress had earlier offered Lieutenant General Burgoyne (who had already been exchanged) for him, that Lieutenant General Cornwallis would be a suitable substitute. Franklin agreed to this exchange, dependent upon the approval of Congress. Though it would be another several months before the formal approval of Congress was received, Laurens considered himself as exchanged from the end of April 1782.[66]

There was one final service, however, that was required of Laurens before he could return to America. After returning from Bath, where he took the waters for the relief of his gout, Laurens conversed often with the Marquis of Rockingham, the Duke of Richmond, Lord Shelburne, and other ministers about the prospects of peace. The instability of British politics following the resignation of Lord North in March 1782 made such discussions frustrating. In his conversations, Laurens repeatedly stressed that the United States would not negotiate without an acknowledgment of independence or separately from the French. The various British ministers were uneasy about both of these conditions and, in April 1782, Lord Shelburne heard rumors that John Adams had hinted that the American commissioners (Adams, Franklin, Laurens, John Jay, and Thomas Jefferson, though the latter never served on the commission) were free to negotiate without the participation of the French. Shelburne suggested to Laurens that he visit Adams in The Hague (where Adams had replaced the imprisoned Laurens as commissioner) in order that they both could obtain a clearer understanding of the American position. When Laurens undertook this mission, Adams assured him that he properly understood the American position: the independence of the United States must be guaranteed and the commissioners would not negotiate apart from the French. For his part, Adams was impressed by Laurens and informed Franklin that "I found the old gentleman perfectly sound in his system of politics." Adams wrote that Laurens had little respect for the new ministry, "that they are spoiled by the same insincerity, duplicity, falsehood, and corruption with the former," and that Lord Shelburne still had hopes for reconciliation and a separate peace. Such thoughts were shattered by the reports of Laurens and Richard Oswald, who had undertaken a similar mission to Franklin in Paris. These reports convinced the ministers that the Empire was irrevocably split and that chances of a separate peace were slim.[67]

Despite his long stay in the Tower, Laurens's diplomatic appointment had never been withdrawn by Congress. Nevertheless, feeling that American interests in Europe were in the capable hands of Adams, Franklin, and Jay, Laurens decided to return home after a visit to his brother and daughters at Vigan, in the south of France. Thus, as he informed Franklin, he declined to act as a peace commissioner.[68] The visit to his brother was satisfying, though hardly pleasurable, as he suffered another sharp attack of gout and spent much of his time confined to bed. To add to his trouble, Laurens found that the British were not prepared to grant safe passage for his voyage back to America. Unwilling to risk capture and the threat of another tour of duty in the Tower, Laurens decided to remain in Europe a while longer.[69] As Congress had refused to accept his resignation, Laurens dutifully traveled to Paris for the peace conference.[70]

While Laurens was attempting to decline service on the peace commission, there were members of Congress who were demanding his recall. Only two days after Congress had refused Laurens's resignation, James Madison rose and read a copy of the petition that Laurens submitted to the House of Commons on December 1, which had been published, along with the debates of Parliament on the subject, in the *Parliamentary Register*. Madison was disappointed by the petition and concluded that Laurens's conduct during his captivity was "far from unexceptionable." In a letter to Edmund Randolph, Madison declared that "there are so many circumstances relating to this gentleman during his captivity, which speaks a bias toward the British nation, and an undue cordiality with its new leaders, that I dread his participation in the work of peace." Thus, Madison denounced the petition and insisted that Laurens be recalled immediately if it could be established as genuine.[71]

This caused a serious debate on the floor of Congress. Madison led one group, which argued that the petition was unworthy of a private citizen and absolutely unacceptable from an accredited representative of the United States. Madison was upset that Laurens had directed his petition to the House of Commons, "whose authority we denied and whose usurpations had compelled us to have recourse to arms." He was also upset that Laurens had petitioned as a private citizen from South Carolina, rather than in his public character as an official representative of the United States. By contrast, the defenders of Laurens, led by John Rutledge, argued that the authenticity of the petition was doubtful at best and, even if it was genuine, there was nothing in it to warrant a recall. Rutledge reminded the House that Laurens had spent fifteen months in the Tower of London with little prospect of relief. Under these circumstances, he felt that Laurens might be excused for penning a petition designed to appeal to Parliament. Even then, he saw nothing in the petition that was dishonorable to either Laurens or Congress. In the end, the issue turned on whether or not the petition was genuine. Since this was a disputed question, the members gave Laurens the benefit of the doubt and the motion for recall was lost. It appears likely that, had Congress known that the petition was indeed genuine, Henry Laurens probably would have suffered the humiliation of an undeserved recall.[72]

Such a course would have been devastating to Laurens, as he was already faced with the heartbreaking news that John Laurens had lost his life while leading a pointless raid against the British at Combahee Ferry, near Charles Town, on August 27, 1782. News of this tragedy reached Europe in early November and left Laurens heartbroken. As Ralph Izard observed to his wife, "I pity his [John Laurens's] Father exceedingly: he has already had more than a sufficient number of misfortunes to contend with." The tributes to the gallant young colonel were many. George Washington declared that young Laurens "had not a fault that I could ever discover, unless intrepidity bordering upon rashness could come under that denomination; and to this he was excited by the purest of motives." David Ramsay, who would later have become his brother-in-law, agreed, adding that "Wherever the war raged most; there was he to be found. A dauntless bravery was the least of his virtues and excess of it was his greatest foible." Alexander Hamilton felt "the deepest affliction" at "the loss of a friend I truly and most tenderly loved, and one of a very small number." Hamilton added that the young United States had lost "a citizen whose heart realized that patriotism of which others only talk." John Adams attempted to console his grieving friend, writing that

> I feel for you more than I can or ought to express. Our country has lost its most promising character, in a manner, however, that was worthy of the cause. I can say nothing more to you, but that you have much greater reasons to say, in this case, as a Duke of Ormond said of an Earl of Ossory, "I would not exchange my dead son for any living son in the world."

Even the enemy paid tribute to John Laurens, as the Charles Town *Royal Gazette* mourned his death. Citing his generosity in treating the Loyalists, the *Royal Gazette* noted that, besides the "single deviation from the path of rectitude" of taking arms against the king, "we know of no one trait of his history which can tarnish his reputation as a man of honour, or affect his character as a gentleman."[73]

Yet, these words of condolence could hardly comfort Henry Laurens, a man who had tied so many of his future hopes to his eldest son. Not only was this promising career at an end, but so was that of his best friend and confidant, the man upon whom he was depending to succeed him in his public and private concerns. He had repeatedly warned his son against rashness, though he knew that his warnings had little effect. Now he sat, broken by tragedy, but proud of the war record compiled by his son. In answer to John Adams, he wrote, "Thank God, I had a son who dared to die in defence of his country." To others, he could not hide his sorrow. To his sister-in-law, Laurens wrote that

> My dear Son was afar off, he is placed at a little further distance from me. . . . He dutiful Son, affectionate friend, sensible honest Counsellor, would have fled across the Globe to conduct and to serve his father; I was striving to go to him, he loved his country, he bled and died for it. I shall soon quit this globe and meet him beyond it: happy never more to separate.

Several months later, Laurens was still feeling the shock of this event. Looking back upon the incident, he wrote

> that almost insupportable stroke fell upon me, the account of my Dear Son's Death in Carolina, this was a little too heavy for my poor battered head, I cannot yet surmount the Shock, your friendly Notes respecting that great and worthy young Man have opened my Wounds afresh, tis unsafe for me to keep the Subject in View, let me close it for the present by saying he was universally beloved by his Compatriots, his fall was lamented by his political Enemies, others he had none.[74]

Though Laurens dutifully traveled to Paris for the peace conference, he was downcast and his health was poor and declining. He experienced a severe attack of gout in 1782 and 1783, during which he feared that he would "perhaps be crippled for life." The gout soon moved to his head, causing his daughter Martha to be heartbroken when she visited him in February 1783. She was shocked by his physical decline and severely shaken when he offered directions for steps to be taken in the event of his death. For this situation, she blamed the death of her brother, observing that "though we have hardly mentioned the dr. relation an untimely Stroke has deprived us of, I can perceive his heart is bowed down & he does indeed stand in need of some kind friend to soothe his Sorrows."[75]

Despite his emotional and physical burdens, Laurens traveled to Paris during November 1782. Though he arrived only two days before the signing of the preliminary treaty, Laurens did have some impact on the document. His influence was felt in two significant clauses. Adams wrote that, on his arrival, Laurens examined the treaty and insisted that an article be inserted that would prevent the British from carrying off American property when their armed forces evacuated their American bases. Of course, Laurens's main concern here was to prevent the British from carrying off any more southern slaves. He was not naive enough to think that his article would protect all American property, but felt that it could serve as the basis for future claims against the British for any property they did take. In an ironic twist, the second major contribution came on the issue of the Newfoundland fisheries, the question that had caused Laurens so much grief with the

North Carolina delegation in Congress. Years later, Adams recalled that Laurens had been the crucial figure in guaranteeing American access to the fisheries. Until the arrival of Laurens, Adams alone insisted that the article be a treaty requirement, while Franklin and Jay were prepared to agree to a treaty without it. When Laurens sided with Adams, the American delegation was divided, delaying agreement on the treaty. The British, anxious for a treaty with the United States, relented and allowed the new nation access to the fisheries.[76] As valuable as these services were, Laurens felt that his most significant contribution to the peace process was one that transcended his limited role in the actual negotiations. Both he and Adams reported to Congress that his work in London had been invaluable in laying the groundwork for the treaty. Laurens wrote that the English people and ministry were "amazingly ignorant" of the true facts of the American situation. They seemed incapable of understanding that American independence was essential to any peace, and it took great effort to finally bring them to this realization. Without such groundwork, the serious work of peace negotiation could not have commenced. Thus, while his contributions to the Treaty of Paris may not have equaled those of Adams, Franklin, or Jay, Laurens did play an important role in the peace process.[77]

The one facet of the agreement on which Laurens registered his disapproval was the commissioners' disobedience regarding the instruction to negotiate only in concert with the French. Among the first questions he raised upon his arrival in Paris was whether the commissioners had complied with this requirement. Though he was not satisfied with the answer, he realized that "the Evil, if any, had taken place and could not be remedied." Laurens was unsure of what action the French would take in response, though he felt that there was a good chance that they would simply overlook the incident. If this were the case, there would be no damage done. If the French did complain, however, Laurens asked the South Carolina delegation to Congress to withhold judgment until the commissioners could explain their conduct. Still, he remained uncomfortable with this action of the delegation:

> I mean not to cast or even insinuate the smallest degree of Censure upon any one of the Gentlemen, every one appears to me to have acted with Zeal and disinterestedness for his Country's good, but for my own part I would have paid strict obedience to the solemn Act of Congress in assurance to the Court of France of so recent a date as the 3d of October last.[78]

Even after he returned to England to await the signing of the definitive treaty, Laurens continued to champion the French alliance. On Christmas Eve 1782, he informed Robert R. Livingston of his suspicions that the British were not yet resigned to the loss of America and had only signed the preliminary treaty in hopes of driving a wedge between the United States and France.[79]

As Laurens waited for the signing of the definitive peace treaty, he was again greatly troubled with gout. Indeed, Laurens was so ill in June and July 1783 that his life was again thought to be in danger.[80] When healthy, Laurens divided his time between London and Paris, keeping himself and the ministry abreast of American developments. Still, he was frustrated by the slow pace of the final negotiations and blamed this largely upon British insincerity and chicanery. Nevertheless, after the ministry of the Duke of Portland and Charles James Fox came to power, he was prepared to open negotiations for a commercial treaty. In August 1783, he began talking to Fox about the possibility of reopening the British West Indies to American trade. Though Fox seemed interested in a treaty, he feared that Laurens was negotiating under the auspices of the French, and he would agree to no concessions as long as he believed this to be the case.[81]

While engaged in these negotiations, Laurens finally received, on June 25, 1783, the permission of Congress to return to America. As the negotiations with Fox seemed hopeless, Laurens began making preparations to return home. First, however, he decided to take a final visit to his dying brother in the south of France. After receiving news that the definitive treaty had been signed, Laurens left England and, after a brief consultation with Franklin in Paris, spent the next two and a half months with his brother.[82] Back in England in early 1784, Laurens was forced by illness and the death of James Laurens to further postpone his trip. It was not until June 6 that he finally left England for good, landing in New York on August 3, 1784.[83]

Laurens had long awaited his return to South Carolina. Yet, his anticipation was mixed with anxiety as he heard stories about the destruction caused by the British in his home state. John Lewis Gervais had informed Laurens that the Gervais estate had been plundered to such an extent that all he retained was the land itself. From other sources, Laurens learned that his own property was in an equally disordered condition. He lamented that

> I may find the Lead upon which the Houses stood, but neither House nor Furniture, all burnt stolen or destroyed. I do not expect even to find the Title Deeds, for my Lands or any other of my Papers, I have been told these Savages called British officers & soldiers destroyed or took them all away.

At the same time, Laurens realized that he had been away for a long time and sadly reflected that he had "become a stranger in my native Land."[84] Thus, after landing at New York, Laurens hoped to return home as soon as possible. First, however, he hoped to repair to Congress and report on his activities, particularly the prospects of a commercial treaty with Britain. When he arrived in Philadelphia, he was disappointed to learn that Congress was in recess and would next meet in Trenton, New Jersey on November 1. After presenting himself to Congress, amid rumors that he would be returned to the presidency, Laurens declined further service and left for South Carolina in late November. He arrived in Charles Town on January 14, 1785.[85]

Henry Laurens and Christopher Gadsden were both back home in Charles Town. For the first time in a decade, they could both enjoy life at home without any fear of trouble with Great Britain. Both men were entitled to a rest, for, though the British occupation had been unpleasant for many, few had suffered to the extent of these two patriots. Bitter political enemies, they had found their names joined once again, this time as symbols of British vengeance. Thousands of miles apart, Laurens and Gadsden had shared the physical and psychological burdens of close confinement in British prisons. Neither man had emerged from his ordeal as quite the man he had been when he entered it. Both had courageously and honorably upheld the American cause and refused to retract any of their services to the patriot movement, despite strong pressure to do so. Each had also emerged with his health undermined to such an extent that he was unable to resume a leading role in public affairs. Thus, when the peace treaty was signed and patriot control was firmly reestablished in South Carolina, both Gadsden and Laurens went into retirement. This retirement would prove much more gratifying to Gadsden than to Laurens. Though both men faced difficult tasks in rebuilding their private affairs, Gadsden could at least do so surrounded by his wife and sons. Although Laurens could take comfort in the presence of his daughters, his sole surviving son, and his granddaughter, he was never able to recover from the blow inflicted by the death of his eldest son. The tragic death of John Laurens left a deep void in the life of Henry Laurens that could never be filled. For Laurens, it could be truly said that the "earth was undone by one grave in it."[86]

15

Patriots in Retirement, 1785–1805

B<small>Y</small> 1785, <small>BOTH</small> C<small>HRISTOPHER</small> G<small>ADSDEN AND</small> H<small>ENRY</small> L<small>AURENS WERE ANXIOUS</small> to retire from active public service and devote the remainder of their lives to rebuilding their private affairs. While both could proudly look back upon decades of disinterested public service, both also realized that they no longer possessed the health or the energy of their youth. Both complained that imprisonment had severely impaired their health and offered this to excuse themselves from further active participation in the new government. While Laurens could retire on his return to South Carolina, Gadsden returned in 1781, while Charles Town was still occupied and the war still in progress. Thus, there remained a few pieces of unfinished business for both men: while Laurens remained in Europe to finalize the international peace, Gadsden was in South Carolina helping to shape the peace at home.

By the time that Gadsden and other exiled leaders returned in November, Cornwallis had surrendered at Yorktown and patriot victory was imminent. John Rutledge was ready to issue writs for the election of a new legislature. These elections, held in December 1781, as the partisan civil war was winding to a close, were sparsely attended and could hardly have been labeled democratic. But, given the circumstances, the legislature that met at Jacksonborough, a small town about thirty-five miles from Charles Town, was a good one. When the Jacksonborough assembly met in January 1782, Gadsden resigned as lieutenant governor and qualified as a member of the assembly. Shortly afterwards, perhaps as a reward for past services, Gadsden was elected by a majority of two votes to serve as governor. He refused this honor, explaining to the assembly that

> I have served you in a variety of stations for thirty years, and I would now chearfully make one of a forlorn hope in an assault on the lines of Charlestown, if it was probable, that with the certain loss of my life you would be reinstated in the possession of your capital. What I can do for my country I am willing to do: My sentiments of the American cause, from the Stamp Act downwards, have never changed; I am still of opinion that it is the cause of liberty and of human nature. If my acceptance of the office of Governour would serve my country, though my administration would be attended with the loss of personal credit and reputation, I would chearfully undertake it, but the

present times require the vigour and activity of the prime of life; I feel the increasing infirmities of old age, to such a degree that I am conscious I cannot serve you to advantage; I therefore beg for your sakes and for the sake of the publick, that you would indulge me with the liberty of declining this arduous trust.

This speech seemed to satisfy everyone, as the old hero could enjoy the honor of his election, while the office could be filled by a younger, more even-tempered individual. Aedanus Burke reflected the views of many when he observed that Gadsden's "declining the office, & his manner of doing it, is the most illustrious action of his Life. I am glad the Complt. was paid him, but more so he did not accept it." However, Gadsden did accept a seat on the Privy Council, and would serve as an advisor to the newly elected governor, John Mathews.[1]

There was a feeling of vindictiveness in the air as the new legislature gathered, an attitude that might have been expected, as South Carolina had been ravaged by the war and it would have taken an almost supernatural understanding for the legislature to forgive past sins before the conflict had ended. Christopher Gadsden now assumed an uncharacteristically moderate stance on the Tory issue. Though his position would not be without its inconsistencies, Gadsden's basic policy was one of mercy and compassion. From Philadelphia, he had declared

That we may pursue every prudent, reasonable, humble and truly political step, devoid of passions and vindictive resolutions is my warmest wish. Revenge is below a brave man; vengence belongeth to the Almighty; He has claimed it expressly as His Right, wisely foreseeing the shocking havoc man would make with such a weapon left to his discretion.[2]

The fate of the Tories was the most serious business of the Jacksonborough assembly. The desire for revenge combined with the emptiness of the treasury made some sort of confiscation act a foregone conclusion. Still, which names to include on a confiscation list proved difficult, as each member submitted his own list, often in pursuit of personal vendettas. Clearly some sort of criteria had to be established for drawing up the confiscation list, as the legislature had to decide the fate of almost seven hundred individuals. It was agreed that there would be six groups, including 237 men who would be subject to confiscation and banishment: those who remained subjects of the British crown; those who signed the address to Clinton and Arbuthnot after the fall of Charles Town; men who served voluntarily in the royal militia; congratulators of Cornwallis after his victory at Camden; individuals who held British civil or military commissions; and men whose conduct was "obnoxious" or suspected. In addition, those individuals who had refused to take the oath of allegiance in 1779 and were obliged to leave the state because of this refusal were also banished and their property confiscated. Finally, it was ordered that those who had abandoned the American cause, but had not acted as infamously as those whose property was confiscated, were to have their property amerced at the rate of 12 percent.[3]

The question of which names belonged on the confiscation list, the amercement list, or no list at all, was controversial and the selection process was arbitrary. For example, fifty-three estates were confiscated because their holders had signed either the address to Clinton and Arbuthnot or that to Cornwallis. Yet, over three hundred fifty names appear on these addresses. What happened to the other three hundred? Why were they not placed on the confiscation list? While it is true that some were listed under a different category, it is also true that some escaped entirely. The explanation is largely political. As the lists were debated, the various members used their influence to save friends and relatives, while including the names of rivals and others they disliked. Though Gadsden was ostensibly an opponent of the entire confiscation process, he nevertheless joined in this political game and appears to have played it as well as anyone. It was to his influence that Rawlins Lowndes, who had taken protection after the fall of Charles Town, owed his escape from placement on any of the lists. There was little to distinguish the conduct of Lowndes from that of many on the confiscation list. But Lowndes had Gadsden for his champion, and this fortunate circumstance saved him from ruin and disgrace. There were others, however, who might have escaped the lists had it not been for Gadsden. Prominent among these was Colonel Charles Pinckney, who had been active in the revolutionary assemblies of 1774 and 1775, and had been one of the counselors who had left with John Rutledge shortly before the fall of Charles Town. Later, giving up the cause as lost, Pinckney returned to Charles Town and not only took British protection, but also signed the congratulatory address to Cornwallis. Such conduct clearly should have earned Pinckney a place upon the confiscation list. Instead, he was the beneficiary of the many services of the Pinckney family and, as a testimonial to these, was placed upon the amercement list. He might have escaped punishment altogether were it not for the efforts of Gadsden, who "said a great deal against him."[4]

Though he was not above using the confiscation laws to extract revenge on those men he felt had betrayed the patriot cause, Gadsden generally opposed the laws and pressed for a more merciful and conciliatory policy. Several months later, Gadsden informed General Francis Marion that, since his release from St. Augustine, he had done everything possible to restrain the vindictiveness of his friends. He opposed the Confiscation Acts as "unjust, impolitic, cruel, premature, oppressing numbers of innocent for one man supposed to be guilty." He insisted that such a harsh act would harm the patriot cause, as it would force the Tories to remain attached to the British and would delay the evacuation of Charles Town. Thus, he repeatedly moved that consideration of the question should be suspended until the patriots had regained control of the capital. Gadsden was upset when the assembly refused his motions and he declared that he would rather have both of his hands cut off than raise them in assent to the Confiscation Acts. Such moderation was unusual coming from Gadsden, and many of his colleagues were surprised by it, attributing his leniency to the effects of his long confinement at St. Augustine.[5]

A major factor in Gadsden's opposition to the confiscation laws was his sympathy for those who had taken protection under severe pressure from the British. Cornwallis and his minions had placed severe economic pressure on the mechanics, the former Sons of Liberty who had done so much for the patriot cause, in an effort to force their return to British allegiance. Gadsden was not surprised that some of the artisans had cracked under such pressure, as he realized that, for some, the choice had come down to either taking the oath or allowing their families to starve. The British could be even more persuasive in other areas of the state, as they sometimes forced the oath on inhabitants at bayonet point. Gadsden saw no reason why these men should be treated harshly, particularly when leniency was granted to men such as Charles Pinckney.[6]

As Gadsden considered the situation, he remained convinced that mercy was the best course for all but the worst offenders. Stating that "he that forgets and forgives most, such times as these, in my opinion, is the best citizen," Gadsden sought to alleviate the severity of the confiscation laws. Thus, he could often be found presenting petitions to the assembly from those, particularly the mechanics, whose property had been confiscated or amerced. Among these were several friends and relatives. His final marriage had been to Ann Wragg, a member of one of the most prominent Tory families in South Carolina. While Ann Gadsden was a firm supporter of her husband and his patriot views, many of her relations were not and suffered the consequences in the confiscation legislation. In addition, both his daughter Ann, and his son Thomas had married into families with strong Tory connections. Gadsden was active in sponsoring petitions from these sufferers and often, though not always, was successful in obtaining compensation for their losses. The general movement for relaxation of the Confiscation Acts also met with success, as the laws were gradually repealed and most of those who had lost their property either had it returned or were compensated for their losses. Most of those who had been expelled were eventually allowed to return, and even former lieutenant governor William Bull was allowed to return in 1787. Though Bull never did return, he appreciated the efforts of Christopher Gadsden and, before he died in 1791, named Gadsden as one of the executors of his will in South Carolina.[7]

As it became evident that the British were preparing to evacuate Charles

Town, Governor Mathews concluded an agreement with the British that, he hoped, would allow a peaceful departure. Many South Carolinians feared that the British would take as much property, particularly slaves, as they could carry when they finally left the capital. On the other hand, the British were concerned with the fate of the £412,000 in debts that South Carolinians owed to British and Tory merchants. Thus, an agreement was reached in which the British promised to return all slaves within their lines and agreed to seize no more property. In return, Mathews offered two concessions. First, Mathews agreed to allow British creditors the same rights enjoyed by Carolinians in suing for the collection of debts. This concession was not a point of controversy, as it proved to be milder than the debt agreement contained in the Treaty of Paris. While the latter treaty mandated that no legal impediment be placed in the way of the collection of British debts, Mathews' agreement contained no such clause. This was important, for the inhabitants of a state that had been as devastated as South Carolina would find it difficult to pay any debts, foreign or domestic. Under Mathews's agreement, the British would have no legitimate complaint against legislation for debtor relief, provided that such laws were not discriminatory. The second concession was not as favorable, however, and would create a great deal of trouble during the next few years: British merchants would be allowed six months after the evacuation to sell their merchandise and collect their debts. This upset the local patriot merchants who understood the difficulty of competition with the well-stocked British merchants for the business of planters anxious to rebuild their plantations.[8]

Christopher Gadsden was among the most determined critics of the latter agreement. As a merchant who looked forward to reconstructing his business after the war, Gadsden could hardly have been expected to applaud an agreement that placed him at such a severe competitive disadvantage. Beyond this, Gadsden criticized the agreement as unfair and supportive of the interests of those individuals who were least deserving of consideration. He felt that the agreement clearly favored the low-country elite, as it would allow them to recover their slaves. Yet he saw nothing in the conduct of this group during the past few years to merit special consideration. Indeed, the opposite was true. Not only had the low-country slave owners been lethargic in the service of their country, but, Gadsden insisted, they were now precisely the ones most responsible for prolonging the conflict through their trade with the enemy in the capital. No, said Gadsden, these gentlemen were not entitled to any special privileges. Rather, he proposed that a few of them be indicted and hanged under the Sedition Act to serve as an example to the rest.[9]

Gadsden's fear that the agreement would unnecessarily delay the evacuation of Charles Town proved unfounded, as the long-awaited departure of the British came on December 14, 1782. The British, however, reneged on their promise to return the slaves they had appropriated from the Carolinians. The commissioners sent to recover the slaves were allowed aboard the fleet bound for St. Augustine, but were refused the opportunity to search the ships bearing the king's pendant. On board the latter ships, according to David Ramsay, were thousands of slaves who would be sold in the West Indies as personal profit for the British officers. Aboard the fleet bound for St. Augustine, the commissioners could claim only one hundred thirty-six blacks, only seventy-three of whom were delivered to them. This was a ridiculously low number, considering it was estimated that twenty-five thousand slaves had been confiscated and carried off during the occupation. Whether the British sold these slaves for profit or, as they claimed, kept their promises of freedom to them, the agreement had been violated. Nevertheless, the British boarded their transports at Gadsden's wharf and left the capital to Gadsden and the patriots.[10]

The repossession of the capital served to intensify the problems surrounding both the Tories and the British merchants. With the protection of the British army gone, these individuals were left to face the wrath of the patriots, many of whom had suffered grievously under British occupation. While many of these thirsted for revenge, Gadsden remained a prominent voice for moderation. Elected to his final two-year term in the South Carolina House of Representatives in 1782, Gadsden faithfully attended the House and worked to scale down the confiscation and amercement lists. His moderation did not appeal to the mechanics, who were anxious to avenge themselves on their former persecutors. There were a series of anti-Tory riots during 1783 and 1784, in which several Tories were killed. Nor were the mechanics ignorant of the fact that their old comrade Gadsden had again seemed to turn against them. At one point, the mob burned an effigy of a Tory who had been removed from the confiscation list, at Gadsden's wharf, as a protest against his leniency. Things turned even uglier when, on September 20, 1783, the radicals set fire to a warehouse on Gadsden's wharf. This proved to be an expensive protest for Gadsden. Though the contents of the warehouse were insured, Gadsden had to personally bear the damages, estimated at one thousand pounds, to the wharf.[11]

Gadsden was less sympathetic to the complaints of the British merchants, though he still assumed a more moderate position than the radical mechanics. The agreement with the British merchants came as a great disappointment to Gadsden and other local merchants, who had hoped to reestablish their businesses while helping the planters rebuild their plantations. The anxious planters had no choice but to turn to the well-stocked shelves of the British merchants for supplies. Before long, the British were monopolizing a trade that brought them five hundred thousands pounds in credit. The furious Carolina merchants bitterly complained that the British were taking advantage of the situation to violate the spirit and the letter of the agreement when they raised prices and purchased new stock.[12] The local merchants found strong support for their position among the people of Charles Town, as many remembered the refusal of the British to allow them to pursue their business during the occupation. It was this discrimination that had brought many of the British merchants to Charles Town in the first place, and the local merchants were unwilling to allow it to continue any longer. Thus, Gadsden and the merchants strenuously opposed the application for an extension of the agreement, as proposed by the British merchants in January 1783. These efforts were in vain, as the legislature agreed to give the British until January 1, 1784, and later to March 1, to dispose of their goods. Tempers were further inflamed when the British merchants, inspired by their vast profits, began to apply for, and receive citizenship. It seemed unfair to Gadsden that British merchants had first been allowed to reap windfall profits repairing the damages caused by their own troops, and now were being allowed to settle permanently in the state and drive the patriot merchants out of business. The adjournment of the legislature at the end of March 1784 marked the end of Gadsden's long service in the assembly. As he now refused to consider any action outside of the legitimate sources of authority, Gadsden dropped the matter, leaving it to the wisdom of the legislature.[13]

Neither the merchants nor the mechanics had fought British rule in order to create a foreign monopoly over Charles Town trade. Since the legislature seemed unresponsive to their demands concerning the Tories and British merchants, members of these groups formed the Marine Anti-Britannic Society under the leadership of Alexander Gillon. In April 1784, the Marine Anti-Britannic Society introduced a new wave of violence against the Tories. Again, the tumult spilled over to include even government officials, who, like John Rutledge, were insulted in the streets.[14] Gadsden again entered the public press, this time with a plea for law, order, and respect for the authority of the government. He and Gillon entered into another abuse-filled free-for-all, reminiscent of the 1760s, which did not finally come to a close until Gillon was soundly trounced by Richard Hutson in the race for the newly established position of intendant of the newly incorporated Charleston. Thereafter, tempers cooled and order was restored to the capital.[15]

As conditions began returning to something approaching normalcy, both Gadsden and Laurens could assess their estates. The war had caused considerable damage to the property of both men. Of the two, Gadsden was in a much better position to repair his losses: his wharf, though not completely free from damage, was operational and, as the largest wharf in Charleston, placed him in a position to handle a considerable amount of business. Gadsden was finally able to establish the factoring business that he had so long desired, a partnership called "Christopher Gadsden and Company," which he organized with his sons Thomas and Philip in August 1783. Gadsden's company prospered during the trade boom of the 1780s, as the Gadsdens claimed their share of meeting the demands of rebuilding the war-torn state. In addition to his factoring income, Gadsden continued to own several plantations near Georgetown that remained quite productive. Thus, Gadsden was able to live well during the remaining twenty years of his life and, at his death, he left an estate valued at over two hundred and fifty thousand dollars.[16]

Still, Gadsden did experience financial problems during the 1780s and 1790s. Though he, like Laurens, emerged from the war as a creditor with an estate free from debt, he suffered the fate of most other creditors during the 1780s. He reported that he had difficulty collecting his debts, and that those debts that were paid were settled in such depreciated currency that they were almost worthless. Due to such debts and the necessity of repairing damaged property, Gadsden was forced to put most of his factoring earnings into plantation reconstruction. By 1791, however, he was prepared to pay his remaining debts and retire, leaving his business in the hands of his sons. At this point, catastrophe struck with the sudden death of his son Thomas on November 4, 1791. Gadsden had once before experienced the loss of a beloved son for whom he held high hopes, when Christopher Gadsden, Jr. died in 1766. Yet the loss of Thomas Gadsden transcended even this earlier tragedy, as the death of Thomas represented a blow to his father's plans comparable to that which the death of John Laurens had inflicted upon the hopes of Henry Laurens. Only thirty-five years old at his death, Thomas Gadsden had already served a term as lieutenant governor of South Carolina and was the son upon whom Gadsden was depending to carry forward his political and economic legacy. The death of Thomas Gadsden forced Gadsden to reconsider his own retirement, and he never did retire completely from business. A second problem that stemmed from the death of his son was a large debt of several thousand dollars that had been incurred by Thomas Gadsden, and that was now assumed by his father. This left Gadsden in debt for much of the 1790s. Still, his business flourished, enabling Gadsden to lead a comfortable life and to reduce his active participation in business affairs after 1795.[17]

Things were more difficult for Henry Laurens, even though he held a more extensive estate than Gadsden. He had closed his mercantile career before his trip to England in 1771 and was now dependent upon income from his extensive credit and plantations. This would have been no problem if the war had not intervened to practically destroy the economy. Noting the impossibility of collecting his debts, and viewing the ruin of his estates, Laurens reported in 1786 that he was forced to live on about one-fifth of the income he had previously enjoyed and that he often lacked even one dollar in ready cash.[18] From England, Laurens estimated that the damage to his property would probably exceed forty thousand pounds. Upon his return to South Carolina, he found that his fears had not been exaggerated. He reported that serious damage had been done to his real estate holdings in Charleston, and that all of the movable property there, except a few slaves, had been carried away. The damage at Mepkin was even worse, as several buildings needed extensive repairs, while others had to be replaced entirely.[19]

When he returned to South Carolina, Laurens was determined to decline any further public appointments and concentrate his efforts on his private affairs. Not only was he determined to retire from politics, but Laurens also decided to forsake the crowds and high prices of Charleston (so named when the town was incorporated in 1784) for the peace and quiet of Mepkin. Thus, Laurens lived the remainder of his life at his plantation seat, with only occasional visits to Charleston. This was, at first, a problem, because of the ruined state of his plantation. Yet Laurens was prepared to live modestly. He lived in an overseer's cottage as he oversaw the reconstruction of his mansion house at Mepkin. Though he often complained about his finances, Laurens was able to construct a beautiful nine-room mansion, built of the finest materials, some of which were imported from Philadelphia and London. Here Laurens spent his days overseeing his financial affairs, perhaps remembering friends from bygone days, and visiting the grave of John Laurens, which he had moved to Mepkin upon his return. As efficient as ever, Laurens lived largely from the produce of his own plantation.[20]

Laurens's most important concerns were the careers and marriage prospects of his three remaining children. He had always recognized the versatile talents of his eldest daughter, Martha Laurens, and he encouraged her to develop these abilities. Termed "a republican treasure" by one historian, Martha Laurens was one of the outstanding women of the early republic. As intelligent and devoted to republican principles as her brother John, her temperament and deep religious faith were more reminiscent of her father. Thus, Martha Laurens understood that she was blessed with impressive intellectual gifts, but she also respected the constraints placed upon her sex by the society of the day. She devoted her considerable gifts to the service of her father and uncle and, later, to her husband and large family. Martha Laurens demonstrated her respect and obedience to her father when, in 1782, she broke off her engagement to a young Frenchman whom, her father believed, wished to marry her for her money. Laurens was happier with her second choice, the patriot physician and historian David Ramsay, whom she married in 1787. Though Ramsay had risen to political prominence as a protege of Christopher Gadsden, he held a great deal of respect for Henry Laurens and his republican philosophy was similar to that of his father-in-law. The match between Martha and David Ramsay was a good one, and Martha Ramsay bore eleven children, eight of whom survived infancy, before her death in 1811.[21]

Laurens loved his sole surviving son, Henry Laurens, Jr., but he never entertained the hopes and expectations that he had held for his eldest son. He was proud that Henry, Jr. had won election to the assembly, but he saw in him little of the talent, energy, or ambition that had been so characteristic of John Laurens. He was disappointed that young Henry showed so little inclination for either politics or planting. He had hoped that Henry would establish his own plantation seat upon Laurens's Georgian lands, and finally offered these lands for sale (unsuccessfully) when his son refused to have anything to do with them. Though Laurens continually pressed his son to marry and settle down, young Henry resisted this pressure until May 1792, when he pleased his father by marrying Eliza Rutledge, the daughter of Laurens's old friend and associate, John Rutledge.[22]

He was not so pleased with the decision of his youngest daughter, Mary Eleanor, to marry, nor, one might suspect, with her choice of a partner. Born in a rough childbirth that resulted in the death of her mother, Mary Eleanor blossomed into a beautiful and accomplished young woman. In 1786 at the age of sixteen, she asked her father for permission to marry Charles Pinckney, the rising young politician who would play an important role in the federal Constitutional Convention, contribute to the founding of the Jeffersonian Republican party in South Carolina, and serve four terms as governor of the state. Laurens objected to the match on the ostensible grounds of the youth of his daughter and because she was thirteen-and-a-half-years younger than Pinckney, though one suspects that political differences might also have played a role. Laurens managed to delay this marriage for two years, but finally relented and witnessed the marriage of the couple upon her eighteenth birthday in 1788. This couple spent only a brief, but happy, life together before, in an ironic twist of fate, Mary Eleanor died following a difficult childbirth in 1794.[23]

Though Gadsden and Laurens were both predominantly concerned with private affairs after 1785, they maintained an interest in public affairs. The idea of a stronger and more effective central government was one that appealed to both men. Indeed, Laurens had proposed the creation of a more effective government while serving in Congress in 1779. Though he considered the call for the Constitutional Convention to be belated, Laurens was happy that it had finally come and hoped that a government could be established that could effectively deal with the pressing problems of debts, trade, and defense. He was offered the opportunity of serving in the Constitutional Convention, as the assembly elected him to serve as a member of the South Carolina delegation. Though he was pleased by the appointment and would have liked to travel to Philadelphia to renew old friendships and again serve his country, his declining health made such service impossible.[24]

Both Gadsden and Laurens applauded the new constitution. Gadsden was "struck with amazement" by the document, as he had expected little from a meeting of people with so many divergent interests. He declared that such a wonderful document could have been the result of "nothing less than the superintending hand of providence." In addition to the beneficial effects that the new Constitution would have upon American trade, Gadsden publicly praised the political aspects of the document. Realizing that the Constitution faced considerable opposition, Gadsden published a letter in the *Gazette of the State of South Carolina* of May 5, 1788, a few weeks before the opening of the South Carolina ratifying convention. In this letter, he praised the Constitution as a democratic document that placed ultimate power in the hands of the people. He approved of the system of checks and balances, insisting that this would allow the president and Congress to be granted substantial powers, but would prevent either from becoming tyrannical or arbitrary. He was particularly pleased with the presidential veto. Though he had been influential in stripping the South Carolina executive of this power in 1778, he had since grown to fear the unchecked power of the assembly and reversed his position. All in all, Gadsden assured his readers that the "essentials to a republican government, are, in my opinion, well secured" by the Constitution, and he urged his fellow citizens to support ratification.[25]

Laurens also approved of the new Constitution, declaring it to be "infinitely better than our present Confederation," though he doubted that it would attain the consent of all thirteen states, "because it is calculated to make them honest." Like Gadsden, Laurens felt that the new government would be able to more effectively promote and protect trade, and hoped that this would be a significant step in the direction of responsible debt management. Though Laurens did not see all of the "Bugbears" imagined by some, he felt that the Constitution would benefit from some revision. Unlike most who favored revision, however, Laurens's idea was to strengthen the power of the government, primarily through allowing the president an absolute veto.[26]

There remained considerable opposition to ratification of the Constitution, as antifederalist sentiment, which probably represented the views of a majority of the voters in the state, centered in the backcountry. The Constitution quickly became caught up in the continuing internal struggle within state politics, particularly the power struggle between east and west. The people of Charleston and the low country overwhelmingly favored ratification, as the new Constitution promised to provide a stronger central government, one that could promote and protect commerce. The backcountry, on the other hand, was concerned that the Constitution gave too much power to the federal government, benefited special eastern interests, and did not include a bill of rights. Despite their numerical strength, however, the prospects of the antifederalists received a blow when it was decided that representation in the ratifying convention would be based upon representation in the legislature, which remained heavily weighted in favor of the east. The decision—by the narrow vote of seventy-six to seventy-five—to hold the convention in Charleston doomed the antifederalist cause to failure. Thus, when the convention met in May 1788, with Laurens and Gadsden both present, the Constitution was easily ratified by a vote of 149 to 73, with Laurens and Gadsden voting with the majority. A short time later, both men were again honored by their selection as two of the seven individuals chosen to cast the electoral vote of South Carolina in the first presidential election. This was to be the final formal public service performed by Laurens, and he and Gadsden both cast their ballots for George Washington.[27]

While Laurens had now completed his public service, there was still one more issue that Gadsden wished to address. After the ratification of the federal Constitution, Gadsden turned his attention to the constitution of South Carolina. For years he had felt the need for constitutional revision, most particularly to assure a more complete separation of the three branches of government. He disliked the fact that judges were allowed to sit in the assembly, observing that this was "very improper and has a natural Tendency to introduce a Confusion of Departments." He also felt that the assembly had grown too powerful and was interfering too much in judicial affairs. To combat this tendency, Gadsden reversed his position of 1778 and supported the restoration of the presidential veto. A state constitutional convention was called in 1790, for reasons different from those pressed by Gadsden. First, there was the location of the capital. The growing influence of the western regions was demonstrated in 1786, when the assembly moved the capital from Charleston to the new settlement of Columbia.[28] This move upset Gadsden and other low-country leaders, who were anxious that the capital be returned to Charleston. The second major issue concerned the continuing battle over representation, as the west clamored for representation that more accurately reflected its overwhelming majority of the white population of the state. Thus, a convention was called at Columbia on May 10, 1790 to prepare a new constitution.[29]

When the convention met, Gadsden was chosen to act as president of the meeting. Though honored by the selection, Gadsden presided over the convention for only one day before stepping down so that he could engage in the debate. Though he was unsuccessful in regaining either the presidential veto or the capital for Charleston, he was generally pleased with the results. He was disappointed that the capital would remain at Columbia, but candidly admitted that his stance was based largely upon convenience. Since he was now retired from active participation in the legislature, the issue was not of such great concern to him as it would have been ten or twenty years earlier. Gadsden reported that the question of representation was again a divisive one that occasioned a long and heated debate. While prepared to make concessions, Gadsden rejected the western demand for a majority of seats in both houses of the legislature. Though satisfied with the final compromise, Gadsden felt that Charleston might have obtained a better settlement if its delegates had attended the Convention more diligently. In terms of representation, the low country managed to retain control over the legislature, though the representation of Charleston was reduced to about 38 percent in the assembly. Thus, Georgetown and Beaufort would now play the critical swing role, as their votes could bring victory to either Charleston or the backcountry. The constitution of 1790, though not based upon proportional representation, did finally break the domination of the legislature by Charleston, an important step along the road to equal representation.[30]

Henry Laurens was not present at this meeting and had little comment on the proceedings, though as a longtime champion of backcountry interests, he was likely satisfied with the results. While he remained aloof from politics, Laurens likely favored the Hamiltonian cause, as he expressed satisfaction with the strengthening of the federal government and even purchased twenty-four shares of the Charleston branch of the Bank of the United States.[31] His poor health continued during the 1780s and early 1790s and he suffered several serious attacks of gout. By 1792, he was clearly in decline, and was often confined to bed. His visits to Charleston became less frequent as his health declined and it was only with great difficulty that he was able to travel there for the wedding of his son in May 1792. Thereafter, his health steadily deteriorated until finally, on the morning of December 8, 1792, Henry Laurens died at the age of sixty-eight, in the presence of his daughter Martha, at Mepkin.[32] In his will, Laurens included a request that was strange for his time: that his body not be buried, but cremated. He had heard stories of people who had been buried alive under the mistaken presumption that they were dead. Indeed, his own daughter Martha had been pronounced dead as an infant, only to be revived by a cool breeze as her small body was laid out before a window. Determined not to be the victim of a similar mistake, Laurens directed that his body be cremated. This wish was carried out and his ashes were buried beside the body of John Laurens on the bluff overlooking the Cooper River.[33]

What effect the passing of Henry Laurens had upon Christopher Gadsden is unknown, as his surviving papers contain no mention of the event. It is unlikely that the two men had seen much of each other after the war, as Laurens spent most of his time at Mepkin, while Gadsden rarely left

Charleston. Still, their paths must have crossed from time to time, as their Charleston homes were near to each other. What was said when they did meet is unknown, for neither man mentioned any meetings in his surviving correspondence. There is no evidence that either man made any effort to settle the longstanding dispute between them, and it is clear that they never resurrected their old friendship. Gadsden must have felt something at the death of the man who had once been one of his closest friends, only to become his most bitter rival. But Gadsden was not a man to put such thoughts into writing and, however interesting they might have been, these thoughts have been lost to posterity.

As he grew older, Gadsden remained active and continued to comment upon the political events of the 1790s. During these years, Gadsden could be labeled a moderate Federalist, one who generally supported Federalist policy, but who retained his independence and was willing to oppose Federalist policies he disliked. This independence was prominently displayed in July 1795, when news of the terms of Jay's Treaty reached Charleston. Though John Jay had avoided war with Great Britain, many Charlestonians, including Gadsden, felt that war might have been preferable to such humiliating terms. Even at the advanced age of seventy-one, Gadsden was at the center of the opposition to the treaty. In a scene reminiscent of bygone days, Gadsden presided over a mass meeting at the exchange and declared that he would "as soon send a favourite virgin to a Brothel, as a man to England to make a treaty." Gadsden then joined a gathering of more prominent citizens at a meeting held at St. Michael's Church. When this group selected a committee to draw up a petition against the treaty to be sent to President Washington, Gadsden and John Rutledge each received 792 votes to head the list. The reaction to Jay's Treaty in Charleston was comparable to that which had greeted the Stamp Act. The mob was again aroused and effigies of John Jay, John Adams, William Loughton Smith, and other prominent supporters of the treaty were hanged and burned. The home of Senator Jacob Read, one of only two southern senators to vote to ratify the treaty, was attacked by a mob that was only dissuaded from further violence by the timely intervention of Charles Cotesworth Pinckney. Tempers were so high that several angry opponents sent Smith an anonymous letter promising to murder him for his role in the making of the treaty. John Rutledge, already displaying the erratic behavior that characterized his declining years and finally led to suicide in 1800, publicly damned both Jay and the treaty and even expressed the wish that Washington would die rather than consent to the treaty. Though Gadsden made no public comment on these disorders, his denunciation of similar disturbances a decade earlier suggests that he probably disapproved of them.[34]

While Gadsden was a bitter opponent of Jay's Treaty, he demonstrated little sympathy for the radicalism of the French Revolution. He staunchly supported the principles of Washington's Farewell Address, insisting that Americans should remain aloof from European affairs while protecting themselves against the interference of foreigners in domestic politics. Thus, he was furious when the French repeatedly interfered in American politics during the election of 1796. He was upset when Thomas Paine launched his scathing attack on President Washington, and was driven to act when the French minister, Pierre Auguste Adet, actively worked for the defeat of John Adams in the presidential election. Waiting until after the election in order to avoid charges of party manipulation, Gadsden published a pamphlet entitled *A Few Observations on Some Late Public Transactions* in early 1797. First, he addressed the issue of Paine. Crediting this old friend with "a great service" in the publication of *Common Sense*, Gadsden sadly observed that Paine's talents seemed limited to those of the "pull-down politicians." He noted that Paine had proved to be quite skillful in overthrowing governments, but seemed incompetent when confronted with the task of building them. Gadsden insisted that Paine was now engaged in the futility of pulling down the American Constitution and, though his efforts were bound to fail, the attempt canceled all of the obligations owed to him for past services. As for Adet, Gadsden considered it highly improper for any foreign minister to bypass the government and make direct appeals to the American people. At the same time, however, Gadsden realized that many Americans maintained a "zealous, uncommon attachment to the French nation" for their help in the winning of American independence. Though he felt that "they had a right to our gratitude," Gadsden reminded his readers that the French had always acted selfishly and consulted only their own interests in supporting the American cause. Thus, Gadsden joined Washington in urging the American people to think with their heads rather than their hearts, and to continue making decisions based upon American principles and interests.[35]

Gadsden grew even angrier with the French when the XYZ Affair brought the United States and France to the brink of war. He was pleased with the way that John Adams handled the crisis and stated "that a better and firmer piece of live Oak was not to be found in the United States" than in the president.[36] When Adams faced a difficult reelection bid in 1800, Gadsden proved to be among his firmest supporters, certain that Adams did not deserve the humiliation of being turned out of office after only one term.[37] Genuinely surprised by the defeat of Adams, Gadsden was now faced with the sad reality that his day had passed, and that a new era, in which there was little place for men like himself and Adams, was dawning. In light of the electoral results, Gadsden wrote a letter of consolation to Adams in which he expressed his bewilderment:

Long have I been led to think our planet a mere bedlam, and the uncommonly extravagant ravings of our own times, especially for a few years past, and still in the highest rant, have greatly increased and confirmed that opinion. Look around our whirling globe, my friend, where you will, east, west, north, or south, where is the spot in which are not many thousands of these mad lunatics?

Under these circumstances, Gadsden was relieved that

I every day feel myself to find that my passage over this life's Atlantic is almost gained, having been in soundings for some time, not far from my wished-for port, waiting only for a favorable breeze from our kind Savior to waft me to that pleasing and expected land for which I cheerfully and humbly hope.[38]

With Jefferson and the Republicans in power, Gadsden's interest in politics waned, and he enjoyed his final years relaxing in the comfort of his family. Though he did not experience such extreme health problems as Laurens, Gadsden's stay in the St. Augustine dungeon had permanently affected his health. Since this time, Gadsden reported, he had been subject to dizzy spells and memory lapses that made it difficult for him to speak in public.[39] Besides these annoying problems, however, Gadsden enjoyed good health and remained vigorous until the end. He exercised daily, usually by taking a brisk walk. These walks generally covered the same route, which included a ditch that Gadsden crossed by means of a narrow plank. One day in late August 1805, Gadsden slipped from the plank and hit his head, causing his confinement in bed for a few days. On August 28, he attempted to rise and dress himself. In the process, he apparently suffered one of his dizzy spells, for he fell and further injured himself. Within hours, surrounded by his family, Christopher Gadsden died at the age of eighty-one. The death of Gadsden, one of the last and foremost patriots of the Revolution in South Carolina, brought great tributes from the press and public. The governor declared a thirty-day mourning period, and the commander of Fort Johnson hung the colors in mourning. The next day, when the body was to be buried, a salute was fired from Fort Johnson every ten minutes from dawn until the interment at 1:00 P.M. At 11:00 A.M., the funeral procession gathered at the Gadsden residence. With the artillery company Gadsden had founded fifty years before leading the way, the procession—family, friends, the governor, and all public officials present in the city—made its way to St. Philip's. Here, in accordance with the instructions left in his will, Christopher Gadsden was buried in an unmarked grave near those of his parents.[40]

The lives of Henry Laurens and Christopher Gadsden had featured so many parallels that it is almost striking that their deaths were so markedly different. Whereas Laurens had spent much of his last decade suffering in sometimes excruciating pain, Gadsden experienced little physical pain during his declining years. While Laurens died a slow death, Gadsden passed away quickly and peacefully. The death of Gadsden also received far more attention than that of Laurens. This is partially explained by Gadsden's greater public activity during his declining years and by the fact that he died and was buried in Charleston, while Laurens passed away at the more remote location of Mepkin. Yet there was more to it than this. When Laurens died in 1792, the revolutionary generation was still very much alive and vigorously active in local, state, and national affairs. By the time of Gadsden's death thirteen years later, this was no longer the case. A few of the younger revolutionaries were still active, and Jefferson was in the presidency, but most of the leadership of the South Carolina protest movement during the 1760s and 1770s had passed from the scene. Several, such as Thomas Lynch, John Mackenzie, and William Henry Drayton, had not even lived to see the final establishment of American independence. Others had died since then: Arthur Middleton died in 1787; Rawlins Lowndes and Edward and John Rutledge both died in 1800; John Mathews died in 1802. Thus, the death of Gadsden, perhaps the most visible of all the patriots of the revolutionary era, symbolized the close of one era and the opening of a new one in South Carolina. The funeral procession of Christopher Gadsden was not just that of a man, but also of a bygone age.

Notes

Abbreviations

CG	Christopher Gadsden
FWW	John C. Fitzpatrick, ed., *The Writings of George Washington*
HL	Henry Laurens
HLP	Henry Laurens Papers, South Carolina Historical Society, Charleston, South Carolina
JCC	Worthington C. Ford et al. *Journals of the Continental Congress, 1774–1789*
JCH	Journals of the Commons House of Assembly, South Caroliniana Library, Columbia, South Carolina
LD	Paul H. Smith et al., eds., *Letters of Delegates to Congress, 1775–1789*
LP	Philip M. Hamer et al. *The Papers of Henry Laurens*
PRO	Records in the British Public Records Office Relating to South Carolina
SCG	*South Carolina Gazette*
SCHM	*South Carolina Historical Magazine* (formerly *South Carolina Historical and Genealogical Magazine*)
SCHS	South Carolina Historical Society, Charleston, South Carolina
WCG	Richard Walsh, ed., *The Writings of Christopher Gadsden, 1746–1805*

1. Early Lives and Business Interests, 1724–1758

1. David Duncan Wallace, *The Life of Henry Laurens* (New York: G. P. Putnam's Sons, 1915), 14n; E. Stanly Godbold and Robert H. Woody, *Christopher Gadsden and the American Revolution* (Knoxville: University of Tennessee Press, 1982), 4, 10.

2. Robert M. Weir, *Colonial South Carolina: A History* (Millwood, N.Y.: KTO Press, 1983), 141. Robert M. Weir, *"A Most Important Epocha": The Coming of the Revolution in South Carolina* (Columbia: University of South Carolina Press, 1970), 4.

3. According to Thomas Barrow, it was the first lord of the admiralty, Sir Charles Wager, who used his influence with Walpole to obtain this position for Thomas Gadsden; see Thomas C. Barrow, *Trade and Empire: The British Customs Service in Colonial America, 1660–1775* (Cambridge: Harvard University Press, 1967), 120.

4. Christopher Gadsden, "A Few Observations on Some Late Public Transactions," January 30, 1797, in *WCG*, ed. Richard Walsh (Columbia: University of South Carolina Press, 1966), 278; Godbold and Woody, *Gadsden*, 3–4.

5. HL to Messieurs and Madame Laurence, February 25, 1774, *The Papers of Henry Laurens*, ed. Philip M. Hamer, et al. (Columbia: University of South Carolina Press, 1968) 9:309–11; Wallace, *Laurens*, 2–8.

6. HL to Messieurs and Madame Laurence, February 25, 1774, *LP*, 9:309.

7. Wallace, *Laurens*, 11–12; see *LP*, 1:3n; Will of John Laurens, *Charleston County Will Transcripts*, 5:665 (will proved June 19, 1747).

8. Godbold and Woody, *Gadsden*, 5–9; Will of Thomas Gadsden, *Charleston County Will Transcripts*, 5:37–38 (will recorded August 21, 1741).

9. Godbold and Woody, *Gadsden*, 4–7; Wallace, *Laurens*, insert between 502–3.

10. David Ramsay, *Ramsay's History of South Carolina: From It's [sic] First Settlement in 1670 to the Year 1808* (808; reprint, Newberry, S.C.), 1858, 2:253.

11. Godbold and Woody, *Gadsden*, 7–11; HL to CG, December 28, 1747, *LP*, 1:94.

12. HL to Messieurs and Madame Laurence, February 25, 1774, *LP*, 9:309–10.

13. CG to HL, September 11, 1746, *WCG*, 4; Godbold and Woody, *Gadsden*, 11–12; Leila Sellers, *Charleston Business on the Eve of the American Revolution* (Chapel Hill: University of North Carolina Press,1934), 81.

14. HL to James Crokatt, June 3, 1747, *LP*, 1:2–5; HL to Richard Grubb, June 23, 1747, *LP*, I, 7–8; HL to James Crokatt, June 24, 1747, *LP*, 1:8–12.

15. HL to William Flower, July 10, 1747, *LP*, 1:22–24.

16. HL to James Crokatt, July 14, 1747, *LP*, 1:28.

17. HL to James Laurens, December 15, 1748, *LP*, 1:178.

18. HL to Elizabeth Laurens, December 16, 1748, *LP*, 1:179–81. Laurens never explained the nature of these charges, but Joseph Barnwell has written that they could only have been incurred through his dealings with his uncle, Auguste Laurens: Joseph W. Barnwell, "Correspondence of Henry Laurens," *SCHM* 30, no. 4 (October 1929): 197–214.

19. HL to Elizabeth Laurens, December 16, 1748, *LP*, 1:179–81.

20. HL to John Lewis Gervais, March 4, 1774, *LP*, 9:336.

21. Weir, *Most Important Epocha*, 4.

22. David Duncan Wallace, *South Carolina: A Short History, 1520–1948* (Chapel Hill: University of North Carolina Press, 1951), 195; Weir, *Colonial South Carolina*, 160, 172; Sylvia R. Frey, *Water from the Rock: Black Resistance in a Revolutionary Age* (Princeton: Princeton University Press, 1991), 7.

23. Sellers, *Charleston Business*, 10–11; Walter J. Fraser, Jr., *Charleston ! Charleston ! The History of a Southern City* (Columbia: University of South Carolina Press, 1989), 128; Josiah Quincy, Jr., "Journal of Josiah Quincy, Jr.," in *Proceedings of the Massachusetts Historical Society, 1915–1916* ed. Mark DeWolfe Howe, 49:441.

24. Stuart O. Stumpf, "South Carolina Importers of General Merchandise, 1735–1765," *SCHM* 84, no. 1 (January 1983): 3–10.

25. HL to George Austin, February 11, 1748 [1749], *LP*, 1:208–10; HL to Foster Cunliffe, January 20, 1749, *LP*, 1:202–3; HL to John Knight, January 20, 1748 [1749], *LP*, 1:204–6; HL to Isaac Hobhouse, March 16, 1748 [1749], *LP*, 1:226–27.

26. Due to the shortage of specie in South Carolina, paper money was the main currency of the colony. The value of the currency varied, but was usually valued at a 7:1 ratio to pounds sterling: Sellers, *Charleston Business*, 76.

27. W. Robert Higgins, "Charles Town Merchants and Factors Dealing in the External Negro Trade, 1735–1775," *SCHM* 65, no. 4 (October 1964): 205–17.

28. According to South Carolina law, all slaves were required to be landed at the

pest house on Sullivan's Island for ten days so that the slaves and ships could be cleansed to prevent the spread of disease: *LP,* 2:223–24n.

29. HL to Smith and Clifton, May 26, 1755, *LP,* 1:255–57; HL to Wells, Wharton, and Doran, May 27, 1755, *LP,* 1:257–59.

30. HL to Thomas Mears, June 27, 1755, *LP,* 1:272–75; HL to John Lewis Gervais, February 28, 1772, in Elizabeth Donnan, *Documents Illustrative of the History of the Slave Trade to America,* (1935; reprint, New York: Octagon Books, 1969) 4:446–49.

31. HL to William Reeve, October 2, 1767, *LP,* 5:322–27.

32. HL to Richard Oswald, May 24, 1768, Donnan, *Documents Illustrative of Slave Trade,* 4:422–23.

33. HL to Smith and Clifton, July 17, 1755, *LP,* 1:295. It was very important to Carolinians which section of Africa their slaves came from, and this was reflected in the prices. Africans from Gambia and the Gold Coast were preferred because they were familiar with rice production. Indeed, some believed African rice to be superior to South Carolinian. The difference between Gambian slaves and less-desirable Calabars could be three to four pounds sterling: Sellers, *Charleston Business,* 143; Elizabeth Donnan, "The Slave Trade into South Carolina before the Revolution," *American Historical Review* 33, no. 4 (July 1928): 816–17; Daniel Littlefield, "Charleston and Internal Slave Redistribution," *SCHM* 87, no. 2 (April 1986): 99.

34. Sellers, *Charleston Business,* 118–19; HL to John Pagan, Alexander Brown, and Co., March 16, 1768, *LP,* 5:625–32.

35. Sellers, *Charleston Business,* 121; Wallace, *Laurens,* 47.

36. Higgins, "Charles Town Merchants and the Slave Trade," 205–17; Sellers, *Charleston Business,* 109.

37. Wallace, *Laurens,* 88–90.

38. Sellers, *Charleston Business,* 138.

39. HL to Smith and Baillies, February 9, 1764, *LP,* 4:167–68.

40. Higgins, "Charles Town Merchants and the Slave Trade," 207–14.

41. This act raised the duty by one hundred pounds currency for a period of three years. HL to John Knight, August 24, 1764, *LP,* 4:381–82; HL to Henry Bright, September 12, 1764, *LP,* 4:420; HL to Smith and Baillies, October 22, 1767, *LP,* 5:373–76; HL to Clay and Habersham, October 26, 1767, *LP,* 5:377–78; HL to Smith and Baillies, January 15, 1768, *LP,* 5:546–48.

42. Laurens was among the largest landowners in South Carolina and, before his death, he had amassed over twenty-four thousand acres in South Carolina and Georgia: N. Louise Bailey, Mary L. Morgan, and Carolyn R. Taylor, eds. *Biographical Directory of the South Carolina Senate, 1776–1985* (Columbia: University of South Carolina Press, 1986), 893.

43. HL to William Fisher, November 9, 1768, *LP,* 6:149.

44. HL to John Holman, September 8, 1770, *LP,* 7:344.

45. HL to John Lewis Gervais, February 28, 1772, *LP,* 8:196–99; HL to John Lewis Gervais, February 5, 1774, *LP,* 9:264; HL to Felix Warley, August 11, 1783, in Donnan, *Documents Illustrative of the Slave Trade to America,* 4:472.

46. Egerton Leigh, *The Man UnMasked* (1769), reprinted in *LP,* 6:450–567; Henry Laurens, *Appendix to the Extracts* (1769), reprinted in *LP,* 7:2–114, 99–100.

47. David Ramsay, *Memoirs of Martha Laurens* (Philadelphia, 1845), 251; Laura P. Frech, "The Republicanism of Henry Laurens," *SCHM* 76, no. 2 (April 1975): 70; HL to Marquis de Lafayette, December 6, 1777, in Paul H. Smith, ed., *Letters of Delegates to Congress, 1774–1789,* (Washington, D.C.: Library of Congress, 1976–present), 8:384.

48. Ramsay, *History of South Carolina,* 2:260.

49. HL to James Wright, December 17, 1763, *LP*, 5:517; HL to Felix Warley, September 6, 1770, *LP*, 7:357.

50. Wallace, *Laurens*, 57; *LP*, 1:241; Wallace, *Short History*, 195; Sara Bertha Townsend, *An American Soldier: The Life of John Laurens* (Raleigh, N.C.: Edwards and Broughton Co., 1958), 10.

51. *LP*, 3:116–17, 221–22; Wallace, *Laurens*, 62; George C. Rogers, Jr., *Charleston in the Age of the Pinckneys* (Norman: University of Oklahoma Press, 1969), 60; For a description of the Laurens town house, see Harriette Kershaw Leiding, *Historic Houses of South Carolina* (Philadelphia: J. B. Lippincott Company, 1921), 44–45.

52. *LP*, 2:180.

53. *LP*, 3:100; HL to Richard Oswald, April 27, 1768, *LP*, 5:668.

54. HL to John Coming Ball, January 7, 1763, *LP*, 3:207–8.

55. Of French Huguenot descent, Gervais migrated to South Carolina from Hanover in 1764, recommended to Laurens by Richard Oswald. The two became fast friends and Gervais handled Laurens's affairs in Carolina during the latter's long absences between 1771 and 1785: *LP*, 4:xviii.

56. Bailey, *Biographical Directory of the South Carolina Senate*, 893. Laurens's holdings in Georgia were extensive and perhaps more valuable than those in South Carolina. He estimated that the war cost him about ten thousand guineas annually from his Georgia estates: Sellers, *Charleston Business*, 61.

57. *LP*, 6:609–13; HL to John Laurens, February 8, 1774, *LP*, 9:272; Fraser, *Charleston*, 111; Robert M. Weir, "Slavery and the Structure of the Union," in *Ratifying the Constitution*, ed. Michael Allen Gillespie and Michael Lienesch (Lawrence: University Press of Kansas, 1989), 201–34.

58. Godbold and Woody, *Gadsden*, 12; George C. Rogers, Jr., *The History of Georgetown County, South Carolina* (Columbia: University of South Carolina Press, 1970), 50; *SCG*, January 24, 1761.

59. Stumpf, "South Carolina Importers," 3–10.

60. Godbold and Woody, *Gadsden*, 14–15; *WCG*, 316; Rogers, *Charleston in the Age of the Pinckneys*, 60.

61. *SCG*, March 7, 1774.

62. According to family tradition, the total cost of construction was twenty thousand dollars: Godbold and Woody, *Gadsden*, 74.

63. CG to Samuel Adams, May 23, 1774, in *WCG*, 92. This was a reference to Christopher Gadsden, Jr., who died August 20, 1766, at age sixteen.

64. *SCG*, October 11, 1773.

65. *SCG*, March 8, 1773.

66. *SCG*, June 7, 1770.

67. Quincy, "Journal," 49:456–63.

68. Ramsay, *History of South Carolina*, 2:255, 261; *LP*, 3:18 n.; Godbold and Woody, *Gadsden*, 16, 19–20; Fraser, *Charleston*, 134; Wallace, *Laurens*, 438–40.

69. Gadsden was a member of the Charleston Library Society (1750–1785) and the South Carolina Society (1754–1805): Walter B. Edgar and N. Louise Bailey, eds., *Biographical Directory of the South Carolina House of Representatives, vol. 2 of The Commons House of Assembly, 1692–1775* (Columbia: University of South Carolina Press, 1977), 260. Laurens belonged to the Charleston Library Society (1759–1788), serving as vice-president from 1767 to 1769, and the South Carolina Society (1753–1792), serving as junior warden (1754–1755), senior warden (1755–1756), and steward (1756–1757); Bailey, *Biographical Directory of the South Carolina Senate*, 891. On the Charleston Library Society, see M. Eugene Sirmans, *Colonial South Carolina: A Political History, 1663–1763* (Chapel Hill: University of North Carolina Press, 1966), 240. On the South Carolina Society, see Hennig

Cohen, *The South Carolina Gazette, 1732–1775* (Columbia: University of South Carolina Press, 1953), 17–18; Rogers, *Charleston in the Age of the Pinckneys*, 99–102; Arthur H. Shaffer, *To Be an American: David Ramsay and the Making of the American Consciousness* (Columbia: University of South Carolina Press, 1991), 135.

70. Bailey, *Biographical Directory of the South Carolina Senate*, 891; Edgar and Bailey, *Biographical Directory of the South Carolina House*, 260.

71. *SCG*, February 2, 1760; *JCH*, August 15, 1764; Godbold and Woody, *Gadsden*, 29.

72. *JCH*, October 7, 1757.

73. *LP*, 2:537–44.

74. HL to Richard St. John, November 11, 1747, *LP*, 1:80–81.

2. The End of a Friendship: The Cherokee War, 1759–1762

1. HL to Lewis DeRosset, October 12, 1755, *LP*, 1:357–59.

2. Ramsay, *History of South Carolina*, 1:95; Wallace, *Laurens*, 99; Edward McCrady, *The History of South Carolina under the Royal Government, 1719–1776* (New York: Macmillan Company, 1899), 336–40.

3. Weir, *Colonial South Carolina*, 269; Ramsay, *History of South Carolina*, 1:95–96.

4. *JCH*, March 18, 1758; Geraldine M. Meroney, *Inseperable Loyalty: A Biography of William Bull* (Norcross, Ga: Harrison Company, 1991), 61.

5. *JCH*, July 5, 9, 11–13, 1759.

6. *JCH*, October 9, 11, 13, 1759; *LP*, 3:16–17; Alan Calmes, "The Lyttelton Expedition of 1759: Military Failures and Financial Successes," *SCHM* 77, no. 1 (January 1976): 19n; Ramsay, *History of South Carolina*, 1:99.

7. *LP*, 3:16–17: The Commons House did, in 1760, appropriate money to reimburse these subscribers: *WCG* 30–33.

8. Godbold and Woody, *Gadsden*, 26–27; Ramsay, *History of South Carolina*, 1:96–99; Weir, *Colonial South Carolina*, 269–70.

9. Citizens of Charles Town to Governor Lyttelton, March 22, 1760, *LP*, 3:30–33.

10. Fraser, *Charleston*, 93–94; Rogers, *Charleston in the Age of the Pinckneys*, 26–27.

11. John Richard Alden, *John Stuart and the Southern Colonial Frontier* (New York: Gordian Press, 1944), 106–7; Godbold and Woody, *Gadsden*, 28; David H. Corkran, *The Cherokee Frontier: Conflict and Survival, 1740–62* (Norman: University of Oklahoma Press, 1962), 198–99; Paul David Nelson, *General James Grant: Scottish Soldier and Royal Governor of East Florida* (Gainesville: University of Florida Press, 1993), 26

12. Ramsay, *History of South Carolina*, 1:100–102; Alden, *John Stuart*, 112–13; Robert L. Meriwether, *The Expansion of South Carolina, 1729–1765* (Kingsport, Tenn.: Southern Publishers, 1940), 231–32; Weir, *Colonial South Carolina*, 270–71; Corkran, *Cherokee Frontier*, 213–15; Nelson, *James Grant*, 28.

13. *JCH*, July 31, 1760.

14. Lt. Colonel James Grant to Lt. Governor William Bull, July 3, 1760, "Gadsden Miscellany," South Caroliniana Library, Columbia (microfilm).

15. *JCH*, August 1, 5, 1760; Alden, *John Stuart*, 114.

16. *LP*, 3:46–47, 52–53, 59; Ramsay, *History of South Carolina*, I, 106–7.

17. James Grant, "Journal of Lieutenant-Colonel James Grant, Commanding an Expedition against the Cherokee Indians, June-July, 1761," *Florida Historical So-*

ciety Quarterly 12, no. 1 (July 1933): 35; Corkran, *Cherokee Frontier*, 246–54; Nelson, *James Grant*, 35–36.

18. James Grant to Jeffrey Amherst, July 10, 1761, Grant, "Journal," *Florida Historical Quarterly* (July 1933): 25.

19. *JCH*, August 6, 1761; Godbold and Woody, *Gadsden*, 30.

20. *JCH*, September 15, 1761; Godbold and Woody, *Gadsden*, 30–31; Alden, *John Stuart*, 131; Weir, *Colonial South Carolina*, 272–73.

21. There is no remaining record of the incident with which Laurens confronted Gadsden, nor does the apology survive. Gadsden to Peter Timothy, March 12, 1763, in *WCG*, 55; *LP*, 3:271.

22. *JCH*, September 16, 1761; Weir, *Colonial South Carolina*, 273.

23. *JCH*, September 18, 1761.

24. James Grant to Jeffrey Amherst, December 24, 1761, in George C. Rogers, Jr., "The Papers of James Grant of Ballindalloch Castle, Scotland," *SCHM* 77, no. 3 (July 1976): 145–69, 148.

25. Philopatrios to Peter Timothy, *SCG*, December 18, 1761; Gadsden, "Some Observations on the Two Campaigns against the Cherokee Indians, in 1760 and 1761: In a Second Letter from Philopatrios to the Printer of the South Carolina Gazette" (Charles Town, 1762), "Gadsden Miscellany," South Caroliniana Library, Columbia. This latter essay was printed as a pamphlet by Peter Timothy, printer of the *SCG*.

26. Gadsden, "Some Observations on Two Campaigns."

27. Henry Laurens, "Manuscript of Philolethes," unpublished manuscript in *HLP* (South Carolina Historical Society, Charleston, S.C., 1966, 19 reels of microfilm), reel 17, 17.

28. Laurens, "Manuscript of Philolethes," *HLP*, reel 17, 14–16, 49–50, 60–66.

29. Gadsden, "Some Observations on Two Campaigns," "Gadsden Miscellany," South Caroliniana Library, Columbia.

30. Ibid.

31. Philopatrios to Peter Timothy, *SCG*, December 18, 1761.

32. Laurens, "Manuscript of Philolethes," *HLP*, reel 17, 42–43.

33. Ibid., 23–27. When the shocked Grant informed Bull of Middleton's departure, the embarrassed lieutenant governor was forced to admit that he had given Middleton permission to leave the regiment. But, added Bull, he did not consider Middleton's stated reasons for leaving as sufficient and the colonel was suspended from his command.

34. Ibid., 25–26, 30.

35. Ibid., 118–19, 80–81.

36. Ibid., 17, 122.

37. Laurens to James Grant, December 22, 1768, *LP*, 6:233–34.

38. Wallace, *Laurens*, 109.

3. Christopher Gadsden and the Birth of the Protest Movement, 1762–1764

1. The struggle between the assemblies and governors for control of the southern colonies is explained very well by Jack P. Greene in *The Quest for Power: The Lower Houses of Assembly in the Southern Royal Colonies, 1689–1776* (Chapel Hill: University of North Carolina Press, 1963). For this notation see 5, 37–38, 134–38. Greene has also provided the authoritative account of the Gadsden election controversy in his article, "The Gadsden Election Controversy and the Revolution-

ary Movement in South Carolina," *Mississippi Valley Historical Review* 46, no. 3 (December 1959): 469–92, which has been important in the preparation of this chapter.

2. Weir, *Colonial South Carolina*, 265–67; Wallace, *Short History*, 176–77.

3. Weir, *Colonial South Carolina*, 288–89; *JCH*, November 22, 1762.

4. Greene, "Gadsden Election Controversy," 470.

5. Ibid., 473–74; Godbold and Woody, *Gadsden*, 35.

6. Gadsden to the Gentlemen Electors of the Parish of St. Paul, Stono, *SCG*, February 5, 1763; Walsh, *WCG*, 38–39; Greene, "Gadsden Election Controversy," 474.

7. *JCH*, September 13, 1762.

8. Greene, "Gadsden Election Controversy," 471–72, 477; Sirmans, *Colonial South Carolina*, 352–53.

9. *JCH*, November 22–24, 1762; Greene, "Gadsden Election Controversy," 475–76; Godbold and Woody, *Gadsden*, 37.

10. *JCH*, November 30, 1762.

11. *JCH*, November 30, 1762; Greene, "Gadsden Election Controversy," 476–78.

12. *JCH*, December 7, 1762.

13. *JCH*, December 9, 1762; Greene, "Gadsden Election Controversy," 479.

14. *JCH*, December 11, 1762.

15. *JCH*, December 16, 1762.

16. Weir, *Colonial South Carolina*, 293.

17. Board of Trade to Thomas Boone, December 3, 1762, *Records in the British Public Records Office Relating to South Carolina* (microfilm) reel 9, vol. 29.

18. Interestingly, the three thousand acres assigned to Laurens was also coveted by Thomas Middleton, Laurens's former antagonist from the Cherokee War controversy. Only by some tricky maneuvering did Laurens manage to survey the land first and, thus, win title to it: Harvey H. Jackson, *Lachlan McIntosh and the Politics of Revolutionary Georgia* (Athens: University of Georgia Press, 1979), 12–13; Laurens to John Rutherford, April 4, 1763, *LP*, 3:404–5. Laurens received the warrant of survey for three thousand acres south of the Altamaha on April 5, 1763: *LP*, 3:405. Laurens described his plans for completing his survey before that of Middleton in Laurens to Edmund Egan, May 4, 1763, *LP*, 3:433; Laurens to Lachlan McIntosh, May 4, 1763, *LP*, 3:433–37. Laurens received the final grant for the three thousand acres on the Altamaha on May 18, 1763: *LP*, 3:454.

19. "An Advertisement," *SCG*, December 11, 1762, *WCG*, 16.

20. There is no extant copy of the January 5,1763 issue of the *South Carolina Weekly Gazette*, but Wragg's letter was reprinted in the February 5, 1763, issue of the *SCG*, as quoted in Godbold and Woody, *Gadsden*, 39–40; Greene, "Gadsden Election Controversy," 480–81.

21. Gadsden to the Gentlemen Electors of the Parish of St. Paul, Stono, *SCG*, February 5, 1763, *WCG*, 25–27.

22. Ibid., 18–19.

23. Ibid., 23.

24. Ibid., 30.

25. Ibid., 30–34.

26. Ibid., 46–47.

27. Ibid., 48.

28. Gadsden to Peter Timothy, *SCG*, March 12, 1763, *WCG*, 55–56.

29. Ibid., 60–61.

30. Greene, "Gadsden Election Controversy," 483.

31. Laurens to John Rutherford, June 1, 1763, *LP*, 3:467–68.

32. *JCH*, September 3, 10, 13, 1763; McCrady, *Royal Government*, 363–65.

33. *JCH*, January 4–6, 1764.

34. Laurens to Christopher Rowe, February 8, 1764, *LP*, 4:164–65.

35. *JCH*, May 23, 1764.

36. *PRO*, reel 10, vol. 30.

37. *JCH*, August 16, 22, 1764.

38. *JCH*, August 23, 1764.

39. Journal of the Board of Trade, February 25, 1766, *PRO*, reel 10 vol. 31; *JCH*, June 17, 20, 1766; Lord Charles Montagu to Board of Trade, June 29, 1766, *PRO*, reel 10, vol. 31.

4. The Stamp Act Crisis, 1764–1766

1. P. D. G. Thomas, *British Politics and the Stamp Act Crisis* (Oxford: Clarendon Press, 1975), 32; John C. Miller, *Origins of the American Revolution* (Stanford,Calif.: Stanford University Press, 1943), 208–10.

2. Edmund S. and Helen M. Morgan, *The Stamp Act Crisis: Prologue to Revolution* (New York: Macmillan Company, 1953), 36; Miller, *Origins*, 89. It was calculated that the British debt per person was eighteen pounds in 1763, while in America it was only eighteen shillings. In 1775, Lord North stated that the average Englishman paid twenty-five shillings a year in taxes while the average American paid six pence: Miller, *Origins*, 89.

3. Edmund and Helen Morgan, *Stamp Act Crisis*, 37–38; Thomas, *British Politics*, 44–45, 53–54. Thomas estimated the annual cost of the army at £359,000, but the Morgans found that this figure was the estimated cost of total American expenses, not solely the army's.

4. Thomas, *British Politics*, 53–54, 69, 99; Thomas C. Barrow, *Trade and Empire: The British Customs Service in Colonial America, 1660–1775* (Cambridge: Harvard University Press, 1967), 102–4.

5. Edmund and Helen Morgan, *Stamp Act Crisis*, 76–82; Thomas, *British Politics*, 72–76.

6. Committee of Correspondence to Charles Garth, September 4, 1764, as quoted in R. W. Gibbes, *Documentary History of the American Revolution* (New York: D. Appleton and Company, 1855), 1:2–3.

7. Ibid., 1:1–2. This request, along with another of November 27, 1766, asking permission to print fifty thousand pounds currency, was refused: *JCH*, November 27, 1766. Henry Laurens frequently commented on the shortage of money during late 1763 and 1764. Typical of these comments was this: "in these times of necessity when money is scarser than ever was known in Carolina,": HL to Cowles and Harford, May 5, 1764, *LP*, 4:264–65.

8. Walter J. Fraser, Jr., "The City Elite, 'Disorder,' and the Poor Children of Pre-Revolutionary Charleston," *SCHM* 84, no. 3 (July 1983): 167–79, 167–68.

9. Committee of Correspondence to Charles Garth, September 4, 1764, *Documentary History*, Gibbs, 1:5.

10. Franklin was so sure that America would accept the stamp tax that he used his influence to secure positions as stamp distributors for his friends. Among the Americans who attempted to gain these positions was Richard Henry Lee: John Richard Alden, *The South in the Revolution, 1763–1789* (Baton Rouge: Louisiana State University Press, 1957), 66.

11. C. A. Weslager, *The Stamp Act Congress* (Newark: University of Delaware Press, 1976), 91–92. It is interesting that Lowndes, who was always a conservative

and would later take British protection after the fall of Charles Town, remained a good friend of both Laurens and Gadsden. Surprisingly, Lowndes was particularly close to the radical Gadsden, who championed Lowndes at the Jacksonborough assembly, saving his property from confiscation. The respect between the two men was demonstrated by Lowndes, who named one of his children for Gadsden, while the latter named Lowndes as one of the executors of his will: Carl Vipperman, *The Rise of Rawlins Lowndes, 1721–1800* (Columbia: University of South Carolina Press, 1978), 87, 118; Harriott Horry Ravenel, *Charleston: The Place and the People* (London: Macmillan Company, 1906), 178.

12. *JCH,* July 19, 26, August 2, 1765; Godbold and Woody, *Gadsden,* 52–53; Wallace, *Laurens,* 122; George C. Rogers, Jr., *Evolution of a Federalist: William Loughton Smith of Charleston, 1758–1812* (Columbia: University of South Carolina Press, 1962), 43.

13. Ramsay, *History of South Carolina,* 2:253.

14. CG to William Henry Drayton, June 1, 1778, *WCG,* 128.

15. CG to Samuel Adams, April 4, 1779, *WCG,* 161–62.

16. Godbold and Woody, *Gadsden,* 53–54; Weslager, *Stamp Act Congress,* 93.

17. Miller, *Origins,* 174–75; Weslager, *Stamp Act Congress,* 134; CG to William Samuel Johnson and Charles Garth, December 2, 1765, *WCG,* 66–67.

18. CG to William Samuel Johnson and Charles Garth, December 2, 1765, *WCG,* 67–68; Godbold and Woody, *Gadsden,* 54–55; Miller, *Origins,* 138; Edmund and Helen Morgan, *Stamp Act Crisis,* 147–48; Weslager, *Stamp Act Congress,* 143.

19. Edmund and Helen Morgan, *Stamp Act Crisis,* 142–44; Weslager, *Stamp Act Congress,* 200–214.

20. The one dissenting member has been identified as William Wragg: Godbold and Woody, *Gadsden,* 59; CG to William Samuel Johnson and Charles Garth, December 2, 1765, *WCG,* 65; *JCH,* November 26, 1765.

21. Thomas, *British Politics,* 189–90.

22. Richard Walsh, *Charleston's Sons of Liberty: A Study of the Artisans* (Columbia: University of South Carolina Press, 1959), 17–25; Godbold and Woody, *Gadsden,* 57.

23. Walsh, *Sons of Liberty,* 31; Godbold and Woody, *Gadsden,* 57–58.

24. CG to the *State Gazette,* October 8, 1800, Walsh, *WCG,* 301–2.

25. Walsh, *Sons of Liberty,* 32–33.

26. *SCG,* September 28, 1765.

27. *SCG,* October 31, 1765.

28. HL to Joseph Brown, October 11, 1765, *LP,* 5:25.

29. HL to Joseph Brown, October 22, 1765, *LP,* 5:27.

30. Eleanor Laurens gave birth to a son, James, on November 26. John Lewis Gervais, in humorous reference to the events of this night, referred to the boy as 'George Liberty': HL to John Lewis Gervais, January 29, 1766, *LP,* 5:55.

31. HL to James Grant, November 1, 1765, *LP,* 5:39; HL to Joseph Brown, October 28, 1765, *LP,* 5:29–31.

32. HL to Joseph Brown, October 28, 1765, *LP,* 5:30.

33. Wallace, *Laurens,* 119n.; Godbold and Woody, *Gadsden,* 59.

34. HL to James Grant, November 1, 1765, *LP,* 5:36. In fairness to those who have misidentified Gadsden as the "malicious Villain" referred to by Laurens, it must be pointed out that this letter has only recently been published, as it was for years hidden away in the Grant papers at Ballindalloch Castle in Scotland. As for Timothy, his leadership in the Sons of Liberty is unquestionable, though he may have exaggerated when he informed Benjamin Franklin that the "Opposition to Tyranny was raised by a single inconsiderable Man here [himself], under all the Discouragements

imaginable, even Gadsden doubting whether it could be attempted.": Peter Timothy to Benjamin Franklin, June 12, 1777, Peter Timothy, *Letters of Peter Timothy, Printer of Charleston, South Carolina, to Benjamin Franklin*, ed. by Douglas C. McMurtrie (Chicago: Black Cat Press, 1935), 17–18.

35. CG to William Samuel Johnson and Charles Garth, December 2, 1765, *WCG*, 66.

36. *South Carolina and American General Gazette*, October 31, 1765; William Bull to Board of Trade, November 3, 1765, *PRO*, reel 10, vol. 30.

37. *SCG*, October 31, 1765; McCrady *Royal Government*, 571–72.

38. Timothy would regret this action, however, for, as he explained to Benjamin Franklin, this caused him to be "from the most *popular* reduced to the most *unpopular* Man in the Province": quoted in Jeffery A. Smith, "Impartiality and Revolutionary Ideology: Editorial Policies of the *South Carolina Gazette*, 1732–1775," *Journal of Southern History* 49, no.4 (November 1983): 511–26. Opposition leaders responded by encouraging Charles Crouch, a former apprentice to Timothy, to open a new newspaper. When Crouch's *South Carolina Gazette and Country Journal* appeared in December 1765 it "immediately attracted a large list of patrons," including Henry Laurens and John Lewis Gervais. Timothy reported that his business was still suffering three years later: Arthur M. Schlesinger, "The Colonial Newspapers and the Stamp Act," *New England Quarterly* 8 (March 1935): 63–83; Edmund and Helen Morgan, *Stamp Act Crisis*, 242; HL to John Lewis Gervais, January 29, 1766, *LP*, 5:54.

39. William Bull to Board of Trade, November 3, 1765, *PRO*, v. 30, reel 10; Fraser, *Charleston*, 110; Meroney, *William Bull*, 84–85.

40. Charles Garth to Committee of Correspondence, December 23, 1765, *LP*, 5:47–48.

41. *JCH*, April 22, 1766.

42. HL to John Lewis Gervais, January 29, 1766, *LP*, 5:52–53; William Bull to Board of Trade, December 17, 1765, *Documents Illustrative of Slave Trade*, 4:415; Carl Bridenbaugh, *Cities in Revolt: Urban Life in America, 1743–1776* (New York: Alfred A. Knopf, 1955), 313; Pauline Maier, "The Charleston Mob and the Evolution of Popular Politics in Revolutionary South Carolina, 1765–1784," *Perspectives in American History*, 4 (1970): 173–96.

43. CG to William Samuel Johnson and Charles Garth, December 2, 1765, *WCG*, 66; CG to William Samuel Johnson, April 16, 1766, *WCG*, 72.

44. Maier, "Charleston Mob," 176.

45. *JCH*, January 22, 24, 28, 1766; HL to Rossel and Gervais, February 4, 1766, *LP*, 5:62–64. It was Bull himself who had set the precedent for demanding official notification before enforcing a law. In early 1761, while Bull and the assembly were providing for the Grant expedition against the Cherokee, unofficial news was received of the death of King George II. By law this news required the dissolution of the assembly and new elections, a process that could take months. Thus, Bull declared that he would not act until the news was confirmed by official sources. In the meantime, the preparations were completed: Meroney, *William Bull*, 66.

46. *South Carolina Gazette and Country Journal*, February 11, 1766.

47. *South Carolina Gazette and Country Journal*, March 4, 1766. Georgia was the only colony in which the stamps were actually sold and used. The Stamp Act was only in operation in Georgia for a few days during January 1766, as threats of violence forced Governor James Wright to transfer the stamps to safer places: Kenneth Coleman, *Colonial Georgia: A History* (New York: Charles Scribner's Sons, 1976), 248–50.

48. John Moultrie to James Grant, February 16, 1766, in George C. Rogers, Jr.,

"The Papers of James Grant of Ballindalloch Castle, Scotland," *SCHM* 77, no. 3 (July 1976): 145–60.

49. CG to James Pearson, February 20, 1766, *SCHM* 75, no. 3 (July 1974): 173–76.

50. CG to James Pearson, February 13, 1766, *SCHM* 75, no. 3 (July 1974), 172–73; CG to James Pearson, February 20, 1766, 175.

51. Vipperman, *Rawlins Lowndes*, 116–22; Edmund and Helen Morgan, *Stamp Act Crisis*, 225–28; *JCH*, April 23, 28, 1766.

52. CG to William Samuel Johnson April 16, 1766, *WCG*, 71.

53. Shinner was suspended pending approval by the British authorities, but died shortly before this was received: Vipperman, *Rawlins Lowndes*, 123–24; *JCH*, April 9, May 19, 1767; Weir, *Most Important Epocha*, 21; for Shinner's defense see *JCH*, May 27, 1767.

54. HL to John Lewis Gervais, May 12, 1766, *LP,* 5:128; Peter Manigault to Thomas Gadsden, May 17, 1766, Peter Manigault, "The Letterbook of Peter Manigault, 1763–1773," ed. by Maurice A. Crouse, *SCHM* 70, no. 2 (April 1969): 79–96.

55. *JCH*, May 7, 1766; HL to John Lewis Gervais, May 12, 1766, *LP,* 5:128–29.

56. *SCG*, June 9, 1766.

57. Charles Garth to Committee of Correspondence, February 25, 1766, *LP,* 5:76; Thomas, *British Politics*, 33, 212–15.

58. HL to John Lewis Gervais, May 12, 1766, *LP,* 5:129–30; HL to John Lewis Gervais, September 1, 1766, *LP,* 5:184.

59. The Liberty Tree, often the site of patriotic meetings, was a "beautiful live-oak" standing in Isaac Mazyck's pasture outside the city limits. The tree was cut down and the stump burned until only "a low black stump" was left after the British captured Charles Town during the war. The site is now a square bounded by Charlotte, Washington, Calhoun, and Alexander streets: "On the Liberty Tree: A Revolutionary Poem from South Carolina." (unpublished by Jay B. Hubbell. *SCHM* 41 no. 3 (July 1940): 117.

60. Quoted in Walsh, *Sons of Liberty*, 40.

61. HL to Joseph Brown, August 21, 1766, *LP,* 5:171; *SCG*, August 25, 1766. Christopher Gadsden Jr. was born on September 5, 1750, and died August 20, 1766. Ironically, reminiscent of his father, one of this boy's young playmates was John Laurens, eldest son of Henry Laurens: Godbold and Woody, *Gadsden*, 72.

62. Godbold and Woody, *Gadsden*, 69.

63. Wallace, *Laurens*, 122.

5. The Making of a Rebel: Henry Laurens and the Vice-Admiralty Court, 1767–1770

1. Arthur M. Schlesinger, *The Colonial Merchants and the American Revolution* (New York: Facsimile Library, 1918), 47–49.

2. Carl Ubbelohde, *The Vice-Admiralty Courts and the American Revolution* (Chapel Hill: University of North Caroliina Press, 1960), 50–51, 210–11.

3. Moore was a placeman who received this appointment as a reward for his support of the Stamp Act: Ubbelohde, *Vice-Admiralty Courts*, 100; Schlesinger, *Colonial Merchants*, 101–2; Carl Bridenbaugh, *Cities in Revolt: Urban Life in America, 1743–1776* (New York: Alfred A. Knopf, 1955), 66; Sellers, *Charleston Business*, 178; Edward McCrady, *The History of South Carolina under the Royal Government, 1719–1776* (New York: Macmillan Company, 1899), 264–65; Warner O. Moore, Jr., "Henry Laurens: A Charleston Merchant in the Eighteenth Century, 1747–1771" (Ph.D. diss., University of Alabama, 1974), 117–19.

4. Ubbelohde, *Vice-Admiralty Courts*, 100.

5. Quoted in McCrady, *Royal Government*, 539.

6. HL to George Appleby, October 18, 1764, *LP*, 4:477; HL to Richard Oswald, October 10, 1764, *LP*, 4:467; In 1757, Christopher Gadsden had been nominated by Governor Lyttelton as one of three men qualified for a vacant seat on the council, but did not receive the appointment: *PRO*, reel 9, vol. 27–28.

7. William Bull to Earl of Hillsborough, October 20, 1770, *PRO*, reel 10, vol. 32.

8. McCrady, *Royal Government*, 280–81.

9. Leigh's law practice was worth between one thousand and twelve hundred pounds sterling annually, and the income from his official positions probably doubled this. This income allowed Leigh to purchase a plantation and a Charles Town home, which he furnished expensively with, among other things, an organ, a fine collection of paintings, and a library of over eight hundred volumes: Robert M. Calhoon and Robert M. Weir, "The Scandalous History of Sir Egerton Leigh," *William and Mary Quarterly* 26, no. 1 (January 1969): 47–74; Robert M. Calhoon, *The Loyalists in Revolutionary America, 1760–1781* (New York: Harcourt Brace Jovanovich, 1965), 76–77.

10. Calhoon and Weir, "Sir Egerton Leigh," 52–53; Committee of Correspondence to Charles Garth, July 2, 1766, "Garth Correspondence," *SCHM* 28, no. 4 (October 1927): 228.

11. Quoted in Godbold and Woody, *Gadsden*, 76.

12. Ubbelohde, *Vice-Admiralty Courts*, 100–102; Sellers, *Charleston Business*, 193–94; Barrow, *Trade and Empire*, 205–6.

13. Henry Laurens, *A Representation of Facts* (Charles Town, 1768), *LP*, 5:406–10; Ubbelohde, *Vice-Admiralty Courts*, 106; Sellers, *Charleston Business*, 194.

14. The *Wambaw* was seized on July 17 and the *Broughton Island Packet* on July 31, 1767: *LP*, 5:273–76.

15. This duel never took place because, according to Laurens, Moore issued the challenge but never took any steps to proceed upon it: Laurens, *A Representation of Facts*, *LP*, 5:412; HL to James Habersham, October 14, 1767, *LP*, 5:365.

16. Laurens, *A Representation of Facts*, *LP*, 5:410–11; Sellers, *Charleston Business*, 195.

17. Laurens, *A Representation of Facts*, *LP*, 5:412–13; Ubbelohde, *Vice-Admiralty Courts*, 107; Egerton Leigh, *The Man Unmasked*, *LP*, 6:473–74.

18. Laurens bought the *Wambaw* at public vendue for twenty-five pounds sterling: *LP*, 5:274–76; Wallace, *Laurens*, 138–39.

19. HL to James Habersham, September 5, 1767, *LP*, 5:297–98.

20. HL to James Habersham, September 5, 1767, *LP*, 5:296–97. Shortly after Moore's arrival, the merchants appointed a committee of seven to reach agreement with the collector on a table of fees and consistent rules of trade. Though the merchants thought that an understanding had been reached, Laurens reported, Moore soon became even more "determined to accomplish his Purpose of accumulating Money by every arbitrary and oppressive Method he could devise": Laurens, *A Representation of Facts*, *LP*, 5:396–97.

21. HL to James Habersham, September 5, 1767, *LP*, 5:298.

22. HL to William Fisher, October 3, 1767, *LP*, 5:328–29; Laurens sent similar accounts of this publicized incident to other friends: HL to Ross and Mill, October 8, 1767, *LP*, 5:338–39; HL to James Habersham, October 14, 1767, *LP*, 5:365–66.

23. *LP*, 5:391–92; Committee of Correspondence to Charles Garth, September 29, 1767, *SCHM* 29 (October 1928): 304–5. These efforts proved successful and Moore was relieved of his post during the summer of 1769: Wallace, *Laurens*, 142.

24. *LP*, 5:679–80; HL to George Appleby, May 24, 1768, *LP*, 5:689.

25. HL to Richard Oswald, April 27, 1768, *LP,* 5:669.

26. *LP,* 5:722; HL to Peter Timothy, July 6, 1768, *LP,* 5:730–33 (public letter which appeared in the *SCG,* July 11, 1768).

27. Laurens, *Extracts* (Philadelphia) *LP,* 6:198–204.

28. Laurens, *Extracts* (Charles Town), *LP,* 6:327–28.

29. *SCG,* July 11, 1768 (also printed in *LP,* 5:737–42).

30. George Roupell to Commissioners of Customs in America, July 11, 1768, *LP,* 5:737–42.

31. HL to William Cowles and Company and William Freeman, July 13, 1768, *LP,* 5:744–47.

32. HL to James Wright, August 8, 1768, *LP,* 6:54; HL to Andrew Turnbull, August 17, 1768, *LP,* 6:72.

33. The correspondence between Laurens and Leigh over this matter can be found, in edited form, in Egerton Leigh, *The Man Unmasked, LP,* 6:552–55. Laurens published an unedited version in his *Appendix to the Extracts, LP,* 7:48–55; see also HL to Leigh, July 28, 1768, *LP,* 5:759–61.

34. HL to William Fisher, August 1, 1768, *LP,* 6:8.

35. Ibid., 5–6.

36. Ibid., 30–37.

37. Ibid., 39–40.

38. Ibid., 38–43.

39. Ibid., 44–49.

40. Ibid., 63.

41. *Extracts from the Proceedings of the Court of Vice-Admiralty in Charles-Town, South Carolina* (Philadelphia, 1768), reprinted in *LP,* 6:191–216; Wallace, *Laurens,* 145. On the authorship of the introduction and conclusion of the *Extracts,* Laurens later wrote to Fisher that "I intend to play the Plagarist in The Introduction & conclusion of my Publication by adopting those in yours, for which I trust your friend will forgive me & accept it as a Tribute.": HL to William Fisher, February 1, 1769, *LP,* 6:263. The editors of the *Laurens Papers* identify Chew as this friend: *LP,* 6:186, 263.

42. HL to William Fisher, December 14, 1768, *LP,* 6:228.

43. HL to William Cowles and Company, December 24, 1768, *LP,* 6:238; the Charles Town edition of the *Extracts* is reprinted in *LP,* 6:295–383.

44. Laurens, *Extracts* (Charles Town, 1769), *LP,* 6:383.

45. Egerton Leigh, *The Man Unmasked, LP,* 6:455–67.

46. Ibid., 464–65.

47. Ibid., 457–58, 467–68.

48. Ibid., 465–67.

49. Ibid., 511–12.

50. Ibid., 563.

51. Ibid., 520.

52. Ibid., 528.

53. Ibid., 531–32.

54. HL to William Fisher, June 26, 1769, *LP,* 6:594–95. The relationship between Laurens and Leigh deteriorated to the extent that a duel was arranged in May 1769. The two never met in the field, however, as Leigh canceled because he had been "bound over": Egerton Leigh to HL, May 29, 1769, *LP,* 6:580.

55. Laurens, *Appendix to the Extracts from the Proceedings of the High Court of Vice-Admiralty in Charlestown, South Carolina, LP,* 7:6–114.

56. For Leigh's record of this correspondence, see *The Man Unmasked, LP,* 6:552–55. For Laurens's version, see *Appendix to the Extracts, LP,* 7:48–55.

57. Ibid., 94–97.

58. Ibid., 99–100.

59. Ibid., 101.

60. Ibid., 105–6.

61. HL to Ross and Mill, October 31, 1769, *LP,* 7:188.

62. HL to Jeremiah Meyler, January 23, 1770, *LP,* 7:220–21; HL to Magnus Watson, February 15, 1770, *LP,* 7:232. The customs service seems to have learned a lesson from this controversy, as the vice-admiralty court under Judge Augustus Johnston, who took office in May 1769, did little business. In fact, the customs board reported that no money in fines and forfeitures was remitted from Charles Town between September 1771 and November 1772: Ubbelohde, *Vice-Admiralty Courts,* 150–51, 155.

63. James Laurens to HL, December 19, 1772, *LP,* 8:506–9; HL to James Laurens, February 1, 1773, *LP,* 8:569.

64. HL to Egerton Leigh, January 30, 1773, *LP,* 8:556–63. It is not exactly clear who seduced whom in this scandal, as Robert Calhoon and Robert M. Weir have noted that Molly Bremar was "something of a hellion in her own right." The fact remains, however, that Leigh impregnated the young sister of his wife and then put her aboard a ship to England without a midwife and refused to allow her to be put ashore when she went into labor. If Leigh did not hope that both mother and baby would die during the voyage, he certainly left himself open to charges of this nature: Calhoon and Weir, "Sir Egerton Leigh," 63–64.

65. HL to James Laurens, January 27, 1774, *LP,* 9:254.

66. James Laurens to HL, November 2, 1773, *LP,* 9:138–41; Laurens to John Laurens, November 19, 1773, *LP,* 9:153–54.

67. James Laurens to HL, November 29, 1773, *LP,* 9:181–82; James Laurens to HL, May 4, 1774, *LP,* 9:427; James Laurens to HL, June 21, 1774, *LP,* 9:476–77.

68. HL to James Laurens, September 15, 1774, *LP,* 9:559–61.

6. The Nonimportation Movement, 1769–1770

1. Wallace, *Laurens,* 150–51; Thomas, *British Politics,* 292–99, 361. Thomas Barrow reported that the Townshend duties were not complete failures, as thirty thousand pounds were collected between September 1767 and September 1769. With expenses of sixteen thousand pounds, the treasury was left with a profit of fourteen thousand pounds that, while by no means overwhelming, was more than had been collected in the past: Barrow, *Trade and Empire,* 240.

2. John Dickinson, *Letters from a Farmer in Pennsylvania to the Inhabitants of the British Colonies,* (1768; reprint, with an introduction by R. T. H. Halsey, New York: Outlook Company, 1903), 13–26.

3. Barrow, *Trade and Empire,* 217–18, 226–27; Thomas, *British Politics,* 361–63.

4. By 1769, South Carolina was in the midst of a desperate currency crisis. The permanent fund of £106,500 was greatly reduced by lost or worn-out bills, and the Commons House responded by illegally replacing the lost or damaged notes. When the act for replacing this currency was disallowed in 1770, the Commons refused to withdraw the reprinted currency. Instead, they printed more: Godbold and Woody, *Gadsden,* 77.

5. *JCH,* April 12, 1768.

6. McCrady, *Royal Government,* 596–604; George C. Rogers, Jr., *Evolution of a Federalist: William Loughton Smith of Charleston, 1758–1812* (Columbia: University of South Carolina Press, 1962), 48–49; Barrow, *Trade and Empire,* 242.

7. *SCG*, October 3, 1768. The *Gazette's* description of this event is reprinted in *LP*, 6:122–23; Wilkes had first become a hero in America after his biting attacks on the Crown and the ministry in the *North Briton No. 45*. After fleeing to France to avoid prison in 1764, Wilkes returned to England four years later and ran for Parliament. After winning the election, Wilkes was repeatedly expelled and reelected, serving as an example of resistance to the dictation of a corrupt ministry.

8. The "Grand simpleton" reference was to Christopher Gadsden: HL to James Grant, October 1, 1768, *LP*, 6:119–20.

9. *SCG*, October 3, 1768.

10. *LP*, 6:119–20n. Peter Timothy also identified Laurens as one of several candidates in whose behalf a considerable amount of campaigning had been conducted during the October 1768 elections: *SCG*, October 3, 1768.

11. *SCG*, October 10, 1768; HL to James Grant, December 22, 1768, *LP*, 6:231–32.

12. HL to Lachlan McIntosh, October 15, 1768, *LP*, 6:126–28.

13. *JCH*, November 17–18, 1768.

14. *JCH*, November 19, 1768.

15. *JCH*, June 28, 1769.

16. *JCH*, August 19, 1769.

17. William Bull to Earl of Hillsborough, October 18, 1768, *PRO*, reel 10, vol. 32.

18. *SCG*, February 2, 1769.

19. *SCG*, February 2, March 2, 1769; Godbold and Woody, *Gadsden*, 81–82.

20. HL to Ross & Mill, March 11, 1769, *LP*, 6:407–8.

21. *SCG*, June 8, 15, 1769.

22. CG to the Planters, Mechanics, and Freeholders of the Province of South Carolina, *SCG*, June 22, 1769, reprinted in Walsh, *WCG*, 80–81.

23. Ibid., 81–82.

24. Ibid., 84–88; Gadsden often displayed an antipathy toward the Scots, which was by no means unusual in Charles Town. The "general bias against Scots" proceeded largely from their relatively late arrival, their tendency to remain largely among themselves and resist integration into the wider community, and their business and political contacts in Britain, which often contributed to their success: J. Russell Snapp, *John Stuart and the Struggle for Empire on the Southern Frontier* (Baton Rouge: Louisiana State University Press, 1996), 46, 153–58.

25. *SCG*, July 6, 13, 1769.

26. *SCG*, July 27, 1769. The Nonimportation Agreement is also printed in Robert M. Weir, ed., *The Letters of Freeman, Etc.: Essays on the Nonimportation Movement in South Carolina, Collected by William Henry Drayton* (Columbia: University of South Carolina Press, 1977), 9–11.

27. HL to James Habersham, October 16, 1769, *LP*, 7:165.

28. *SCG*, August 10, September 14, November 14, 1769.

29. Weir, *Letters of Freeman*, xiii.

30. *SCG*, August 3, 1769, reprinted in Weir, *Letters of Freeman*, 7–9. A complete text of the ensuing newspaper battle was collected and published by Drayton as *The Letters of Freeman*. Future references will be made to the Robert M. Weir edition of *The Letters of Freeman*.

31. John Mackenzie was a young lawyer and planter, born in 1738 and sent to England to be educated at Cambridge and the Middle Temple. He was a capable and wealthy man, but died young in 1771, leaving an estate valued at twelve thousand pounds sterling: Weir, *Letters of Freeman*, xiii–xiv.

32. *SCG*, August 10, 1769 in Weir, *Letters of Freeman*, 11–14.

33. *SCG*, September 21, 1769 in Weir, *Letters of Freeman*, 26–29. As a reward for championing British interests, the government offered Wragg the office of chief

justice of South Carolina. Wragg, however, declined the appointment after Gadsden charged that desire for such preferment had motivated Wragg's conduct: Robert M. Weir, "The South Carolinian as Extremist" *South Atlantic Quarterly* 74, no. 1 (Winter 1975): 86–103.

34. *SCG*, September 21, 1769 in Weir, *Letters of Freeman*, 29–32.

35. *SCG*, September 28, 1769 in Weir, *Letters of Freeman*, 39–41.

36. *SCG*, October 5, 1769 in Weir, *Letters of Freeman*, 111–14.

37. *SCG*, October 12, 1769 in Weir, *Letters of Freeman*, 42–49.

38. *SCG*, October 26, 1769 in Weir, *Letters of Freeman*, 53–57.

39. *SCG*, October 26, 1769 in Weir, *Letters of Freeman*, 57–64.

40. *SCG*, October 26, November 9, 1769 in Weir, *Letters of Freeman*, 58–74.

41. HL to James Habersham, October 16, 1769, *LP*, 7:165.

42. McCrady, *Royal Government*, 672–74; Sellers, *Charleston Business*, 214–15.

43. *SCG*, February 1, 1770; Weir, *Most Important Epocha*, 37.

44. *SCG*, March 8 and March 29, 1770. Later, Timothy would add that the boycott had cost Britain three hundred thousand pounds sterling. He thought this was an unreasonable sacrifice in an effort to raise an annual revenue of thirteen thousand pounds: *SCG*, May 24, 1770.

45. William Bull to Earl of Hillsborough, March 6, 1770, *PRO*, reel 10, vol. 32.

46. *SCG*, May 17, 1770.

47. HL to Henry Humphries, May 19, 1770, *LP*, 7:298.

48. The death of Eleanor Laurens on May 22, 1770, shortly after giving birth to a daughter, was an unexpected calamity that almost completely immobilized her grief-stricken husband. For months Laurens remained mired in grief, with little inclination for either business or politics. He treasured the memory of his faithful wife, and even a year later, "the bare mention of her Name hurries reflexions upon my mind which betrays a weakness that I can not yet conquer.": HL to John Moultrie, June 27, 1771, *LP*, 7:544.

49. *South Carolina and American General Gazette*, June 15, 1770; *SCG*, June 21, 1770.

50. *SCG*, June 28, August 23, October 25, 1770; *South Carolina and American General Gazette*, July 11, 1770.

51. HL to William Fisher, November 2, 1770, *LP*, 7:396.

52. William Bull to Earl of Hillsborough, December 5, 1770, *PRO*, reel 10, vol. 32.

53. William Bull to Earl of Hillsborough, December 13, 1770, *PRO*, reel 10, vol. 32; *SCG*, December 13, 27, 1770; *LP*, 7:411.

54. Arthur Schlesinger presented figures that show how imports to New York fell from £490,673 in 1768 to £75,930 in 1769. In Philadelphia, they dropped from £441,829 in 1768 to £204,978 in 1769 to £134,881 in 1770. Imports in New England dropped from £430,806 in 1768 to £223,694 in 1769, while in the Carolinas they went from £306,600 in 1769 to £146,273 in 1770: Arthur M. Schlesinger, *The Colonial Merchants and the American Revolution, 1763–1776* (New York: Facsimile Library, 1918), 182–208.

55. John C. Miller, *Origins*, 276; Jack M. Sosin, *Agents and Merchants: British Colonial Policy and the Origins of the American Revolution, 1763–1775* (Lincoln: University of Nebraska Press, 1965), 109–10.

7. The Wilkes Fund Crisis, 1770–1774

1. Godbold and Woody, *Gadsden*, 99–101; John Brooke, *King George III* (New York: McGraw-Hill, 1972), 144–49. The best study of John Wilkes and his movement

in England remains George Rude's, *Wilkes and Liberty* (Oxford: Clarendon Press, 1962).

2. *JCH*, December 8, 1769; *SCG*, December 8, 1769; *South Carolina and American General Gazette*, December 13, 1769; Weir, *Colonial South Carolina*, 305. It seems that Wilkes was not very grateful for the American contributions. Horne Tooke—a fellow radical and a leading organizer of the Society of the Gentlemen Supporters of the Bill of Rights—broke with Wilkes over the appropriation of these funds. Tooke insisted that the money be used to defray Wilkes's legal expenses, while the latter, who had amassed large debts gambling, drinking, and womanizing, wished to put it toward more fun-seeking. Tooke wrote that Wilkes, rather than expressing gratitude for the contribution, was angry at the Carolinians for sending the money to the society, rather than to him personally. Tooke insisted that Wilkes then demonstrated his well-known contempt for Americans by writing a sarcastic reply, which was suppressed by the society and replaced by a letter of thanks: Miller, *Origins of the Revolution*, 324–25; Jack Greene, "Bridge to Revolution: The Wilkes Fund Controversy in South Carolina, 1769–1775," *Journal of Southern History* 29, no. 1 (February 1963): 24.

3. Petition to Lords Hillsborough, Stormont, and Germain, June 23, 1781, Simms (Kendall) Collection, South Caroliniana Library, Columbia, reel 4 (microfilm).

4. William Henry Drayton to Peter Timothy, *SCG*, December 28, 1769, reprinted in Weir, *The Letters of Freeman*, 109–10; *SCG*, December 8, 1769.

5. William Bull to Earl of Hillsborough, December 12, 1769, *PRO*, reel 10, vol. 32, 132–35; William Bull to Earl of Hillsborough, December 16, 1769, *PRO*, reel 10, vol. 32, 136. What Bull did not add was that he had never personally disputed the authority of the Commons to unilaterally order money from the treasury. Indeed, Bull had supported this authority during his tenure as speaker of the Commons House and, as acting governor during the Cherokee War, had encouraged the House to utilize this power. Thus, though Bull was strongly offended by the purpose of the grant, he did not denounce the power of the Commons to grant money: Meroney, *William Bull*, 94.

6. Opinion of William de Grey, February 13, 1770, *PRO*, reel 10, vol. 32, 166–82; Earl of Hillsborough to William Bull, April 14, 1770, *PRO*, reel 10, vol. 32, 253–55; John Drayton, *Memoirs of the American Revolution, from its Commencement to the Year 1776, Inclusive: As Relating to the State of South Carolina* (Charleston: A. E. Miller, 1821), 1:92–94.

7. *JCH*, April 9, 1770.

8. *JCH*, April 10, 1770.

9. *SCG*. April 19, 1770; *South Carolina Gazette and Country Journal*, April 24, 1770. The numbers ninety-two and twenty-six were celebrated in South Carolina as references to the members of the Massachusetts assembly who refused to rescind their circular letter of February 1768 under orders from Hillsborough, and the twenty-six members of the South Carolina Commons House who ignored Hillsborough's order to ignore the Massachusetts letter.

10. *SCG*, July 5, 1770; *SCG*, June 7, 1770.

11. HL to Thomas Franklin, December 26, 1771, *LP*, 7:21.

12. *JCH*, August 16, 29, 1770.

13. *JCH*, August 29, September 6–8, 1770.

14. William Bull to Earl of Hillsborough, August 23, 1770, *PRO*, reel 10, vol. 32, 316–19; William Bull to Earl of Hillsborough, September 8, 1770, *PRO*, reel 10, vol. 32, 320–21; Earl of Hillsborough to William Bull, October 19, 1770, *PRO*, reel 10, vol. 32, 339–40; Earl of Hillsborough to William Bull, November 15, 1770, *PRO*, reel 10, 32, 353; Earl of Hillsborough to Lord Charles Montagu, November 21, 1770,

PRO, reel 10, vol. 32; Charles Garth to Committee of Correspondence, March 27, 1771, *LP*, 7:462.

15. *JCH*, January 24–25, 31, February 7, 1771.

16. HL to James Laurens, December 12, 1771, *LP*, 8:91–94; see also HL to William Fisher, September 6, 1770, *LP*, 7:335–36; HL to William Williamson, November 28, 1771, *LP*, 8:57–58; HL to Alexander Garden, May 24, 1772, *LP*, 8:328.

17. HL to James Laurens, December 12, 1771, *LP*, 8:96.

18. HL to Thomas Franklin, December 26, 1771, *LP*, 8:121; Greene, "Bridge to Revolution," 32.

19. Ibid., 29–30; *JCH*, November 11, 1771; *South Carolina and American General Gazette*, November 11, 1771.

20. HL to James Laurens, April 1, 1772, *LP*, 8:238; HL to Peter Mazyck, April 10, 1772, *LP*, 8:259–60; HL to Samuel Wainwright, September 23, 1772, *LP*, 8:473.

21. Charles Montagu to Earl of Hillsborough, July 27, 1772, *PRO*, reel 11, vol. 33; Charles Montagu to Earl of Hillsborough, September 24, 1772, *PRO*, reel 11, vol. 33; Lord Dartmouth to Charles Montagu, September 27, 1772, *PRO*, reel 11, vol. 33; McCrady, *Royal Government*, 696–99.

22. *SCG*, September 3, 17, 1772, October 8, 1772.

23. *SCG*, October 15, 1772; *JCH*, October 10, 1772. After this disconcerting incident, Manigault sadly observed of Montagu that "it was not impossible for a Man to be too great a Fool to make a good Governor": quoted in Weir, *Colonial South Carolina*, 307.

24. *JCH*, October 23–24, 1772; Greene, "Bridge to Revolution," 38–39.

25. It was Gadsden who nominated Lowndes to replace Manigault in the speaker's chair: Carl Vipperman, *The Rise of Rawlins Lowndes* (Columbia: University of South Carolina Press, 1978), 165; Godbold and Woody, *Gadsden*, 106. Peter Manigault left shortly afterwards on a trip to England to recover his health. While there, he enjoyed the company of his close friend, Henry Laurens, who observed the gradual deterioration of Manigault's health. Laurens sat with his friend on the night of his death in November 1773 and added a codicil to Manigault's will before taking a final, affectionate leave. It was Laurens who, with Ralph Izard and Benjamin Stead, then sent Manigault's body home to Charles Town for burial: Laurens to Gabriel Manigault, November 12, 1773, "Letters Concerning Peter Manigualt, 1773," *SCHM* 21, no. 2 (April 1920): 48–49; HL to Edward Neufville, November 13, 1773, *LP*, 9:147–48.

26. *JCH*, October 29, November 9, 1772; Greene, "Bridge to Revolution," 39.

27. *SCG*, February 22, 1773; *JCH*, January 6, 8, 1773; Greene, "Bridge to Revolution," 40.

28. *SCG*, August 9, 1773; HL to Alexander Garden, April 8, 1773, *LP*, 8:669; Quincy, "Journal", 452.

29. Greene, "Bridge to Revolution," 43–44.

30. *JCH*, September 11, 13, 1773; Greene, "Bridge to Revolution," 43–44.

31. William Bull to Earl of Dartmouth, September 18, 1773, *PRO*, reel 11, vol. 33, 303–10.

32. Egerton Leigh, *Considerations on Certain Political Transactions of the Province of South Carolina* (London, 1774), reprinted in Jack Greene, *The Nature of Colony Constitutions: Two Pamphlets on the Wilkes Fund Controversy in South Carolina by Sir Egerton Leigh and Arthur Lee* (Columbia: University of South Carolina Press, 1970), 63–123.

33. HL to John Lewis Gervais, January 24, 1774, *LP*, 9:250–53.

34. Arthur Lee, *Answer to Considerations on Certain Political Transactions of the Province of South Carolina* (London, 1774), reprinted in Greene, *Nature of*

Colony Constitutions, 127–205; HL to George Appleby, February 15, 1774, *LP,* 9:275–76; HL to James Laurens, February 17, 1774, *LP,* 9:288–89; HL to John Lewis Gervais, April 9, 1774, *LP,* 9:393–94; HL to Alexander Garden, April 13, 1774, *LP,* 9:400–401; HL to James Laurens, April 13, 1774, *LP,* 9:405. Laurens hoped to regain his investment in this pamphlet and sent accounts for £103 sterling to his brother in Charles Town, asking him to show them to Gadsden, Lowndes, and other opposition leaders. A public subscription raised over half of this sum, but despite efforts as late as 1777, Laurens never regained the rest: HL to James Laurens, May 18, 1774, *LP,* 9:453–54; HL to Ralph Izard, February 10, 1775, *LP,* 10:65–66; HL to John Lewis Gervais, June 26, 1777, *LP,* 11:390.

35. William Bull to Earl of Dartmouth, May 3, 1774, *PRO,* reel 11, vol. 34, 36–40.

36. HL to John Lewis Gervais, May 18, 1774, *LP,* 9:456–57; HL to George Appleby, June 18, 1774, *LP,* 9:472.

37. HL to John Lewis Gervais, April 9, 1774, *LP,* 9:390; HL to John Lewis Gervais, April 16, 1774, *LP,* 9:415; Earl of Dartmouth to William Bull, May 4, 1774, *PRO,* reel 11, vol. 34, Greene, "Bridge to Revolution," 49–50.

38. HL to John Lewis Gervais, April 16, 1774, *LP,* 9:415.

8. The Breakdown of British Authority, 1774–1775

1. HL to John Laurens, January 17, 1774, *LP,* 9:231.

2. *SCG,* November 15, 22, 1773.

3. James Laurens to HL, December 4, 1773, *LP,* 8:190–91; *SCG,* December 6, 1773; Godbold and Woody, *Gadsden,* 110–11.

4. *SCG,* December 27, 1773; Drayton, *Memoirs of the Revolution,* 1:99–100; Earl of Dartmouth to William Bull, February 5, 1774, *PRO,* reel 11, vol. 34; Sellers, *Charleston Business,* 224–25.

5. *SCG,* January 17, 24, March 21, 1774; CG to Samuel Adams, May 23, 1774, Walsh, *WCG,* 92–94; Godbold and Woody, *Gadsden,* 112; George C. Rogers, Jr., "The Charleston Tea Party: The Significance of December 3, 1773," *SCHM* 75, no. 3 (July 1974): 164–65.

6. HL to John Laurens, January 21, 1774, *LP,* 9:243–45; HL to James Air, February 25, 1774, *LP,* 9:314.

7. HL to George Appleby, May 4, 1774, *LP,* 9:428; HL to James Laurens, May 7, 1774, *LP,* 9:434–38.

8. HL to James Laurens, February 5, 1774, *LP,* 9:264–69; HL to John Laurens, February 8, 1774, *LP,* 9:271–72; HL to George Appleby, March 10, 1774, *LP,* 9:349.

9. HL to John Laurens, February 21, 1774, *LP,* 9:300.

10. HL to John Laurens, March 11, 1774, *LP,* 9:350–52; HL to John Knight, March 17, 1774, *LP,* 9:360.

11. HL to James Laurens, March 16, 1774, *LP,* 9:352–54: Laurens directed John Lewis Gervais to make a sizable contribution in his name to any subscription raised to pay for the tea: HL to John Lewis Gervais, April 9, 1774, *LP,* 9:389–92; HL to John Lewis Gervais, April 16, 1774, *LP,* 9:414–15.

12. The petitions can be found in *LP,* 9:368–76. The *SCG* proudly reported that, of the twenty-nine signers of the petitions to Parliament, eleven were from South Carolina. In addition to Laurens, other signers included Ralph Izard, Thomas Pinckney, and John F. Grimke: *SCG,* June 6, 1774.

13. HL to George Appleby, June 18, 1774, *LP,* 9:472.

14. Ramsay, *History of the Revolution,* 1:109; Miller, *Origins of the Revolution,* 361; Greene, *Quest for Power,* 443; William M. Dabney and Marion Dargan, *William*

Henry Drayton and the American Revolution (Albuquerque: University of New Mexico Press, 1962), 23.

15. CG to Samuel Adams, June 28, 1774, in *WCG*, 99; *SCG*, June 27, 1774; Drayton, *Memoirs of the Revolution*, 1:226; McCrady, *Royal Government*, 742–43; Godbold and Woody, *Gadsden*, 113.

16. CG to Samuel Adams, June 5, 1774, in *WCG*, 94–96.

17. CG to Samuel Adams, June 14, 1774, in *WCG*, 97–98.

18. CG to Samuel Adams, June 28, 1774, in *WCG*, 100–101.

19. Ramsay, *History of South Carolina*, 2:253–54.

20. *SCG*, July 11, 1774, Godbold and Woody, *Gadsden*, 117–18; Rogers, "Charleston Tea Party," 165.

21. *SCG*, July 11, 1774; Godbold and Woody, *Gadsden*, 118–19; Drayton, *Memoirs of the Revolution*, 1:130; Rogers, "Charleston Tea Party," 166; Schlesinger, *Colonial Merchants*, 376–78; McCrady, *Royal Government*, 738–41; Edward Rutledge to Ralph Izard, July 21, 1774, Anne Izard Deas, ed., *Correspondence of Mr. Ralph Izard of South Carolina, from the Year 1774 to 1804: With a Short Memoir* (New York, 1844), 2–6.

22. *SCG*, July 11, 1774; Godbold and Woody, *Gadsden*, 120; Rogers, "Charleston Tea Party," 166–67.

23. William Bull to Earl of Dartmouth, August 3, 1774, *PRO*, reel 11, vol. 34; *JCH*, August 2, 1774.

24. *South Carolina Gazette and Country Journal*, August 16, 30, 1774; *SCG*, September 17, 1774; Godbold and Woody, *Gadsden*, 120–21.

25. Silas Deane to Elizabeth Deane, August 31, 1774, *LD* 1:15; Godbold and Woody, *Gadsden*, 121–22.

26. Frank W. Ryan, Jr., "The Role of South Carolina in the First Continental Congress," *SCHM* 60, no. 3 (July 1959): 148–49; Godbold and Woody, *Gadsden*, 122–23; L. H. Butterfield, ed., *Diary and Autobiography of John Adams* (Cambridge: Harvard University Press, 1961), 2:133–34: Adams described Edward Rutledge as "a perfect Bob o' Lincoln—a Swallow—a Sparrow—a Peacock—excessively vain, excessively weak, and excessively variable and unsteady—jejune, inane, and puerile." Of John Rutledge, Adams wrote that there "is no keenness in his Eye. No Depth in his Countenance. Nothing of the profound, sagacious, brilliant, or sparkling" in his appearance. Adams later noticed "the Air of Reserve, Design, and Cunning" in John Rutledge and compared him to Joseph Galloway: Butterfield, ed., *Diary of John Adams*, 2:119, 121, 150. Patrick Henry placed John Rutledge in the conservative group with Galloway and John Jay that would "ruin the cause of America,": Ryan, "Role of South Carolina," 150–51.

27. Miller, *Origins of the Revolution*, 379–80; Ryan, "Role of South Carolina," 150.

28. Silas Deane to Elizabeth Deane, September 7, 1774, *LD*, 1:35; Godbold and Woody, *Gadsden*, 125.

29. Quoted in Godbold and Woody, *Gadsden*, 127.

30. Butterfield, *Diary of John Adams*, 2:139; "John Adams' Notes of Debates" September 26–27(?), 1774, *LD*, 1:104.

31. Edward Rutledge to Thomas Bee, October (no date), 1774, *LD*, 1:254–55; Godbold and Woody, *Gadsden*, 126–27. For a copy of the Continental Association see William Moultrie, *Memoirs of the American Revolution* (1802; reprint, New York: Arno Press, 1968), 1:27–36; Sellers, *Charleston Business*, 227.

32. *SCG*, November 21, December 12, 1774; Godbold and Woody, *Gadsden*, 128–29.

33. James Laurens to HL, November 29, 1773, *LP*, 9:183.

34. HL to John Laurens, July 5, 1774, *LP*, 9:479–81.

35. HL to John Petrie, September 7, 1774, *LP*, 9:550–53; HL to John Lewis Gervais, September 14, 1774, *LP*, 9:558–59; HL to George Appleby, September 17, 1774, *LP*, 9:564; HL to John Delagaye, October 21, 1774, *LP*, 9:596–97; HL to John Laurens, December 12, 1774, *LP*, 10:1–4.

9. The Collapse of British Rule, 1775

1. HL to Richard Oswald, January 4, 1775, *LP*, 10:22; HL to John Laurens, January 8, 1775, *LP*, 10:25–26.

2. Godbold and Woody, *Gadsden*, 129; Rogers, "Charleston Tea Party," 166–67; HL to John Laurens, January 18, 1775, *LP*, 10:27–28; Klein, *Unification of Slave State*, 83.

3. "South Carolina Delegates Report to the South Carolina Provinvial Congress", January 11, 1775, Smith, *LD*, 1:292–95; CG to Thomas and William Bradford, March 28, 1775, *WCG*, 102; HL to John Laurens, January 18, 1775, *LP*, 10:28; Drayton, *Memoirs*, 1:168–70; Rutledge had a point, as South Carolina exports were far in excess of the combined exports of all of the colonies north of Maryland: Wallace, *Short History*, 256–57.

4. Rice would be valued at fifty-five shillings currency per hundred and the value of the other commodities would rise and fall with this price. The value of the other products was indigo, thirty shillings per pound; hemp, eight shillings per hundred weight; corn, twelve shillings six pence per bushel; flour, the best at four pounds ten shillings, secondary at four pounds per hundred weight; lumber, inch pine boards (per one thousand feet) at twenty pounds at Charles Town, fifteen pounds at Beaufort and Georgetown, with other plank and scantling in proportion; pork, thirteen pounds per barrel; butter, three shillings per pound: Drayton, *Memoirs*, 1:170–74; Schlesinger, *Colonial Merchants*, 465–69. Though a member of the committee that framed this plan, Laurens thought it was a ridiculous and impractical program that was certain to fail: HL to John Laurens, January 18, 1775, *LP*, 10:28–30.

5. HL to John Laurens, January 18, 1775, *LP*, 10:28–29; *WCG*, 117–18; Godbold and Woody, *Gadsden*, 73, 129.

6. HL to John Laurens, January 18, 1775, *LP*, 10:29. Laurens's reference to the Cherokees was to his public dispute with Gadsden over the Grant expedition during 1761 and 1762.

7. HL to John Laurens, January 18, 1775, *LP*, 10:30; HL to John Laurens, January 22, 1775, *LP*, 10:43–44.

8. HL to John Laurens, January 18, 1775, *LP*, 10:31; Drayton, *Memoirs*, 1:177–80, 221; Godbold and Woody, *Gadsden*, 130. For the complete resolutions of the First Provincial Congress, see Moultrie, *Memoirs*, 1:36–52.

9. HL to John Laurens, January 22, 1775, *LP*, 10:40–45.

10. John Laurens to HL, December 3, 1774, *LP*, 9:647; HL to John Laurens, January 4, 1775, "Letters from Hon. Henry Laurens to his Son John, 1773–1776," *SCHM* 4, no. 4 (October 1903): 269; HL to John Laurens, February 6, 1775, *LP*, 10:57–59.

11. *JCH*, January 26, February 3, 1775; Jerome J. Nadelhaft, *The Disorders of War: The Revolution in South Carolina* (Orono: University of Maine at Orono Press, 1981), 23–24.

12. Drayton, *Memoirs*, 1:180.

13. Imports in other areas declined as follows:

	1774	*1775*
New England	£562,476	£71,625
New York	£437,937	£ 1,228
Philadelphia	£625,652	£ 1,366
Maryland/Virginia	£528,738	£ 1,921

Schlesinger, *Colonial Merchants*, 535–36; Sellers, *Charleston Business*, 229–30.

14. HL to William Manning, May 9, 1775, *LP*, 10:117; McCrady, *Royal Government*, 774; Schlesinger, *Colonial Merchants*, 527.

15. The conversion of Drayton to the radical cause is a seemingly baffling problem. It appears that several factors were involved in this development. Included among these was a desire to avoid some sizeable debts owed to British officials, the loss of several positions and favors to British placemen, and a genuine revulsion toward the Intolerable Acts. See Dabney and Dargan, *Drayton*, 44–47, 57–58, 63–64; William M. Dabney, "Drayton and Laurens in the Continental Congress," *SCHM* 60, no. 2 (April 1959): 76–77.

16. David H. Villers, "The Smythe Horses Affair and the Association," *SCHM* 70, no. 3 (July 1969): 137–43; McCrady, *Royal Government*, 775–77; Schlesinger, *Colonial Merchants*, 527; Walsh, *Sons of Liberty*, 67–68; William Bull to Earl of Dartmouth, March 28, 1775, *PRO*, reel 11, vol. 35, 78–83.

17. Drayton, *Memoirs*, 1:222; Ravenel, *Charleston*, 199; *JCH*, April 25, 27, 1775; Moultrie, *Memoirs*, 1:57–58.

18. Alexander Innes to Lord Dartmouth, May 1, 1775, *PRO*, reel 11, vol. 35.

19. William Bull to Earl of Dartmouth, May 15, 1775, *PRO*, reel 11, vol. 35; Alexander Innes to Earl of Dartmouth, May 16, 1775, B. D. Bargar, ed., "Charles Town Loyalism in 1775: The Secret Reports of Alexander Innes," *SCHM* 63, no. 3 (July 1962): 127–30.

20. HL to John Laurens, May 15, 1775, *LP*, 10:118–19; HL to William Manning, May 22, 1775, *LP*, 10:127–31; HL to John Laurens, May 27, 1775, *LP*, 10:155.

21. William Edwin Hemphill and Wylma Anne Wates, eds., *Extracts from the Journals of the Provincial Congresses of South Carolina, 1775–1776* (Columbia: South Carolina Archives Department, 1960), 33; HL to James Laurens, June 7, 1775, *LP*, 10:102.

22. HL to John Laurens, June 8, 1775, *LP*, 10:166; Alexander Innes to Lord Dartmouth, June 3, 1775, in Bargar, "Charles Town Loyalism," 130–31.

23. A copy of the Association is presented in Drayton, *Memoirs*, 1:285–86; Wallace, *Laurens*, 205–6.

24. HL to John Laurens, June 8, 1775, *LP*, 10:173–74. Laurens included a copy of his speech, with notes in the margin, in this letter to his son: 172–79. David Duncan Wallace also reprinted the speech in its entirety: Wallace, *Laurens*, 207–12. Despite Laurens's plea, the Association was not amended to include a declaration of loyalty to the king.

25. HL to John Laurens, June 8, 1775, *LP*, 10:174–79. Laurens reported in the same letter that when the Association was circulated in Charles Town, only about thirty men refused to sign. Since these were almost entirely royal officials, no official censure was attached to these refusals. As for Tennent, Laurens was unimpressed, writing in the margin of his speech that "Mr. Tennent I am told holds the most absolute & rigid principles on the doctrine of Predistination—he claims toleration, he is intitled to it—but alas! from my short acquaintance with him I have found him totally void of Charity for other Men": *LP*, 10:178–79 n.

26. Hemphill and Wates, *Extracts from the Provincial Congresses*, June 6, 10, 1775, 39, 45; *South Carolina and American General Gazette*, June 9, 1775; Drayton, *Memoirs*, 1:255; McCrady, *Royal Government*, 792.

27. HL to John Laurens, June 8, 1775, *LP*, 10:170. Laurens's fears that the military policy of the Provincial Congress might not be approved by the Continental Congress were realized as he informed his son ten days later that the Philadelphia Congress had censured South Carolina's conduct in this area: HL to John Laurens, June 18, 1775, *LP*, 10:185.

28. HL to John Laurens, May 30, 1775, *LP*, 10:159–60; HL to John Laurens, June 7, 1775, *LP*, 10:163; HL to John Laurens, June 8, 1775, *LP*, 10:165; HL to John Laurens, June 18, 1775, *LP*, 10:185.

29. HL to John Laurens, June 8, 1775, *LP*, 10:169–70.

30. Alexander Innes to Lord Dartmouth, June 10, 1775, Bargar, "Charles Town Loyalism," 133; HL to John Laurens, June 8, 1775, *LP*, 10:164–65.

31. Hemphill and Wates, *Extracts from the Provincial Congresses*, June 13, 17, 1775, 49–51, 55–56; Drayton, *Memoirs*, 1:255; McCrady, *Royal Government*, 792–93; *Journal of the Council of Safety*, June 16, 1775, *HLP*, reel 12; HL to John Laurens, June 18, 1775, *LP*, 10:182.

32. *HLP*, reel 18; *South Carolina and American General Gazette*, June 23, 1775.

33. Despite the suspicions of British officials, there was no evidence that Bull had betrayed his office. Rather, Geraldine Meroney is probably correct in attributing his unlikely behavior to a growing despondency at the collapse of royal government, the cause to which he had dedicated his life: Meroney, *William Bull*, 113–17.

34. Provincial Congress to Lord William Campbell, June 20, 1775, Drayton, *Memoirs*, 1:259–61; Lord William Campbell to Provincial Congress, June 21, 1775, Drayton, *Memoirs*, 1:261–62.

35. *JCH*, July 10–12, 21, 1775. The correspondence between Campbell and the assembly was published in Drayton, *Memoirs*, 2:5–12. The Commons House formally expired when Governor Campbell dissolved it on September 15 before fleeing to the *Tamar*.

36. Drayton, *Memoirs*, 1:318–21; Edward McCrady, *The History of South Carolina in the Revolution, 1775–1780* (New York: Macmillan Company, 1902), 30–31; HL to John Laurens, July 14, 1775, *LP*, 10:221.

37. HL to Clement Lempriere, July 27, 1775, *LP*, 10:249. While Laurens hoped to preserve the peace, he supported rational war preparations and was prepared to help finance these plans. In July 1775, the Council of Safety repaid him one thousand pounds currency, which he had advanced to help outfit Lempriere's ship: *Journal of the Council of Safety*, July 26, 1775; *HLP*, reel 12.

38. Ramsay, *History of the Revolution*, 1:256; Drayton, *Memoirs*, 1:310–11; Moultrie, *Memoirs*, 1:59–61. The texts of the letters sent by Wright and the forgeries substituted for them by the patriots can be found in R. W. Gibbes, *Documentary History of the American Revolution* (New York, 1855), 1:98–102.

39. William Campbell to Earl of Dartmouth, July 19–20, 1775, *PRO*, reel 11, vol. 35.

40. HL to Thomas Fletchall, July 14, 1775, *LP*, 10:214–18.

41. Gibbes, *Documentary History*, 1:106.

42. *LP*, 10:xvi; HL to Robert Deans, January 8, 1776, *LP*, 11:11. For a complete account of the Drayton mission, see Dabney and Dargan, *Drayton*, 89–106. Perhaps the best account of the backcountry during this period can be found in Klein, *Unification of a Slave State*, 78–79. The text of Drayton's treaty with the backcountry Loyalists can be found in Gibbes, *Documentary History*, 1:184–91.

43. Sylvia Frey estimated the white population of South Carolina to be seventy thousand in 1775 and the black population to be one hundred thousand. For the lowcountry, she reports 14,302 whites and 72,743 blacks in 1775: Frey, *Water from a Rock*, 9–10.

44. For accounts of the relationship between politics and slavery in South Carolina, see Peter Wood, "'Taking Care of Business' in Revolutionary South Carolina: Republicanism and the Slave Society" in *The Southern Experience in the American Revolution*, ed. Jeffrey J. Crow and Larry B. Tise (Chapel Hill: University of North Carolina Press, 1978), 268–93; Robert A. Olwell, "'Domestick Enemies': Slavery and Political Independence in South Carolina, May 1775–March 1776" *Journal of Southern History* 55, no. 1 (February 1989): 21–48; Weir, *Colonial South Carolina*, 196–203; Frey, *Water From a Rock*, 45–80.

45. Jeremiah was hanged and burned on August 18, 1775. Laurens included a complete copy of his correspondence with Governor Campbell and Alexander Innes in HL to John Laurens, August 20, 1775, *LP,* 10:320–35. For the governor's side of the story, see Lord William Campbell to Earl of Dartmouth, August 31, 1775, *PRO*, reel 11, vol. 35; Good secondary accounts include Olwell, "Domestick Enemies," 30–40; Wood, "Taking Care of Business," 278–87; Weir, *Colonial South Carolina*, 200–203.

46. Among those who believed that Stuart was engineering an Indian uprising was Henry Laurens: HL to William Henry Drayton, September 21, 1775, *LP,* 10:411–12. Stuart's activities remain a subject of controversy. For more information, see Gary O. Olson, "Loyalists and the American Revolution: Thomas Brown and the South Carolina Backcountry, 1775–1776," *SCHM* 69, no. 1 (January 1968): 44–56 and Snapp, *John Stuart*, 158–80. For a speech that Stuart made to the Creeks in August 1775, advocating neutrality, see Gibbes, *Documentary History*, 1:159–62.

47. The spy who had insinuated himself with the governor has been identified as Captain Adam McDonald: Moultrie, *Memoirs*, 1:67–74. Drayton, *Memoirs*, 2:34–36; Ramsay, *History of South Carolina*, 1:142; William Campbell to Earl of Dartmouth, September 19, 1775, *PRO*, reel 11, vol. 36; Council of Safety to William Henry Drayton, September 15, 1775, *LP,* 10:386–87; Council of Safety to South Carolina Delegates in Congress, September 18, 1775, *LP,* 10:397–403; *South Carolina and American General Gazette*, September 22, 1775.

48. HL to John Laurens, September 23, 1775, *LP,* 10:422–23; HL to John Laurens, September 26, 1775, *LP,* 10:426–27; Drayton, *Memoirs*, 2:55–56; Wallace, *Laurens*, 214; Thomas Ferguson to CG, October 5, 1775, Gibbes, *Documentary History*, 1:200–201.

49. HL to John Laurens, September 18, 1775, *LP,* 10:396–97; HL to John Laurens, September 26, 1775, *LP,* 10:426–27.

50. HL to Arthur George Karr, October 21, 1775, *LP,* 10:487.

51. HL to John Laurens, October 20, 1775, *LP,* 10:476–81; HL to John Laurens, October 21, 1775, *LP,* 10:487–90; HL to John Laurens, October 23, 1775, *LP,* 10:492–97.

52. Drayton, *Memoirs*, 2:60, 78–79; McCrady, *Revolution*, 1:72; Wallace, *Laurens*, 218–19; HL to John Laurens, December 6, 1775, *LP,* 10:543.

53. *South Carolina and American General Gazette*, November 24, 1775; HL to John Laurens, November 26, 1775, *LP,* 10:519–20; HL to William Manning, November 26, 1775, *LP,* 10:521.

54. Godbold and Woody, *Gadsden*, 134–35.

55. John Adams to Thomas Jefferson, May 29, 1818, Lester J. Cappon, ed., *The Adams-Jefferson Letters: The Complete Correspondence between Thomas Jefferson and Abigail and John Adams* (Chapel Hill: University of North Carolina Press, 1959), 525; Godbold and Woody, *Gadsden*, 135–36; Butterfield, ed., *Autobiography of John Adams*, 3:330.

56. Butterfield, ed., *Autobiography of John Adams*, 3:314–17, 328–30; "John Adams Notes on Debates," October 21, 1775, *Journals of the Continental Congress, 1774–1789*, ed. Worthington C. Ford et al. (Washington, D.C., 1904–37), 1:501.

57. Butterfield, *Autobiography of John Adams*, 3:317; John Adams to Abigail Adams, August 18, 1776, *LD*, 5:17.

58. *JCC* (1775) 2:177; South Carolina Delegates to the South Carolina Secret Committee, July 1, 1775, *WCG*, 105–6; Gibbes, *Documentary History*, 1:116–17; Godbold and Woody, *Gadsden*, 136–38; Schlesinger, *Colonial Merchants*, 578.

59. John Adams to Elbridge Gerry, June 7, 1775, *LD*, 1:450–51; *JCC* (1775) 3:420, 427–28, 443–44 (1775) 6:1065–1066.

60. Godbold and Woody, *Gadsden*, 139–42; Naval Committee to Dudley Saltonstall, November 27, 1775, *WCG*, 106–7.

61. Godbold and Woody, *Gadsden*, 141–43; *WCG*, 316.

10. Independence Proclaimed, 1776

1. HL to James Laurens, January 6, 1776, *LP*, 9:4–7. Laurens exonerated his grieving eldest son, John Laurens, from all blame for the death of his brother and directed him to await happier times and then send the remains of the young boy home to be buried beside his mother. There is no evidence that this wish was ever carried out: HL to John Laurens, January 4, 1776, *LP*, 10:616–17. Laurens sent this letter to his son under the protection of Lady William Campbell, who, in a nice expression of sympathy for the bereaved father, ignored her husband's order that all patriot correspondence be seized and hid the letter among her personal effects before delivering it to John Laurens: HL to John Laurens, January 4, 1776, *LP*, 10:617, 617 n.

2. CG to Esek Hopkins, January 15, 1776, *LD*, 3:96; *WCG*, 111.

3. Thomas Lynch to Philip Schuyler, January 20, 1776, *LD*, 3:125; Thomas Nelson to Thomas Jefferson, February 4, 1776, *LD*, 3:194.

4. Gadsden's copy of *Common Sense* still exists and is in the possession of the College of Charleston.

5. HL to Georgia Council of Safety, February 13, 1776, *LP*, 11:99–100; HL to John Laurens, February 22, 1776, *LP*, 11:115–16; *South Carolina and American General Gazette*, February 9, 1776.

6. Charles Cotesworth Pinckney to HL, January 11, 1776, *LP*, 11:23–24; HL to Joseph Glover, January 12, 1776, *LP*, 11:25; HL to Richard Richardson, January 13, 1776, *LP*, 11:26; HL to Job Rothmahler, January 13, 1776, *LP*, 11:26–27; HL to John Laurens, January 16, 1776, *LP*, 11:32–36; HL to Stephen Bull, January 20, 1776, *LP*, 11:49–50; HL to Stephen Bull, January 25, 1776, *LP*, 11:67–69.

7. *JCC* (1775) 3:319, 325–27; Hemphill and Wates, *Extracts from the Provincial Congresses*, 181–83; Godbold and Woody, *Gadsden*, 149–50.

8. Drayton, *Memoirs*, 2:172–73; McCrady, *Revolution*, 1:108–9; Fletcher M. Green, *Constitutional Development in the South Atlantic States, 1776–1860: A Study in the Evolution of Democracy* (Chapel Hill: University of North Carolina Press, 1930), 60–61; Vipperman, *Rawlins Lowndes*, 190; Godbold and Woody, *Gadsden*, 150–51.

9. HL to John Laurens, February 22, 1776, *LP*, 11:114–21. It appears that Laurens's supposition that Paine stole his ideas for *Common Sense* from the "Apology," delivered by William of Orange to the Dutch estates general in 1580 to justify the revolt of the low countries against Spanish rule, was incorrect. The editors of the *Laurens Papers* demonstrate that The "Apology" was concerned largely with feudal, dynastic, and religious concerns and that there is no evidence that Paine was influenced by this work. Rather, Paine drew his ideas from the Enlightenment: *LP*, 11:115n. Laurens's denunication of the doctrines asserted in *Common Sense* had

little effect upon his son, as John Laurens warmly embraced them: John Laurens to James Laurens, undated (marked "received June 26, 1776"), Kendall Collection, South Caroliniana Library, Columbia, South Carolina, reel 3.

10. HL to William Manning, February 27, 1776, *LP*, 11:122–28.

11. Hemphill and Wates, eds., *Extracts from the Provincial Congresses*, 184–85; Drayton, *Memoirs*, 2:173–74; McCrady, *Revolution*, 1:109–10; Nadelhaft, *Disorders of War*, 28–29.

12. McCrady, *Revolution*, 1:114; Nadelhaft, *Disorders of War*, 29–31; Weir, *Colonial South Carolina*, 333; Alden, *South in Revolution*, 313. There has been some disagreement among historians over the proportion of seats between the low country and the backcountry. Jerome Nadelhaft has effectively made the point that the low country did not always act as a unit and, due to differences in settlement and agriculture, twelve of the seats generally thought to have been dominated by the low country should be transferred to the backcountry. This would give the low country a majority of 126 to 76.

13. Hemphill and Wates, eds., *Extracts from the Provincial Congresses*, 263; McCrady, *Revolution*, 1:111–12; Nadelhaft, *Disorders of War*, 29–34; Elisha Douglass, *Rebels and Democrats: The Struggle for Equal Political Rights and Majority Rule during the American Revolution* (Chapel Hill: University of North Carolina Press, 1955), 42–43; Green, *Constitutional Development*, 61. The South Carolina constitution of 1776 can be found in its entirety in Drayton, *Memoirs*, 2:186–97.

14. William Edwin Hemphill, Wylma Anne Wates, and R. Nicholas Olsberg, eds., *Journals of the General Assembly and House of Representatives, 1776–1780* (Columbia: University of South Carolina Press, 1970), 3–4; Drayton, *Memoirs*, 2:239–40; HL to John Laurens, March 16, 1776, *LP*, 11:174–75; HL to John Laurens, March 28, 1776, *LP*, 11:193–95. In accepting the constitution, both President Rutledge and the legislature joined Laurens in emphasizing the temporary nature of the new government and the desirability of reconciliation with the mother country: Moultrie, *Memoirs*, 1:132–33; Gibbes, *Documentary History*, 1:273–75.

15. HL to John Laurens, March 26, 1776, *LP*, 11:192.

16. Hemphill and Wates, *Extracts from the Provincial Congresses*, 248; *JCC* (1776) 4:305–6.

17. HL to James Laurens, March 19, 1776, *LP*, 11:178–79; Alden, *South in Revolution*, 202–3; Marvin R. Zahniser, *Charles Cotesworth Pinckney: Founding Father* (Chapel Hill: University of North Carolina Press, 1967), 48–49.

18. Ramsay, *History of South Carolina*. 2:254.

19. HL to John Laurens, August 14, 1776, *LP*, 11:225–26; Drayton, *Memoirs*, 2:282; Godbold and Woody, *Gadsden*, 156.

20. HL to John Laurens, August 14, 1776, *LP*, 11:226–27; Moultrie, *Memoirs*, 1:141–44; Alden, *South in Revolution*, 204; Godbold and Woody, *Gadsden*, 157–59.

21. *South Carolina and American General Gazette*, August 2, 1776; Ramsay, *History of South Carolina*, 1:155–56; CG to William Moultrie, July 1, 1776, *WCG*, 114–15; CG to Charles Lee, August 2, 1776, *WCG*, 115–16; Alden, *South in Revolution*, 203–6; Godbold and Woody, *Gadsden*, 159–60. Laurens sent a complete account of the battle to his son in HL to John Laurens, August 14, 1776, *LP*, 11:236–45.

22. The territory surrendered by the Cherokees encompassed what is now Pendleton and Greenville counties: Ramsay, *History of South Carolina*, 1:157–59; HL to John Laurens, August 14, 1776, *LP*, 11:228–31; HL to Hope & Co., August 17, 1776, *LP*, 11:248.

23. McCrady, *Revolution*, 1:170–79; Alden, *South in Revolution*, 211–13.

24. HL to John Laurens, August 14, 1776, *LP*, 11:228; Drayton, *Memoirs*, 2:315.

25. HL to John Laurens, August 14, 1776, *LP,* 11:234; HL to Martha Laurens, August 17, 1776, *LP,* 11:252–56; HL to James Laurens, August 23, 1776, *LP,* 11:260–61.

26. John Laurens to HL, October 20, 1775, *LP,* 10:476–83; John Laurens to James Laurens, November 13, 1775, quoted in John Laurens, *The Army Correspondence of Colonel John Laurens* (New York: Bradford Club, 1867), 17–18; Ralph Izard to Laurens, July 25, 1778, Francis Wharton, ed., *The Revolutionary Diplomatic Correspondence of the United States* (Washington, D.C.: Government Printing Office, 1889), 2:663.

27. HL to John Laurens, January 8, 1776, *LP,* 11:13–14.

28. HL to John Laurens, August 14, 1776, *LP,* 11:234–35; HL to Jacob Read, August 16, 1776, ALS, South Caroliniana Library, Columbia. For information on John Laurens's temperament and ideas see Richard J. Hargrove, "Portrait of a Southern Patriot," in Higgins, ed., *The Revolutionary War in the South,* 182–202. Durham, N.C.: Duke University Press, 1979.

29. John Laurens to James Laurens, October 25, 1776, *LP,* 11:277n.; John Laurens to HL, October 26, 1776, *LP,* 11:275–77; *South Carolina and American General Gazette,* April 17, 1777; Townsend, *John Laurens,* 48–56.

11. The Eclipse of Christopher Gadsden, 1776–1778

1. HL to Elias Ball, Jr., April 15, 1776, *LP,* 11:202; Godbold and Woody, *Gadsden,* 154. William Wragg was banished during 1777 for his refusal to support the war against Great Britain. He drowned during his voyage to England: Godbold and Woody, *Gadsden,* 154.

2. *JCC* (1776): 5:761; Arthur Middleton to William Henry Drayton, September 18, 1776, *LD,* 5:191; McCrady, *Revolution,* 1:204; Godbold and Woody, *Gadsden,* 166.

3. *WCG,* 118n.; Godbold and Woody, *Gadsden,* 164.

4. CG to John Rutledge, December 14, 1776, *WCG,* 118–19; CG to Thomas Mumford, February 19, 1777, *WCG,* 120; CG to William Henry Drayton, August 15, 1778, *WCG,* 147–48; Godbold and Woody, *Gadsden,* 165.

5. Godbold and Woody, *Gadsden,* 178–80; Charles E. Bennett and Donald R. Lennon, *A Quest for Glory: Major General Robert Howe and the American Revolution* (Chapel Hill: University of North Carolina Press, 1991), 7–8.

6. John Lewis Gervais to HL, August 16, 1777, *LP,* 11:461–62; Godbold and Woody, *Gadsden,* 180.

7. HL to John Laurens, September 30, 1777, *LP,* 11:539–40.

8. Robert Howe to Continental Congress, August 28, 1777, "Gadsden Miscellany," South Caroliniana Library, Columbia; Robert Howe to HL, August 28, 1777, *HLP,* Charleston, reel 9; Bennett and Lennon, *Robert Howe,* 56–58.

9. *JCC* (1777) 8:757; CG to William Henry Drayton, July 4, 1778, *WCG,* 143; CG to William Henry Drayton, August 15, 1778, *WCG,* 147.

10. HL to John Rutledge, October 19, 1777, *LD,* 8:144–45.

11. CG to William Henry Drayton, June 1, 1778, *WCG,* 128–29.

12. CG to William Henry Drayton, July 4, 1778, *WCG,* 135–36.

13. Ibid., 136–44.

14. Ibid.

15. HL to John Lewis Gervais, August 7, 1778, *LD,* 10:399.

16. HL to John Lewis Gervais, September 10, 1778, *LD,* 10:614–15.

17. John Lewis Gervais to HL, September 21, 1778, *SCHM* 66 (January 1965): 36.

18. CG to William Henry Drayton and John Neufville, September 22, 1778, *WCG*, 153.

19. CG to William Henry Drayton, September 9, 1778, *WCG*, 151; *South Carolina and American General Gazette*, September 3, 1778; Godbold and Woody, *Gadsden*, 185–87; Bennett and Lennon, *Robert Howe*, 58–60.

20. Ramsay, *History of South Carolina*, 2:255.

21. John Lewis Gervais to HL, March 16, 1778, *SCHM* 66(January 1965), 29; Green, *Constitutional Development*, 111; Nadelhaft, *Disorders of War*, 37; Vipperman, *Rawlins Lowndes*, 202.

22. Green, *Constitutional Development*, 111; Nadelhaft, *Disorders of War*, 39.

23. Green, *Constitutional Development*, 113–14; Nadelhaft, *Disorders of War*, 38–39; Douglass, *Rebels and Democrats*, 44; Weir, *Colonial South Carolina*, 333. It was not until the 1790s that Jews and Catholics received the right to organize on the same basis as Protestants: Rogers, *Charleston in the Age of the Pinckneys*, 92.

24. Nadelhaft, *Disorders of War*, 39–40; Godbold and Woody, *Gadsden*, 169. Hugh Rutledge, brother of John Rutledge, currently held the position of speaker of the Privy Council, a position that he used to support his brother in the upper house: Clow, "Edward Rutledge," 129–30.

25. Nadelhaft, *Disorders of War*, 40; Green, *Constitutional Development*, 115; Alden, *South in Revolution*, 313–14.

26. All officeholders had to be adult white Protestants. The other qualifications were as follows: for the assembly, at least twenty-one years of age with three years' residence in the state, and holding five hundred acres and ten slaves if a resident of the parish, or, if a nonresident, property worth thirty-five hundred pounds; for the Senate, at least thirty years of age with five years residence in the state and a freehold worth two thousand pounds if a resident of the district, seven thousand pounds if not. The governor had to be a ten-year resident with an estate worth at least ten thousand pounds: Green, *Constitutional Development*, 114–15; Smith, *South Carolina as a Royal Province*, 97–98.

27. Nadelhaft, *Disorders of War*, 41.

28. A copy of Rutledge's speech to the General Assembly is in the "Gadsden Miscellany," South Caroliniana Library, Columbia. Edward McCrady also reprinted parts of the speech in McCrady, *Revolution*, 1:235–39. Rutledge defended his resignation in a letter to HL: John Rutledge to HL, March 8, 1778, *LP*, 12::527–29.

29. John Lewis Gervais to HL, March 16, 1778, *SCHM* 66 (January 1965): 28–29; Vipperman, *Rawlins Lowndes*, 204–5.

30. John Lewis Gervais to HL, March 16, 1778, *SCHM* 66 (January 1965): 27–28; CG to William Henry Drayton, March 7, 1778, *WCG*, 122; Vipperman, *Rawlins Lowndes*, 205.

31. John Lewis Gervais to HL, March 16, 1778, *SCHM* 66 (January 1965): 28–29. John Rutledge to HL, March 8, 1778, *LP*, 12:529.

32. CG to William Henry Drayton, June 1, 1778, *WCG*, 126.

33. HL to John Rutledge, May 4, 1778, *LD*, 9:598; HL to John Laurens, March 29, 1778, *LD*, 9:352.

34. McCrady, *Revolution*, 1:241–42.

35. Vipperman, *Rawlins Lowndes*, 209–11; Robert Stansbury Lambert, *South Carolina Loyalists in the American Revolution* (Columbia: University of South Carolina Press, 1987), 62.

36. Rawlins Lowndes to HL, June 17, 1778, *HLP*, SCHS, Charleston, reel 9; Vipperman, *Rawlins Lowndes*, 211; Nadelhaft, *Disorders of War*, 45–46.

37. CG to William Henry Drayton, June 15, 1778, *WCG*, 131–32; John Lewis Gervais to HL, June 26, 1778, *SCHM* 66 (January 1965): 31.

38. John Wells to HL, June 10, 1778, Kendall Collection (microfilm), South Caroliniana Library, Columbia, reel 2; John Wells to HL, September 6, 1778, Kendall Collection (microfilm), South Caroliniana Library, Columbia, reel 2.

39. CG to Peter Timothy, June 8, 1778, *WCG*, 130–31; Rawlins Lowndes to HL, June 17, 1778, *HLP*, SCHS, reel 9; McCrady, *Revolution*, 1:272.

40. CG to William Henry Drayton, June 15, 1778, *WCG*, 133; John Lewis Gervais to HL, June 26, 1778, *SCHM* 66 (January 1965): 32.

41. Quoted in Walsh, *Sons of Liberty*, 87.

42. Walsh, *Sons of Liberty*, 86–87; Godbold and Woody, *Gadsden*, 174–76.

43. John Lewis Gervais to HL, September 21, 1778, *SCHM* 66 (January 1965): 36.

44. CG to Thomas Bee, October 5, 1778, *WCG*, 154–58; CG to William Henry Drayton, October 14, 1778, *WCG*, 159.

12. A Nationalist at Philadelphia: Henry Laurens in the Continental Congress, 1777–1778

1. HL to John Laurens, September 16, 1776, *LP*, 11:268–69; HL to Lachlan McIntosh, October 28, 1776, *LP*, 11:279; HL to Ralph Izard, April 2, 1777, *LP*, 11:328–32; HL to Joseph Clay, May 10, 1777, *LP*, 11:336.

2. *JCC* (1777) 7:129–30; *JCC* (1777) 8:570; HL to John Laurens, February 3, 1777, *LP*, 11:294; HL to John Rutledge, August 12, 1777, Smith, ed., *LD*, 7:466; Wallace, *Laurens*, 226–27.

3. John Adams to Abigail Adams, August 17, 1777, *LD*, 7:492.

4. *JCC* (1777) 8:579, 596, 599, 631–32, 660.

5. HL to Lachlan McIntosh, August 11, 1777, *LD*, 7:456; HL to John Rutledge, August 12, 1777, *LD*, 7:466–68; HL to John Houstoun, August 27, 1778, *LD*, 10:509. Most South Carolina leaders, including Gadsden and Lowndes, joined Laurens in the belief that South Carolina and Georgia could never be safe as long as the British retained control of the Floridas, particularly St. Augustine. All three men supported expeditions against St. Augustine, but each was amazed by the "imbecility" of the Georgians in planning these campaigns for the spring and summer, when the unhealthy climate would be as fatal as British bullets: HL to John Houstoun, August 27, 1778, *LD*, 10:509, Rawlins Lowndes to HL, May 28, 1778, *HLP*, SCHS, reel 9; Rawlins Lowndes to HL, September 23, 1778, *HLP*, SCHS, reel 9; CG to William Henry Drayton, June 1, 1778, *WCG*, 126–27; CG to William Henry Drayton, June 15, 1778, *WCG*, 134. Laurens clearly hoped that South Carolina and Georgia could conquer the Floridas and annex them to their own states. He was extremely distrustful of Spanish motives toward the Floridas, even before that country formally entered the war: HL to William Livingston, August 21, 1778, *LD*, 10:486–87.

6. HL to John Rutledge, August 12, 1777, *LP*, 11:446.

7. HL to John Lewis Gervais, August 5, 1777, *LD*, 7:420, 423.

8. HL to John Rutledge, August 12, 1777, *LD*, 7:469. It is interesting that Laurens and Gadsden were both leading champions of Benedict Arnold. In fact, it was Gadsden who, in January 1776, had moved that Arnold be promoted from colonel to brigadier general as a reward for his services during the Canadian campaign: "Diary of Richard Smith," January 8, 1776, *LD*, 3:60. Also interesting is that Laurens, despite his commentary on Arnold, does not appear to have voted on the motion to promote the general: *JCC* (1777) 8:623–24.

9. HL to John Lewis Gervais, September 5, 1777, *LP*, 11:485–489; HL to John Laurens, October 10, 1777, *LP*, 11:551.

10. HL to Joseph Clay, September 2, 1777, *LD*, 7:593–94; Joseph Clay to HL, October 16, 1777, *LP*, 11:557–58. For Laurens's letter giving Clay power of attorney over his Georgia lands, see HL to Joseph Clay, May 10, 1777, *LP*, 11:336. Laurens was, in the words of Kenneth Coleman, "Georgia's best delegate in Congress." Georgia was usually underrepresented and, sometimes, not represented at all in Congress. Realizing the importance of Georgia to the security of South Carolina and kept abreast of Georgian affairs by Clay and other correspondents, Laurens was careful to protect Georgian interests in Congress: Kenneth Coleman, *The American Revolution in Georgia, 1763–1789* (Athens.:University of Georgia Press, 1958), 92, 166.

11. HL to John Lewis Gervais, August 9, 1777, *LD*, 7:444, HL to Gabriel Manigault, August 15, 1777, *LD*, 7:485–87; HL to William Manning, August 16, 1777, *LP*, 11:459–60; Townsend, *John Laurens*, 57–59.

12. HL to John Lewis Gervais, July 25, 1777, *LD*, 7:372; HL to John Lewis Gervais, August 21, 1777, *LD*, 7:522–23.

13. *JCC* (1777) 8:666; HL to Lachlan McIntosh, September 1, 1777, *LD*, 7:586.

14. HL to John Rutledge, September 16, 1777, *LP*, 11:524–27; HL to John Lewis Gervais, September 18, 1777, *LP*, 11:527–29; HL to John Lewis Gervais, October 8, 1777, *LP*, 11:545–48; *JCC* (1777) 8:742, 755, 756.

15. HL to John Lewis Gervais, October 16, 1777, *LD*, 8:124; HL to John Hancock, November 3, 1777, *LP*, 12:13, 13n.; *South Carolina and American General Gazette*, November 27, 1777; *JCC* (1777) 9:846, 853–54; Wallace, *Laurens*, 234–35.

16. HL to John Laurens, November 30, 1777, *LD*, 8:350; HL to Marquis de Lafayette, March 7, 1778, *HLP*, SCHS, reel 7; HL to Francis Dana, March 1, 1778, *LP*, 12:489–91; HL to John Laurens, June 7, 1778, *LD*, 10:43; HL to William Nichols, May 23, 1778, *LD*, 9:735; HL to John Burnet, July 24, 1778, *LD*, 10:345; Edmund Cody Burnett, *The Continental Congress* (New York: Macmillan Co., 1941), 321–22. In contrasting Laurens to his successor, John Jay, James Lovell commented that "the Manners of the Men differ. One was flush of Pen & Ink the other quite the Reverse; one was with his Candle burning in the Morning almost thro the year, the other has a lovely wife to amuse him in these Hours": James Lovell to Horatio Gates, June 5, 1779, *LD*, 13:29.

17. HL to Horatio Gates, November 23, 1777, *LP*, 12:78–79; *LD*, 8:486n.; Wallace, *Laurens*, 243–45; Burnett, *Continental Congress*, 261–62.

18. John Burgoyne to Horatio Gates, November 14, 1777, *HLP*, SCHS, reel 9.

19. *LD*, 8:542–44. It seems that Howe did not actually intend to use these unexchanged soldiers in battle as Laurens and Congress suspected. Instead, he hoped to quickly exchange them and have them present for immediate service. Even this, however, would be a violation of the terms of the convention, as this document required the troops to be transported to England, a measure that would diminish the number of troops that Howe would have present for service. It must also be noted that Howe's directions to Burgoyne came to light only after the issue had been decided and played no role in Congress's decision to suspend the Convention: *LD*, 8:544n.

20. *LP*, 12:229n.

21. HL to Congress, December 12, 1777, *LP*, 12:140–41; HL to John Lewis Gervais, December 20, 1777, *LP*, 12:140–41; HL to Marquis de Lafayette, December 20, 1777, *LP*, 12:163–64; HL to John Lewis Gervais, December 30, 1777, *LP*, 12:220–25; *JCC* (1777) 9:1022, 1058–1064.

22. *JCC* (1778) 10:16–17, 29–35; *LD*, 8:486n.

23. HL to William Heath, December 27, 1777, *LP*, 12:214–17. The resolutions of Congress were in accord with the suggestions of General Washington: George

Washington to HL, December 14, 1777, *LP,* 12:152–55. Laurens sent the formal congressional resolutions to Heath on January 14: HL to William Heath, January 14, 1778, *LP,* 12:300–301.

24. HL to John Laurens, January 14, 1778, *LD,* 8:592; HL to Rawlins Lowndes, August 11, 1778, *LD,* 10:428–30. Though Burgoyne himself was allowed to return to England on his parole, the British government recognized the consequences of a formal ratification of the convention and refused to ratify the agreement. Thus, the army remained in America as prisoners until the end of the war: *LD,* 8:487n. Congress agreed to allow Burgoyne and his staff to depart on March 3, 1778: *JCC* (1778) 10:218; HL to John Burgoyne, March 6, 1778, *LD,* 9:227.

25. HL to John Laurens, January 8, 1778, *LD,* 8:546–47.

26. HL to John Laurens, October 16, 1777, *LD,* 8:125–26.

27. HL to Benjamin Huger, November 15, 1777, *LD,* 8:270.

28. George Washington to Thomas Conway, November 9, 1777, John C. Fitzpatrick, ed., *The Writings of George Washington* (Washington, D.C.: United States Government Printing Office, 1931–1944), 10:29; James Thomas Flexner, *Washington: The Indispensable Man* (New York: Little, Brown, and Company, 1969), 108–15; Burnett, *Continental Congress,* 282–83; H. James Henderson, *Party Politics in the Continental Congress* (New York: McGraw-Hill Company, 1974), 118–20. Whether or not there was a formal conspiracy, several members of Congress were extremely critical of Washington during this period. A few examples include Richard Henry Lee to Samuel Adams, November 23, 1777, *LD,* 8:310–15; Thomas Mifflin to Horatio Gates, November 17, 1777, *LD,* 8:314–15n.; James Lovell to Patrick Henry, November 27, 1777, *LD,* 8:329.

29. Thomas Conway to George Washington, December 31, 1777, *HLP,* SCHS, reel 10; *JCC* (1777) 9:874, 959–60. Conway was elected inspector general on December 13: *JCC* (1777) 9:1026.

30. John Laurens to HL, January 1, 1778, *LP,* 12:231; John Laurens to HL, January 3, 1778, *LP,* 12:244–47.

31. George Washington to Congress, January 2, 1778, *FWW,* 10:249–50; George Washington to Horatio Gates, January 4, 1778, *FWW,* 10:263–65. Washington also answered Gates's accusations that someone had searched his private papers to discover these remarks by informing his rival that he had received this information from General Lord Stirling, who had in turn received it from a drunken Colonel James Wilkinson, Gates's own aide. This caused a dispute between Gates and Wilkinson that nearly ended in a duel: George Washington to Horatio Gates, January 4, 1778, *FWW,* 10:263–65; Burnett, *Continental Congress,* 283.

32. HL to John Laurens, January 8, 1778, *LP,* 12:269–75. Laurens was not the only one who numbered Mifflin among the war profiteers: "John Adams' Notes of Debates," September 23, 1775, *JCC* (1775) 3:473.

33. Marquis de Lafayette to HL, January 5, 1778, *LP,* 12:253–57; HL to Marquis de Lafayette, January 12, 1778, *LP,* 12:283–87.

34. HL to John Laurens, January 25, 1778, *LD,* 8:647.

35. HL to George Washington, January 27, 1778, *LP,* 12:359–62; George Washington to HL, January 31, 1778, *FWW,* 10:410–11; Wallace, *Laurens,* 270–71. The Conway Cabal cemented a fast friendship between Laurens and Washington, characterized by mutual respect and affection. When Laurens resigned the presidency in December 1778, Washington sent him an affectionate letter of thanks for his support: George Washington to HL, December 18, 1778, *FWW,* 13:421. Even more indicative of the relationship that developed between the two men, however, is the fact that when Washington visited Philadelphia between December 22, 1778 and

February 2, 1779, he stayed as the guest of the former president: *FWW*, XIV, 129n.; George Washington to HL, February 17, 1779, George Washington Papers, Library of Congress, reel 28.

36. HL to John Laurens, January 25, 1778, *LD*, 8:647; HL to Isaac Motte, January 26, 1778, *LD*, 8:656.

37. HL to Marquis de Lafayette, January 25, 1778, *LP*, 12:341; Marquis de Lafayette to HL, January 26, 1778, *LP*, 12:350–54; Marquis de Lafayette to HL, January 27, 1778, *LP*, 12:363–66; HL to Marquis de Lafayette, January 28, 1778, *LP*, 12:366–67; Marquis de Lafayette to HL, January 31, 1778, *LP*, 12:386–88; Marquis de Lafayette to HL, February 19, 1778, *Lafayette in the Age of the American Revolution: Selected Letters and Papers, 1776–1790*, ed. Stanley Izerda et al. (Ithaca: Cornell University Press, 1977), 1:295–97; Marquis de Lafayette to HL, February 23, 1778, *Lafayette*, 1:318–19; Marquis de Lafayette to George Washington, February 23, 1778, *Lafayette*, 1:321–22; HL to Marquis de Lafayette, March 4, 1778, *LP*, 12:511–15; Marquis de Lafayette to HL, March 12, 1778, *Lafayette*, 1:350–51; Marquis de Lafayette to HL, March 20, 1778, *Lafayette*, 1:366–69; HL to Marquis de Lafayette, March 24, 1778, *LP*, 13:27–30; *JCC* (1778) 10:87, 107, 217, 253–54.

38. HL to Rawlins Lowndes, May 17, 1778, *LD*, 9:700–701.

39. Congress accepted Conway's resignation on April 28, 1778: *JCC* (1778) 10:399; HL to Rawlins Lowndes, May 1, 1778, *LD*, 9:556; HL to Thomas Conway, May 7, 1778, *LD* , 9:619; HL to Marquis de Lafayette, June 5, 1778, *LD*, 10:25–27; HL to John Laurens, June 5, 1778, *LD*, 10:28–29; Burnett, *Continental Congress*, 297.

40. George Washington to HL, April 10, 1778, *FWW*, 11:235–41; George Washington to HL, April 30, 1778, *FWW*, 11:327.

41. HL to George Washington, May 5, 1778, *LD*, 9:606–09.

42. *JCC* (1778) 10:502; HL to William Livingston, April 19, 1778, *LD*, 9:442–45; Burnett, *Continental Congress*, 312–15; Henderson, *Party Politics*, 122–24.

43. HL to Isaac Motte, January 26, 1778, *LD*, 8:656; HL to John Rutledge, January 30, 1778, *LP*, 12:375–81; HL to William Livingston, January 27, 1778, *LP*, 12:354–58.

44. HL to Isaac Motte, January 26, 1778, *LD*, 8:654; HL to John Rutledge, January 30, 1778, *LP*, 12:375–81; Laurens was granted permission to return to South Carolina on January 19, 1778: *LD*, 9:xxi–xxii; HL to John Rutledge, May 4, 1778, *LP*, 13:247–48.

45. The distrust that many in South Carolina still felt toward the French during the Revolutionary War was demonstrated by a riot that broke out between French sailors and the Charles Town mob on September 6, 1778. In this riot four men, three of them Frenchmen, were killed: Nadelhaft, *Disorders of War*, 47; CG to William Henry Drayton, September 9, 1778, *WCG*, 150; John Lewis Gervais to HL, September 9, 1778, SCHM 66 (January 1965): 34. HL to Babut and Co., August 5, 1776, *LP*, 11:216–20; HL to Babut and Co., August 21, 1776, *LP*, 11:257; HL to Jacob Sandilands, February 4, 1777, *LP*, 11:296–98; HL to Babut and Labouchere, February 25, 1777, *LP*, 11:301–2; HL to Delaire and Richmond, February 25, 1777, *LP*, 11:303–4; HL to Babut and Labouchere, March 16, 1777, *LP*, 11:306–9; HL to Noodingh and Alaret, March 19, 1777, *LP*, 11:309–11; HL to Jacob Sandilands, March 21, 1777, *LP*, 11:311–12.

46. HL to James Laurens, September 8, 1776, *LP*, 11:266.

47. HL to William Brisbane, August 14, 1777, *LP*, 11:453–58; HL to Gabriel Manigault, August 15, 1777, *LD*, 7:486–87; HL to John Rutledge, September 10, 1777, *LD*, 7:642–45.

48. HL to John Lewis Gervais, May 3, 1778, *LD*, 9:578; HL to Baron Von Steuben, May 11, 1778, *LD*, 9:647–48; HL to Lieutenant Colonel Duplessis, May 11, 1778, *LD*,

9:640; HL to John Laurens, May 16, 1778, *LD*, 9:684–85. The Treaty of Alliance arrived at York on May 2, 1778 and was ratified unanimously on May 4: *JCC* (1778) 11:418–57.

49. George Washington to HL, November 14, 1778, *FWW*, 13:254–58; HL to George Washington, November 20, 1778, *LD*, 11:229–30.

50. George Washington to HL, June 7, 1778, *FWW*, 12:27–28; HL to George Johnstone, June 14, 1778, *LD*; British Commissioners to HL, July 11, 1778, Kendall Collection, South Caroliniana Library, Columbia, reel 1; *JCC* (1778) 11:585, 604–5.

51. William Manning to HL, April 11, 1778, *LP*, 13:103–5; Richard Oswald to HL, April 12, 1778, *LP*, 13:107–13; HL to George Washington, June 18, 1778, *LP*, 13:484–88; Ramsay, *History of the Revolution*, 2:72–73.

52. *JCC* (1778) 11:770; HL to George Washington, July 31, 1778, *LD*, 10:377; HL to Rawlins Lowndes, August 7, 1778, *LD*, 10:401; Ramsay, *History of the Revolution*, 2:78; Wallace, *Laurens*, 297–98.

53. Quoted in Ramsay, *History of the Revolution*, 2:79–80.

54. HL to Rawlins Lowndes, May 17, 1778, *LP*, 13:314–24. General Washington informed Congress that the enemy evacuated Philadelphia on June 18, 1778: *JCC* (1778) 11:626. Congress resolved to adjourn from York on June 27 and meet again in Philadelphia on July 2: *JCC* (1778) 11:641, 671; HL to Rawlins Lowndes, June 27, 1778, *LP*, 13:521; HL to Rawlins Lowndes, July 15, 1778, *LD*, 10:283–84.

13. Contention in Congress: Henry Laurens and the Continental Congress, 1778–1779

1. HL to John Lewis Gervais, September 5, 1777, *LP*, 11:498.

2. *JCC* 6 (1776): 897; Wallace, *Laurens*, 305–7.

3. HL to John Lewis Gervais, September 5, 1777, *LP*, 11:493. Laurens's main complaint against Deane, at this point, concerned the vast number of Frenchmen who were promised high positions in the Continental Army by Deane. Laurens noted that it was impossible to honor most of these promises, and that Deane's conduct was embarrassing and expensive to Congress: HL to John Lewis Gervais, August 5, 1777, *LD*, 7:421.

4. Ralph Izard to HL, February 16, 1778, *The Revolutionary Diplomatic Correspondence of the United States*, ed. Francis Wharton (Washington, D.C.: Government Printing Office, 1989), 2:497–501.

5. Ralph Izard to HL, April 1, 1778, *Diplomatic Correspondence*, 2:532.

6. Ralph Izard to HL, undated 1778, *HLP*, SCHS, reel 14.

7. Ralph Izard to HL, June 28, 1778, *Diplomatic Correspondence*, 2:629–32. Izard reported that, even after the departure of Deane, there was no improvement in Franklin's behavior. He finally became convinced that "no man of honour can do his duty, and serve his Country properly, who has any connexion with Dr. Franklin": Ralph Izard to HL, January 16, 1779, "Izard-Laurens Correspondence," *SCHM* 22, no. 3 (July 1921): 78. In assessing Izard's charges, it must be pointed out that the above letters contain a bitterness that might be attributed to the fact that he, like Lee, claimed to have been slighted and mistreated by Franklin and Deane.

8. *JCC* (1777) 9:946–47, 1008–9. John Adams was appointed to serve in Deane's place on November 28, 1777: *JCC* (1777) 9:975.

9. HL to George Washington, June 8, 1778, *LD*, 10:46; HL to Rawlins Lowndes, July 15, 1778, *LD*, 10:285–86.

10. *JCC* (1777) 11:799–801, 802, 813, 826: HL to Rawlins Lowndes, August 18, 1778, *LD*, 10:473–74; Laurens, "Notes on Resignation," December 9, 1778, *LD*, 11:317.

11. HL to Silas Deane, December 5, 1778, *LD*, 11:290; *JCC* (1778) 12:1200–1206; Laurens, "Speech to Congress," December 9, 1778, *LD*, 11:312–15; Wallace, *Laurens*, 309–13; Burnett, *Continental Congress*, 362–65; Louis W. Potts, *Arthur Lee: A Virtuous Revolutionary* (Baton Rouge: Louisiana State University Press, 1981), 212–15.

12. HL to Rawlins Lowndes, May 2, 1778, *LD*, 9:565–66; HL to John Lewis Gervais, July 15, 1778, *LD*, 10:283; HL to John Lewis Gervais, September 15, 1778, *LD*, 10:647; HL to John Laurens, September 17, 1778, *LD*, 10:655–56.

13. HL to John Lewis Gervais, September 15, 1778, *LD*, 10:647. It appears that Mathews's reasons for leaving were no more pressing than those of Laurens, as his main complaint was the general one that service in Congress was a disagreeable waste of time. Mathews, however, was one of the strongest critics of Congress: John Mathews to Thomas Bee, July 7, 1778, *LD*, 10:236; John Mathews to Thomas Bee, September 22, 1778, *LD*, 10:682–83; John Mathews to Thomas Bee, October 17, 1778, *LD*, 11:70.

14. "Charles Thomson's Draft Resolution of Congress," October 31, 1778, *LD*, 11:153; Laurens, "Notes on Resignation," December 9, 1778, *LD*, 11:319–20.

15. Laurens, "Speech to Congress," December 9, 1778, *LD*, 11:312–15. Laurens's sentiments were shared by many of the anti-Deane party. Even John Adams, in France, reacted warmly to Deane's paper. He told Franklin that "it was one of the most wicked and abominable Productions that ever sprung from an human Heart." To Edward Bancroft, Adams called the article "Evidence of such a Complication of vile Passions, of Vanity, Arrogance and Presumption, of Malice, Envy and Revenge, and at the same Time of such weakness, Indiscretion and Folly, as ought to unite every honest and wise Man against him. That there appeared to me no Alternative left but the Ruin of Mr. Deane, or the Ruin of his Country. That he appeared to me in Light of a wild boar that ought to be hunted down for the Benefit of Mankind": Butterfield, *Diary of John Adams*, 2:345.

16. *JCC* (1778) 12:1221–1222; HL to Rawlins Lowndes, December 16, 1778, *LD*, 11:350–52; John Jay to HL, December 15, 1778, *LD*, 11:344; HL to Congress, December 16, 1778, *LD*, 11:349–50.

17. Laurens, "Notes in Congress," April 21(?), 1779, *LD*, 11:364–67; "Statement of Thomas Burke, April 16(?), 1779, *LD*, 12:336–39; William Paca and William Henry Drayton to Congress, April 30, 1779, *LD*, 12:410–11; *JCC* (1779) 14:533–37; Wallace, *Laurens*, 320–21.

18. *JCC* (1779) 14:712, 930; *JCC* (1779) 15:1166; Laurens, "Notes on Debates," June 11, 1779, *LD*, 13:47–49; Laurens, "Notes on Debates," May 6, 1779, *LD*, 12:433–35; "Diary of John Fell," October 21, 1779, *LD*, 14:102; Wallace, *Laurens*, 323–28.

19. HL to Robert Morris, January 10(?), 1778, *LD*, 11:448. Laurens was not the only one who suspected Morris's business practices. John Adams was critical of Morris as early as September 1775: *JCC* (1775) 3:473.

20. Ralph Izard to HL, February 16, 1778, *Diplomatic Correspondence*, 2:498–99; HL to George Washington, November 20, 1778, *LD*, 11:231; Robert Morris to HL, December 26, 1777, *LP*, 12:203–13; Jennings B. Sanders, *Evolution of Executive Departments of the Continental Congress, 1774–1789* (Chapel Hill: University of North Carolina Press, 1935), 84–86; Wallace, *Laurens*, 329–30.

21. HL to Robert Morris, January 10(?), 1779, *LD*, 11:448–49.

22. HL to Robert Morris, January 10(?), 1779, *LD*, 11:448–50.

23. Paine's publication raised a storm in Congress that resulted in his resignation

as secretary to the Committee for Foreign Affairs: *JCC* (1779) 13:30–31, 36–38, 545. For evidence of Laurens' collaboration with Paine, see *LD*, 11:425n.

24. Robert Morris to the Public, January 7, 1779, *LD*, 11:430–35; *JCC* (1779) 13:46–47; Laurens, "Notes on Remarks in Congress," January 9, 1779, *LD*, 11:439–40; HL to Robert Morris, January 10(?), 1779, *LD*, 11:447; Laurens, "Statement to Congress," January 11, 1779, *LD*, 11:451–52.

25. *LD*, 11:425n.; HL to Robert Morris, January 10(?), 1779, *LD*, 11:448; Robert Morris to HL, January 11, 1779, *LD*, 11:452–54.

26. *JCC* (1779) 13:86, 158–59, 163–76; "Diary of John Fell," February 11, 1779, *LD*, 12:52; Wallace, *Laurens*, 333.

27. HL to Robert Morris, July 8, 1779, *LD*, 13:163–64; Wallace, *Laurens*, 334.

28. *LD*, 12:226; Jack N. Rakove, *The Beginnings of National Politics: An Interpretive History of the Continental Congress* (New York: Alfred A. Knopf, 1976), 262; Wallace, *Laurens*, 340–41.

29. Alexander Hamilton to John Laurens, May 22, 1779, *The Papers of Alexander Hamilton*, ed. Harold C. Syrett (New York: Columbia University Press, 1961–1987), 2:53; Rakove, *Beginnings of National Politics*, 263.

30. Laurens had already experienced several problems with John Penn. Charles Thomson, the secretary of Congress, later charged that, as president, Laurens had openly taunted Penn from the chair: Charles Thomson to a Committee of Congress, *LD*, 13:460. More seriously, during the Robert Morris investigation, Laurens became angry when Penn did not provide the support for his allegations against Morris, which Laurens felt that he could have and should have provided. This led to a duel between the two men in which both men fired, though neither was hit: *LD*, 11:440–41n.

31. North Carolina Delegates to South Carolina Delegates, April 2, 1779, *LD*, 12:277–79; North Carolina Delegates to Richard Caswell, April 2, 1779, *LD*, 12:274–76. It appears that this letter to Caswell was composed merely to apply pressure against Laurens and was probably never sent: *LD*, 12:277n.

32. The reference to voting and acting systematically concerned a conversation that Drayton held with Samuel Adams, a friend to Laurens. Adams asked Drayton if he could explain why he always seemed to vote opposite to Laurens. Drayton replied that "we vote systematically." Laurens added on this note that, since he always voted first, any system must be confined to Drayton: *LD*, 12:291n.

33. HL to William Henry Drayton, April 4, 1779, *LD*, 12:290–91. Further correspondence in this affair can be found in William Henry Drayton to North Carolina Delegates, April 3, 1779, *LD*, 12:282; HL to William Henry Drayton, April 3, 1779, *LD*, 12:283–84; William Henry Drayton to HL, April 4, 1779, *LD*, 12:285.

34. HL to Richard Caswell, April 4, 1779, *LD*, 12:288–89; HL to North Carolina Delegates, April 4, 1779, *LD*, 12:291.

35. North Carolina Delegates to HL, April 8, 1779, *LD*, 12:312–14; HL to North Carolina Delegates, April 8, 1779, *LD*, 12:310–11; HL to John Laurens, April 16, 1779, *LD*, 12:340.

36. HL to John Laurens, September 21, 1779, *LD*, 13:523–24.

37. Smith, ed., *LD*, 12:297n.; HL to John Laurens, April 16, 1779, *LD*, 12: 341; Laurens, "Notes on Debates," May 8, 1779, *LD*, 12:439–40; Alden, *South in Revolution*, 300–301.

38. *JCC* (1778) 10:294; HL to John Laurens, May 5, 1778, *LD*, 9:603; HL to Baron Von Steuben, May 5, 1778, *LD*, 9:606.

39. "Note by Moses Young, March 10, 1779," *HLP*, SCHS, reel 10; Dabney and Dargan, *Drayton*, 159–60; William Henry Drayton to HL, September 16, 1778, *LD*, 10:649–50; HL to William Henry Drayton, September 16(?), 1778, *LD*, 10:650–51.

40. Laurens, "Notes on the Conduct of William Henry Drayton," April 12(?), 1779, *LD*, 12:326; Laurens, "Notes on Debates," June 3(?), 1779, *LD*, 13:18–21; Dabney and Dargan, *Drayton*, 169.

41. "Henry Laurens on the Olympic Games," SCHM 61, no. 3 (July 1960): 146–47 also in *LD*, 13:135–36; HL to William Livingston, July 5, 1779, *LD*, 13:150–51.

42. HL to John Laurens, July 17, 1779, *LD*, 13:249.

43. It was John Drayton who, using the remaining papers, wrote the history of the Revolution in South Carolina. John Drayton was convinced that Laurens had destroyed these documents not, as Laurens claimed, out of fear that secrets might fall into the hands of the enemy, but to protect himself against unflattering material: Drayton, *Memoirs*, 1:vii; HL to Richard Henry Lee, August 31, 1779, *LD*, 13:434; William M. Dabney, "Drayton and Laurens in the Continental Congress," SCHM 60, no. 2 (April 1959): 81–82; *JCC* (1779) 15:1020; "Samuel Holten's Diary," September 4, 1779, *LD*, 13:451.

44. The editors of the *Laurens Papers* cite no particular incident that set off the feud between Laurens and Thomson. Rather, they attribute it to "fundamental differences in character and political outlook": *LP*, 12:547–48n. Thomson, however, seems to have been a foe of the Adamses and Lees. John Adams accused him of supporting the "opposition," while Richard Henry Lee insisted that Thomson was "as unfit to be Secretary of Congress as any other W-h-e [whore] in Philadelphia": Richard Henry Lee to HL, May 27, 1779, *LD*, 11:550; J. Edwin Hendricks, *Charles Thomson and the Making of a New Nation, 1729—1824* (London: Associated University Presses, 1979), 132–33.

45. *JCC* (1779) 14:1008; HL to a Committee of Congress, September 1, 1779, *LD*, 13:442–46.

46. *LD*, 13:444n.

47. Charles Thomson to a Committee of Congress, September 6, 1779, *LD*, 13:458–66, 466n.

48. *LD*, 13:445n.

49. *JCC* (1779) 15:1196, 1230, 1232–36, 1248; HL to Richard Henry Lee, August 31, 1779, *LD*, 13:434; "Diary of John Fell," October 21, 1779, *LD*, 14:102; Nathaniel Peabody to William Whipple, November 1, 1779, *LD*, 14:141; Wallace, *Laurens*, 349–50. Laurens received his commission and instructions from the new president in Samuel Huntington to HL, October 30, 1779, *LD*, 14:133–34.

50. Nathaniel Peabody to William Whipple, November 9, 1779, *LD*, 14:171; *South Carolina and American General Gazette*, December 10, 1779.

14. Tribulation and Triumph, 1780–1785

1. CG, daybook entry, September 18, 1778, *WCG* 125; John Wells to HL, January 23, 1778, *LP*, 12:331–34; John Lewis Gervais to HL, February 18, 1778, *HLP*, SCHS, reel 19; Hennig Cohen, *The South Carolina Gazette, 1732–1775* (Columbia: University of South Carolina Press, 1953), 247.

2. *JCC* (1778) 13:949–51; HL to Rawlins Lowndes, May 17, 1778, *LD*, 9:696–702; HL to Rawlins Lowndes, September 15, 1778, *LD*, 10:647–48; HL to Rawlins Lowndes, September 23, 1778, *LD*, 10:687–88; HL to George Washington, September 23, 1778, *LD*, 10:689–90; George Washington to HL, October 3, 1778, *FWW*, 13:15–16; HL to George Washington, October 10, 1778, *LD*, 11:46; "Diary of Samuel Holten," September 25, 1778, *LD*, 10:692.

3. Rawlins Lowndes to HL, December 24, 1778, *HLP*, SCHS, reel 9; HL to Rawlins Lowndes, January 29, 1779, *LD*, 11:533–34.

4. Laurens, "Notes on a Speech in Congress," December ?, 1778, *LD*, 11:392–93.

5. CG to Thomas Bee, February 4, 1779, *WCG*, 160; Godbold and Woody, *Gadsden*, 191. Gadsden was related by marriage to both Ferguson and Edwards. Thomas Ferguson had married Gadsden's daughter Elizabeth in 1774, shortly after the death of her first husband, Andrew Rutledge. She died in 1777. Catharine Edwards, daughter of John Edwards, was married to Philip Gadsden, youngest son of Christopher Gadsden: Godbold and Woody, *Gadsden*, 161–64.

6. Ramsay, *History of South Carolina*, 1:173–74; Godbold and Woody, *Gadsden*, 191–92; David B. Mattern, *Benjamin Lincoln and the American Revolution* (Columbia: University of South Carolina Press, 1995), 64–65.

7. Godbold and Woody, *Gadsden*, 192; CG to Samuel Adams, April 4, 1779, *WCG*, 161–64. Other South Carolinians wrote similar letters at this time. Thomas Bee threatened that if no aid were forthcoming, South Carolinians might be forced to "make the best Terms for ourselves we can": Thomas Bee to William Henry Drayton, April 5, 1779, *LD*, 12:400; Page Smith, *A New Age Now Begins: A People's History of the American Revolution* (New York: Penguin Books, 1989, 2:1318;

8. Ramsay, History of *South Carolina*, 1:173–74; Godbold and Woody, *Gadsden*, 193; Washington recommended John Laurens highly to Governor Rutledge, noting that "the whole tenor of his conduct has been such as to entitle him to my particular friendship and to give me a high opinion of his talents and merit": George Washington to John Rutledge, March 15, 1779, *FWW*, 14:245–46.

9. This action resulted in serious casualties, including a minor wound for John Laurens: Smith, *New Age Now Begins*, 2:1319–1320; Alexander Garden, *Anecdotes of the American Revolution* (Charleston, 1822), 1:xxii; Ramsay, *History of South Carolina*, 1:174; Moultrie, *Memoirs*, 1:402–4; *JCC* (1779) 8:388–89; Townsend, *John Laurens*, 4.

10. *HLP*, SCHS, reel 16; Moultrie, *Memoirs*, 1:426–32; McCrady, *Revolution*, 2:372–73; Walsh, *WCG*, 165n.; Godbold and Woody, *Gadsden*, 193–94.

11. *HLP*, SCHS, reel 16; HL to Jonathan Trumbull, Sr., July 8, 1778, *LD*, 13:166; McCrady, *Revolution*, 2:373–76; Moultrie, *Memoirs*, 1:432–35; Godbold and Woody, *Gadsden*, 194–95; Mattern, *Benjamin Lincoln*, 71. Henry Laurens was proud of his son's performance during the Prevost raid. He also suggested that Rutledge may have offered his terms to the British as a delay tactic: HL to William Livingston, July 10, 1779, *LD*, 13:188–89.

12. Ramsay, *History of South Carolina*, 1:176; Nadelhaft, *Disorders of War*, 50; Smith, *New Age Now Begins*, 2:1329–1330.

13. CG to Samuel Adams, July 6, 1779, Walsh, *WCG*, 165–66; *JCC* (1779) 13:385–86.

14. Moultrie, *Memoirs*, 2:40–43; Smith, *New Age Now Begins*, 2:1331–1337.

15. Smith, *New Age Now Begins*, 2:1380–1381; Godbold and Woody, *Gadsden*, 196.

16. Moultrie, *Memoirs*, 2:65; Ramsay, *History of South Carolina*, 1:183; Smith, *New Age Now Begins*, 2:1380–1381; Godbold and Woody, *Gadsden*, 196–97.

17. William Edwin Hemphill, Wylma Anne Wates, and R. Nicholas Olsberg, eds., *Journals of the General Assembly and House of Representatives, 1776–1780* (Columbia: University of South Carolina Press, 1970), 242–76.

18. Godbold and Woody, *Gadsden*, 196–97; Smith, *New Age Now Begins*, 2:1381; Clow, *Edward Rutledge*, 144. Lincoln continued to hope for further reinforcements from Virginia and North Carolina, which would have left him with an army of nearly ten thousand men. Given the unreliability of such promises in the past, it is difficult to understand why he placed such faith in them at this point: Mattern, *Benjamin Lincoln*, 97–98.

19. HL to Committee for Foreign Affairs, July 1, 1780, *LD*, 15:397.

20. McCrady, *Revolution*, 2:465; Godbold and Woody, *Gadsden*, 197–98.

21. Moultrie, *Memoirs*, 2:65–73; Godbold and Woody, *Gadsden*, 198–99; Smith, *New Age Now Begins*, 2:1381–1385. Congress had earlier authorized Lincoln to appeal to Spanish authorities at Havana for aid: *JCC* (1779) 15:1388.

22. McCrady, *Revolution*, 2:473–76; Ravenel, *Charleston*, 268–69; Mattern, *Benjamin Lincoln*, 93–95, 102–3, 108.

23. Moultrie, *Memoirs*, 2:87–89; McCrady, *Revolution*, 2:495–98; CG to Benjamin Lincoln, May 8, 1780, *WCG*, 167–68; Smith, *New Age Now Begins*, 2:1386–1388.

24. Moultrie, *Memoirs*, 2:89–93; McCrady, *Revolution*, 2:498–502; CG to Benjamin Lincoln, May 9, 1780, *WCG*, 167n.

25. Moultrie, *Memoirs*, 2:93–112; McCrady, *Revolution*, 2:502–4; CG to Benjamin Lincoln, May 11, 1780, *WCG*, 169; CG to Benjamin Lincoln, May 12, 1780, *WCG*, 169; Smith, *New Age Now Begins*, 2:1388–1392; Godbold and Woody, *Gadsden*, 201–2. It was at this time that Gadsden probably destroyed most of his papers in an effort to ensure that they did not fall into the hands of the British: John Hammond Moore, ed., "Jared Sparks Visits South Carolina," *SCHM* 72, no. 3 (July 1971): 154. David Mattern numbers American casualties at eighty-nine killed and one hundred thirty-eight wounded during the siege. Approximately twenty-two hundred continentals were surrendered, of whom five hundred were sick or wounded. About five hundred militia were also surrendered. The British suffered seventy-six killed and one hundred eighty-nine wounded: Mattern, *Benjamin Lincoln*, 108.

26. McCrady, *Revolution*, 2:512–14.

27. John Laurens to HL, May 25, 1780, Kendall Collection, South Caroliniana Library, Columbia, reel 3. The British did raid Laurens's plantation at Mepkin, destroying many valuable papers: *LD*, 12:555n.

28. George Smith McCowen, Jr., *The British Occupation of Charleston, 1780–82* (Columbia: University of South Carolina Press, 1972), 55–56; Godbold and Woody, *Gadsden*, 202.

29. Ramsay, *History of South Carolina*, 1:253; McCrady, *Revolution*, 2:713–16; Godbold and Woody, *Gadsden*, 202–3. For more recent discussions of British efforts at pacification and its problems see Klein, *Unification of a Slave State*, 100–108; Frey, *Water from a Rock*, 108–42.

30. Josiah Smith, "Josiah Smith's Diary, 1780–1781," *SCHM* 33, no. 1 (January 1932): 2–3; McCrady, *Revolution*, 2:716–17.

31. McCrady, *Revolution*, 2:722–23; Wallace, *Short History*, 305. McCrady provided a copy of one of the paroles taken by the British: McCrady, *Revolution*, 2:718n. A copy of the letter from the prisoners to Balfour can be found in Smith, "Josiah Smith's Diary," 4–5.

32. Smith, "Josiah Smith's Diary," 5.

33. McCrady, *Revolution*, 2:719–21; Godbold and Woody, *Gadsden*, 204; Smith, "Josiah Smith's Diary," 5–6.

34. Smith, "Josiah Smith's Diary," 6–8; McCrady, *Revolution*, 2:723–25.

35. Garden, *Anecdotes*, 1:152; Smith, "Josiah Smith's Diary," 9–10; McCrady, *Revolution*, 2:725–26; Godbold and Woody, *Gadsden*, 205–8.

36. *JCC* (1780) 17:534–38; HL to Committee for Foreign Affairs, July 1, 1780, *LD*, 15:399; Wallace, *Laurens*, 355–57. While in Philadelphia awaiting passage, Laurens attended Congress between July 1 and August 12, 1780, *LD*, 15:xxii.

37. HL to Richard Henry Lee, August 1, 1780, *LD*, 15:532; Henry Laurens, "Narrative of the Capture of Henry Laurens, of his Confinement in the Tower of London, &c, 1780, 1781, 1782," *Firelands Pioneer* 16 (1907): 1259; Wallace, *Laurens*, 357–58.

38. Laurens, "Narrative of Capture and Confinement," 1259–62; Wallace, *Laurens*, 358–59.

39. Laurens, "Narrative of Capture and Confinement," 1262.

40. Ibid., 1262–63.

41. Ibid., 1263–65; "Records of the Tower of London," Henry and John Laurens Papers, Library of Congress.

42. Laurens, "Narrative of Capture and Confinement," 1265–66.

43. Ibid., 1266–67; "Excerpts from London to Dumas," October 17, 1780, *Diplomatic Correspondence*, 4:84–85.

44. *JCC* (1780) 18:1179; John Adams to Benjamin Franklin, October 24,1780, John Adams, *The Works of John Adams*, ed. Charles Francis Adams (Boston: Little, Brown, and Company, 1856), 7:320; Benjamin Franklin to Sir Grey Cooper, November 7, 1780, *Diplomatic Correspondence*, 4:151; Samuel Huntington to Benjamin Franklin, January 4, 1781, *LD*, 16:545–46. Offers of assistance came from various sources, including the wife of the Marquis de Lafayette, who wrote to Vergennes and, reminding him of Laurens's assistance to her husband after his wound at Brandywine, asked him to use his influence on behalf of Laurens: Marchioness de Lafayette to Count de Vergennes, October 18, 1780, Wharton, *Diplomatic Correspondence*, 5:454n.

45. It is likely that this woman was either the wife or the daughter of James Futerell, one of his wardens in the Tower. In his "Narrative," Laurens affectionately referred to the woman who smuggled his writings as a "good woman" and as "a very faithful friend." He remained very close to all of the Futerells after his release and always remembered their kindness to him. These relations were so close that, after the war, the daughter spent a long period of time living with the family of Martha Laurens and her husband, David Ramsay, in South Carolina. As for the mother, Laurens left a legacy to her in his will: Laurens, "Narrative of Capture and Confinement," 1267; Wallace, *Laurens*, 363–64; "Will of Henry Laurens," *Charleston County Transcripts of Wills*, State Archives, Columbia, South Carolina, 24:1152–58.

46. Laurens, "Narrative of Capture and Confinement," 1267–68, 1271, 1280–82.

47. Ibid., 1268–69.

48. Ibid., 1270–72.

49. Ibid., 1273–75. A copy of the pertinent records of the Tower of London, including all visits to Laurens, is in "Henry and John Laurens Papers," Library of Congress.

50. Ibid., 1275–76. John Laurens was sent to France to impress upon the court the necessity of a quick loan. The impatient and impetuous young colonel, frustrated by the repeated delays of the French, shocked everyone by presenting his case to the king at a levee, at which no business was supposed to be conducted. The king was quite pleasant and presented young Laurens with a fancy snuffbox which remains in the possession of the Laurens family, as well as promises of a loan and military supplies. Benjamin Franklin was offended by Laurens' conduct and wrote that several prominent Frenchmen shared this resentment, though he was able to soothe their tempers and complete the negotiations for the loan: Benjamin Franklin to William Carmichael, August 24, 1781, Wharton, *Diplomatic Correspondence*, 4:660; James Madison to Edmund Pendleton, September 3, 1781, *LD*, 18:4–5; Thomas McKean to Thomas Rodney, September 6, 1781, *LD*, 18:20; Townsend, *John Laurens*, 160–85. On a personal note, Laurens's wife and daughter managed to cross the Channel to visit him. Little is known of their trip, but it would be the last time that both mother and daughter would see John Laurens, as Matilda Laurens died in November 1781, while John Laurens was killed before he could again see his daughter: Townsend, *John Laurens*, 182–83.

51. John Laurens to President of Congress, September 6, 1781, Wharton, *Diplomatic Correspondence*, 4:700–701.

52. *LD*, xiv–xv; Samuel Huntington to George Washington, April 5, 1781, *LD*, 17:132–33; Samuel Huntington to George Washington, June 20, 1781, *LD*, 17:334–35: Benjamin Franklin to John Adams, November 7, 1781, *Works of John Adams*, 7:476.

53. Laurens, "Narrative of Capture and Confinement," 1275, 1279–80; Wallace, *Laurens*, 368.

54. Laurens, "Narrative of Capture and Confinement," 1280; Wallace, *Laurens*, 374–80.

55. Laurens, "Narrative of Capture and Confinement," 1280. David Duncan Wallace printed Laurens's representation, along with his notes, in its entirety: Wallace, *Laurens*, 374–80. In support of his statement that he did not persecute the Loyalists, Laurens submitted a deposition from Peter Bachop, himself a Loyalist: *LP*, 11:215n.

56. CG to George Washington, August 10, 1781, *WCG*, 170–71; Godbold and Woody, *Gadsden*, 209.

57. Garden, *Anecdotes*, 1:155; Ramsay, *History of the Revolution*, 2:200, 212–13; Smith, "Josiah Smith's Diary," 104–5; McCrady, *Revolution*, 2:371–73.

58. Nisbet Balfour to South Carolina leaders, May 17, 1781, *HLP*, SCHS, reel 18; *Royal South Carolina Gazette*, November 21, 1780; *South Carolina and American General Gazette*, November 22, 1780; McCrady, *Revolution*, 2:727–30; McCrady, *Revolution*, 3:373; Shaffer, *David Ramsay*, 56–58.

59. The exchange was agreed to by Greene and Cornwallis on May 3 and ratified on June 22: Smith, "Josiah Smith's Diary," 287–88; McCrady, *Revolution*, 2:375–76; Godbold and Woody, *Gadsden*, 211–12; Thomas McKean to Samuel Adams, July 8, 1781, *LD*, 17:387.

60. Smith, "Josiah Smith's Diary," 31, 67–68, 83–84; CG to George Washington, August 10, 1781, *WCG*, 170–73; McCrady, *Revolution*, 3:379–80; Godbold and Woody, *Gadsden*, 214–16.

61. Laurens, "Narrative of Capture and Confinement," 1283–85; Benjamin Franklin to Benjamin Vaughan, December 22, 1781, *Diplomatic Correspondence*, 4:856; John Adams to President of Congress, December 4, 1781, C.F. Adams, ed., *Work of John Adams*, 7:488.

62. Laurens, "Narrative of Capture and Confinement," 1285–86.

63. Ibid., 1287.

64. Ibid., 1289–92; Benjamin Franklin to Benjamin Vaughan, November 22, 1781, *Diplomatic Correspondence*, 4:856; Benjamin Franklin to Martha Laurens, December 29, 1781, Wharton, *Diplomatic Correspondence*, 5:75–76. It is clear that the copy of the petition that Laurens directed to be sent to Congress was either never sent or lost along the way, for when Congress considered the question, they referred to an account published in a London newspaper: Charles Thomson, "The Papers of Charles Thomson, Secretary of the Continental Congress," *Collections of the New York Historical Society* (1878), 155.

65. "Records of the Tower of London," Henry and John Laurens Papers, Library of Congress; Laurens, "Narrative of Capture and Confinement," 1293–95; Laurens to President of Congress, May 30, 1781, *Diplomatic Correspondence*, 6:455–56; Wallace, *Laurens*, 387–88.

66. HL to Richard Oswald, August 7, 1782, Kendall Collection, South Caroliniana Library, Columbia, reel 4; HL to Benjamin Franklin, April 30, 1782, *HLP*, SCHS, reel 15; Benjamin Franklin to HL, May 25, 1782, *HLP*, SCHS, reel 15; Benjamin Franklin to HL, June 9, 1782, *HLP*, SCHS, reel 15; Wallace, *Laurens*, 394–95. Congress held lengthy debates on the subject of exchanging Cornwallis for Laurens. Ironically, it

was John Rutledge and the South Carolinians, burning to avenge themselves upon Cornwallis for his treatment of the Carolinas, who led the opposition to the exchange: "Charles Thomson's Notes," August 12, 1782, *LD*, 19:57–58; Arthur Lee to John Adams, August 7, 1782, *LD*, 19:37; "James Madison's Notes of Debates," November 22, 1782, *LD*, 19:411–13; James Madison to Edmund Randolph, November 26, 1782, *LD*, 19:420–23.

67. Laurens, "Narrative of Capture and Confinement," 1295–1300; John Adams to Benjamin Franklin, April 16, 1782, *Works of John Adams*, 7:569–70; Wallace, *Laurens*, 391–93. Despite his imprisonment, Laurens was appointed to the peace commission on June 14, 1781: Thomas Rodney to Caesar Rodney, June 14, 1781, *LD*, 17:319–21, 321n.

68. *JCC* (1780) 18:1204–17; HL to Benjamin Franklin, May 6, 1782, Kendall Collection, South Caroliniana Library, Columbia, reel 4.

69. HL to William Manning, August 3, 1782, Kendall Collection, South Caroliniana Library, Columbia, reel 4; HL to Richard Oswald, August 15, 1782, Kendall Collection, South Caroliniana Library, Columbia, reel 4; HL to William Lee, August 22, 1782, Kendall Collection, South Caroliniana Library, Columbia, reel 4.

70. HL to John Adams, August 27, 1782, *Works of John Adams*, 7:616; Proceedings of Congress, September 17, 1782, Thomson, "Charles Thomson Papers," *Collections of the New York Historical Society*, 154–55; John Adams to HL, November 6, 1782, *Diplomatic Correspondence*, 5:853–54; HL to John Adams, November 12, 1782, Kendall Collection, South Caroliniana Library, Columbia, reel 4.

71. "Charles Thomson's Notes of Debates," September 19–20, 1782, *LD*, 19:182–92 James Madison to Edmund Randolph, September 24, 1782, *LD*, 19:200–203.

72. The debate took place in Congress on September 20, 1782, and a record of it, along with the roll call vote on recall, can be found in Thomson, "Charles Thomson Papers," *Collections of the New York Historical Society*, 155–69. Massachusetts delegate Samuel Osgood believed that politics played a critical role in the vote and that the eastern states would have voted for recall had they not needed Laurens's assistance in obtaining use of the Newfoundland fisheries: Samuel Osgood to John Adams, December 7, 1783, *LD*, 21:192.

73. Ralph Izard to Alice Izard, October 7, 1782, *LD*, 19:231: George Washington to Reverend William Gordon, March 8, 1785, *FWW*, 28:97; Ramsay, *History of the Revolution*, 2:291; Alexander Hamilton to Nathanael Greene, October 12, 1782, *The Papers of Alexander Hamilton*, 3:183–84; John Adams to HL, November 6, 1782, *Diplomatic Correspondence*, 5:854; *Royal Gazette* (Charles Town), September 7, 1782. One man who did not pay tribute to John Laurens was General Moultrie, who viewed the action at Combahee Ferry as yet another example of Laurens' dangerous rashness. Moultrie wrote that Laurens, in command of the advance guard of a force sent to resist a British foraging raid, caused his own death and those of many of his men by pushing too far in front of the main body and then attacking a superior enemy force: Moultrie, *Memoirs*, 2:342–43; Townsend, *John Laurens*, 216–20.

74. HL to John Adams, November 12, 1782, *Works of John Adams*, 8:10–11; HL to Mrs. James Laurens, December 30, 1782, *HLP*, SCHS, reel 8; HL to Mr. Himeli, May 2, 1783, *HLP*, SCHS, reel 7.

75. HL to George Appleby, December 9, 1782, *HLP*, SCHS, reel 8; HL to Mrs. James Laurens, December 30, 1782, *HLP*, SCHS, reel 8; HL to Martha Laurens, January 9, 1782, *HLP*, SCHS, reel 7; Martha Laurens to Mrs. James Laurens, February 15, 1783, *HLP*, SCHS, reel 15.

76. Butterfield, *Diary of John Adams*, 3:82–83; HL to South Carolina Delegates in Congress, December 16, 1782, *HLP*, SCHS, reel 8; John Adams to James Lloyd, March 12, 1815, *Works of John Adams*, 10:137–38.

77. HL to Robert R. Livingston, December 15, 1782, *Diplomatic Correspondence*, 6:138–40; John Adams to Robert R. Livingston, January 23, 1783, *Works of John Adams*, 8:27; HL to South Carolina Delegates to Congress, December 16, 1782, *HLP*, SCHS, reel 8.

78. HL to South Carolina Delegates to Congress, December 16, 1782, *HLP*, SCHS, reel 8.

79. HL to Robert R. Livingston, December 24, 1782, *HLP*, SCHS, reel 8.

80. HL to Robert R. Livingston, January 9, 1783, Wharton, *Diplomatic Correspondence*, 6:200; Martha Laurens to Mrs. James Laurens, June 28, 1783, *HLP*, SCHS, reel 15; HL to Richard Oswald, July 15, 1783, *HLP*, SCHS, reel 7.

81. HL to Robert R. Livingston, March 15, 1783, *HLP*, SCHS, reel 7; HL to John Adams, March 26, 1783, *Diplomatic Correspondence*, 6:343; HL to John Lewis Gervais, April 1, 1783, *HLP*, SCHS, reel 7; HL to Benjamin Franklin, April 4, 1783, *HLP*, SCHS, reel 7; HL to John Lewis Gervais, April 7, 1783, *HLP*, SCHS, reel 7; HL to American Peace Commissioners, August 9, 1783, *HLP*, SCHS, reel 7.

82. Congress granted Laurens permission to return to America on April 1, 1783: "James Madison's Notes on Debates," April 1, 1783, *LD*, 20:128; HL to Robert R. Livingston, August 9, 1783, *Diplomatic Correspondence*, 6:641; HL to Francis Bremar, August 15, 1783, *HLP*, SCHS, reel 7; HL to Robert R. Livingston, September 11, 1783, *Diplomatic Correspondence*, 6:693; Wallace, *Laurens*, 418. The definitive peace treaty was signed on September 3, 1783: Benjamin Franklin to Laurens, *HLP*, SCHS, reel 15.

83. Samuel Hardy to Benjamin Harrison, August 13, 1784, *LD*, 21:764; Wallace, *Laurens*, 418–19.

84. John Lewis Gervais to HL, September 27, 1782, ALS, South Caroliniana Library, Columbia; HL to Mr. I. Desagaye, June 6, 1783, *HLP*, SCHS, reel 7; HL to James Harford, February 4, 1783, *HLP*, SCHS, reel 7; HL to Monsieur Mathy, December 25, 1782, *HLP*, SCHS, reel 8. Laurens also wrote that the British "had spitefully destroyed all my papers. This will be a great and irreparable Loss to me.": HL to John Delagaye, March 27, 1784, Kendall Collection, South Caroliniana Library, Columbia, reel 7. Fortunately for posterity, most of Laurens's papers had been moved to Mepkin and the damage to these records was not nearly so great as he had feared.

85. HL to Martha Laurens, August 19, 1784, Kendall Collection, South Caroliniana Library, Columbia, reel 7; HL to Martha Laurens, September 30, 1784, Kendall Collection, South Caroliniana Library, Columbia, reel 7; HL to John Dart, October 7, 1784, Kendall Collection, South Caroliniana Library, Columbia, reel 7; Wallace, *Laurens*, 420–21; Charles Thomson to Thomas Jefferson, October 1, 1784, *LD*, 21:808; Samuel Hardy to Benjamin Harrison, November 7, 1784, *LD*, 22:12; James Monroe to James Madison, November 15, 1784, *LD*, 22:20–21; Jacob Read to Benjamin Guerard, November 20, 1784, *LD*, 22:29–30, 30n.

86. Quoted in Ravenel, *Charleston*, 331–32.

15. Patriots in Retirement, 1785–1805

1. For Gadsden's speech see *Charles Town Royal Gazette*, May 1, 1782; A. S. Salley, Jr., ed., *Journal of the House of Representatives of South Carolina, January 8, 1782–February 26, 1782* (Columbia: State Company, 1916), 33–34; Aedanus Burke to Arthur Middleton, January 25, 1782, in Arthur Middleton, "Correspondence of Hon. Arthur Middleton, signer of the Declaration of Independence," annotated by Joseph W. Barnwell, *SCHM* XXVI (October 1925), 193–94; John Rutledge to South Carolina Delegates in Congress, January 29, 1782, "Letters of John Rutledge," 167.

2. CG to Morton Wilkinson, September ?, 1781; Walsh, *WCG*, 174–75.

3. Aedanus Burke to Arthur Middleton, January 25, 1782, "Correspondence of Arthur Middleton," 192–93; McCowan, *British Occupation of Charleston*, 136–37; Nadelhaft, *Disorders of War*, 81–83; Smith, "Josiah Smith's Diary," 194–99.

4. Edward Rutledge to Arthur Middleton, February 26, 1782, "Correspondence of Arthur Middleton," 7–9; Vipperman, *Rawlins Lowndes*, 234; McCowen, *British Occupation of Charleston*, 71–73, 137–38; Nadelhaft, *Disorders of War*, 83. A complete list of those confiscated and amerced by the Jacksonborough Assembly can be found in Smith, "Josiah Smith's Diary," 194–99.

5. CG to Francis Marion, November 17, 1782, *WCG*, 194–95.

6. CG to Francis Marion, November 17, 1782, *WCG*, 196–97; Ramsay, *History of South Carolina*, 1:194–96; McCrady, *Revolution*, 3:580–82; Walsh, *Sons of Liberty*, 112–13.

7. CG to Francis Marion, November 17, 1782, *WCG*, 197. Gadsden submitted many petitions for redress to the South Carolina House of Representatives during 1783 and 1784: see Theodora J. Thompson, ed., *Journals of the House of Representatives, 1783–1784* (Columbia: University of South Carolina Press, 1977), 1–762; McCrady, *Revolution*, 3:588; Alden, *South in Revolution*, 326–28; Godbold and Woody, *Gadsden*, 227–28, 251; Lambert, *South Carolina Loyalists*, 280, 295.

8. Ramsay, *History of South Carolina*, 1:270–71; Nadelhaft, *Disorders of War*, 88–89, 92.

9. CG to John Mathews, October 16, 1782, *WCG*, 181–82; CG to Francis Marion, October 29, 1782, *WCG*, 188.

10. CG to John Mathews, October 16, 1782, *WCG*, 181–82; John Lewis Gervais to Battaile Muse, February 10, 1783, *LD*, 19:667; Ramsay, *History of South Carolina*, 1:271–72; Moultrie, *Memoirs*, 2:351–52, 358–61; Nadelhaft, *Disorders of War*, 91; Godbold and Woody, *Gadsden*, 224; Lambert, *South Carolina Loyalists*, 250–52; Frey, *Water From the Rock*, 172–79.

11. Alden, *South in Revolution*, 326–28; Nadelhaft, *Disorders of War*, 109; Godbold and Woody, *Gadsden*, 228.

12. Though the agreement between Mathews and the British said nothing about price levels, the merchants had not been given permission to restock their shelves: Nadelhaft, *Disorders of War*, 92–93.

13. Nadelhaft, *Disorders of War*, 91–95; Godbold and Woody, *Gadsden*, 229.

14. Godbold and Woody, *Gadsden*, 229–30.

15. CG to the Public, *Gazette of the State of South Carolina*, May 6, 1784, *WCG*, 200–206; CG to the Public, *Gazette of the State of South Carolina*, July 17, 1784, *WCG*, 206–12; CG to the Public in General and to Commodore Gillon in Particular, *Gazette of the State of South Carolina*, August 5, 1784, *WCG*, 228–38; Godbold and Woody, *Gadsden*, 231–36; Walsh, *WCG*, 224n.

16. Walsh, *WCG*, 253n.; Godbold and Woody, *Gadsden*, 237–39, 252.

17. After the death of his son, Gadsden reorganized his business by taking in Thomas Morris, a Philadelphia merchant who had moved to Charleston and married Gadsden's daughter Mary in 1787: Godbold and Woody, *Gadsden*, 239–41; "Marriage and Death Notices from *State Gazette of South Carolina*," SCHM 51 (April 1950): 100; CG to John Adams, July 24, 1787, *WCG*, 243–44; CG to Robert Burton, March 28, 1796, Walsh, *WCG*, 260–61.

18. HL to Baron Von Steuben, January 5, 1786, *HLP*, SCHS, reel 8; HL to Michael Hillegas, April 14, 1786, *HLP*, SCHS, reel 8.

19. HL to John Lewis Gervais, March 4, 1784, Kendall Collection, South Caroliniana Library, Columbia, reel 7; HL to Countess of Huntingdon, March 26, 1785,

Kendall Collection, South Caroliniana Library, Columbia, reel 7; HL to William Bell, December 7, 1785, *HLP*, SCHS, reel 15.

20. HL to James Bourdieu, August 5, 1785, *HLP*, SCHS, reel 8; Wallace, *Laurens*, 424–25.

21. David Ramsay, *Memoirs of Martha Laurens Ramsay* (Boston: S. T. Armstrong, 1812), 11–280; HL to Messrs. Manning and Vaughan, February 8, 1787, *HLP*, SCHS, reel 8; "Marriage and Death Notices from *State Gazette of South Carolina*," *SCHM* 36 (October 1935): 136–37; Wallace, *Laurens*, 415–16. The best secondary account of the married life of Martha and David Ramsay can be found in Shaffer, *David Ramsay*, 206–17.

22. HL to William Bell, December 2, 1786, *HLP*, SCHS, reel 8; HL to Messrs. Mannings and Vaughan, June 30, 1787, *HLP*, SCHS, reel 8; HL to William Bell, May 30, 1792, *HLP*, SCHS, reel 15; Wallace, *Laurens*, 422.

23. Wallace, *Laurens*, 430–31, 503; Frances Leigh Williams, *A Founding Family: The Pinckneys of South Carolina* (New York: Harcourt Brace Jovanovich, 1978), 283.

24. James Madison to Thomas Jefferson, June 6, 1787, *LD*, 24:303; HL to William Bell, April 28, 1787, *HLP*, SCHS, reel 8; HL to John Vaughan, July 13, 1787, *HLP*, SCHS, reel 8; Wallace, *Laurens*, 422; Shaffer, *David Ramsay*, 154.

25. CG to Thomas Jefferson, October 29, 1787, *WCG*, 245–47; CG to Mrs. Ann Timothy, *Gazette of the State of South Carolina*, May 5, 1788, *WCG*, 248–50; CG to John Adams, July 24, 1787, *WCG*, 244.

26. HL to Edward Bridgen, October 8, 1787, *HLP*, SCHS, reel 8; HL to William Bell, October 11, 1787, *HLP*, SCHS, reel 8; HL to William Bell, November 29, 1787, *HLP*, SCHS, reel 8.

27. *Journal of the Convention of South Carolina which Ratified the Constitution of the United States, May 23, 1788* (Atlanta: Foote and Davies Company, 1928); Nadelhaft, *Disorders of War*, 180; Rogers, *Evolution of a Federalist*, 151–55; Godbold and Woody, *Gadsden*, 241–42; Klein, *Unification of a Slave State*, 164–71; Lewright B. Sikes, *The Public Life of Pierce Butler, South Carolina Statesman* (Washington, D.C.: University Press of America, 1979), 47; Lisle A. Rose, *Prologue to Democracy: The Federalists in the South, 1789–1800* (Lexington: University of Kentucky Press, 1968), 54–55.

28. It was John Lewis Gervais who suggested that the capital be moved inland to a site to be named Columbia: Klein, *Unification of a Slave State*, 145.

29. CG to John Adams, July 24, 1787, *WCG*, 244; Godbold and Woody, *Gadsden*, 242. According to figures presented by Jerome J. Nadelhaft, the white population of the low country in 1790 was 28,644, while that of the backcountry was 111,534: Nadelhaft, *Disorders of War*, 180.

30. CG to Thomas Morris, May 30, 1790, Walsh, *WCG*, 251–52, 252n.; Godbold and Woody, *Gadsden*, 243–44; Nadelhaft, *Disorders of War*, 216–17; Klein, *Unification of a Slave State*, 145–48.

31. HL to William Bell, February 17, 1792, *HLP*, SCHS, reel 15.

32. HL to William Bell, May 30, 1792, *HLP*, SCHS, reel 15; Wallace, *Laurens*, 457.

33. Wallace, *Laurens*, 457–58; Ramsay, *Martha Laurens Ramsay*, 13–14.

34. Godbold and Woody, *Gadsden*, 246–47; Rogers, *Evolution of a Federalist*, 276–77; David Hackett Fischer, *The Revolution of American Conservatism: The Federalist Party in the Era of Jeffersonian Democracy* (New York: Harper and Row, 1965), 398; Clow, *Edward Rutledge*, 269–70, 283. In an interesting demonstration of Gadsden's independence, it should be pointed out that Gadsden had published a public letter in support of the reelection of William Loughton Smith in 1793: CG to *City Gazette*, February 4, 1793, *WCG*, 257–58.

35. CG, *A Few Observations on Some Late Public Transactions* (Charleston, 1797), *WCG*, 262–80.

36. CG to the Citizens of South Carolina, *South Carolina Gazette and Timothy's Daily Advertiser*, April 23, 1798, *WCG*, 280–81; CG to Jacob Read, July 16, 1798, *WCG*, 282.

37. CG to the *South Carolina Gazette and Timothy's Daily Advertiser*, August 29, 1800, *WCG*, 299; CG to the *South Carolina Gazette and Timothy's Daily Advertiser*, October 8, 1800; *WCG*, 303.

38. CG to John Adams, March 11, 1801, *WCG*, 305–7. Adams was touched by Gadsden's support and noted that, while he had been deserted by most of his old colleagues, "Gadsden was almost the only staunch old companion who was faithful found": Page Smith, *John Adams* (Garden City, N.J.: Doubleday and Co., 1962), 2 vols., 2:1068.

39. CG to John Adams, June 24, 1801, *WCG*, 308–9; CG to the *South Carolina Gazette and Timothy's Daily Advertiser*, October 8, 1800; *WCG*, 302.

40. Godbold and Woody, *Gadsden*, 252–53; *Charleston City Gazette*, August 31, 1805; "Will of Christopher Gadsden," *WCG*, 311–14.

Bibliography

Unpublished Primary Sources

Charleston County Transcripts of Wills. State Archives. Columbia, South Carolina.

Gadsden Christopher. "South Carolina Miscellany." South Caroliniana Library. Columbia, South Carolina.

Great Britain. *Records in the British Public Records Office Relating to South Carolina.*

Journal of the Commons House of Assembly, 1757–1775. State Archives: Columbia, South Carolina.

Laurens, Henry. *Henry Laurens Papers.* South Carolina Historical Society: Charleston.

———. *Henry Laurens Papers: Correspondence of the Revolution, Military, and Civil, 1771–1792, collected, arranged, and annotated by William Gilmore Simms* (Kendall Collection). South Caroliniana Library: Columbia, South Carolina.

Newspapers

Charleston City Gazette
Gazette of the State of South Carolina
South Carolina and American General Gazette
South Carolina Gazette
South Carolina Gazette and Country Journal
South Carolina Gazette and Timothy's Daily Advertiser

Manuscript Collections

Bee, Thomas. Papers. Library of Congress.

Greene, Nathanael. Papers. Library of Congress.

Izard, Ralph. Papers. Library of Congress.

Laurens, John and Henry. Papers. Library of Congress.

Lincoln, Benjamin. Journals. Library of Congress.

Lowndes, Rawlins. Papers. Library of Congress.

Lynch, Thomas. Papers. Library of Congress.

Madison, James. Papers. Library of Congress.

Morris, Robert. Papers. Library of Congress.

Moultrie, William. Papers. Library of Congress.

Rutledge, Edward. Papers. Library of Congress.

Rutledge, John. Papers. Library of Congress.

Thomson, Charles. Papers. Library of Congress.

Washington, George. Papers. Library of Congress.

Published Primary Sources

Adams, John. *The Works of John Adams*. Edited by Charles Francis Adams. 10 vols. Boston: Little, Brown, and Company, 1850–1856.

———. *Diary and Autobiography of John Adams*. Edited by L. H. Butterfield. 4 vols. Cambridge: Harvard University Press, 1961.

Bargar, B. D. "Charles Town Loyalism in 1775: The Secret Reports of Alexander Innes." *South Carolina Historical Magazine* 63, no. 3 (July 1962): 125–36.

Barnhart, Eleanor L. "Thunderstorm of 1771." *South Carolina Historical Magazine, 74, no. 1 (January 1973): 37–38.*

Bull, William. *"Governor William Bull's Representation of the Colony, 1770." In The Colonial South Carolina Scene: Contemporary Views, 1697–1774,* edited by H. Roy Merrens. Columbia: University of South Carolina Press, 1977.

Cappon, Lester J., ed. *The Adams-Jefferson Letters: The Complete Correspondence between Thomas Jefferson and Abigail and John Adams.* Chapel Hill: University of North Carolina Press, 1959.

Continental Congress. *Journals of the Continental Congress, 1774–1789.* Edited by Worthington C. Ford 34 vols. Washington, D.C., 1904–37.

Deas, Anne Izard, ed. *Correspondence of Mr. Ralph Izard of South Carolina, from the Year 1774 to 1804: With a Short Memoir.* New York: 1844.

"Death Notices from the *South Carolina Gazette* from September 29, 1766 to December 19, 1774." *South Carolina Historical and Genealogical Magazine* (later became *South Carolina Historical Magazine*), 34, no. 2 (April 1933): 88–95.

Dickinson, John. *Letters from a Farmer in Pennsylvania to the Inhabitants of the British Colonies.* 1768. Reprint, with an introduction by R. T. H. Halsey, New York: Outlook Company, 1903.

Donnan, Elizabeth. *Documents Illustrative of the Slave Trade to America.* 4 vols. New York: Octagon Books, 1969.

Drayton, John. *Memoirs of the American Revolution, from its Commencement to the Year 1776, Inclusive: As Relating to the State of South Carolina.* 2 vols. Charleston, 1821.

Gadsden, Christopher. "Two Letters of Christopher Gadsden." Edited by Robert M. Weir. *South Carolina Historical Magazine,* 75 no. 3 (July 1974): 169–76

Garden, Alexander. *Anecdotes of the American Revolution.* 3 vols. Charleston, Charleston: A. E. Miller, 1822.

———. "Garth Correspondence." Annotated by Joseph W. Barnwell. *South Carolina Historical and Genealogical Magazine* 28, no. 4 (October 1927): 226–35; 29, no. 4 (October 1928): 295–305; 30, no. 1 (January 1929): 27–49; 30, no. 2 (April 1929): 105–16; 31, no. 2 (April 1930): 124–53; 33, no. 4 (October 1932): 262–80.

Garth, Charles. "Stamp Act Papers." *Maryland Historical Magazine* 6 (September 1911): 282–305.

Gervais, John Lewis. "Letters from John Lewis Gervais to Henry Laurens, 1777–1778." Edited by Raymond Starr. *South Carolina Historical Magazine* 66, no. 1 (January 1965): 15–37.

Gibbes, R. W. *Documentary History of the American Revolution.* 2 vols. New York: D. Appleton and Company, 1855.

Grant, James. "Journal of Lieutenant-Colonel James Grant, Commanding an Expedition against the Cherokee Indians, June-July, 1761." *Florida Historical Society Quarterly* 12, no. 1 (July 1933): 25–36.

Hamilton, Alexander. *The Papers of Alexander Hamilton.* Edited by Harold C. Syrett. 27 vols. New York: Columbia University Press, 1961–1987.

Hayne, Isaac. "Records kept by Colonel Isaac Hayne." *South Carolina Historical and Genealogical Magazine* 10, no. 4 (October 1909): 220–35; 11, no. 1 (January 1910): 27–38; 11, no. 2 (April 1910): 92–106; 11, no. 3 (July 1910): 160–70.

Hazard, Ebenezer. "A View of Coastal South Carolina in 1778: The Journal of Ebenezer Hazard." Edited by H. Roy Merrens. *South Carolina Historical Magazine* 73, no. 4 (October 1972): 177–93.

Hemphill, William Edwin and Wylma Anne Wates, eds. *Extracts from the Journals of the Provincial Congresses of South Carolina, 1775–1776.* Columbia: South Carolina Archives Department, 1960.

Hemphill, William Edwin and R. Nicholas Olsberg, eds. *Journals of the General Assembly and House of Representatives, 1776–1780.* Columbia: University of South Carolina Press, 1970.

Hooker, Richard J., ed. *The Carolina Backcountry on the Eve of the Revolution: The Journal and Other Writings of Charles Woodmason, Anglican Itinerant.* Chapel Hill: University of North Carolina Press, 1953.

Izard, Ralph. "Izard-Laurens Correspondence." *South Carolina Historical and Genealogical Magazine* 22 no. 2 (April 1921): 39–52; 22, no. 3 (July 1921): 73–89.

Journal of the Convention of South Carolina which Ratified the Constitution of the United States, May 23, 1788. Indexed by A. S. Salley, Jr. Atlanta: Foote and Davies Company, 1928.

Kaminski, John P. and Gaspare J. Saladino, eds. *The Documentary History of the Ratification of the Constitution.* 15 vols. Madison: Historical Society of Wisconsin, 1981.

Lafayette, Marquis de. *Lafayette in the Age of the American Revolution: Selected Letters and Papers, 1776–1790.* Edited by Stanley Izerda; Roger E. Smith, associate editor; Linda J. Pike and Mary Ann Quinn, associate editors. 5 vols. Ithaca, N.Y.: Cornell University Press, 1977.

——— "Letters from the Marquis de Lafayette to Hon. Henry Laurens, 1777–1780." *South Carolina Historical and Genealogical Magazine* 7, no. 4 (October 1906): 180–93.

Laurens, Henry. "Correspondence Between Hon. Henry Laurens and His Son, John, 1777–1780." *South Carolina Historical and Genealogical Magazine* 4, no. 4 (October 1903): 263–77; 6, no. 2 (April 1905): 47–52.

———. "Narrative of the Capture of Henry Laurens, of His Confinement in the Tower of London, etc.. 1780, 1781, 1782." *Firelands Pioneer* 16 (1907): 1259–1302.

———. Laurens, Henry. "Correspondence of Henry Laurens." Annotated by Joseph W. Barnwell. *South Carolina Historical and Genealogical Magazine* 30 no. 4 (October 1929): 197–14.

————. "Letters from Henry Laurens to William Bell of Philadelphia." *South Carolina Historical and Genealogical Magazine* 24, no. 2 (July 1923): 53–68; 25, no. 1 (January 1924): 23–35.

————. "Henry Laurens on the Olympic Games." *South Carolina Historical Magazine* 61, no. 3 (July 1960): 146–47.

————. *The Papers of Henry Laurens*. Edited by Philip M. Hamer, George C. Rogers, Jr., David R. Chesnutt, C. James Taylor; Assistant editors: David Fischer, Peggy J. Clark, Walter B. Edgar, Maude E. Lyles, Peggy H. Wehage. 15 vols. to date. Columbia: University of South Carolina Press, 1968–.

Laurens, John. *The Army Correspondence of John Laurens*. New York: Bradford Club, 1867.

————. "Letters from John Laurens to his Father, Hon. Henry Laurens, 1774–1776." *South Carolina Historical and Genealogical Magazine* 5, no. 4 (October 1904): 197–208.

Lee, Arthur. "Answer to Considerations on Certain Political Transactions of the Province of South Carolina." Jack P. Greene, ed., *The Nature of Colony Constitutions*. Columbia: University of South Carolina Press, 1970.

Lee, Richard Henry. *The Letters of Richard Henry Lee*. Edited by James Curtis Ballagh. 2 vols. New York: Macmillan Company, 1911.

Leigh, Egerton. "Considerations on Certain Political Transactions of the Province of South Carolina." In *The Nature of Colony Constitutions*, edited by Jack P. Greene.

Livingston, William. *The Papers of William Livingston*. Edited by Carl E. Prince and Dennis P. Ryan. 5 vols. Trenton: New Jersey Historical Commission, 1979–1988.

Madison, James. *The Papers of James Madison*. Edited by Wiliam T. Hutchinson, William M. E. Rachal. 10 vols. Chicago: University of Chicago Press, 1967–.

Manigault, Ann. "Extracts from the Journal of Mrs. Ann Manigault, 1754–1781." Notes by Mabel L. Webber. *South Carolina Historical and Genealogical Magazine* 20, no. 3 (July 1919): 204–12; 21, no. 1 (January 1920): 10–23; 21, no. 3 (July 1920): 112–20.

Manigault, Peter. "Letters Concerning Peter Manigault, 1773." In *South Carolina Historical and Genealogical Magazine* 21, no. 2 (April 1920): 39–49.

————. "The Letterbook of Peter Manigault, 1763–1773." Edited by Maurice A. Crouse. *South Carolina Historical Magazine* 70, no. 2 (April 1969): 79–96.

"Marriage and Death Notices from the *State Gazette* of South Carolina." *South Carolina Historical and Genealogical Magazine* 36, no. 4 (October 1935): 134–38; 51, no. 2 (April 1950): 97–102.

Middleton, Arthur. "Correspondence of Hon. Arthur Middleton, Signer of the Declaration of Independence." Annotated by Joseph W. Barnwell. *South Carolina Historical and Genealogical Magazine* 26, no. 4 (October 1925): 183–13; 27, no. 1 (January 1926): 1–29.

"Miscellaneous Papers of the General Committee, Secret Committee, and Provincial Congress, 1775." *South Carolina Historical and Genealogical Magazine* 8, no. 4 (October 1907): 189–94.

Moultrie, William. *Memoirs of the American Revolution*. 2 vols. 1802. Reprint, New York: Arno Press, 1968.

"'On Liberty Tree': A Revolutionary Poem from South Carolina." Contributed by Jay B. Hubbell. *South Carolina Historical and Genealogical Magazine* 41, no. 3 (July 1940): 117–22.

"Papers of the Second Council of Safety of the Revolutionary Party in South Carolina, November 1775–March 1776." *South Carolina Historical and Genealogical Magazine* 4, no. 2 (April 1903): 83–95.

Quincy, Josiah, Jr. "Journal of Josiah Quincy, Jr." Edited by Mark DeWolfe Howe. In *Proceedings of the Massachusetts Historical Society* 49 (1915–1916): 424–81.

Ramsay, David. *Memoirs of Martha Laurens Ramsay.* Boston: S. T. Armstrong, 1812.

———. *The History of the American Revolution.* 2 vols. 1789. Reprint, New York: Russell and Russell, 1968.

Rutledge, John. "Letters of John Rutledge." *South Carolina Historical and Genealogical Magazine* 17, no. 4 (October 1916): 131–46; 18, no. 4 (October 1917): 155–67.

Salley, A. S., Jr., ed. *Journal of the House of Representatives of South Carolina, January 8, 1782–February 26, 1782.* Columbia: State Commercial Printing Company, 1916.

——— *Journal of the Commons House of Assembly of South Carolina, January 8, 1765–August 9, 1765.* Columbia: State Commercial Printing Company, 1949.

Smith, Josiah. "Josiah Smith's Diary." Annotated by Mabel L. Webber. *South Carolina Historical and Genealogical Magazine* 33, no. 1 (January 1932): 1–28; 33, no. 2 (April 1932): 79–116; 33, no. 3 (July 1932): 197–207; 33, no. 4 (October 1932): 281–89; 34, no. 1 (January 1933): 31–39; 34, no. 2 (April 1933): 67–84; 34, no. 4 (October 1933): 194–210.

Smith, Paul H., ed. *Letters of Delegates to Congress, 1774–1789.* 25 vols. Washington, D.C.: Library of Congress, 1976–1998.

"South Carolina Contributors to the College of Philadelphia: Extracts from the Minutes of the Board of Trustees, April 15, 1772." *South Carolina Historical and Genealogical Magazine,* 65, no. 4 (October 1944): 189–92.

Sparks, Jared. "Jared Sparks Visits South Carolina." Edited by John Hammond Moore. *South Carolina Historical Magazine* 72, no. 3 (July 1971): 150–60.

Thompson, Theodora J., ed. *Journals of the House of Representatives, 1783–1784.* Columbia: University of South Carolina Press, 1977.

Thomson, Charles. "The Papers of Charles Thomson." *Collections of the New York Historical Society* (1878), New York: New York Historical Society, 1878, 1–286.

Timothy, Peter. *Letters of Peter Timothy Printer of Charleston, South Carolina, to Benjamin Franklin.* Edited by Douglas C. McMurtrie. Chicago: Black Cat Press, 1935.

Walsh, Richard. *The Writings of Christopher Gadsden.* Columbia: University of South Carolina Press, 1966.

Washington, George. *The Writings of George Washington.* Edited by John C. Fitzpatrick. 39 vols. Washington, D.C.: Government Printing Office, 1931–1944.

Weir, Robert M., ed. *The Letters of Freeman, Etc.: Essays on the Non-Importation Movement in South Carolina, Collected by William Henry Drayton.* Columbia: University of South Carolina Press, 1977.

Wharton, Francis, ed. *The Revolutionary Diplomatic Correspondence of the United States.* 6 vols. Washington, D.C.: Government Printing Office, 1889.

Secondary Sources

Alden, John Richard. *John Stuart and the Southern Colonial Frontier.* New York: Gordian Press, 1944.

————. *The South in the Revolution, 1763–1789*. Baton Rouge: Louisiana State University Press, 1957.

Bailey, N. Louise, Mary L. Morgan, and Carolyn R. Taylor, eds. *Biographical Directory of the South Carolina Senate, 1776–1985*. Columbia: University of South Carolina Press, 1986.

Bailyn, Bernard. *The Ideological Origins of the American Revolution*. Cambridge: Harvard University Press, 1967.

————. "The Central Themes of the American Revolution: An Interpretation." In *Essays on the American Revolution*, edited by Stephen G. Kurt and James H. Hutson. Chapel Hill: University of North Carolina Press, 1973.

Barrow, Thomas C. *Trade and Empire: The British Customs Service in Colonial America, 1660–1775*. Cambridge: Harvard University Press, 1967.

Becker, Robert A. "Salus Populi Suprema Lex: Public Peace and South Carolina Debtor Relief Laws, 1783–1788." *South Carolina Historical Magazine* 80, no. 1 (January 1979): 65–75.

Bell, Malcolm, Jr. *Major Butler's Legacy: Five Generations of Slaveholding Family*. Athens: University of Georgia Press, 1987.

Bennett, Charles E. and Donald R. Lennon. *A Quest for Glory: Major General Robert Howe and the American Revolution*. Chapel Hill: University of North Carolina Press, 1991.

Brady, Patrick S. "The Slave Trade and Sectionalism in South Carolina, 1787–1808." *Journal of Southern History* 38, no. 4 (November 1972): 601–20.

Bridenbaugh, Carl. *Cities in Revolt: Urban Life in America, 1743–1776*. New York: Alfred A. Knopf, 1955.

————. *Myths and Realities: Societies of the Colonial South*. New York: Atheneum, 1966.

Brooke, John. *King George III*. New York: McGraw-Hill, 1972.

Brown, Richard Maxwell. *The South Carolina Regulators*. Cambridge: Belknap Press of Harvard University Press, 1963.

Burnett, Edmund Cody. *The Continental Congress*. New York: Macmillan Company, 1941.

Calhoon, Robert M. *The Loyalists in Revolutionary America, 1760–1781*. New York: Harcourt Brace Jovanovich, 1965.

Calhoon, Robert M. and Robert M. Weir. "The Scandalous History of Sir Egerton Leigh." *William and Mary Quarterly* 26, no. 1 (January 1969): 47–74.

Calmes, Alan. "The Lyttelton Expedition of 1759: Military Failures and Financial Successes." *South Carolina Historical Magazine* 77, no. 1 (January 1976): 10–33.

Chaplin, Joyce E. "Slavery and the Principle of Humanity: A Modern Idea in the Early Lower South." *Journal of Social History* (Winter 1990): 299–315.

————. *An Anxious Pursuit: Agricultural Innovation and Modernity in the Lower South, 1730–1815*. Chapel Hill: University of North Carolina Press, 1993.

Chesnutt, David R. "South Carolina's Penetration of Georgia in the 1760s: Henry Laurens as a Case Study." *South Carolina Historical Magazine* 73, no. 4 (October 1972): 194–208.

Clow, Brent Richard. "Edward Rutledge of South Carolina, 1749–1800: Unproclaimed Statesman." Ph.D. diss., University of Georgia, 1976.

Cohen, Hennig. *The South Carolina Gazette 1732–1775*. Columbia: University of South Carolina Press, 1953.

Coleman, Kenneth. *The American Revolution in Georgia, 1763–1789.* Athens: University of Georgia Press, 1958.

———. *Colonial Georgia: A History.* New York: Charles Scribner's Sons, 1976.

Corkran, David H. *The Cherokee Frontier: Conflict and Survival, 1740–62.* Norman: University of Oklahoma Press, 1962.

Crouse, Maurice A. "Gabriel Manigault: Charleston Merchant." *South Carolina Historical Magazine* 68, no.4 (October 1967): 220–31.

———. "Cautious Rebellion: South Carolina's Opposition to the Stamp Act." *South Carolina Historical Magazine* 73, no. 2 (April 1972): 59–71.

Dabney, William M. "Drayton and Laurens in the Continental Congress." *South Carolina Historical Magazine* 60, no. 2 (April 1959): 74–82.

Dabney, William M. and Marion Dargan. *William Henry Drayton and the American Revolution.* Albuquerque: University of New Mexico Press, 1962.

Davis, David Brion. *The Problem of Slavery in the Age of Revolution, 1770–1823.* Ithaca, N.Y.: Cornell University Press, 1975.

Dickerson, Oliver M. *The Navigation Acts and the American Revolution.* Philadelphia: University of Pennsylvania Press, 1951.

Donnan, Elizabeth. "The Slave Trade into South Carolina before the Revolution." *American Historical Review* 33, no. 4 (July 1928): 804–28.

Douglass, Elisha P. *Rebels and Democrats: The Struggle for Equal Political Rights and Majority Rule during the American Revolution.* Chapel Hill: University of North Carolina Press, 1955.

Easterby, J. H., ed. "The South Carolina Education Bill of 1770." *South Carolina Historical and Genealogical Magazine* 48, no. 3 (April 1947): 95–111.

Edgar, Walter B. and N. Louise Bailey, eds. *Biographical Directory of the South Carolina House of Representatives.* 5 vols. Columbia: University of South Carolina Press, 1977.

Farley, M. Foster. "The South Carolina Negro in the American Revolution, 1775–1783." *South Carolina Historical Magazine* 79, no. 2 (April 1978): 75–86.

Fischer, David Hackett. *The Revolution of American Conservatism: The Federalist Party in the Era of Jeffersonian Democracy.* New York: Harper and Row, 1965.

Flexner, James Thomas. *Washington: The Indispensable Man.* Boston, Little, Brown, and Company, 1969.

Frakes, George Edward. *Laboratory for Liberty: The South Carolina Legislative Committee System 1719–1776.* Lexington: University of Kentucky Press, 1970.

Fraser, Walter J., Jr. "The City Elite, 'Disorder,' and the Poor Children of Pre-Revolutionary Charleston." *South Carolina Historical Magazine* 84, no. 3 (July 1983): 167–79.

———. *Charleston ! Charleston ! The History of a Southern City.* Columbia: University of South Carolina Press, 1989.

Frech, Laura P. "The Republicanism of Henry Laurens." *South Carolina Historical Magazine* 76, no. 2 (April 1975): 68–79.

Freehling, William W. "The Founding Fathers and Slavery." *American Historical Review* 77, no. 1 (February 1972): 81–93.

Frey, Sylvia R. "Liberty, Equality, and Slavery: The Paradox of the American Revolution." In *The American Revolution: Its Character and Limits,* edited by Jack P. Greene. New York: New York University Press, 1987.

———. *Water from the Rock: Black Resistance in a Revolutionary Age.* Princeton: Princeton University Press, 1991.

Gallay, Alan. *The Formation of the Planter Elite: Jonathan Bryan and the Southern Colonial Frontier.* Athens: University of Georgia Press, 1989.

Godbold, E. Stanly and Robert H. Woody. *Christopher Gadsden and the American Revolution.* Knoxville: University of Tennessee Press, 1982.

Green, Fletcher M. *Constitutional Development in the South Atlantic States, 1776–1860: A Study in the Evolution of Democracy.* Chapel Hill: University of North Carolina Press, 1930.

Greene, Jack P. "The South Carolina Quartering Dispute, 1757–1758." *South Carolina Historical Magazine* 60, no. 4 (October 1959): 193–204.

———. "The Gadsden Election Controversy and the Revolutionary Movement in South Carolina." *Mississippi Valley Historical Review* 46, no. 3 (December 1959): 469–92.

———. "South Carolina's Colonial Constitution: Two Proposals for Reform." *South Carolina Historical Magazine* 62, no. 2 (April 1961): 72–81.

———. "Bridge to Revolution: The Wilkes Fund Controversy in South Carolina, 1769–1775." *Journal of Southern History* 39, no. 1 (February 1963): 19–52.

———. *The Quest for Power: The Lower Houses of Assembly in the Southern Royal Colonies 1689–1776.* Chapel Hill: University of North Carolina Press, 1963.

Hancock, David. *Citizens of the World: London Merchants and the Integration of the British Atlantic Community, 1735–1785.* New York: Cambridge University Press, 1995.

Hargrove, Richard J. "Portrait of a Southern Patriot: The Life and Death of John Laurens." In *The Revolutionary War in the South: Power, Conflict, and Leadership,* edited by W. Robert Higgins. Durham, N.C.: Duke University Press, 1979.

Henderson, H. James. *Party Politics in the Continental Congress.* New York: McGraw-Hill, 1974.

Hendricks, J. Edwin. *Charles Thomson and the Making of a New Nation, 1729–1824.* London: Associated University Presses, 1979.

Higgins, W. Robert. "Charles Town Merchants and Factors Dealing in the External Negro Trade, 1735–1775." *South Carolina Historical Magazine* 65, no. 4 (October 1964): 205–17.

———. "The South Carolina Revolutionary Debt and Its Holders, 1776–1780." *South Carolina Historical Magazine* 72, no. 1 (January, 1971): 15–29.

Jackson, Harvey H. *Lachlan McIntosh and the Politics of Revolutionary Georgia.* Athens: University of Georgia Press, 1979.

Johnson, Elmer Douglass. "David Ramsay: Historian or Plagiarist?" *South Carolina Historical Magazine* 57, no.4 (October 1956): 189–98.

Klein, Rachel N. *Unification of a Slave State: The Rise of the Planter Class in the South Carolina Backcountry, 1760–1808.* Chapel Hill: University of North Carolina Press, 1990.

Lambert, Robert Stansbury. *South Carolina Loyalists in the American Revolution.* Columbia: University of South Carolina Press, 1987.

Leiding, Harriette Kershaw. *Historic Houses of South Carolina.* Philadelphia: J. B. Lippincott Company, 1921.

Lesesne, J. Mauldin. *The Bank of the State of South Carolina: A General and Political History.* Columbia: University of South Carolina Press, 1970.

Littlefield, Daniel C. *Rice and Slaves: Ethnicity and the Slave Trade in Colonial South Carolina.* Baton Rouge: Louisiana State University Press, 1981.

———. "Charleston and Internal Slave Redistribution." *South Carolina Historical Magazine* 87, no. 2 (April 1986): 93–105.

———. "The Slave Trade to Colonial South Carolina: A Profile." *South Carolina Historical Magazine* 91, no. 2 (April 1990): 68–99.

MacLeod, Duncan J. *Slavery, Race and the American Revolution.* Cambridge: Cambridge University Press, 1974.

Maier, Pauline. "John Wilkes and American Disillusionment with Britain." *William and Mary Quarterly* 20, no. 3 (July 1963): 373–95.

———. "The Charleston Mob and the Evolution of Popular Politics in Revolutionary South Carolina." *Perspectives in American History* 4 (1970): 173–96.

———. "Early Revolutionary Leaders in the South and the Problem of Southern Distinctiveness." In *The Southern Experience in the American Revolution,* edited by Jeffrey J. Crow and Larry E. Tise. Chapel Hill: University of North Carolina Press, 1978): 3–24.

———. *From Resistance to Revolution: Colonial Radicals and the Development of American Opposition to Britain, 1765–1776.* New York: Alfred A. Knopf, 1972.

Martin, James Kirby. *Men in Rebellion: Higher Governmental Leaders and the Coming of the American Revolution.* New Brunswick, N.J.: Rutgers University Press, 1973.

Maslowski, Peter. "National Policy toward the Use of Black Troops in the Revolution." *South Carolina Historical Magazine* 73 (June 1972): 1–17.

Massey, Gregory D. "The Limits of Anti-Slavery Thought in the Revolutionary Lower South: John Laurens and Henry Laurens." *Journal of Southern History* 63, no. 3 (August 1997): 495–530.

Mattern, David B. *Benjamin Lincoln and the American Revolution.* Columbia: University of South Carolina Press, 1995.

McColley, Robert. *Slavery and Jeffersonian Virginia.* Urbana: University of Illinois Press, 1964.

McCowen, George Smith, Jr. *The British Occupation of Charleston, 1780–82.* Columbia: University of South Carolina Press, 1972.

McCrady, Edward. *The History of South Carolina, 1719–1783.* 3 vols. New York: Russell & Russell, 1899–1902 reprint ed [1969].

Meriwether, Robert L. *The Expansion of South Carolina, 1729–1765.* Kingsport, Tenn.: Southern Publishers, 1940.

Meroney, Geraldine M. *Inseperable Loyalty: A Biography of William Bull.* Norcross, Ga.: Harrison Company, 1991.

Mettler, Cecilia. "A Biographical Sketch of Christopher Gadsden." Ph.D. diss., Cornell University, 1938.

Miller, John C. *Origins of the American Revolution.* Stanford, Calif.: Stanford University Press, 1943.

Moore, Warner O., Jr. "The Largest Exporters of Deerskins from Charles Town, 1735–1775." *South Carolina Historical Magazine* 74, no. 3 (July 1973): 144–50.

———. "Henry Laurens: A Charleston Merchant in the Eighteenth Century." Ph.D. diss., University of Alabama, 1974.

Morgan, Edmund S. and Helen M. *The Stamp Act Crisis: Prologue to Revolution.* New York: Macmillan Company, 1953.

Morgan, Philip. "Three Planters and Their Slaves: Perspectives on Slavery in Virginia, South Carolina, and Jamaica, 1750–1790." In *Race and Family in the Col-*

onial South, edited by Winthrop D. Jordan and Sheila L. Skemp. Jackson: University Press of Mississippi, 1987.

Nadelhaft, Jerome J. *The Disorders of War: The Revolution in South Carolina.* Orono: University of Maine Press, 1981.

Nash, Gary B. *Race and Revolution.* Madison: Madison House, 1990.

Nelson, Paul David. *General James Grant: Scottish Soldier and Royal Governor of East Florida.* Gainesville: University Press of Florida, 1993.

Olson, Gary D. "Loyalists and the American Revolution: Thomas Brown and the South Carolina Backcountry, 1775–1776." *South Carolina Historical Magazine* 69, no. 1 (January 1968): 44–56.

Olwell, Robert A. "'Domestick Enemies': Slavery and Political Independence in South Carolina, May 1775–March 1776." *Journal of Southern History* 55, no. 1 (February 1989): 21–48.

Phillips, Ulrich B. "The South Carolina Federalists." *American Historical Review* 14, no. 3 (April 1909): 529–43; 14, no. 4 (July 1909): 731–43.

Potts, James L. "Christopher Gadsden and the American Revolution." Ph.D. diss., George Peabody College for Teachers, 1958.

Potts, Louis W. "Arthur Lee, Autonomy, and Diplomacy in the American Revolution." In *The Revolutionary War in the South: Power, Conflict, and Leadership.* Durham, N.C.: Duke University Press, 1979.

————. Arthur Lee: A Virtuous Revolutionary. Baton Rouge: Louisiana State University Press, 1981.

Rakove, Jack N. *The Beginnings of National Politics: An Interpretive History of the Continental Congress.* New York: Alfred A. Knopf, 1976.

Ramsay, David. *Ramsay's History of South Carolina.* 1808. Reprint, Newberry, S.C.: W. J. Duffie, 1858.

Ravenel, Harriott Horry. *Charleston: The Place and the People.* London: Macmillan Company, 1906.

Rhett, Robert Goodwyn. *Charleston: An Epic of Carolina.* Richmond: Garrett and Massie, 1940.

Robinson, Donald L. *Slavery in the Structure of American Politics, 1765–1820.* New York: Harcourt Brace Jovanovich, 1971.

Rogers, George C., Jr. *Evolution of a Federalist: William Loughton Smith of Charleston, 1758–1812.* Columbia: University of South Carolina Press, 1962.

————. *Charleston in the Age of the Pinckneys.* Norman: University of Oklahoma Press, 1969.

————. *The History of Georgetown County, South Carolina.* Columbia: University of South Carolina Press, 1973.

————. "The Charleston Tea Party: The Significance of December 3, 1773." *South Carolina Historical Magazine* 75, no. 3 (July 1974): 153–68.

————. "The Papers of James Grant of Ballindalloch Castle, Scotland." *South Carolina Historical Magazine* 77, no. 3 (July 1976): 145–60.

Rose, Lisle A. *Prologue to Democracy: The Federalists in the South, 1789–1800.* Lexington: University of Kentucky Press, 1968.

Rossie, Jonathan Gregory. *The Politics of Command in the American Revolution.* Syracuse, N.Y.: Syracuse University Press, 1975.

Rude, George. *Wilkes and Liberty: A Social Study of 1763 to 1774.* Oxford: Clarendon Press, 1962.

Ryan, Frank W., Jr. "The Role of South Carolina in the First Continental Congress." *South Carolina Historical Magazine* 60, no. 3 (July 1959), 147–53.

Sachse, William L. *The Colonial American in Britain*. Madison: University of Wisconsin Press, 1956.

Sanders, Jennings B. *Evolution of Executive Departments of the Continental Congress, 1774–1789*. Chapel Hill: University of North Carolina Press, 1935.

Schlesinger, Arthur M. *The Colonial Merchants and the American Revolution, 1763–1776*. New York: Facsimile Library, 1918.

———. "The Colonial Newspapers and the Stamp Act." *New England Quarterly* 8 (March 1935): 63–83.

Sellers, Leila. *Charleston Business on the Eve of the American Revolution*. Chapel Hill: University of North Carolina Press, 1934.

Shaffer, Arthur H. "Between Two Worlds: David Ramsay and the Politics of Slavery." *Journal of Southern History* 50, no. 2 (May 1984): 175–96.

———. *To Be an American: David Ramsay and the Making of the American Consciousness*. Columbia: University of South Carolina Press, 1991.

Shy, John. *Toward Lexington: The Role of the British Army in the Coming of the American Revolution*. Princeton: Princeton University Press, 1965.

Sikes, Lewright B. *The Public Life of Pierce Butler, South Carolina Statesman*. Washington, D.C.: University Press of America, 1979.

Sirmans, M. Eugene. *Colonial South Carolina: A Political History, 1663–1763*. Chapel Hill: University of North Carolina Press, 1966.

Smith, Henry A. M. "Charleston and Charleston Neck: The Original Grantees and the Settlements along the Ashley and Cooper Rivers." *South Carolina Historical and Genealogical Magazine* 19, no. 1 (January 1918): 3–76.

Smith, Jeffery A. "Impartiality and Revolutionary Ideology: Editorial Policies of the *South Carolina Gazette*, 1732–1775." *Journal of Southern History* 49, no. 4 (November 1983): 511–26.

Smith, Page. *John Adams*. 2 vols. Garden City, N.Y.: Doubleday and Company, 1962.

———. *A New Age Now Begins: A People's History of the American Revolution*. 2 vols. New York: Penguin Books, 1989.

Smith, W. Roy. *South Carolina as a Royal Province, 1719–1776*. New York: Macmillan Company, 1903.

Snapp, J. Russell. *John Stuart and the Struggle for Empire on the Southern Frontier*. Baton Rouge: Louisiana State University Press, 1996.

Sosin, Jack M. *Agents and Merchants: British Colonial Policy and the Origins of the American Revolution, 1763–1775*. Lincoln: University of Nebraska Press, 1965.

Steedman, Marguerite. "Charlestown's Forgotten Tea Party." *Georgia Review* 21, no. 2 (Summer 1867): 244–59.

Stoesen, Alexander R. "The British Occupation of Charleston, 1780–1782." *South Carolina Historical Magazine* 63, no. 2 (April 1962): 71–82.

Stumpf, Stuart O. "South Carolina Importers of General Merchandise, 1735–1765." *South Carolina Historical Magazine* 84, no. 1 (January 1983): 1–10.

Thane, Ellswyth. *The Fighting Quaker: Nathanael Greene*. Mattituck, N.Y.: Aeonian Press, 1977.

Thomas, Peter D. G. *British Politics and the Stamp Act Crisis*. Oxford: Clarendon Press, 1975.

————. *The Townshend Duties Crisis: The Second Phase of the American Revolution, 1767–1773.* Oxford: Clarendon Press, 1987.

————. *Tea Party to Independence: The Third Phase of the American Revolution, 1773–1776.* Oxford: Clarendon Press, 1991.

Townsend, Sara Bertha. *An American Soldier: The Life of John Laurens.* Raleigh, N.C.: Edwards and Broughton Company, 1958.

Ubbelohde, Carl. *The Vice-Admiralty Courts and the American Revolution.* Chapel Hill: University of North Carolina Press, 1960.

Villers, David H. "The Smythe Horses Affair and the Association." *South Carolina Historical Magazine* 70, no. 3 (July 1969): 137–48.

Vipperman, Carl. *The Rise of Rawlins Lowndes, 1721–1800.* Columbia: University of South Carolina Press, 1978.

Wallace, David Duncan. *The Life of Henry Laurens.* New York: G. P. Putnam's Sons, 1915.

————. *South Carolina: A Short History, 1520–1948.* Chapel Hill: University of North Carolina Press, 1951.

Walsh, Richard. "The Charleston Mechanics: A Brief Study, 1760–1776." *South Carolina Historical Magazine* 60, no. 3 (July 1959): 123–44.

————. *Charleston's Sons of Liberty: A Study of the Artisans.* Columbia: University of South Carolina Press, 1959.

————. "Christopher Gadsden: Radical or Conservative Revolutionary?" *South Carolina Historical Magazine* 63, no. 4 (October 1962): 195–203.

Weir, Robert M. *"A Most Important Epocha": The Coming of the Revolution in South Carolina.* Columbia: University of South Carolina Press, 1970.

————. "The South Carolinian as Extremist." South Atlantic Quarterly 74, no. 1 (Winter 1975): 86–103.

————. *Colonial South Carolina: A History.* Millwood, N.Y.: KTO Press, 1983.

————. "Slavery and the Structure of the Union." In *Ratifying the Constitution*, edited by Michael Allen Gillespie and Michael Lienesch. Lawrence: University Press of Kansas, 1989.

Weslager, C. A. *The Stamp Act Congress.* Newark: University of Delaware Press, 1976.

Williams, Frances Leigh. *A Founding Family: The Pinckneys of South Carolina.* New York: Harcourt Brace Jovanovich, 1978.

Wood, Betty. *Slavery in Colonial Georgia, 1730–1775.* Athens: University of Georgia Press, 1984.

Wood, Gordon S. *The Creation of the American Republic, 1776–1787.* Chapel Hill: University of North Carolina Press, 1969.

————. *The Radicalism of the American Revolution.* New York: Alfred A. Knopf, 1992.

Wood, Peter H. *Black Majority: Negroes in Colonial South Carolina from 1670 through the Stono Rebellion.* New York: Alfred A. Knopf, 1972.

————. "'Taking Care of Business' in Revolutionary South Carolina: Republicanism and the Slave Society." In *The Southern Experience in the American Revolution*, edited by Jeffrey J. Crow and Larry E. Tise, 268–93. Chapel Hill: University of North Carolina Press, 1978.

Zahniser, Marvin R. *Charles Cotesworth Pinckney: Founding Father.* Chapel Hill: University of North Carolina Press, 1967.

Index